Public Opinion

CRITICAL MEDIA STUDIES:
INSTITUTIONS, POLITICS, AND CULTURE

Series Editor:
Andrew Calabrese, University of Colorado at Boulder

This series covers a broad range of critical research and theory about media in the modern world. It includes work about the changing structures of the media, focusing particularly on work about the political and economic forces and social relations which shape and are shaped by media institutions, structural changes in policy formation and enforcement, technological transformations in the means of communication, and the relationships of all of these to public and private cultures worldwide. Historical research about the media and intellectual histories pertaining to media research and theory are particularly welcomed. Emphasizing the role of social and political theory for informing and shaping research about communications media, Critical Media Studies seeks to address the politics of media institutions at national, subnational, and transnational levels. The series will also include short, synthetic texts on "Masters and Concepts" in critical media studies.

Advisory Board

Titles in the Series

Interactions: Critical Studies in Communication, Media, and Journalism, Hanno Hardt

Communication, Citizenship, and Social Policy: Rethinking the Limits of the Welfare State, edited by Andrew Calabrese and Jean-Claude Burgelman

Public Opinion: Developments and Controversies in the Twentieth Century, Slavko Splichal

Forthcoming in the Series

Tabloid Tales: Global Debates over Media Standards, edited by Colin Sparks and John Tulloch

The Information Society in Europe: Work and Life in an Age of Globalization, edited by Ken Ducatel, Juliet Webster, and Werner Herrmann

Redeveloping Communication for Social Change: Theory, Practice, and Power, edited by Karin G. Wilkins

Deregulating Telecommunications: A Comparison of American and Canadian Telecommunications, 1844–1997, Kevin G. Wilson

Deliberation, Democracy, and the Media, edited by Simone Chambers and Anne Costain

Public Opinion

Developments and Controversies in the Twentieth Century

Slavko Splichal

ROWMAN & LITTLEFIELD PUBLISHERS, INC.
Lanham • Boulder • New York • Oxford

ROWMAN & LITTLEFIELD PUBLISHERS, INC.

Published in the United States of America
by Rowman & Littlefield Publishers, Inc.
4720 Boston Way, Lanham, Maryland 20706

12 Hid's Copse Road
Cumnor Hill, Oxford OX2 9JJ, England

British Library Cataloguing in Publication Information Available

Library of Congress Cataloging-in-Publication Data

Splichal, Slavko.
    Public opinion : developments and controversies in the Twentieth Century / Slavko
Splichal.
Century / Slavko Splichal.
        p.   cm. — (Critical media studies)
    Includes bibliographical references and index.
    ISBN 0-8476-9162-4 (cloth : alk. paper). — ISBN 0-8476-9163-2
(pbk. : alk. paper)
    1. Public opinion.   2. Public opinion polls.   3. Social
psychology.   I. Title.   II. Series.
HM261.S7515   1999
303.3'8—dc21   99-17452
                                                                          CIP

Printed in the United States of America

♾ ™The paper used in this publication meets the minimum requirements of American National
Standard for Information Sciences—Permanence of Paper for Printed Library Materials, ANSI
Z39.48-1992.

Contents

Illustrations

Preface

Public opinion is believed to be the cornerstone of modern democracy: it ought to be the views expressed by citizens that influence the course of political events, from parliamentary elections to decisions made by institutions of political representation. The irony of contemporary conceptualizations of public opinion is that after centuries of theoretical endeavors in diverse disciplines from political philosophy to sociology, which succeeded neither in defining the concept in a generally accepted, noncontroversial way nor in reaching consensus regarding its political and moral validity, the twentieth century is facing a radical alternative—the empirical approach that pretends to have found the key to solving all conceptual problems in a simplistic behaviorism. A growing interest in the public opinion phenomenon in the twentieth century correlates with a widespread disenchantment with traditional "philosophical" approaches to public opinion, which dominated the period between the seventeenth and early twentieth centuries, and the rise of public opinion polling. Yet this (anti)intellectual turn, marked by an excess of measurement rigor but bereft of the substantive intellectual vigor characteristic of earlier contributions, cannot conceal its shortcomings: its ultimate inability to come to terms with the relation of public opinion to knowledge, cognition, communication, power, control, and politics, which has preoccupied public opinion theorists for centuries.

The irony of contemporary interest in public opinion is clearly reflected in journals and monographs published internationally that are dominated by more or less sophisticated analyses of polling data but lack "serious" theoretical research, broader historical perspectives, and reflections on political and ideological implications. I started to write this book with the aim of contributing to a critical reexamination of public opinion theories in the twentieth century from a nonlinear perspective. The central questions I attempt to answer are not primarily related to theoretical (or otherwise) *progress* (or recession) but rather to *controversies* in theoretical and operational conceptualizations of public opinion. Thus the work is a mixture of a meticulous though "synoptic" marshalling of historical evidence and endeavors to develop innovative and critical perspectives on widely discussed phenomena. I wanted to integrate different intellectual streams and leading traditions of the century and, particularly, "bring back" to the field some forgotten perspectives on public opinion, like those by William A. MacKinnon, Ferdinand Tönnies, Tom Harrison, Lindsay Rogers, or Francis Graham Wilson. The book brings together critical-theoretical and administrative-empirical approaches, and it stresses the importance of social-historical and political contexts in developing theories and conducting research. I do not intend to bridge the gap between historically distant or even exclusive traditions (which could not be achieved in a single book anyway), yet I do argue for building bridges between different perspectives. In contrast to a widespread belief that critical acuteness is proportionate to the time distance, my own insight into twentieth-century developments made me more critical toward the newest empirical developments than toward older theorizations. It is the historical distance that makes more transparent the validity of ideas developed, for example, by Ferdinand Tönnies, John Dewey, and Walter Lippmann in the 1920s, and their significance for the entire development of the twentieth century, although the rise of empiricism placed them at the rear of the "science of public opinion."

When I started to write this book, I did it bilingually, in Slovene and English (the Slovene version of the book has already been published). Yet it soon became apparent that this work was too demanding and time-consuming for one person, so I wrote more than half of the original version partly in Slovene and partly in English. I am much obliged to Vida Zei, Zala Volčič, Mark Andrejevic, Erica Debejak and Andrej Pinter, who translated parts of the manuscript into the opposite language and helped make the manuscript more terse and exact in both versions, which is perhaps the only advantage of writing in two languages at the same time. My teaching assistant, Zala Volčič, was also very helpful in searching for many historical documents and publications that I used in writing the book. For his contribution to the precision of the final text, I am particularly grateful to Hanno Hardt, professor of communications at the University of Iowa and University of Ljubljana, who thoroughly read a large part of the manuscript. I also benefited from stimulating comments and suggestions by John D. Peters of the University of Iowa. Andrew Calabrese, a professor at the University of Colorado at Boulder, checked and edited the manuscript once more. But I did the final editing myself, and I am solely responsible for any imperfections and errors. Without substantial help from two German colleagues of mine—Jörg Becker, director of ComTech Institute in Solingen, and Winfried Schulz, professor of communications at the University of Erlangen-Nürnberg—the chapters discussing two main German contributions to public opinion theories in the twentieth century would have remained a pale draft. For helpful conversations at various stages of the project I wish to thank the participants in a series of EURICOM Colloquia in Communication and Culture in the 1990s in Piran, Slovenia. Special thanks go to Brenda Hadenfeldt and Karen Johnson of Rowman & Littlefield, and particularly to copy editor Chrisona Schmidt. Last but not least, I would like to thank the Slovenian Ministry of Science and Technology for the research grant that enabled me to accomplish the research project that became part of the present book, the Faculty of Social Sciences, University of Ljubljana, and the Library of the University of Iowa, Iowa City, where I found stimulating conditions for my work.

1

✚

Publicity, the Public, and Public Opinion

The hardest problems are those which institutions cannot handle. They are the public's problems.
—Walter Lippmann, *The Phantom Public*

Public opinion is usually, it seems, a slightly embarrassing notion. It is easier to talk about "democracy" or "socialism," for instance, than to in-dicate the conditions under which public opinion creates obligations for a government to follow.
—Francis G. Wilson, *A Theory of Public Opinion*

The concepts of the public, publicness, publicity, public sphere, and public opinion are among the most controversial, ambiguous, and nontransparent concepts in the social sciences. But in spite of the social, historical, and discipli-nary variability and inconsistency of their meanings, these concepts have been used consistently since the eighteenth century. In this chapter different concep-tualizations are analyzed through a critical interpretation of some fundamental contributions to the field, with the aim of identifying persisting questions and concerns that are relevant to social research in general and to democratic theo-ries in particular. The chapter begins with the controversial notions of the fall versus the rise of the public sphere, and the theoretical and empirical validity of the concepts related to it. Five of them are examined in more detail: (1) a/the

1

public, in the sense of a specific social category (collectivity) that appears as a social (political) actor, or subject, specifically in relation to a given activity or project; (2) publicness, in the sense of a specific nature or character of an activity or
a social space; (3) publicity, usually referred to in the sense of a (moral) principle
or human right; (4) the concept of the public sphere (or public domain) as
the "infrastructure" of social integration through public discourse; and (5) the
concept of public opinion, which is considered to correlate with the first four
conceptual dimensions and to add to them a fifth that conceptualizes opinions.

The second part of the chapter discusses the importance of consensus for
the conceptualization of public opinion and fundamental contradictions that
aggravate problems of its definition(s): (1) the internal contradiction that is a
consequence of connecting the two concepts, "public" and "opinion" ("public" implies or refers to the universal, objective, and rational; and "opinion,"
to the individual, subjective, unstable), and (2) the external contradiction resulting from the relationship between the subjects of public opinion and the
subjects opposing it (or being pressured to heed it), or between the expression
and realization of public opinion. The contradictions are examined in relation
to some dominant traditions developed in the conceptualization of public
opinion. Early (normative-political) public opinion theories may be defined as
substantive, in contrast to what Francis G. Wilson named "adjective theories,"
which consider the concept of the public as correlative to opinion (the term
"public" is used as an adjective to describe the specificity or quality of an opinion). The former stress a tight, authoritative singleness ("the public" as the object of a quest for a universal collective subject or a privileged arena of struggle), the latter refer to a more relaxed, decentered pluralism (publicness as
something spread liberally through many irreducibly different collectivities).
Although eighteenth-century rationalism saw the development of a great faith
in the possibility of an enlightened public opinion, the shift from substantive
toward adjective theories in the twentieth century indicates the loss of (a hope
for) a rational-critical nature of public opinion. Instead, the question of social
control became one of the central issues in psychological and sociological theories of public opinion. Early theorizations were focused on the relation between the public and the government, whereas in the nineteenth century the
relation between the public and the mass became central; control over the ruling authorities by the public (majority) as the fundamental principle was "replaced" by the principle of the majority tolerance (the mass) of minority (representative government).

The concept of public belongs to the part of social sciences that is marked by
the absence of a clear, noncontroversial, and positive definition, which could

best demonstrate the theoretical meaningfulness of the concept. In the sense of both a social category and the nature of a certain activity (public as opposed to private and secret), it has been introduced in the language of social-scientific research at least since the late Middle Ages. The concept of public has a distinctive notional heterogeneity that is not defined only (or not primarily) by specific theoretical positions but is specifically defined historically. Habermas's concept of feudal representative publicness, for example, denotes public representation of the gentry or ruling power, that is, social status or "ceremonial control" (Park), in contrast to the ancient understanding of publicity as opposed to privacy, and in contrast to the concept of the bourgeois public as a social category. Almost the same was a "destiny" of the concept of public opinion that made publicness popular in the twentieth century—not just in an everyday and political jargon but also in the expert discourse in different areas and, with the establishment of polling in the United States in the period between the two world wars, in social research. In some languages, conceptual difficulties amplify because of linguistic ambiguities, for example in Slovene or German languages where the terms *javnost* or *Öffentlichkeit* imply "the/a public," "publicness," "publicity," and the "public sphere."

In the early 1920s, Walter Lippmann wrote in his book *Public Opinion* that "since Public Opinion is supposed to be the prime mover in democracies, one might reasonably expect to find a vast literature. One does not find it. . . . The existence of the force called Public Opinion is in the main taken for granted" (Lippmann [1922] 1960, 253). The main reason for such a disillusion lies in the fact that since the earliest dissertations on public opinion in the eighteenth century, "'Public opinion' took form as a political or ideological construct, rather than a discrete sociological referent" (Baker 1990, 172). Although the first disenchantments regarding the omnipotence of the public and public opinion appeared as early as the end of the eighteenth century (Peters 1995, 13), the efforts to (re)discover the discrete sociological referent of public opinion are primarily associated with the sociological thought of the twentieth century. However, the results of these efforts were controversial. The historical and disciplinary semantic heterogeneity of the concepts of public, publicity, and public opinion that is very near questioning their validity is closely related to their plethoric usage, which even the paradigmatic exclusiveness of theories does not limit. It has been symptomatic since the beginning of the second half of the twentieth century that all dissertations on public opinion begin with a note that there is an extensive literature on the public and on public opinion, but clear and unequivocal definition of the concepts are not to be found.

Definitional difficulties led Childs (1965) and after him many others who contributed to the advance of the critical empirical tradition in the conceptualization of public opinion, for example, Valdemar O. Key (1967), Benjamin Ginsberg (1986), James Beniger (1987), and John Zaller (1992), to the conclusion that perhaps the best way out of the growing perplexities would be to substitute the term "mass opinion" for "public opinion" in empirical research. Even earlier, Newcomb (1950, 176) suggested the term "group attitudes" as being more appropriate to name the subject of public opinion surveys.[1] Since the first empirical inquiries into public opinion, there have been several attempts "to define the meaning of the term 'public opinion' in a way that will be generally acceptable. As a result there are about as many definitions as there are studies in the field" (Childs 1939, 327). Philip Converse is one among rare authors who are convinced that "the firm establishment of a public opinion polling industry . . . homogenized the definition and stabilized it for foreseeable future" (Converse 1987, S13). The facts rather prove the contrary: despite the enormous quantities of money and attention devoted to public opinion polling, there are "few theoretical perspectives to guide research on the role of public sentiment in the political process. Perhaps this lack is not so surprising, given that even consistent definitions of the concept 'public opinion' are missing" (Glynn and McLeod 1984, 43). Yet this conceptual perplexity, which results in the absence of an agreed-upon definition of public opinion, is not specific to public opinion; rather, "from the beginning of modern social science, there has been sharp disagreement on most of the questions it has considered," as Wilson (1962, 74) put it.

It should not surprise us that understandings and attempts at defining the public and public opinion were often motivated by (political) interests, commonsense myopia, or theoretical exclusivism. Thus it is understandable that, in accordance with Durkheim's principles of sociological method, it was often proposed to "true" social scientists both in the past and at present to abandon the use of the concept with such unstandardized meanings. Already in the beginning of this century, the problem of definition became so perplexing that the round table on political statistics of the National Conference on the Science of Politics held in the United States in 1924 concluded that it would be wise to "avoid the use of the term public opinion, if possible" (Binkley 1928, 389). Half a century later Luhmann argued, a bit sarcastically, that the classical concept of the public was "too undetermined and for analytic and critic purposes inappropriate category" thus merely an "agrarian-historic concept" without any reference to practical existence or practical object (Luhmann 1971, 339–401). Public opinion supposedly developed into an "inner media" of political system, a mirror "generated by mass media to regulate the watching of the observers." With its help, politicians observe themselves, their adversaries, and ordinary people, who are mere observers (Luhmann 1994, 63). In the same vein, Bourdieu entitled his resounding article first published in 1972 "Public Opinion Doesn't Exist" (Bourdieu [1972] 1979) to express a similar disbelief in the validity of the concept, as did Bentley and Lippmann before him (Price 1992, 18).

One has to agree that the increase in the number of treatises on public opinion did not decrease the opacity of the concept, but this should not be a sufficient argument to renounce the concept itself. At least two reasons speak in disfavor. First, although the concept of public opinion won recognition only in the modern age with parliamentary democracy (which might imply that it is fully valid only within a limited temporal horizon), this does not mean that its conceptual dimensions do not go back to more remote historical periods. In other words, the concept veils a more universal validity than that conferred on it by bourgeois society or, as Negt argues (1980, 71), unduly, restricted by Habermas when he claimed that the idea of the public sphere (*Öffentlichkeit*) should not be pushed back into the sixteenth and seventeenth centuries, since that would change substantially the meaning of the concept (Habermas 1992a, 465). In contrast to Habermas, and with reference to Margaret Mead's discussion of 1937 (1965), Paul Beaud admonishes that in primitive communities, anthropologists have discovered mechanisms of group interaction that advance processes of differentiation in which we could recognize "the individualistic definition of public opinion in which liberalism would like to see the foundations of modern democratic societies alone" (Beaud 1993, 125). A case in point is the ancient Greek city-state, in which citizens directly participated in state (political, public) affairs—basically in the sense of the formation of a specific "realm of social life in which something approaching public opinion can be formed," in which "access is guaranteed to all citizens." According to Habermas ([1964] 1979, 198), this is the most general understanding of the public sphere. Arguments for extending the concept further into history temporally, as suggested by Margaret Mead and Beaud, increase in validity if "public" is not considered a single, homogeneous (bourgeois) public but a differentiated public sphere—which became hierarchically structured and organized, primarily through establishing the difference between the center and periphery, for example, by the exclusion of peripheral or marginal social groups (women, workers, or peasants)—or even a public sphere in which opposing publics simultaneously exist, for example, the idea of an opposition between the bourgeois and proletarian public (Negt 1980, 75) or Jakubowicz's idea of an official, alternative, and oppositional public (Jakubowicz 1994). Thus the concept of public opinion may have universal validity; that is why Tönnies (1992) considers it a "normal concept" which, due to its transcendental nature, is only a matter of pure, ahistorical theory.

Second, the question of the theoretical and empirical import of the concept of public and its derivatives pertains not only to the interpretation of the past

but also to the present and the future. The origin of the liberal model of publicness is closely related to the advancing of the first generation of fundamental
human rights and liberties—political and civil rights related to the public
sphere (freedom of thought and expression, freedom of association, freedom of
the press) and private sphere (privacy rights related to individuals' movement,
residence, and personal communications). In the first half of the twentieth century, which is considered the period of codification of the second generation of
the fundamental—economic and social—rights, the liberal model of the public was already in decline. Should then the end of the twentieth century, which
is marked by the third generation of fundamental human rights—information
and communication rights, directly related to the question of public access to
information and the right to communicate and, at the same time, to the recon-
ceptualization of the private sphere and privacy rights—denote the end of the
public? This paradox demands systematic deliberation. In the first place, the
public/ness must not be reduced to a single conceptual dimension. Yet despite
the insistence on multidimensional conceptualization, an important dimension
of reductionism cannot be avoided here—ethnocentrism, which is commonly
characteristic of a large part of social thought.

The modern concepts of public/ness and public opinion are primarily products of the Enlightenment, but the idea of public/ness is closely related to the
idea of democracy and harks back to the political philosophy of ancient Greece
and Rome. During almost three millennia, but essentially during the last three
centuries, dissertations on public/ness developed five basic semantic dimensions of the general concept:

1. a/the public as a specific social category or collectivity that appears as a
   social actor or agent, particularly in relation to some important social issues (often in contrast to the crowd or the mass);
2. public/ness as the specific nature of a particular activity or space (the characteristic or state of publicness; for example, public service broadcasting,
   public utilities, public schools);
3. publicity as the "incarnation" of publicness embedded in a principle or
   norm, and as a universal human right, thus representing the foundations
   of public opinion and the doctrine of sovereignty;
4. public sphere as specific sphere, domain, or imagined space (e.g., French
   l'espace publique) of social life, a social space between the state and civil
   (initially bourgeois) society, which represents an infrastructure for social
   integration through public discourse or an opinion market; and
5. public opinion as a linkage of the above dimensions while providing a
   fifth one—opining. Opining could be considered a specific dimension in

treatises on public/ness, especially since the vigorous controversies over public opinion contributed most to the popularity of public/ness. In normative theories, public opinion is considered as directly resulting either from the public as a social category (expressed by the public) or from the public sphere (or "public opinion context," as Wilson put it), or both. However, in twentieth-century positivist and, particularly, empiricist approaches, public opinion is commonly "emancipated" from its historical foundations.

I shall elaborate on each of these dimensions and discuss the questions that recur in analyses of public opinion and public/ness.

THE PUBLIC AS A SOCIAL COLLECTIVITY

Sociological (or social-psychological) theorization of public/ness asserted by the Chicago school in the twentieth century does not conceptualize "the public" on the ground of differentiation between public and private spheres but as a loosely organized collectivity or group emerging in a rational discussion, which is very difficult to identify and operationalize as a *specific* group. The classic Enlightenment understanding of the public as a specific social actor was grounded on its restriction to the educated elite—"the public" of addressees, consumers, and critics of arts, which emerged in cities in the period of rising capitalism and bourgeois class—without emphasizing its exclusive character. As Habermas argues ([1962] 1995, 30), cities did not develop into the centers of bourgeois society only in the economic but also in the cultural and political sense with English coffeehouses, French salons, and German (later also Slovene) *Tischgesellschaften*. In those elite societies, debates on literature and art (and later, when the revolution time was approaching, primarily on politics) preferred the authority of arguments over the argument of authority. As press censorship was restricted and gradually abolished, newspapers played an increasingly important role in public debates. With their art, cultural, and political critique, they were transformed from an object and reporter of debates in dispersed publics into an inherent part of the discussions. Debates in publics, based on the rationality and equality of discussants, were public at least in two distinct meanings. First, they were aimed at reaching a consensus in the formation of common will and/or common good; thus they went beyond the confrontation of particularistic interests. Second, participation in discussions in the public was *formally* open. It was not restricted by the social or economic status; however, women and other deprived social groups did not have at their disposal the intellectual skills necessary for an active participation in a rational discourse. It was only when fundamental human political, economic, and social rights were constitutionally enacted that informal restrictions of access to the public became suppressed. But new impediments appeared at the same time.

In the analysis of "basic forms of social units" in his doctoral dissertation (1904), Robert E. Park defined the public as a specific *social group* opposite to the *crowd*. "The behavior of the public which is expressed in public opinion, results from discussion among individuals who assume opposing positions. This discussion is based upon the presentation of facts." It is characteristic of the public that "individual impulses and interests arise out of the undefined basis of the common consciousness and develop further in a peculiar reciprocal interaction" among its members, that is, in a form of critical (rational) discourse—in contrast to the crowd, in which reciprocal interaction results in control over all its members, inhibits individual impulses and interests, and suppresses individual autonomy (Park [1904] 1972, 57, 51). Essential for the public is the process of reciprocity between interests or interest groups in the public, in which differences between them are preserved and one side always presumes the existence of the opposite one: neither of them would be the same without the existence of the other. The process of adaptation through differentiation is perhaps best expressed in political life (e.g., interaction between opposing political parties) and economy (reciprocal relationship between the buyer and seller). However, the public has many characteristics in common with the crowd: both emerge from the processes of social adaptation (imitation) and change; neither is formally organized and both lack of regulation; neither is conscious of itself as a group; both presuppose the prior existence of other functional groups that transform themselves into new groupings through either of the two; both the public and the crowd have no history or common tradition; consequently, they "cannot be viewed as general will in the historical sense of the word, but instead as an empirical preliminary stage to it" (Park [1904] 1972, 79–80).

Park comes at a definition of the difference between the crowd and the public through the difference between "primary reciprocity" (or interaction) and "reciprocity through which a collectivity acts upon itself." Primary reciprocity enables behavior usually initiated by opinion leaders to be diffused throughout society almost mechanically (by imitation) and to become common to all. Through primary reciprocity each generation takes on a large part of its traditions from the preceding generation, for example, language, usages, or ceremonies. According to Park, this process "enables social usages to establish and perpetuate themselves in society." Tönnies associated this process with *Gemeinschaft,* in which a true opinion of the public does not exist. In Beniger's (1987) terms, primary reciprocity is reproduction, which means control of evolution or "becoming." Directly opposite to it is the process in which the group takes a stand on something in its environment—the process generating collective attention through which the group acts upon itself:

> In certain social groupings, such as parliament or a court of law, a kind of reciprocity occurs whose function is not only to carry out collective action, but free from external considerations, to direct the collective action toward changing the disposition of the group itself or of some of its members. This kind of institution thus presents examples of formal processes in which a collectivity act upon itself. . . . [These processes] tend to be more like the process of attention and perception. (Park [1904] 1972, 44–45)

The public denotes a specific form of secondary reciprocity; it differs from the crowd, which is characterized by obedience, in that it requires rational reflection. Park's differentiation between the two forms of interaction may be related to two basic purposes of control, which is aimed at either (1) achieving given ends, such as laying hold of scarce resources (control over environment or extrinsic control) or (2) achieving self-control (intrinsic control) and dealing with (un)expected changes and threats; here control is not aimed toward other ends but is an end in itself. Primary reciprocity represents exogenous control, which is imposed on a system and depends on vertical flows of information and on a centralized capacity to process information, which assure the most appropriate commands to achieve the most effective strategies. Access to exogenous control generates power (e.g., access to production resources or state-controlled allocation of broadcasting frequencies). Endogenous (organic) control depends on horizontal information flows. It distributes the capacity to process information. Consequently, access to endogenous control generates influence rather than power.

Collective attention tends to loosen more stable forms of social interaction, which can eventually be dissolved. In any collectivity, some general concerns that dominate communication are always present; some of them may capture the attention of the whole world. The latter sociological processes operate in different sorts of collectivities or groupings—from parliaments and courts (in which they are very complex and thus more difficult to observe) to a form simple enough to be observed in the crowd.

In the development of a crowd, individuals unconsciously and without reflection join together as a unit. As Park argues ([1904] 1972, 50), "The unity of the crowd is based on the fact that all members of the group are controlled by one common drive evoked by the reciprocal interaction of these members."

In contrast to all other forms of groups, both the crowd and the public represent "individualistic forms of society": they bring individuals out of old ties and into new ones; they represent transition to new, more stable social forms; individuals in them have no common tradition and no common future; thus, in this sense they are both ahistorical. Although individual interests and impulses are inhibited in the crowd, they fully emerge in the public. Therefore, the conditions under which one enters the public are stronger than those of the crowd: not only the ability to feel and empathize is required but also the ability to think and reason with others (Park [1904] 1972, 80). In addition, the public expresses criticism and within it, opinions are divided. *If criticism disappears, the public itself ceases to exist.* Whereas the dominant cohesive factor of the crowd is obedience, the public is guided by prudence and rational reflection. Although the public is, similarly to the crowd, influenced by the collective drive, this collective drive finds individual expression in the individuals. According to Park ([1904] 1972, 81), public opinion is "the insight gained through criticism and the resulting explanation of the drive controlling the public."

> It is a mistake to view public opinion as one which is acceptable to each individual member of the public to the same degree. It is much more an opinion or an attitude which is external to every individual and which is viewed as something objective. Precisely because public opinion is seen as the product of individual critical attitudes, it expresses itself variously in different individuals. (Park 1904] 1972, 59)

Park's disciple Herbert Blumer, like Park, conceived of the public as an elementary collective grouping "(a) who are confronted by an issue, (b) who are divided in their ideas as to how to meet the issue, and (c) who engage in discussion over the issue" (Blumer [1946] 1966, 46). The elementary and spontaneous nature of the public derives from the fact that it occurs as a "natural response" to an issue; it does not exist in an organized form, and its behavior is not prescribed by traditions or cultural patterns. In contrast to Park, Blumer does not define the opposite to the public with the crowd but rather with the mass, which can best be exemplified with the recipients in mass communication interested in an issue. In contrast to the public, the peculiarities of the mass are that (1) its membership may come from different social strata, (2) it is composed of anonymous individuals, (3) in contrast to the crowd, there is little interaction between its members because they are physically separated from each other, and (4) it is very loosely organized and not able to act as effectively as the crowd (Blumer [1946] 1966, 43).

Following Park and Blumer, C. Wright Mills defined the public in contrast to *mass,* which differs both from *public* and *crowd:* "In a *public,* as we may understand the term, (1) virtually as many people express opinion as receive them. (2) Public communications are so organized that there is a chance immediately and effectively to answer back any opinion expressed in public. Opinion formed by such discussion (3) readily finds an outlet in effective action, even against— if necessary—the prevailing system of authority. And (4) authoritative institutions do not penetrate the public, which is thus more or less autonomous in its operations" (Mills [1956] 1968, 303–4). Mills is, however, skeptical with regard to the concept of the public assumed in classical democratic theory and compares it to fairy tale images. Similarly, a bit later Habermas noted that a certain regression occurred in the development of the public sphere—a so-called refeudalization of the public, which was primarily a consequence of the interventionist role of the state and, because of that, the disappearance of a clear line between the state and civil society, the decline of traditional public places, and the homogenization and commercialization of the mass media. Last, but not least, a certain critical distance in relation to the classical concept of the public is reflected in its pluralization: the object of attention is no more "the public" but many (specific) publics, or "a public." The general public, paradoxically, became the publicist synonym for the population, for a kind of sum or statistical average, which actually represents the opposite of the public.

In the most general way, the public as a social category was defined by John Dewey. The starting point of his understanding of the public is the distinction between the results of interpersonal transactions, which the people involved can control by themselves, and indirect consequences, to which people not directly involved are exposed. This difference leads to a distinction between the private and the public. The public as a specific grouping differing from other forms of community life is formed by "those indirectly and seriously affected for good or for evil" by consequences of transactions in which they are not involved— to such a degree that a systematic regulation of the consequences is believed necessary (Dewey [1927] 1991, 35, 16). The interest in implementing a restricting or an encouraging regulation is assumed by public officials,[2] and the public eventually produces a political state as its own political organization identifying with it:

> This public is organized and made effective by means of representatives who as guardians of custom, as legislators, as executives, judges, etc., care for its especial interests by methods intended to regulate the conjoint actions of individuals and groups. Then and in so far as, association adds to itself political organization, and something which may be government comes into being: the public is a political state. (Dewey [1927] 1991, 35)

Dewey's conception of the public as a political state collides with Tönnies's and later with Habermas's understanding of the public, according to which "state authority is, so to speak, the executor of the political public sphere, it is not a part of it" (Habermas [1964] 1979, 198), although in Habermas's conceptualization, "public authority" takes care of the common welfare of all legal persons and is, in this sense, functionally similar to Dewey's political organization of the public. On the other hand, Dewey, like Habermas, emphasizes the role of a "constant watchfulness and criticism of public officials by citizens," which enables the maintenance of the state "in integrity and usefulness" (Dewey [1927] 1991, 69). Dewey has, contrary to Habermas and similarly to Tönnies, emphasized the time and space variability of the public caused by differences in "the consequences of associated action and the knowledge of them" and in "the means by which a public can determine the government to serve its interests." Consequently, he emphasized that "in no two ages or places is there the same public." What different publics have in common is primarily "the function of caring for and regulating the interests which accrue as the result of the complex indirect expansion and radiation of conjoint behavior" (Dewey [1927] 1991, 33, 47).

Contrary to sociological tradition from Park to Mills, which modernized the idea of citizen presence on an antique Greek square or Roman forum, or replaced it by defining the terms of an efficient collective action, especially on the basis of (e.g., parliamentary) representation, German constitutional lawyer Carl Schmitt ([1928] 1954) nostalgically defended the conservative idea of "government by public opinion" founded on the notion of people gathered in a certain space that allows for their direct presence, and thus for a version of direct democracy similar to that expressed by Rousseau in his *Social Contract*. Even Dewey, who was, together with Lippmann and Tönnies, Schmitt's contemporary, we could say that he excessively argued for the importance of direct communication in a local community in which dialogue is only possible: "Unless local communal life can be restored, the public cannot adequately resolve its most urgent problem: to find and identify itself" (Dewey [1927] 1991, 216). However, at the same time, he emphasized the historical urge to overcome the borders of territorial states and political boundaries. Schmitt also claimed, as Blumer did later, that the mere tallying of votes and opinions of individuals cannot build public opinion by itself; but at the same time he argued that only when citizens gather in a shared space can they call to life the essence of public opinion—public acclamation.

Public opinion cannot arise through secret individual polling or by aggregating the opinions of isolated private persons. All these recording methods are only expedients, as such useful and valuable; yet they certainly do not constitute public opinion. *Public opinion is the modern art of acclamation.* . . . There is no democracy and no State without public opinion, as there is no State without acclamation. Public opinion rises and exists 'unorganised;' it would be deprived of its nature, and so would be the acclamation, if it became a sort of official function. (Schmitt [1928] 1954, 246)

In Schmitt's opinion, acclamation means that people can express their agreement or disagreement through exclaiming (or that they can refuse acclamation by keeping quiet or murmuring); to do that, of course, requires physical presence. People produce the public by their very presence, and their specific activity in the public is acclamation, which is, according to Schmitt, linked with the constitutional right of free gathering as a basis of democracy. Demonstrations, public celebrations, theater audiences, spectators at stadiums, and similar modern forms of gathering, whose model is the antique form; they do not represent organized forms but are, potentially, always political and are supposed to contain the basis of the public in the forms that Park viewed as typical examples of the crowd. Schmitt was primarily pointing to the process of "ignoring the gathered people" in bourgeois democracies. He was also emphasizing the nondemocratic quality of secret voting used by "liberal individualism" to compensate for the fundamental assumption of any democracy—which is that the people cannot be represented because only what is absent can be represented, whereas the people always have to be present, which is equated by Schmitt to the "actually gathered people" *(wirklich versammeltes Volk)*.

Practically no contemporary discussion on the public, including radical critiques, can ignore Habermas's intellectual project initiated in the early 1960s by his habilitation work *Strukturwandel der Öffentlichkeit*. In this work, Habermas initially emphasizes that the public (sphere) implies something more than a general accessibility. Later on he realizes that the bourgeois public exists merely through the principle of general accessibility, although he limits validity of the term "public opinion" and the liberal model of the public, only to its historically specific meaning in England at the end of the seventeenth century, and in France in the eighteenth century (Habermas [1962] 1995). In later discussions, in spite of modifications, Habermas's critical view of the fate of the public in a developed capitalist society has not radically changed. In his earliest period, Habermas understood the public as the bearer of public opinion having the function of a critic in relation to power. Later on, he defined the public as a "communication structure which is, through its base in a civil society, rooted in the life-world," and concluded by examining its political functions in relation to "communicative power" and "deliberative politics" as an "alarm system" (Škerlep 1996, 379). As Habermas argues, the contemporary notion of publicness, particularly in the sense of critical publicity, can only play the role of some kind of comparative standard or of a radical democratic vision at the normative level, allowing for a critique of the deficiencies of existing (non)democratic institutions and relationships. Certain proposals of Habermas concerning democratization, however, are almost utopian, and he himself later denied or at least fundamentally modified them (Habermas 1992a).

Habermas's ideas concerning the creation and especially the decline of the bourgeois public and the refeudalization of publicity were systematically criticized by John Thompson, who, by the way, admits at the same time that Habermas "should also be given credit for anticipating, with remarkable prescience, the glittering media campaigns that were to become such a pervasive feature of presidential and general elections in the age of television" (Thompson 1993, 178). Thompson emphasizes in the first place that "the development of mass communication has created new opportunities for the production and diffusion of images and messages, opportunities which exist on a scale and are executed in a manner that precludes any serious comparison with the theatrical practices of feudal courts" (Thompson 1990, 115; 1993, 183). He consequently argues that Habermas's argument regarding the refeudalization of publicity is unjustified. The new possibilities offered by forms of mass communication are, according to Thompson, linked principally with the development of the medium of television and less with the development of information and telecommunication technologies, which allow an ever larger quantity of information to circulate in the information markets. Thompson perhaps took too literally the metaphor of refeudalization. On the other hand, his criticism brings him very close to the trap of equating an information society with an informed society when he argues that the commercialization of the media and the use of quasi-commercial techniques for the presentation of political contents— which, according to Habermas ([1962] 1995), Sennett (1978) or Mills, mark the decline of the public—increase the visibility of political leaders and limit their opportunity to control the conditions of receiving messages and ways of their being interpreted by their receivers. Indeed, the role of mass communication audiences cannot be reduced to that of passive consumers. As Thompson (1993, 183) accurately argues, "This kind of argument exaggerates the passivity of individuals and takes too much for granted concerning the process of reception; a more contextualized and hermeneutically sensitive approach would show that the process of reception is a much more complicated and creative activity." Yet it would be no less presumptuous to equate audiences of modern mass media with critical readers, who represented the core of the liberal bourgeois public, or, as Thompson suggests, to abandon the historical comparison.

The opposition between the critical and the manipulative functions of publicity was globalized due to the development of information and telecommunication technologies. Of course it would be absurd to think that new technologies alone have produced globalization, but they certainly were the basic impelling force. From another perspective we could say that globalization is the "natural" result of the capitalist economy, whose very essence has been global since its beginning: it was developed through the social and spatial (geographical) integration of the production and exchange processes, only consumption remaining local. The differentiation of relationships between the realms of the public and the private in the triangle formed by the state, the economy, and civil society is becoming global itself because of the gradual limiting of the state's political and economic sovereignty and the occurrence of international and transnational political and economic factors in the period of cybercapitalism. Zolo (1992, 170) was right to emphasize that global changes led to new structural changes of the public (sphere), which are even more important than those that were analyzed by Habermas, since they come close to an "anthropological mutation."

At both local and global levels, the conflict between manipulative and critical publicity, between the authoritarian (demonstrative) and emancipatory (democratic) potential of communication, is extremely complex. Primarily due to this complexity, there is a threat of a radical dispersion of the public sphere (Zolo 1992, 114), promoted by the mass media themselves (although, on the other hand, new telecommunication technologies should [re]activate the public). "Global media" develop along with the "global state" and the "global economy" and increase the complexity of communication processes and broach functional and spatial integration processes. Frequently media operate outside the scope of democratic control, which reveals the utopianism of notions of "teledemocracy" and "technologies of freedom" (Pool 1983).

However, globalization does not resolve the conflict at either the local or the global level. If already at the state level it is possible to detect processes of the refeudalization of publicity, the symmetry in the state-economy-civil society triangle being completely destroyed at the global level, as a "global state" (as in the European Union) is created by political elites and bureaucracies, and the global economy of transnational corporations takes rise. No doubt, new forms of global civil society emerge in the processes of globalization, and a "global public sphere" would correspond with it—with functions in international relationships analogous to those of a public within a state organization. However, there is no doubt either that civil society and the public generally retain their national characteristics. In specific circumstances like those in the former socialist states, such characteristics are even strengthened when the public is functionally reduced to the (necessarily locally delimited) "consumption of public opinion" or "created" for acclamation purposes. In a way, this is also proven by international public opinion polls (e.g., the Eurobarometer), which—like the early polls between the world wars—reaffirm the actual processes of opinion (trans)nationalization. These polls are focused on the comparison of national public opinions rather than on processes of "Europeanization" of public opinion, and the aggregation of individual opinions is still confined to the level of the nation-state.

In present times, then, the concept of the public denotes different groups or collectivities in different (research) circumstances. Besides the general public, which is empirically loosely associated with the national population (because this is the only definition that makes survey research based on random sampling possible),[3] there is also a "voting public" (i.e., the body of actual voters), an "attentive public" (characterized by the interest in politics and at least occasional participation in debates on political issues), an "active public" (representing the elite of the attentive public), and "sectoral" or "special publics," which merely by their size (the number of members) differ greatly from each other. Searching for special publics that would be empirically observable is getting dangerously close to rhetorical speculations and commonsense assessments of the public from the world or international one to the domestic or local one, from the political to the cultural, from the professional to the lay—all of which can lead to the conclusions of Luhmann or Bourdieu, since by the creation of an infinite number of different publics, the notion of the public becomes all-encompassing.

Irrespective of all perplexities, the understanding of the public as a national phenomenon prevails fully, though often implicitly. On the one hand, this implies that a large number of publics exist—there are at least as many publics as there are nations—while on the other hand it implicitly denies the possible existence of a kind of special publics. Why should a nation have the privilege of generating the public? Why can't other types of collectivities also have their own publics? A clear answer can only be found within the framework of Dewey's theory of the public and those theories of public opinion that define it in relation to the state, or to state authority. Dewey conceives the public as a consequence of transactions between individuals and (nonpolitical) groups that affect individuals and groups not involved in these transactions. The public therefore occurs because of the need for the (legal) regulation of such consequences, and regulation is only possible through the political organization of the public, that is, the state. The existence of the public is subject to the possibility of efficient political representation and not to the possibility of participation, which is restricted to relatively small groups (communities).[4] Thus we could speak of (the possibility of) a transnationalization of the public that parallels the formation of transnational political communities with their own regulatory means (e.g., the European

Union), although such means do not imply a dying out of nation-states. On the other hand, the idea of political participation limits the public "downward," since the public is, in principle, open to the cooperation of all citizens who want to utter their opinion and participate in the formation of the opinion of the public. Special publics can exist neither by the first nor by the second criterion (1) because they are not regulatively efficient (they have no state of their own) and (2) because in their specificity they limit access (the scientific public, for example, is limited to scientists, the sport public to sports figures and sports fans, etc.).

THE PUBLIC AND THE PRIVATE AS ATTRIBUTES OF SOCIAL ACTIONS AND INSTITUTIONS

The relationship between the public and the private and the boundary between the two realms has changed throughout history. No doubt, the majority of changes were caused by the development of communication and, above all, the mass media. The latter made private life to a large extent public (accessible to audiences), and at the same time they made it possible to witness public issues and events in the private sphere of home, for example, on television screen. Different meanings of publicness that were formed from the Renaissance on were summed up in the famous statement uttered by Abraham Lincoln during the U.S. Civil War, in which he paraphrased the conception of people's governance first outlined by Edmund Burke: "government of the people [with their consent], by the people [through their representatives], for the people [for their common and permanent good] shall not perish from the earth" (see Hoffman and Levack [1949] 1967, xx–xxi).

The first three semantic dimensions of publicness are connected with the public-private dichotomy. In France, the notion of the public was initially defined in opposition to the particular or the individual, and had not yet been defined in opposition to the private. Ozouf (in contrast to, e.g., Gouldner 1976, 101) stated that the meaning of the public as opposed to the private was asserted in the French language only in the middle of the nineteenth century (Ozouf 1987, 2). Both semantic dimensions refer to the development of modern societies characterized by commodity production and representative democracy, first, public in the sense of what is (generally, to all) visible and/or accessible (cf. public space, public notice—in Burke and Lincoln: "*of* the people").

To publish means to make a message accessible, attainable, visible. Public is therefore what can be seen by everyone, what is accessible to everyone or at least to many, what is happening within the sight of the citizens, spectators (readers, listeners, viewers) and buyers—like commodities in the market place, in circulation, but not in the sphere of production or consumption—whereas the private is hidden and confidential, and it is carried out within a narrow circle of individuals (e.g., within a family but also in the institutions of power, as in the case of state secrets). As Hannah Arendt ([1958] 1989, 50) put it, the term public means, first, that "everything that appears in public can be seen and heard by everybody and has the widest possible publicity." Habermas's notion of "representative publicity" ([1964] 1979) in the sense of public (re)presentation similarly refers to making the (feudal) power visible although—since it concerns representations of *power*—it also implies the meaning of matters of general interest.

"For us, appearance—something that is seen and heard by others as well as by ourselves—constitutes reality," Hannah Arendt ([1958] 1989, 50) said. Similarly, Marx ([1842] 1969, 94) argued in his critique of censorship that "what I cannot be for others, I am not for myself and cannot be for myself," that is, I cannot exist as a human being if I am not allowed to "communicate my spiritual here-being." With the development of information and communication technologies, the horizon of publicness in the sense of accessibility, visibility, and audibility is substantially extended (cf. "the right of access to information"); direct (physical) access to an event in a public place is more and more replaced by indirect mediated accessibility through the mass media and new telecommunication technologies. At the same time, accessibility is becoming standardized. For example, the political system has become accessible in the same way as commodities are accessible in the market place; even more so, "the contexts of commodities and politics share the same media and, at least in part, the same metalanguage for constructing our notion of what a public or a people is" (Warner 1992, 386).

Second, public in the sense of referring to matters of general or, specifically, national (state) importance or interest that, of course, has nothing to do with general accessibility but rather with common or general interests (a state as a "public authority"—in Burke and Lincoln: "*for* the people") that should be satisfied by (thus public) actions. Public in this sense refers to the sphere of institutionalized political power, a sovereign state, whereas private refers to the economy and personal relations, which are outside of the state control. Here, the similarity with the division between the state and civil society is more than evident—also in reference to vaguely defined and changing boundaries between the state or public sphere and private (economic) relationships, or civil society, and the formation of public actors that do not entirely belong either to the public (state) or to the private (civil) sphere but remain somewhere in-between (e.g., state-owned companies, nonprofit private firms, interest groups, even political parties). In the classical model of the liberal bourgeois public, the difference between the state and civil society is the difference between the public sphere (public authority embodied in the state) and the private domain composed of the private sphere (civil society in its narrow sense, that is, economy and family), and the public of private people. In modern (post)industrial societies, there is a basic shift of the border between the public and the private spheres, or between the state and civil society, that is opposed to both the state and the economy; the central part of civil society is occupied by associations that form opinion and serve as a focus for "autonomous public spheres" (Habermas 1992a, 454; 1992b, 443).

In both aforementioned meanings, the private denotes not only a border or an opposition to the public but also the basis of the public: "The private sphere is, on the one hand, a sort of arena wherein public rationality was eliminated and within which it is not necessary to give justifications, and on the other hand, the private provides a basis for resistance to the public sphere which can become strong enough to impose upon the private sphere and control it" (Gouldner 1976, 104). Similarly, Hannah Arendt argues that the term "public" signifies also "the world itself" in the sense of human artifacts by which people are gathered together and placed in relation to, or separated from, each other, as far as this world is "common to all of us and distinguished from our privately-owned place in it" (Arendt [1958] 1989, 52). The public realm, as understood by Arendt, has the power to gather and relate people together who are *interested in common world.*

"Public" in the sense of regulating general/state affairs also includes Habermas's and Leforts's notion of "representative publicness," which denotes a special type of public agency that excludes the people: public representation (demonstration) of the power or the status of nobility, clergy, or governing classes *before* the people as some sort of a passive audience—which thus represents a condition for the formation of representative publicness, but it is in no way allowed to participate in power. This semantic dimension of the public was dominant also in the former socialist states, clearly expressed in Lenin's idea of the unity of "collective propaganda, agitation and organization." Habermas's notion of the refeudalization of publicity in developed capitalism refers to this particular semantic dimension of the public, especially in connection with the mass media through which power is represented. Moreover, historically speaking, this dimension of the public seems to be the one that served as the cornerstone of contemporary forms of mass-public communication and their tendency of representing public persons (Warner 1992, 388). In this sense, of course, there is no state without the "public," no matter if this state is a democracy or a monarchy. Although in the former case it is only a residual, essentially overcome form of the public, in the latter case it is its only form (cf. Schmitt [1928] 1954, 244).

Third, John Dewey's conceptualization of the difference between the public and the private is most distinct of all.[5] It is not related to the difference between the individual and the social or socially useful (e.g., in the sense of public interests as social interests). Rather, it is based on the consequences of the individual's action for other individuals. Dewey ([1927] 1991, 12) draws a distinction between consequences that "affect the persons directly engaged in a transaction, and those which affect others beyond those immediately concerned." The former can be controlled by the people involved, but not the latter. If the consequences of human actions are confined to the individuals directly participating in them, the transactions may be considered *private*. If, however, indirect consequences are recognized and somehow regulated, the transactions have a *public* nature. This distinction is the basis of Dewey's definition of the public, which "consists of all those who are affected by the indirect consequences of transactions to such an extent that it is deemed necessary to have those consequences systematically addressed. . . . The public as far as it is organized by means of officials and material agencies to care for the extensive and enduring indirect consequences of transactions between persons is the Populus" (Dewey [1927] 1991, 15–16).

Fourth, "public" also denotes what is created in the public or resulting from the public (in Burke and Lincoln: "*by* the people"). This meaning is the most recent and is determined primarily by the conception of the public as a social category or as a public sphere: it relates to what takes place in the public as a collectivity or some sort of a social network. Thus, for example, *public opinion is much more than publicly expressed opinion or what individuals dare show at a moment;* it is the opinion that is formed in, or by, the public or, as Dewey ([1927] 1991, 177) kept asserting, "public opinion is a judgment which is formed and entertained by those who constitute the public and is about public affairs." There are at least two reasons that help explain the central role that public opinion has in modern developments and conceptualizations of the public: (1) the primary function of the (bourgeois) public crystallized in the very concept of public opinion and (2) empirical public opinion research radically— although not intentionally—impugned the existence of the public.

THE PRINCIPLE OF PUBLICITY

Conceptualizations of publicness as a distinctive attribute of human actions and social institutions culminated in Kant's elaboration of the principle of publicity. Much before "public opinion" and "the public sphere" became commonly used terms, Kant defined *publicity* in his essay "Perpetual Peace" as a "transcendental concept of public right" based on citizens' fundamental dignity and moral sovereignty. Kant conceived of publicity as a moral principle and legal norm, as an "instrument" to achieve both individuals' independent reasoning and legal order in the social realm: "All actions affecting the rights of other human beings are wrong if their maxim is not compatible with their being made public" (Kant [1795] 1983, 135). Much later, John Dewey defined "the public" on similar grounds, arguing that the public consists of "all those who are affected by the indirect consequences of transactions to such an extent that it is deemed necessary to have those consequences systematically cared for" (Dewey [1927] 1991, 15–16), which would imply that a public can be democratically organized only on the basis of full publicity in respect to all "transactions with indirect consequences" concerning the public, and freedom of expression.

The idea of publicity as a fundamental human right in Kant's principle of publicity also represents the fundamental principle of a democratic order. Any regulation of relationships in a (political) community would contradict the public interest and citizens' freedom if citizens cannot be convinced by reason in the public realm, or if they are kept alienated and isolated from public communications that would enable them to discuss matters of common concern in public. (Of course, "citizens" for Kant means property-owning adult males, who alone should be admitted to the "public use of reason" and elections.) The legitimacy of the state can only be grounded on the principle of publicity because the government can only hold authority over people if it represents the general will of the community: Only governments that are not acting in the public interest may fear "independent and public thought." Thus Kant's principle of publicity reconciles politics with democratic legitimacy: whereas politics is coercion, democracy is the moral basis of association. The two spheres can only be reconciled by fundamental human rights embodied in the principle of publicity—freedom of thought and freedom of public expression; neither of them can exist without the other.

Kant's differentiation between politics (power) and morals (justice) is particularly important from the perspective of some twentieth-century reconceptualizations of public opinion into a form of social control and surveillance that assure the functioning of power, that is, its transformation from an associative into a coercive concept. Such a conceptual transformation strongly contradicts Kant's (and generally the Enlightenment as well as pragmatists') belief that citizens must be convinced by reason in the exercise of public debate that public policies are just, or else the state loses its moral legitimacy.

THE PUBLIC SPHERE

The concept of the public sphere that emerges between civil society and the state is the most complex and theoretically specific from among all conceptual dimensions of "public/ness." Although similar ideas can be found elsewhere (notably in Wilson's concept of the public opinion situation), it is based predominantly upon Habermas's (re)conceptualization of the public, which is a concept no less complex itself and, as critics point out, even contradictory. Since the public is, historically, connected with a diversity of economic, political, cultural, social-psychological, system-organizational, and communication dimensions and phenomena, I shall only briefly introduce some key propositions here.

The significance of the public sphere resides in its potential for the creation of social integration on the basis of public discourse (or communicative action)—in the homology in the sphere of politics with political power and in the sphere of economy with market mechanisms, both of which represent specific ways of social integration and competition. It represents the locus at which private citizens engage in "the public use of reason," as conceptualized by Kant. The (political) public sphere is defined by Habermas (1992a, 446) as "all those conditions of communication under which there can come into being a discursive formation of opinion and will on the part of a public composed of the citizens of a state." The public sphere activates itself in the communicative interdependence of those potentially affected, who create the public as a social category in which both the legislated laws of the state and the market laws of the economy are suspended. In order to define the conceptual difference between a/the public as a social category and the public sphere as a form of social integration based on public discourse, the conditions of communication could be conceived of as the "infrastructure" of the (political) public sphere. The public sphere, then, would be a mental space that enables social integration on the basis of open, public discourse on matters of public concern. The necessary infrastructure and an institutional assurance of public sphere autonomy, guaranteed by the state of law, are not enough for the existence of the public sphere. What is also required is the supportive spirit of cultural traditions and socialization patterns, political culture, and (economic) freedom. For Habermas, the public sphere is

> a social phenomenon just as elementary as action, actor, association, or collectivity, but it eludes the conventional sociological concepts of "social order." The public sphere cannot be conceived as an institution and certainly not as an organization. . . . Just as little does it represent a system. . . . The public sphere can best be described as a network for communicating information and points of view (i.e.,

opinions expressing affirmative or negative attitudes); the streams of communication are, in the process, filtered and synthesized in such a way that they coalesce into bundles of topically specified *public opinions*. ([1992] 1997, 360)

The public sphere can be represented metaphorically as a sort of opinion market. The market metaphor is not new—one can find it in J. S. Mill and Park already—but it still undoubtedly presents the specifics of the public sphere in its relation to the public as a social category and as a certain type of activity: the public sphere has a similar meaning for politics as the market has for the economy. In the public sphere, as in the market, many different actors (individuals, groups, organizations) meet. However, these actors do not all have equal access to the market, and their opinions do not have equal weight or value. Just as the economic market, the public sphere also was originally (and up to the modern times) determined by, and restricted to, a specific public space (the agora in ancient Greece and the forum in Rome, for example). In that public space, public life was taking place, which could be quite easily controlled and eventually even abolished. That happened in the medieval era, when only representative publicity existed. With the development of communication technology in the period of the rise of capitalism—similarly again to the changes in the economic market—the public sphere began to liberate itself from its spatial determination and gained the character of a network of spatially detached actors and their relationships. This network is nowadays becoming global. In addition to the newly emergent public places of the period (including cafes, salons, pubs, reading clubs), the first media of public communication played a crucial role in the creation of the public sphere. Newspapers made public affairs and discussions about such affairs accessible to individuals scattered across space. Tönnies coined the term "large public" to refer to the readers among whom the newspapers circulated. The development of the press has, in spite of the resistance it faced from absolutist power, especially in the form of censorship and high taxes, crucially contributed to the establishment of parliamentary democracies.

Even though elements of public sphere can no doubt be found in ancient Greece, the public sphere in the contemporary (strict) sense originates in its separation from the sphere of public power in the seventeenth and eighteenth centuries and with the invocation of the principle of publicity and public reasoning against the arcane practice of the absolute monarchy, which stood over and above the will of the "incompetent people." The implementation of the principle of publicity was crucially important for the transition from absolute rule and monarchical authority to the rule of universal legal norms and the rule of law. The further reshaping of the political public sphere, according to Habermas, is primarily connected to the dialectical relations between the state (public authority) and (civil) society, and in particular to their interpenetration (which leads to the nationalization of society and the socialization of the state) as well as the (in)ability to create an "institutional core of civil society" outside the borders of the state (and later also outside the economy). As Calhoun (1992, 6) points out, state and economy are crucial themes of the democratic public sphere and at the same time its crucial rivals. The public sphere establishes itself between the sphere of the public authority of the state and the private sphere of the economy and the family (civil society). In the latter sphere, private actors appear and discuss the public affairs of both civil society and the state (art, science, economy, and politics). The public sphere, together with its opposing private sphere, shapes civil society against the state from which the bourgeois public has appropriated the public sphere and reshaped it into a sphere for the critique of public authority. In this sense, the public sphere represents a (new) domain for the articulation and execution of social will, a sphere in which the "public opinion situations" are created (Wilson 1962, 278) and "a *public* could form its own opinion that might challenge the state's primacy in setting social purposes and that might expect its understanding to bear weight on what the state did" (Hauser 1997, 278).

The public sphere is closely related to the concept of civil society if the latter is conceived of as the public (particularly mental and, more recently, cybernetic or virtual) space, which is delineated on one side by bureaucratic structures of the state and economy (state institutions and private corporations) and on the other side by the private sphere of family, friendship, and intimacy. Civil society, then, is constituted by organizations and activities that do not have a directly political or commercial character and are not motivated by profit or power. Rather, in civil society opinions and goals are formed and defined to influence opinion formation and decision making in given institutional and normative frameworks (the public and the state). It consists of self-governing organizations and activities like schools and education, the media and (mass) communication, churches and religion, trade unions and workers movements, associations of "men of rank" and charity, movements and associations of national and ethnic minorities, professional associations and chambers, and so on. It is important to note that all these organizations are more or less constantly under the pressure of capital and political power. The mass media are perhaps the best example, since the nature of their activity is in itself neither nonprofitable nor nonpolitical. Yet precisely in the sense of its autonomy from the sphere of economy and politics, civil society is a vitally important force for public opinion formation—for the formation of a consensus that may either influence political decision making or its legitimization. In this sense, civil society is "a *locus* of opinion formation that asserts authority to guide state actions"

(Hauser 1997, 278; emphasis added). In the latter sense, civil society conceptually comes close to the concepts of the public and the public sphere: "*under certain circumstances* civil society can acquire influence in the public sphere, have an effect on the parliamentary complex (and the courts) through its own public opinions, and compel the political system to switch over to the official circulation of power" (Habermas [1992] 1997, 373).

Associations and institutions of civil society are supposed to guarantee the necessary context to help establish political communication in the sense of the communicative generation of legitimate power, for example, against the manipulative use (misuse) of mass media to secure a massive citizen loyalty and promote consumer demand. The communication structures of the public (public sphere) enable actors on the periphery of civil society, who, in contrast to those at the political center (the state), have a higher sensitivity for the identification of problems, to activate new political and nonpolitical themes. Through often controversial discussions in the media, these new themes can become public themes. In contrast to the classical model of the liberal public sphere as a realm of individuals who, as individuals, are all included in the rational discussion, the contemporary public sphere is predominantly characterized by the appearance of identity politics, as manifested in nationalistic, ethnic and religious movements, feminism, youth movements, and so on, which shape a sort of secondary public. In short, against the state there does not stand a general, single, undifferentiated public sphere but rather a network of "specific publics" that preserve the borders to the general public and have relatively strong internal cohesion, not based upon some division of labor but upon specific identity politics.

The assertion that "the *principle* of the public sphere, that is, critical publicity, seemed to lose its strength in the measure that it expanded as a *sphere* and even undermined the private realm" summarizes Habermas's thesis about the decline of the public ([1962] 1995, 140). With the economic and political consolidation of capitalism in the global dimensions, with the development of the mass media and electoral propaganda and public opinion polls, the principle of publicity has radically changed its meaning. The principle of critical publicity, on which the constitution of the public was grounded, has to be strictly distinguished from publicity in its contemporary alternative sense of promoting goods, advertising, and public relations, all of which have nothing in common with the process of rational critical discussion. In a simplified conception of democratic political pluralism, both the pluralism of the mass media (in the sense that every group aspiring after political power can "freely use" the media) and their independence from political authority have been presented as necessary and sufficient conditions for freedom of expression and public opinion.

The principle of publicity has changed from the principle of public critique as a means of public opinion formation (critical public discourse) to the principle of the publicity as a process of directed integration based upon the depolitization of public communications and mediated by public relations, advertising, and propaganda. The reasoning of private individuals, once the cornerstone of the public, has become "one of the production numbers of the stars in radio and television, a salable package ready for the box office; it assumes commodity form even at 'conferences' where anyone can 'participate'" (Habermas [1962] 1995, 164). Along the same lines, the role of political parties and parliaments, in which party bureaucrats meet, has changed. Publicness becomes the attribute of an activity that gathers public opinion support for the representatives of political and economic power and thereby leads to the demise of the critical function of the public. The public sphere, with the development of the mass media, is changing into the sphere of the struggle for influence and control over the media. Through influencing the selection of themes and the way they are presented in the media, representatives of political power endeavor to influence the behavior of citizens (as audiences) who largely are not aware of manipulation. The critique of these changes by Senett, Mills, and the early Habermas had significantly pessimistic overtones, which Habermas later (1992a, 439)—under the influence of the results of research into political behavior and the mass media—relinquished or at least corrected. An ambivalent—either authoritarian or emancipatory—potential is concealed in the development of the media and in the changes in the public sphere. Which side of this potential is realized depends on the development of political, economic, and cultural conditions.

That ambivalence expresses itself also in the very notion of publicity. In contrast to the Enlightenment understanding of publicity as a means of countering the secrecy of autocratic authority, the rise of the advertising industry has turned publicity, in many cases, into a synonym for advertising. In French to date *(publicité)* and also in English from the end of the nineteenth century to the beginning of the twentieth century, both publicity and advertising meant spreading the information in public—a meaning that might today best be expressed by the term "public relations." Publicity in this sense often had extremely negative overtones; publicity stunts were supposed to assure the organizations, individuals, or articles popularity.[6] Only seldom has publicity implied, for example, public exposure of corruption—a meaning close to the classical principle of publicity (Mayhew 1997, 202).

Contemporary communication possibilities and the dominant forms of (mass) communication have stimulated the development of ideas about the postmodern public sphere, which, as opposed to the modern or enlightened public sphere, is not composed of a network of interdependent participatory communications and channels. Instead, it is based upon representations in mass media. It is believed that, at the end of the twentieth century, the public sphere has significantly expanded and transformed into the complex "public space of media culture" (Luthar 1996, 187). But if postmodern expansion and transformation mean political neutralization of the public sphere (or the public) and the loss of critical publicity as its fundamental principle, such consequences are not transferable directly to the public and public opinion, which will be the topic of further discussion.

A GENERAL MODEL OF PUBLIC OPINION

The notion of public/ness is most often present in expressions in which publicity is connected to the public as the carrier of public opinion. The term "public opinion" first appeared in the eighteenth century in the English and French political philosophy of the Enlightenment, which gave rise to the development of the liberal bourgeois public. In the twentieth century, it achieved—especially with opinion polls—such popularity that science has practically renounced itself from the topic, yet it has never stopped critically investigating it. Paul Beaud ironically points out that the well-known American journal *Public Opinion Quarterly*, founded in 1937, still systematically problematizes the very foundation of its own existence, that is, public opinion (Beaud 1993, 121). In its almost four-hundred-year history, a consensus on the social group(s) that create public opinion, or are implicated in it, is far from being reached. But it is obvious that with the domination of empirical sociological and social-psychological research over political-philosophical critique, or else with the administrative research ideology, the social foundation of public opinion is expanding from intellectual elites to the masses or even the whole population of a state. Additionally, public opinion, just like the public, became, already by the end of the eighteenth century, "a political and ideological construct without any clear sociological referent; it provided an implicit new system of authority in which the government and its critics had to claim the support of public opinion in order to secure their respective aims" (Price 1992, 12).

Like democracy, public opinion seems to bestow "an aura of legitimacy" (Held 1989, 1): laws, policies, decisions, even convictions or wars appear justified if they are in accordance with public opinion. Whereas premodern states legitimated their origin and development with divine will, in modern democracies this function is largely assumed by public opinion. Public opinion is indispensable to the legitimacy of governments that claim their power is based on the consent of the governed. In this sense, the functional equivalence of religion and public opinion, according to Tönnies, is obvious. Such a "legitimization pressure" can partly explain why the public and public opinion are so differently, even controversially, interpreted and defined but are often ignored in practice.

In the first political-philosophical dissertations in the period of the Enlightenment, public opinion was considered a political phenomenon of prime importance. In the notion of public opinion, the relationship between citizens and authorities was brought to the forefront: public opinion was supposed to secure a liberal form of government and not the opposite, that a government would secure public opinion, as William A. MacKinnon ([1828] 1971, 9) believed in the first monograph ever written on public opinion. Jean Jacques Rousseau's "model of public opinion" was based on the idea of the absolute sovereignty of the people as a community of equal citizens (irrespective of their status, property, etc.) within the nation-state, although this idea was even at that time clearly utopian. Later, Immanuel Kant in his writings emphasized the sovereignty of the nation-state as a meaningful and realistic guarantor of world peace, but this idea too soon proved a utopia: with the processes of internationalization and globalization of the economy and politics, state sovereignty became de facto more and more confined. These limitations were revealed only in the period of the sociologization of various approaches to public opinion in the beginning of the twentieth century, particularly in the treatises of Ferdinand Tönnies, John Dewey, and Walter Lippmann. At the same time, the significance and controversial nature of professional communication in political processes and consequently in the processes of public opinion formation became manifest. The importance of knowledge and information in decision making increased enormously since Rousseau's times, along with the exponential growth of the quantity of disposable knowledge produced.

Within the framework of the normative theory of democracy the notion of public opinion as a state-legal fiction points toward the unity of a "counterfactual entity" (Habermas 1992a, 440). Public opinion as "the rational opinion which emerges from the civil society and does not therefore mean the same as the opinion of particular groups of voters or the opinion of the electorate globally considered" remains a radical democratic vision, without existing (or even being able to exist) as a real unity. In that sense it is neither a representative for nor an aggregate of individual opinions and it is therefore impossible to operationalize it so as to coincide with the results of opinion polling. However, in everyday language public opinion is most often equated with simple aggregation, "the summing-up of individual opinions," that is, with the direct object of public opinion polling, which represents a sort of the "serialization of individuals," as Jean-Paul Sartre refers to it (Beaud 1993, 134). Such understanding of public opinion is of course in complete contradiction with the (dominant) understanding up to the beginning of the twentieth century, when opinion polling in the contemporary meaning began to develop. In the earlier, dominant understanding, public opinion was never considered in terms of a series of individual public opinions but instead as the opinion of the public resulting from group interactions, and therefore as a "supraindividual phenomenon" (Price 1992, 22). But one has to acknowledge alongside this critique that the empirical equation of the public with the sum of all the members of society (or just voters), at least in the early period, has not been without democratic stimulus: summing up individual opinions was supposed to enable the voice of the people to reach the ears of the authority.

In empirical opinion and communication research the notion of public opinion long ago ceased to mean in reality existing unity. "Political opinion polls provide a certain reflection of 'public opinion' only if they have been preceded by a focused public debate and a corresponding opinion-formation in a mobilized public sphere" (Habermas [1992] 1997, 362). On that account one could talk only about mass opinions (a collection of individual opinions), but definitely not about the unified public opinion. It is not only that the true object of public opinion research is not *public* opinion and not even opinion, but rather that private attitudes[7] are the object of research. Empirical research of public opinion has emerged as the result of the equation of the spheres of politics and consumption, and the decline of a critical public. Politics has begun to be sold just like any other good. As Zolo (1992, 129) claims, "The political market owes its democratic functionality to the existence of a 'public opinion' which is in a position to evaluate the market's offerings and to control its procedures." But consumers of political goods are in a worse position than the consumers of economic goods because they cannot directly control or sanction the quality of the good. Nor is the media plurality characterized by such a high level of competition among producers and the consequent differentiation of goods (contents diversity) that might characterize the economic market. Up to a point, public opinion polling should diminish that asymmetry. Indeed, public opinion became the object of empirical research in the period when the process of commodification of politics was already accomplished. Empirical research has improved and not caused the reliability and efficiency of harmonizing mass consciousness (public opinion) with the dominant opinions and interests (Splichal 1987, 252). The role played by public opinion polling can be compared to the role of the "mature" mass media, which Dewey and Lippmann, and later on Mills and Habermas, described as one that did not provide the public with the kind of information and opinions that could provoke discussion and connect people in a conversational community.

In the endeavors of empirical research, opinion can be considered public opinion in three senses: (1) as an opinion that is publicly expressed; (2) as opinion expressed by the public; (3) as any individual opinion on public affairs. Operationalization of public opinion in empirical research usually actualizes the third meaning (public affairs) and denounces the first two, thus negating the fundamental objective, that is, generating the model of public opinion. The objects of empirical research are not publicly expressed opinions; moreover, the respondent in the survey is always guaranteed the anonymity of his opinion. The object of research is not the opinion(s) of the public in the nonoperational sense, that is, in the sense of implying anything more than the legal age and the legal capacity of the persons surveyed. Such research has completely omitted any endeavor to empirically capture a fluid and complex public, deciding instead for an operational conception of the public as an aggregate of individuals. In addition, even the notion of public affairs, on which the operational understanding of public opinion is built, can be problematized. As Bourdieu ([1972] 1979, 124) establishes, empirical research of public opinion presupposes that there is a consensus in society about which questions are relevant and should be asked by researchers. In reality, there is no such consensus. It could only be formed as a result of a really existing public opinion, which, as Bourdieu points out, simply does not exist or—as Lippmann called it for opposite reasons than Bourdieu—it exists only as a "phantom."

In contemporary societies characterized by the disintegration of the public in the classical or strict sense, it is perhaps more sensible to speak, instead of public opinion, about some kind of opinion temper or climate, in which there are no longer opinions but rather attitudes that are shaped and changed in the processes that derive from the human tendency for cognitive consistency—in short, harmonizing attitudes and behavioral patterns in the organization of the "inner world." Instead of rational discourse, the mechanisms for assuring attention and achieving internal and external consistency come to the fore: selective perception and remembering (up to the collective amnesia), partial perception and problematization of the credibility of opinion leaders—generally, a tendency to avoid information and opinions that could cause cognitive dissonance (Festinger [1957] 1962). This leads to the need for a supply of symbols of identification by the media (Lasswell 1981) and "a sociopsychological calculation of supplies" (Habermas [1962] 1995, 217) on the media side. Using these symbols, political actors try through the media to become attractive to the population and avoid a commitment to "rational arguments which could arouse the critical capacities of the recipient of the message and stimulate his awareness" (Zolo 1992, 146). As a consequence, "governing more than ever becomes a massive public relations exercise" (Axford and Huggins 1999). Mass media, particularly television, "act in a way that is calculated to mobilize the public," which inducts a "perverse form of direct democracy" (Bourdieu 1998, 64)—actions that resemble riots of a mob more than the expression of opinion by an "imagined" public.

In this milieu, empirical opinion research has been implemented as an *institutional actor in the political sphere.* That could diminish the scientific relevance of public opinion—as reflected by the warnings and suggestions, mentioned in the introduction, to expel the notion of public opinion from scientific discussions. However, since at the same time the political importance of public opinion (polling) has increased, public opinion has not lost its scientific relevance.

However, the most frequent "scientific" reactions to the growing complexity of political and public opinion processes are astonishing. On the one hand is the psychologization of public opinion research, the reduction of public opinion to characteristics and effects of group (and later mass) communications, and, on the other hand, the development of public opinion polling, which reduces public opinion to an aggregate of the anonymous answers of isolated individuals to a set of arbitrarily defined questions. All the fundamental dimensions of conceptualizations of public opinion that developed since the eighteenth century were completely excluded from these behaviorist models: the formation of citizen consensus through public discussion (or with acclamation), the role of the state and authoritative institutions in the formation and realization of public opinion, the importance of political and economic organizations and associations within the (nation-) state and international relations, the effects of the professionalization of political and communication processes, and, last but not least, the importance and specific functions of the mass media. The dominant dimensions elaborated in theoretical treatises on public opinion through more than two centuries are schematically presented in figure 1. Some of these dimensions may be found in almost any discussion of public opinion (e.g., the relationship between public opinion and the mass media), whereas others are more theoretically distinctive. The issue of (expert) knowledge is in the forefront of Lippmann's and Dewey's theories, although from opposing starting points. This also applies to their emphasis on the importance of the relationship between the public (and public opinion) and the state. The economic dimension has a prominent place in Tönnies's critique of public opinion as well as contemporary critiques of public opinion polls. The international dimension, which first appeared in Tönnies's discussion of opinion formation by the international public, is largely ignored because public opinion is usually (and uncritically) considered a national phenomenon. Classical theories of public opinion contributed to this perplexing assumption by emphasizing the importance of the relationship between public opinion and the institutional power of the (nation-) state.

The schematic representation in figure 1 basically corresponds to Tönnies's subdivision of his "reflexive will" into three complex forms: (1) the sphere of

Figure 1.1: Key Dimensions in Theorizing Public Opinion

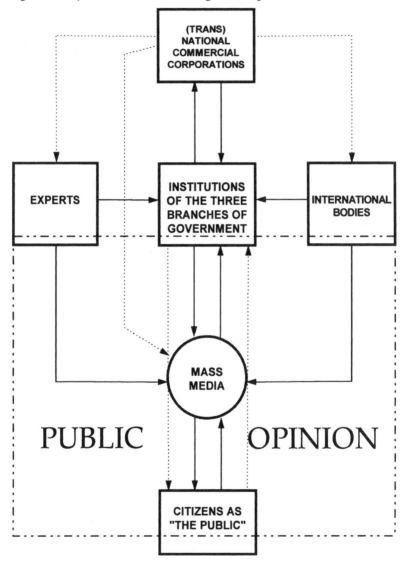

convention, which primarily refers to the economic life of society, (2) the sphere of legislation, which refers to the political life and its main subject, the state, and (3) the sphere of opinion of the public, which refers to moral and ethical issues. Two things have to be emphasized here. First, public opinion cannot be understood and explained if held in isolation from other forms of complex social will as identified by Tönnies—both those belonging to the normative concept of *Gesellschaft* and those that Tönnies has placed into *Gemeinschaft* (concord, custom, and religion). It is only within this broader theoretical framework that the processes of elementary forms of social will—upon which social-psychological approaches to the formation and expression of individual opinions lay great stress—make sense. Second, neither Tönnies's forms of social will nor the components of public opinion presented in figure 1 can be exclusively delimited; for example, mass media typically pertain to the sphere of public opinion formation and expression as well as the spheres of politics and economy, and also to other forms of social will.

One of the most important consequences of the sociologization of public opinion studies in the twentieth century was the repudiation of predominantly unfavorable attitudes toward public opinion that, in contrast to the Enlightenment, developed during the second half of the nineteenth century and reached their peak with Gustave Le Bon's *Study of the Popular Mind* (*The Crowd,* 1895) in which he treated even parliament as a type of crowd characterized by intellectual simplicity, irritability, suggestibility, and exaggeration of sentiments. In a way, the twentieth century restores the tradition beginning with John Milton's assertion that "opinion in good men is but knowledge in the making," that is, a tradition of understanding opinion in general and public opinion in particular as attempting to recognize the truth and the common good. At the same time this century brings about a variety of new approaches and theories, which will be my main concern in this book.

The analysis of the multilayered meanings of the concepts of public/ness and public opinion reveals their distinctive interdisciplinary determination and calls attention to global "structural transformations of the public," that is, to the processes of globalization or the rising of the world economy and political system, which, at least potentially, imply the development of a global public sphere and global public opinion in contrast to the apparently natural and self-evident restriction of public opinion to the (nation-) state. The recognition of the multidimensional nature of public opinion and its historical relativity calls for holistic and multidisciplinary approaches to public/ness and public opinion that should avoid a priori (disciplinary or otherwise) exclusiveness in definitions. It would not make sense to strive for a universally valid definition of public opinion. Yet, perhaps paradoxically, particularly because of such a variety of (often exclusive) understandings and definitions of the concept of public opinion, at least a loose definition is needed—without any pretension to its universal validity, and only in the sense of the Tönniesian "normal concept." The following is such an attempt: *Public opinion is formed and expressed through continual and institutionalized communication processes in which individuals and groups tend to achieve consensus about controversial public issues in order to influence the actions of authoritative institutions.*

Nothing can be more easy to agree with than Tönnies's assertion in *Kritik der öffentlichen Meinung* that it is very difficult to find out what public opinion is but much easier to discover in what form it appears, and even easier, what it is taken for. By common understanding, public opinion is about controversial issues and how they should be resolved. In an idealized (and simplified) notion, public opinion is usually considered a process in which (1) a group of people give salience to some problem, (2) the discussion of the problem results in increased salience and the problem thus becomes a public issue, (3) participants in the discussion formulate alternative solutions to solve the problem and narrow the alternatives, and (4) the commonly agreed opinion (consensus) affects either the collective decision through majority vote, as in an election or referendum, or the assessment of the strength of public opinion by politically acting officials in coming to a decision.

The emphasis on public opinion as primarily a communication phenomenon does not arise from a sort of disciplinary self-deception, as will become clear. The idea goes back at least to the theories of Charles N. Cooley and John Dewey, who emphasized the communicative origin of public opinion and society:

> Even if "society" were as much an organism as some writers have held, it would not on that account be society. Interactions, transactions, occur *de facto* and the results of interdependence follow. But participation in activities and sharing in results are additive concerns. They demand *communication* as a prerequisite. (Dewey [1927] 1991, 152)

Public opinion would remain a mere fiction without the substantial assumptions related to its communicative nature. "In politics communication makes possible public opinion, which, when organized, is democracy" (Cooley 1909, 84). Public opinion presupposes freedom (and courage, as Kant would say) of opinion expression, freedom of the press, and thus human freedom in general; it was and remains inseparably connected with the Enlightenment principle of publicity. Without the double determination of public opinion as the relationship (1) among citizens and (2) with the government, the concept of public opinion would lose its democratic import.

Thus public opinion is more than a subjective "perception imposed by the perceiver on information about citizen attitudes toward a publicly debated issue," as argued by James B. Lemert (1981, 12). (Lemert himself also argues that "opinion input" does influence perceptions of public opinion held by political decision makers, and in that sense the perception is not merely subjective and certainly is not idiosyncratic. Information about opinions comes in whether or not decision-makers want it to.) Although public opinion is also a subjective phenomenon in the sense that opinions are always subjectively formed and expressed and that the perceivers try to estimate and anticipate or predict the state of public opinion, this is not to say that public opinion in an objective sense is a "phantom" or a "myth." On the contrary, we must accept Robert E. Park's recognition that public opinion is external to every individual. Although it manifests itself differently in different individuals (Park [1904] 1972, 59), it is objective or, as Dewey would say, it occurs de facto in the tendency to establish consensus on an initially controversial issue. Nevertheless, I do agree with Lemert that the subjective perceptions by key (political) decision makers of what may be public opinion on a controversial issue represent a fundamental component of public opinion process; their estimation of public opinion is actually the other side of the influence of public opinion upon the authoritative institutions.

THE IMPORTANCE OF CONSENSUS

When forming and expressing (public) opinion, individuals and groups tend to reach consensus on controversial issues. In the first place, consensus presupposes opinion *differentiation* and *conflict*. The controversial nature of public issues is based on the separation of the being and the value of things discussed, as Park ([1904] 1972, 61) maintained: their meaning is accepted as identical (and important) by all members of the public, but the value is different. At the end of the process, public opinion can never result in complete agreement because, at the very least, differences in degree, intensity, or firmness of opinions always exist. Consensus could be considered a counterfactual ideal and presupposition that all participants anticipate in that they strive not merely for empirical agreement but for a consensus motivated by the general interest. It denotes commonly the most acceptable opinion so that the distances between it and all individual opinions are minimized.

Yet a certain degree of mutual agreement is a necessary condition for public opinion to influence institutions of decision making, or, as Dewey would say, for the public to secure, through its officers, the regulation of long-term consequences of transactions among individuals and groups for society. This specific regulative power defines the fundamental difference between the public, which is always directly (politically) related to the state, and civil society, which is a network of organizations and movements independent from the state. In civil society, which links together a variety of groups that develop as self-governing spheres, regulation is intended for internal or intragroup transactions among individuals rather than for the indirect and long-term external consequences of in-group transactions, which lead to the formation of the public. Through public opinion—as a specific institutional form of social will, as Tönnies defined it—civil society acts on the basis of its moral power, in contrast to economy, whose regulative power is enforced by money, and the state (political society), which acts directively through the legislature.

Consensus should not be understood as a simple and static agreement but as a form of coordination; it could be conceptualized in analogy to information, if information is defined as a measure of nonrandomness, reduction of uncertainty,[8] and organization (opposite to entropy). Nor is consensus equivalent to consent: whereas consensus can only result from interaction and coorientation in a collectivity, consent implies a passive, individual or massive, acceptance of an opinion or permission given to somebody. Basically, consensus is a communication phenomenon, since it can only be achieved in communication. Through history, forms, means, and aims of communication evidently are changing, but all the changes do not challenge one of the basic functions of communication—to maintain individuals' adherence to groups and societies. Individuals, groups, and societies are knit together through communication; in this process, consensus has the central importance. It is not only public opinion but also symbols, norms, roles, institutions, society, and culture that derive their significance from consensus. Consensus concerning common action or, as Key named it, "consensus on fundamentals" is *the* necessary condition for any form of human collectivity to exist. Wirth (1948, 4) believed that "the only reasonable equivalent of 'mind' in the individual organism that we can think of as an essential in the social organism can be supplied through consensus":

> Consensus is the sign that [a] partial or complete understanding has been reached on a number of issues confronting the members of a group sufficient to entitle it to be called a society. It implies that a measure of agreement has been reached. The agreement, however, is neither imposed by coercion nor fixed by custom so as no longer to be subject to discussion. It is always partial and developing and has constantly to be won. (Wirth 1948, 4)

In a large number of publications on public opinion, at least a vague idea of the opinion connecting many individuals and/or spreading through many collectivities appear as a fundamental element of its definition. In *The Social Contract*, Rousseau ([1762] 1947) relates *volonté générale* (general will) to the agreement upon the common benefit, which arises from the resistance to the benefit of each individual, in contrast to *volonté de tous* (the will of all) that is merely the sum of all individual wills. In *Critique of Public Opinion*, Tönnies (1922, 301) emphasized that the power of public opinion is "the greater, the higher is the level of its firmness and energy, which make it to move: both together, the mass with the speed factor, make the *momentum* of the public opinion." Whereas the "power" of public opinion is based on the level of consensus, the process of public opinion formation and expression is fundamentally characterized by controversy and dissensus. According to Tönnies, public opinion differs from other forms of complex social will by the nature of "consensus and rational agreement" (Tönnies 1922, 53). He insisted that commonness does not mean merely what people or objects have in common, that is, the properties of agents, but rather the relations between them: "we think of feelings etc. which already are an expression of the boundness among people, and which condition this boundness" (Tönnies 1922, 44).

In *The Phantom Public*, Lippmann related "the method and spirit of reason" in controversies in which the public ought to identify which actor is worthy of public support to the fundamental assumption that "we are maintaining a society based on the principle that all controversies are soluble by peaceable *agreement*. They may not be. But on that dogma our society is founded" (Lippmann 1925, 135; emphasis added). V. O. Key stressed in *Public Opinion and American Democracy* the importance of consensus as "a prerequisite to the existence of representative government," which often seems to be a magic word but nevertheless "may condition the behavior of those in positions of public authority" (Key [1961] 1967, 27). Along with other democratic conditions, like freedom of speech and information, consensus on fundamentals represents a basic requirement for the existence of public opinion. Like Key, Wilson relates the concept of public opinion to consensus and participation:

> Participation is, clearly, the proper avenue of approach to the study of public opinion, for, in various senses, public opinion is participating opinion. But the legitimation of participation rests on the older, broader, and more philosophical proposition that just governments are governments to which, in some sense, the subjects have given their consent. Like participation, consent is never perfect, and like it also there are variations in forms of consent. Since we can hardly say that nonexistent opinion can be public opinion, we can hardly say that a primitive and inarticulate acceptance of a governing order is really consent. (Wilson 1962, 7)

The idea of the central significance of consensus in communication processes also appeared within another research tradition, namely, social psychology. Although in this tradition consensus was often named differently, for example, balance (Heider 1946), symmetry (Newcomb 1953), congruity (Osgood and Tannenbaum 1955), or consonance (Festinger [1957] 1962), all these terms denote a sort of consensus among persons who have a sense of affinity with each other and are connected by affective ties and common concerns or interests, that is, they refer not only to the rational but also to the emotional component of mental processes or common sentiments—they are "sensing together" (Coser 1994, 107). Although early social-psychological approaches primarily focused on interpersonal communication, advanced theorizations dealt specifically with how people tend to use information available from mass media and other sources in their environment. Such extensions were, for example, Westley and MacLean's (1957) application of Newcomb's model of interpersonal symmetry to a mass communication situation and Festinger's theory of cognitive dissonance, which also postulates that "one of the major ways in which [cognitive] dissonance reduction may be accomplished [is] obtaining *agreement from others*" ([1957] 1962, 208).

A number of social-psychological approaches to (mass) communication in the 1950s attributed a significant explanatory power to the idea of cognitive consistency. Basically, consistency may be intraindividual, or interindividual or social; both forms of consistency tend to reduce response variability and thus actually represent two forms of consensus. The idea of consistency assumes that inconsistency generates tension or discomfort within individuals who therefore seek to eliminate or reduce it. In more recent social-psychological analyses consensus is considered as having two important functions for those expressing opinions: (1) to validate opinions and judgments and (2) to provide self-enhancement, reaffirmation of identity (Moscovici 1976, 152). The individual can consider his or her personal opinions valid or correct inasmuch as they correspond to the socially affirmed reality. The second function relates to the transformation of private reality into public reality; the individual tends to have his or her opinions accepted by others to be right. According to Moscovici, both functions are always present in the process of reaching consensus; which one is dominant depends on social norms. If behavior in society is guided by the norm of objectivity, the priority is given to the validation function. The objectivity norm requires that every person think and behave with reference to the public reality that is the same for all individuals; consequently, opinions may be universally accepted. The preference norm views consensus as resulting from comparisons between different opinions that reflect different private realities of individuals and groups; it thus gives priority to the self-assertion function, and consensus is no more than a common denominator to different opinions. The originality norm represents the midway between the other two.

Broadly speaking, we may distinguish two major conceptualizations of consensus. Scheff (1967, 33) argues that the majority of sociological researchers represent a commonsense approach in which consensus is defined or is just implicitly understood simply as agreement among individuals in a group. Even in its dynamic dimension, it still means only the degree (intensity) to which individuals express their agreement with a statement. According to Key, for example, "In its most uncomplicated form 'consensus' means *an overwhelming public agreement upon a question of public policy*" whose main function is "to limit and guide, within a broad range, governmental action on specific matters" (Key [1961] 1967, 41, 28). Consensus, for Key, represents a "significant type of distribution of public opinion" whose importance is attributed to the potential influence it may have on public authorities, and it can be simply identified from the opinion data. In this way, Key arrives at a simplistic operational definition of consensus, according to which "unimodality of the distribution . . . constitutes the essence of consensus" (Key [1961] 1967, 28). Different opinion distributions within the population may be expected to have different influence on governmental action, and in different situations—when different issues are at stake—government may interpret agreements differently. Key's typology of functions of consensus is more a description of a variety of empirical situations than a discussion of specific aims of public opinion and reasons for different consequences induced by agreement.[9] Apart from integrative functions, Key mentions an important negative aspect of the efforts to achieve agreement in public opinion: the suppression of conflicting issues that are beyond a general agreement and not susceptible to compromise. Yet, as a pragmatic author, Key believes that it is appropriate and reasonable to place issues in which a compromise is clearly out of reach, for example, in the matters of religious beliefs,[10] outside governmental actions and consequently—according to Key's understanding of public opinion—outside public opinion.

In the individual agreement approach, the dynamism of consensus is limited to different types of distribution of opinions, as Key put it, or to the degree to which individuals agree with an opinion. With such a conceptualization of consensus in public opinion, we would be facing two main problems. First, the idea of consensus as the "lowest common denominator"(when every one is partly right and partly wrong at the end) is, according to Moscovici and Doise (1994, 15), a tacitly accepted convention that, however, is in essence wrong. Consensus is not necessarily a compromise; it may be reached also at an extreme position. (The criticism does not apply only to the behavior in a crowd, which, by definition, behaves in an extreme way [i.e., violently] but also to the public.)

Even more, consensus is normally established at one of the extreme positions preferred by the group, provided that the discussion is not restrained by the external factors.[11] The main reason for this is that a group is less inclined than individuals to silence conflicts and avoid differences. Yet this criticism does not undermine the general idea of consensus as the central tendency in public opinion formation; rather, it helps us better explain the development of, and changes in, public opinion.

Second, another difficulty with the individual agreement definition of consensus is that it makes no provision for perceptions of agreement. Lippmann made the point that "we cannot fully understand the acts of other people, until *we know what they think they know*" (Lippmann [1922] 1960, 85). Perceptions of agreement actually affect individual behavior, rather than agreement itself; the two will not necessarily correlate, although they often do. This became known as the paradox of pluralistic ignorance: If no one agrees with an opinion, but everyone believes that all but himself do agree, he or she would behave as if everyone actually agreed. In terms of individual agreement definition, obviously no consensus would exist in the above situation and such an opinion could not be effective in a practical action. But in fact, in a situation in which everyone believes that all the others do agree (although they actually do not), a minority opinion could be as effective as an actual agreement or majority opinion: the perception of agreement may affect the behavior of individuals even more than the agreement itself. Opinions published in the media are so important because they became widely socially visible.

In contrast to the individual agreement stream, the tradition stemming from the pragmatism and interactionism of Mead and Dewey stresses the consequences of the process of coorientation of individuals in a given group. Unlike the former linear model, interactionism does not conceive communication as "an operation as simple as the transportation of a commodity like bricks" but rather as a cultural process with two fundamental dimensions—diffusion, or transmission, and acculturation, or assimilation (Park [1939] 1966, 171–72). According to Mead, interaction is a stepwise, self-regulating process through which an individual can experience another's subjective state and act accordingly: "It involves not only communication in the sense in which birds and animals communicate with each other, but also an arousal in the individual himself of the response which he is calling out in the other individual, a taking of the rôle of the other, a tendency to act as the other person acts" (Mead [1934] 1962, 159). In this perspective, empathy—the ability to put oneself into another person's position and to understand his or her perspectives and behavior—is an important condition that facilitates effective communication or reduces barriers to it. In his conceptualization of public opinion Blumer thus emphasized that the formation of public opinion "implies that people share one another's experience and are willing to make compromises and concessions. It is only in this way that the public, divided as it is, can come to act as a unit" (Blumer [1946] 1966, 49).

Lippmann's significant idea that "we cannot fully understand the acts of other people, until *we know what they think they know*" may be considered the invisible birthplace of Chaffee's (1969) cognitive coorientation model. The coorientation school of thought surmounted the individual as the unit of analysis and introduced higher-level units created in interactions of two or more individuals who are cooriented toward each other and toward common attitude objects. According to the Chaffee model, a person who is cooriented with a second person has at least two distinguishable sets of cognitions: (1) one person knows what the other person thinks and (2) one person estimates what the other person thinks. This gives three distinct types of coorientational relations between two persons: (1) cognitive overlap—both persons have the same cognitions; (2) congruency—a person's internal perception that his or her cognitions match the other person's; and (3) accuracy—a person's cognitions match the other person's estimate of them. Furthermore, cognitive overlap has two distinct forms. First, understanding is defined as the two persons perceiving in the same way the "objective" relation between two objects, based on comparing them on a relevant attribute, that is, when both persons have identical "pertinence." This dimension is what Park named "the being of things," that is, their "objective" meaning, which in the case of the public is supposed to be *identical* for all members of the group (Park [1904] 1972, 61). Second, agreement is defined as two persons holding the same general evaluation of each object to which they are cooriented, that is, they have identical salience.[12] This is the second dimension in Park's understanding of the "two-sidedness of the public's attitudes," which he named "the value of things"; according to Park, it is different for individual members of the public. The being and the value of things diverge as soon as the public comes into existence, whereas in the crowd they characteristically coincide. Starting from divergent evaluations, the public continually attempts to reach a "supra-individual viewpoint."[13] In the coorientational framework, consensus could be defined as a multidimensional coorientation process. Combination of the simple dichotomous values in two dimensions—dis/agreement and non/accuracy—results in four possible outcomes of an opinion process, one of them being consensus (Scheff 1967, 38): (1) *monolithic consensus* if the majority of individuals in a group agree with an opinion and perceive accurately ("understand," according to Scheff) that there is an agreement; (2) *pluralistic ignorance* if the majority of individuals actually agree but they think they disagree, or vice versa; (3) *dissensus* if the majority do not agree and perceive accurately they do not agree; and (4) *false consensus* if the majority disagree but they think they agree.

A situation of complete consensus is never achieved in practice—irrespective of the size of the social entity—since a complete or perfect consensus would imply, in Chaffee's terms, (1) a complete cognitive overlapping (which refers to a unanimous agreement of all individuals in a group, the highest possible intensity or degree of agreement, and the highest possible degree of mutual understanding), and (2) the highest possible degree of accuracy. A situation of cognitive overlapping and perfect accuracy, by definition, assumes also congruency for the persons interacting. All these assumptions would be totally unrealistic, with a possible exception of the probability of a perfect mutual understanding. As Lippmann argues in his conceptualization of public opinion, "the conflicts and differences are so real that we cannot deny them and instead of looking for *identity of purpose* we look simply for an *accommodation of purposes*," for a modus vivendi of conflicting interests in the process of opinion formation (Lippmann 1925, 98; emphasis added). A public discussion may only result in the adjustment of different interests and compromises. In view of the plurality of interests, opinions, and orientations characteristic of modern complex societies, *it would not make much sense to try to build a theory of public opinion on the assumption that a complete consensus may (or should) exist.* Usually, the form of consensus we may find is one in which a large majority would partially (to some extent) agree, or no more than a simple majority (just above 50 percent) would largely (or, in rare occasions, even perfectly) agree.

There are no absolute criteria in terms of the level and the degree of agreement that could be used as indicators of consensus. There is a similar problem with Chaffee's second dimension, that is, the degree of accuracy. In both operational dimensions of coorientation, the relative criterion that could be effectively used is that proposed already by Rousseau in *Social Contract* ([1762] 1947, 96) in which he argued that the majority of votes needed to pass a decision should approach unanimity, "the more serious and important deliberations are." Similarly, Allport (1937, 13) related the number of individuals who must express public opinion in order to make it effective, to the importance of the issue (i.e., more individuals are needed as a more important issue is discussed). Or, according to Scheff's (1967, 41) general proposition, "the type and extent of consensus is dependent on the type and extent of coordination required between the members of the group."

The idea of the interactive substance of attaining consensus relates consensus to mutual understanding and interaction (discussion); it cannot be imposed by coercion or determined by custom. As Tönnies and pragmatists would have suggested, rationality of public opinion cannot originate from any form of physical or psychic coercion exhibited in conformity pressures but rather from empathy and coorientation. Coercion would degrade the rationality of consensus to the individual's rational decision to consent to a given opinion. It is true that in a broad sense even an individual's decision to conform may be a purely rational decision; yet, an opinion adopted by conformity cannot be a rationally formed opinion. Thus consensus

> generally implies a process through which agreement between participant actors is brought about. It is to be conceived as an active process and must hence be distinguished from acquiescence, resigned acceptance or simple conformism. . . . Unreflective conformity and the habitual acceptance of social commands cannot be taken as the equivalent of consensus. (Coser 1994, 107)

The issues of conformity and coercion bring to the fore the notion of influence, that is, the questions of who or what is influenced by public opinion, and to what influences public opinion itself is exposed—issues vividly discussed already by the classic public opinion theorists, and particularly in the twentieth century. Influence is attributed to all institutionalized forms of public opinion from parliaments and newspapers to contemporary public opinion polling. Tönnies, for example, saw the fundamental characteristic of newspapers as both an instrument of, and against, public opinion in the difference from science: whereas the characteristic of science is the will for the truth, the mass media are characterized by the intention to influence. Similar distinctions between the function of science and the press may be found in Lippmann and in Dewey. In his critique of journalism practicing sensational news reporting Dewey pointed out the difference between journalism and science, which should be, according to Dewey, abolished in favor of science. The idea that the press, in the first place, is able to incite the movement of the public and therefore has to enable or influence it to align itself for or against a proposal was expressed by both Tönnies and Lippmann. For Dewey, a fundamental problem was the influence of the public on the regulation of indirect consequences of interactions among individuals and groups, that is, on the state. More recent conceptualizations of public opinion (e.g., the Noelle-Neumann model of the spiral of silence) and their critiques lay stress on the (manipulative) processes through which individuals fall under the sway of the media and social control.

Cognitive consistency and coorientation models seem to be particularly appropriate for group interactions and not directly applicable to a public opinion situation. The question of influence primarily pertains to social relationship and social structure. Although (social) influence is sometimes considered an aspect of power or a (direct) execution or manifestation of power (when it does not rely on argument but on authoritative status), it is usually understood as a form of control that is not based on power and the possibility of coercion (and threat) but on the capacity to induce changes in individuals' opinions and, consequently, their behavior. Influence of one agent over another means that the former causes changes in the behavior of the latter not by force but on the basis of his or her competence to change beliefs and opinions. In this, influence denotes the absence of resistance in the process of carrying out the will of an individual or social group, that is, a willing participation in the process. Influence may be considered the result of the division of labor when extended to information activities: "Individuals give up their informational self sufficiency at the cost of becoming dependent on information provided by others. . . . They must rely on the credibility of that information, not to reproduce all the knowledge that went into producing and supplying it" (Mayhew 1997, 109). By definition, then, influence cannot be reduced to a one-way relationship or, even less, to conformity of those being influenced. Conformity is only one modality of social influence, or only one possible motivation for the limitation of informational self-sufficiency. In addition to conformity, which is individual tendency to integrate with others, influence also includes manifest conflicting relations that take place in interaction. According to Moscovici (1976, 166), two specific influence modalities arising from conflict are normalization and innovation. Normalization is a process in which individuals or groups achieve compromises on the basis of reciprocal influence. Normalization does not imply a majority-minority relation and conformity but rather a plurality of opinions and norms that are all considered equivalent. Interaction results in a compromise because the actors

> seek to discover what is "reasonable," rather than what is true; no one wishes to dominate, but no one wishes to be left in the wrong. Such a situation not only induces a positive movement toward *cooperation* and *mutual understanding,* but also offers an escape from choices between incompatible terms. The process essentially consists of the suppression of differences and the acceptance of the lowest common denominator. (Moscovici 1976, 171; emphasis added)

Conformity is focused on the control or resolution of conflicts, and normalization on the avoidance of conflicts; innovation creates them. It is based on the intensification of differences by the minority, which wants to obtain social visibility. Like Lippmann, Key believes that innovation is beyond the capacity of public opinion, since by its very nature it tends toward agreement by compromise or the lowest common denominator: "The public cannot innovate; it can only acclaim or reject innovation" (Key [1961] 1967, 286). Yet such an understanding of the (limited) capacities of the public would reduce it to an aggregate of individuals, and public opinion to "the modern art of acclamation" (as Carl Schmitt defined it), with an inhibited intelligence and exaggerated affectivity as typically exhibited by the crowd. If public opinion is not primarily oriented toward the creation of conflicts, it does not follow that it is reduced to what Moscovici calls "normalization." The definition of public opinion as a process arising from or related to controversial issues indicates that it may well induce innovations. However, it is important to see public opinion as a process connecting the public with the institutions of power rather than merely expressing opinions: in the former case, conflicts are created (primarily) between the public and the government, whereas in the latter case, only internal conflicts in the public would have to appear.

Nevertheless, the creation of conflicts as the source of innovation and originality is not in the core of public opinion process; rather, public opinion aims primarily at transcending social conflicts and producing consensus, which may influence governments to heed it. The same holds true for the coorientation approach which was mostly used for analysis of interpersonal (two-person) relationship rather than for more complex interactions, for example, between the public and its representative. In contrast, for example, to Scheff, who is primarily interested in possible applications of his model of consensus and coordination for the measurement of social integration in a group, in public opinion situations we must concentrate on a different, more specific, and perhaps more complex case of (political) representation or interaction between the constituency and its representatives or, in Dewey's terms, between the public and the state. Generally, the process of formation and the degree of consensus between the representative and his or her constituency may help us explain, as Wilson put it, how "public opinion creates obligations for a government to follow" (Wilson 1962, 39), that is, how public opinion influences the behavior of the representatives and the government. Scheff stresses the importance of higher-level coorientation in this process, for example, the representative will wish to know what are the opinions of his or her constituency on issues in discussion ("first-level coorientation") but also what the constituency thinks his or her opinions are ("second-level coorientation"). However, this is not the only typical relationship in public opinion process to which the general model of consensus could be applied. Another situation would represent the relationship between the media and their publics. We may also consider the relationship between the media and the political representatives and, of course, we should not neglect coorientation processes within social (sub)groups (which may, at the same time, represent specific publics). Conflicting representations of public opinion are inescapable. That is why the anticipation of a full agreement between the representatives and the constituencies is not grounded at all. Rather, the relationship between the leaders and the followers is asymmetric. Typically, leaders are more often and intensely faced with the problem of coordination than followers, and that is so for quite a simple reason: the leader has to coordinate his or her actions with all (a large number of) the followers, whereas the follower has to coordinate his or her actions with only one leader, or a few of them. This may help to explain Newcomb's finding that leaders are somewhat more perceptive of followers' views than vice versa. That was clear to Lippmann when he wrote that "every leader must consider his decision not only on 'the merits,' but also in its effect on any part of his following whose continued support he requires" ([1922] 1960, 239).

Still, it is possible to conceive of a model of public opinion that would allow for an enduring process of achieving consensus among dissenting opinions and, at the same time, for creating dissenting opinions, which is the fundamental condition for a democratic society to exist. Even if we consent to Moscovici and Doise's (1994, 13) argument that consensus is not likely to be a compromise between the opposing positions (i.e., the "average") but rather a more extreme and biased solution, closer to the values shared by the group that established itself during debates, this does not represent a solution to the question of how dissenting opinions start to develop. When consensus is established, it does not stimulate individuals to seek new information and, thus it reinforces the existing opinions; social interaction in such a biased environment would obviously support the status quo. The more homogeneous is the individual's environment, the more likely interaction will generate (opinion) stability rather than change. The reason is that we regularly look for (additional) information in the same environment in which we live and which provided us with information already, thus perpetuating the same bias. Even if information is supplied by the depoliticized mass media, a distinctive bias is unavoidable. "Social and economic structures accidentally, but nevertheless systematically, mould homogeneity by repeatedly triggering individual reassessments of political beliefs" (Huckfeldt and Sprague 1995, 51).

How, then, can social interaction result in dissenting opinions generating innovations and changes? According to Huckfeldt and Sprague (1995, 54), there are essentially two sources of a potential dissent. First, dissenting opinions may originate from the perceived differences between the local (microenvironment) and the global (external) environment, which provide individuals with information. The more the two environments differ from each other, the more likely this will be to generate some changes in individuals' opinions. Comparing the two (or many) informational environments is essential for the identification of controversial issues, which unleashes the spiraling process of (rational) discourse aimed at reconciliation by consensus. Second, dissenting opinions may be a consequence of newly developed interest and attentiveness. For example, dramatic political events may attract the attention of individuals who ordinarily do not pay any attention to politics. However, such rapid changes in interest and attention are more likely to appear among those who heed the existing public opinion rather than participate in opinion formation and expression. As attitude theory postulates, "the commitment of more extreme individuals is stronger than that of moderate individuals, who therefore find it easier to shift" (Moscovici 1985, 401). In other words, it is not very likely that "we might expect to see occasional but dramatic episodes of socially stimulated change occurring among them," as Huckfeldt and Sprague (1995, 55) believe;[14] and even if we may expect some sudden changes, it is more likely that they would be directed toward a sort of bandwagon effect (e.g., a massive political support to the government in war) rather than to an increase in dissenting opinions. Yet if the rise of attention is pulled by an external environment, that may imply "dramatic episodes" in the microenvironment.

To the argumentation developed by Huckfeldt and Sprague may be added the third source of a potential dissent—the inflation of influence (Mayhew 1997). The inflation of influence is a consequence of the reduced objective sufficiency or certainty of the substantive arguments expressed in persuasive communication, and the dissociation of public discussion organized by political elites from what Dewey would call important indirect and long-term consequences on the public as issues of discussion. The less the arguments are plausible, logical, and concordant with recipients' experiences and needs, the more persuasion depends on the communicator's influence, and the less effective the influence becomes. According to Mayhew, in such circumstances, influence of opinion leaders may "have too little value to provide resources for social integration." Disagreements about the validity of arguments do not directly weaken "influence as a medium," which could be compared with the arguments about prices of goods on the market, in which disagreements about prices do not reduce the use of money as a medium of exchange. One can always refuse to buy an argument, thus implicitly saying that the communicator's prestige does not provide sufficient credibility to his or her assertions (Mayhew 1997, 103). However, a consistent loss of arguments' credibility may undercut, in the long run, the trust in the medium of influence—for example, in a newspaper, a political party, or an opinion leader—and its opinions would become systematically rejected, and its information sources replaced.[15]

However, all these factors causing individual dissenting opinions are less significant than the overwhelming political culture. To use Moscovici's simple dichotomy for illustration, we could simply argue that societies regulated by the norm of objectivity would impede dissenting opinions while the "rule" of the preference norm would stimulate alternative voices. If in a democratic political environment spontaneous group discussion is encouraged, significant group polarization may occur. In less formal conditions, groups tend to make more extreme judgments than in more formal conditions. Generally, tendency toward polarization correlates with free interaction, but an important regulating factor is the rules and norms individuals have to obey even in the most spontaneous groups. The types of political culture based on the two norms significantly differ in the dominant modality of social influence: while a typical one-way influence—conformity—is dominant under the rule of the objectivity norm, the rule of the preference norm stimulates a symmetrical relationship and interaction in which each participant (e.g., both majority and minority) simultaneously emits and receives influence. The process of interactive influence can only be based on nonconformity (to a certain degree, of course) and competence of those interacting. Such a perspective may help us to see consensus as a possible means of changes: in striving for consensus, groups, societies, or public opinion may change their decisions and opinions without external intervention. Consensus, then, is the very mechanism of change rather than status quo. Its function is not to maintain the balance between opposing opinions but to make them operate reciprocally and achieve mutual modifications.

THE CONTRADICTION BETWEEN *PUBLIC* AND *OPINION*

At the beginning of the century Binkley suggested that "it may serve some useful purpose to bring together in their relation to each other various concepts of public opinion, and to set forth their similarities and differences" (Binkley 1928, 389) and his proposition had influenced many others in the field. His endeavors were relatively unsuccessful due to two fundamental contradictions, which had burdened the notion of public opinion and still are the main source for controversies about the definition of public opinion:

1. Internal, or semantic, contradiction is a consequence of connecting the concepts of public and opinion. Additional problems are caused by semantic ambiguities of the two constitutive elements themselves, that is, opinion (e.g., in contrast to attitude) and public (e.g., as opposed to private). The problems are expanding due to linguistic differences (e.g., between German *Meinung* and French *l'opinion,* which has been adopted by the English language).

2. External contradiction stems from the relationship between subjects of public opinion and subjects to whom it is addressed, *alias* between expressing and realizing the (public) opinion; with the rise of mass media, an additional dimension of opinion reception aggravates the contradiction.

On the strictly theoretical level the problem of the definition of public opinion is, according to Binkley, simply a matter of combining two terms: "Here is one entity: an *opinion;* there is another: a *public*" (Binkley 1928, 389). But the combination is hardly simple because of internal or semantic contradiction between the two concepts, by which the notion of public opinion has been marked since its first appearances. Within the concept of public opinion, or the public sphere more generally, as Robbins (1993, xxi) put it, "there is an unresolved and perhaps unresolvable tension between a tight, authoritative singleness (the public as object of a quest for a universal collective subject or a privileged arena of struggle) and a more relaxed, decentered pluralism (publicness as something spread liberally through many irreducibly different collectivities)."

As a political and philosophical concept, public opinion did not appear before the eighteenth century, but both elements of the notion—public and opinion—originated in the ancient era. The meanings of the concepts public and opinion have not only been changing in the last few centuries but have also been different in the different linguistic communities. Liberal-philosophical attempt to conceptually link opinion to public has appeared as an attempt to unite in reality absolutely incompatible—one with many, individual rights (liberal state) with public interest (social welfare state). The concept of opinion implies unity (*the* opinion), whereas its specific characterization (public) denotes many individuals and thus opinions (Jordan 1918 in Tönnies 1922, 132). Whereas public aspires to achieve the universal, objective, and rational, opinion is marked by the variable, subjective, and uncertain (Baker 1990; Otto 1966). Opinion (*doxa* in Greek, *alias opinio* in Latin) is typically individual in nature, for it is the reflection of the subjectivity of human beings: the content, intensity, and duration of opinion is determined by the individual. "Opining" lacks of certainty; it is, as Kant argued, subjectively and objectively insufficient form of "holding for true" (unlike believing and knowing). Hegel considered opinion *(Meinung)* as something peculiarly "mine" *(mein)*.[16] Tönnies, however, explicitly linked opinion with human reason; in contrast to Kant, he placed rational opining superior to affective believing. Ever since Plato "opinion" has been understood more as a conviction not based on a firm philosophical procedure of cognition, in contrast to factual knowledge (*episteme* in Greek alias *scientia* in Latin) that is based on scientific procedures and is thus accessible to only a few. Regardless of its (scientific) value opinion is thus distinctively individual.

The notion of public has the opposite sign of opinion: it implies the presence of the others (i.e., a larger number of people), which fundamentally questions the character of individuality within the opinion. Holscher identifies in ancient Rome and Greece already two versions of the concept of public: (1) social-political (related to polis or the whole body of the people who are involved in public process of discussion) and (2) visual-intellectual (fame or open exhibition—as something visible or known to all the people). Accordingly, "public" has been a distinctively multidimensional and ambiguous concept since ancient times, so, for example, the Latin verb *publicare* means to make public property, to place at the disposal of the community or exhibit publicly, or to prostitute (see Peters 1995, 7). An exceptional and unusual character of public origins from that time on, in both a good (fame) and a bad (shame, *iniuria*) sense, which is much later actualized in the notion of public opinion in the sense of opinion about public issues as important and controversial issues for the public, which do not leave anybody indifferent.

Public opinion must not be thought of as a single, unified opinion of a relatively large group of people (crowd, mass, public, audience, or even population, people, or nation). It can only be a conglomerate of different, often conflicting opinions. Therefore it is not surprising that during the three centuries, understanding of public opinion has been oscillating between holistic endeavors to place the public opinion in the sphere of collective, and reductionist endeavors to attribute the public opinion exclusively to the individual (Price 1992, 2). Indeed, public opinion seems to be more a poetical than scientific term because only in poetry may the incompatible become united.

The second—external—contradiction of the concept of public opinion that causes opacity in definitions originates from its political dimension: public opinion should express and assert the will of the people. As argued by Key ([1961] 1967, 547), "If a democracy is to exist, the belief must be widespread that public opinion, at least in the long run, affects the course of public action." But many theorists and particularly empiricists would strongly disagree.

Ever since Rousseau the idea of public opinion has been linked to the ideal of the rule of law and thus to democracy. Public opinion refers to people's sovereignty, the principle of rule by majority, political representation, and formal, constitutionally established ways of participation in the decision-making process. But that relationship is also contradictory in nature. First, as emphasized by Wilson, the development of ideas about people's sovereignty and participation has not developed simultaneously and in accordance with the development of the idea of free speech:

Historically, formal participation has run far ahead of the idea of free opinion, and free opinion is logically perfect only when there is no mechanism of political censorship or coercion. Probably only the anarchists can say that they really believe in a completely free opinion, while believers in government and its attendant coercion can be forceful supporters of mass participation in decision-making. . . . In support of public decisions, the majority is ready to deny the right of expression to certain opinions, especially when it is believed they contradict the principle of the continued existence of the community itself. (Wilson 1962, 5)

The relationship between public opinion and the idea of rule of law is also contradictory because public opinion has never been understood as direct participation in the execution of state power but rather as a critique of state power. Even public opinion as people's opinion or socialist public opinion (Splichal 1981a) could not become "government by the people" except in the revolutionary periods of people's democracy, which have always turned against its own origin and changed from people's democracy to democratic tyranny or totalitarian rule. This contradiction is only seemingly resolved in behavioristic conceptions (in which public opinion is only an aggregation of individual opinions) and in the constitutionalistic conceptualization of Carl Schmitt, who sees the fundamental (and unique) function, or political significance, of public opinion as the factor of "state life" in the acclamation of physically aggregated people (Schmitt [1928] 1954, 242–47).

With the development of mass media, a new contradiction with regard to the subject of public opinion—the public—has been established. Although formerly the public was predominantly understood as a normative foundation of democracy, as public forum shaped in critical discussions about public affairs by constantly interacting, educated, and informed individuals, modern mass media have created a new type of public that is entirely depoliticized and independent from participation in political decision making. Changes in the communication sphere are homologous to what happened in the sphere of politics, in which representative (electoral) democracy—with parliament providing the space for discussions among political leaders visible to individuals outside of parliament—has replaced the direct participatory democracy as known in antique Athens, where every citizen had the right to speak in the sovereign assembly. In the same way, the dominant forms of communication became far more effective in public representation before the people than involving them in public discussions as active participants-communicators. "The mass media . . . can offer a vast population a vision of the public sphere without giving them means for acting in it. Public . . . can mean both spectacle and participation; it has both theatrical and political senses" (Peters 1995, 3).

Tönnies and Dewey were the last vigorous defenders of the normative concept of opinion of the public in the sense of a common judgment formed and expressed by those who constitute the public, "the public" being expressly singularized. Later on, plurality and diversity of opinions typical of democratic societies preponderated over the unity of the public in conceptualizations of public opinion. Scholarly attention was redirected from the final state and normative goal (consensus) to the everyday processes of opinion formation and expression. Even in political theories, *the* public opinion was understood in the sense of V. O. Key's consensus on fundamentals (which must exist in any human collectivity) that permits and limits rather than directs certain governmental actions. In other words, *the* ("solid") public opinion (or opinion of the public) is not an organized, active opinion directly entangled in (political) discussions but a judgment—formed and entertained by those who constitute the public, and about public affairs—that may be activated if organized by a specific (political) actor, for example, an interest group, political party, or the media. A further step away from the traditional normative concept of public opinion is represented by blurring out the difference between public and private opinions brought about by Lippmann's concept of public opinions.

The increase in the number of discussions on public opinion in the twentieth century also enhanced controversies on what exactly constitutes the object of discussion. In the 1920s, American political scientists still managed to reach a consensus on the meaning of "opinion," which was already in strong opposition to Tönnies's understanding of *Meinung*. Whereas American political scientists agreed that "opinion needs not be result of rational process" (Binkley 1928, 389), Tönnies (1922, 19) emphasized that "believing pertains to the heart, and opining to the head." The public–opinion and public–public opinion relationships had at that time already become matters of dispute among American political scientists themselves.[17] In the next decades the list of controversial questions has extended over every border. If we do not want to relinquish the idea of public opinion, we have to reconcile ourselves to the fact that universal definitions of the public and public opinion cannot be attained. The reason for that is not primarily in the existence of too numerous, as well as exclusive, definitions (which would make it impossible to formulate a universal definition or establish a common denominator); it derives instead from the contradictions inherent in the very concept of public opinion. Universal definition of public opinion does not exist—but public opinion does!

2

+

Public Opinion: The Substance or Phantom of Democracy?

Regarded as an idea, democracy is not an alternative to other principles of associated life. It is the idea of community life itself. It is an ideal in the only intelligible sense of an ideal: namely, the tendency and movement of some thing which exists carried to its final limit, viewed as completed, perfected. Since things do not attain such fulfilment but are in actuality distracted and interfered with, democracy in this sense is not a fact and never will be.

—John Dewey, *The Public and Its Problems*

Nonpublic opinions are at work in great numbers, and "the" public opinion is indeed a fiction. Nevertheless, in a comparative sense the concept of public opinion is to be retained because the constitutional reality of the social-welfare state must be conceived as a process in the course of which a public sphere that functions effectively in the political realm is realized, that is to say, as a process in which the exercise of social power and political domination is effectively subjected to the mandate of democratic publicity.

—Jürgen Habermas, *The Structural Transformation of the Public Sphere*

This chapter briefly presents early normative-political theorizations of public opinion in the eighteenth and nineteenth centuries and concentrates on general developments in the twentieth century, when public opinion became the subject of systematic social inquiry. Public opinion has been rather clearly and noncontroversially understood as long as its meaning has been "controlled" by normative political theories, but nowadays any attempt to bring together various concepts of public opinion in order to set forth their similarities and differences would be senseless.

Sociological conceptualizations of public opinion that prevailed at the beginning of the twentieth century shared many characteristics with social-psychological models of group interaction. The most prominent sociological theorists of public opinion of the time (e.g., Ferdinand Tönnies and Wilhelm Bauer in Germany and John Dewey, Robert Park, and Walter Lippmann in the United States) explicitly referred to psychological research as a source as valuable as normative political theories. Early sociological theorists conceived of public opinion as an organic social process, but the concept was soon radically reconceived as a measurable quantity that could be identified and measured in survey research. The interest in questions of communication and media changed from theoretical considerations and social criticism based upon the expectation of progressive thought to practical concerns and specific problems within the scope of emerging research methodologies. That was a period of orchestrated attempts in social sciences to reject social-problem and reform-oriented theory and research and to develop disciplinary knowledge with the help of empirical research. Specifically, this chapter preliminarily discusses the shift from the emphasis on public opinion theory to practical applications in survey research and polling—from contributions by American pragmatism and Walter Lippmann's critique of limitations of democracy based on the belief that the people cannot "find a way of acting effectively upon highly complex affairs by very simple means" to Paul F. Lazarsfeld's plea for progress in theorizing public opinion, which "consists in leaving the ashes and taking the flames from the altars of one's forebears," the real-typical approach in Germany, and recurrent controversies on empirical research. Different traditions demonstrate that public opinion has been, since the very beginning, both politically relevant—since it always implies a certain relation toward the government— and politically problematic—because this relation is always historically biased. The question of the (impossibility of) convergence of the dominant paradigms of the twentieth century is, consequently, not only a question of theoretical and methodological but also ideological (in)compatibility.

The concept, the nature, and indeed the function of public opinion have undergone a radical transformation from early theorizations in the eighteenth century to contemporary times. No doubt concrete historical changes have exerted an important influence on changes in the understanding of, and in the development of theories on, the public/ness and public opinion. Such changes have been noticeable both in those studies of public opinion dealing above all with the "ideal public opinion" in the sense of normative political theory, which focuses primarily on characteristics of political values, and in sociological theories and empirical discussions directed toward constitutional factuality, at least since Childs's search for the definition (Childs 1939). Particularly in more recent periods one can also find several efforts to formally classify concepts (and definitions) of public opinion. In an attempt to examine the most important constructs of public opinion "which have won respectful hearings . . . among opinion researchers," Zaller (1994) distinguishes between "the currently dominant construct" (i. e., "public opinion as the aggregation of respondents to survey questions" or, more specifically, to "nationally representative polls") and "two alternatives to the dominant construct": (1) the concept of enlightened and rational opinion and (2) public opinion defined in terms of latent opinions with political relevance. In her own classification, Susan Herbst (1993, 44) expands on all the conceptualizations of public opinion (not only those that are empirically useful) and states that the various meanings of public opinion can be sorted into four definitional categories: aggregation, majoritarian, discursive/consensual, and reification.

Similar to the history of the public/ness and public opinion itself, the history of its research can be roughly divided into certain key periods or dominant paradigms, starting with the eighteenth century, when the expression "public opinion" was coined. The dominant paradigms, which will be presented below, partly proceed in clear chronological sequence and partly synchronically, but all reflect the social context from which they emerged. It is noteworthy that early debates about public opinion were generally linked to theories about freedom of the press. Both the eighteenth-century idea of public opinion and the idea of freedom of the press paralleled the economic idea of a free market (Mills [1956] 1968, 299). The theories of freedom of the press alternatively substantiated press freedom by the God-given ability of free thought, the utilitarian principle of the pursuit of happiness, freedom as natural right, or by the postutilitarian idea that Truth can only be attained through unfettered public debate among educated citizens. Concepts of public opinion can also be classified into similar categories. Traces of the connection between public opinion and freedom of the press can also be found in American pragmatism and later in Habermas's *Structural Transformation of the Public Sphere* ([1962] 1995). In recent times, however, after the constitutional guarantee for a free press in parliamentary democracies, the concept of freedom of the press has been ideologically frozen, and public opinion studies have taken off in their own independent way.

The concepts of public/ness and public opinion throughout all historical periods have been limited in two respects: (1) taken in their entirety, they have only been valid in certain historical periods and (2) they have always denoted specific social categories of individuals (the middle class) even though the public/ness was based on the principle of general accessibility. As Francis G. Wilson concluded, the concept of public opinion was always in a decisive manner linked to (or even limited by) the idea of the middle class, even though there have always been important differences, as well as opposition, between the two. With the advent of the bourgeois revolution, these two phenomena were joined together in "close doctrinal union at the height of a historical crisis" (Williams [1962] 1976, 200). Even more, as Champagne argues, public opinion was "a machine of an ideological war, made by intellectual elites and bourgeoisie during the eighteenth century to legitimise their own political pretensions and to impair royal absolutism" (Champagne, quoted in Blondiaux [1998] 1976, 45). The close connection between public opinion and the flowering of the middle class was exhaustively discussed at the beginning of the nineteenth century by William MacKinnon (1828), who argued that the power of public opinion is "in proportion to the information, proper religious feeling, facility of communication and capital that exist amongst the individuals of which the community is composed, which may be styled the requisites for public opinion" (MacKinnon [1828] 1971, 5). "As most of these requisites are to be found in the middle class of society as well as in the upper, it follows that the power of public opinion depends in a great measure on the proportion that the upper and middle class of society bear to the lower, or on the quantity of intelligence and wealth that exists in the community" (MacKinnon [1828] 1971, 15).

Similarly, for example, the rise of public opinion is an "entirely modern phenomenon," according to Tönnies, and related to the formation of "the people" (*das Volk*) and "bourgeois economic society" (Tönnies 1922, 220; 1928a, 36). In contrast to MacKinnon, Tönnies defines public opinion as a negation of religion, rather than its affirmation. Notwithstanding, the rudiments of public opinion can be identified already in the formation of the ancient Greek city square (*agora*) as a public space (but not the public as a social collectivity). The literature from ancient times on abounds in ideas and questions contemporarily discussed in the framework of public opinion. Some authors (e.g., William Albig 1956, 20) believe that public opinion was related to controversial issues that developed among the Greeks to an extent unequalled until modern times. However, the size of these "publics" was small, and there was no belief in general equality—only the ruling elite participated in democratic life. In Athens of the fourth century B.C., there were approximately 120,000 adults, of whom 40,000 were citizens (but only men with political rights and freedoms), 25,000 unenfranchised free foreigners, and 55,000 slaves. Wilhelm Bauer ([1933] 1963, 671) searches for the first predecessors of public opinion in the early civilizations of Egypt and Asia Minor, and among the early Hebrew prophets, who "made direct appeals to crowds [and] canalized popular attitudes. But there was little opportunity for popular discussion, and the role of the individual was that of a recipient of the supposedly revealed truth that the prophets trumpeted" (Albig 1956, 20). Thus it may be argued that in this early interlacing of politics and religion, one may identify predecessors of propaganda rather than predecessors of public opinion.

Tönnies was convinced that, due to its universal nature, the public is connected with every developed (i.e., democratic) political life, particularly with the "life of the States," and in this particular sense it has its predecessors in the Greek polis. Yet neither in the polis nor in the medieval towns (which resembled the polis in their civilization and political conflicts) existed newspapers, and it is the newspapers that brought about public life not restricted to a narrow circle of chosen individuals (Tönnies 1922, 100). Public opinion starts to develop into a new world power by the end of the sixteenth century, when the government begins to get more popular, as Tönnies (1916, 421) resumes after Bryce. Great faith in the possibility of an enlightened public opinion further developed with eighteenth-century rationalism when it was particularly popularized by the prophets of liberal democracy. Freedom of thought and opinion was declared a preeminent value. The great proponents of democratic government did not declare that public opinion was always right, but they did place faith in the ultimate soundness of popular judgments. The contradiction between the attribution of the origin of public opinion to the new Europe and the findings of certain forms of public opinion in the antiquity are easily reconcilable if, as Tönnies (1916, 419) suggests, "the natural fact is distinguished from the slogan in the concept." Thus public opinion has always and everywhere existed, but with different degrees of influence; however, it fully developed only with the rise of the bourgeoisie.

Yet forms of bourgeois public/ness have also remained trapped in a fundamental contradiction, as Negt and Kluge pointed out (1973, 10–11). On the one hand, the bourgeois public pretends to represent or express the opinion of the whole but, on the other hand, excludes two fundamental areas of life, "the entire industrial apparatus of the business and the socialization in the family." The public and public opinion are thus universal categories only in the sense of universal interest but not, for example, in the sense of universal accessibility. Because there is no external hindrance or limitation on debate (such as censor-

ship), debate can be thematically universal in the sense that the subject of debate and the formation of opinion can cover all kinds of events from art to politics. At the same time, the Enlightenment required that public opinion contain a certain moral judgment and concern the common (public) interests.

EARLY CONCEPTUALIZATIONS: BETWEEN CENSORSHIP
AND POPULAR CONTROL OF GOVERNMENT

The history of public opinion theories only interests us here to the extent that
it is needed for a better understanding of the theoretical development and controversies in the study of public opinion in the twentieth century,[1] which will
be discussed in detail in the chapters to follow, that is, from the particular standpoint of the well-developed assumptions that contributed to the later sociological theorizations of public opinion. The most important of these were articulated within the British liberal utilitarian theory of public opinion that
prevailed from the end of the eighteenth century to the beginning of the nineteenth century, and in the liberal critique of the tyranny of the majority from
the second half of the nineteenth century. These two paradigms are chronolog-
ically separated by the German legal-political philosophy spanning the end of
the eighteenth century and the first half of the nineteenth. The earliest articu-
lations in Rousseau's *Social Contract* must, of course, not be overlooked.

Classical liberal theories of the reign of public opinion were advanced during the Enlightenment, for the most part in England and France, and with some
delay in Germany. It came out of the utilitarian theory of the free press pro-
mulgated by James Mill and Jeremy Bentham, who saw in public opinion the
emergence of reasoned individuals against absolutist authority (Keane 1992,
66–71; Wilson 1962, 208). To this end, autonomy, competence, morality, and
responsibility for the common good were demanded of the individual. It was
no coincidence that these qualities materialized in the nascent bourgeoisie,
since the origins as well as the disintegration of the liberal public are connected
to the development of capitalism. In terms of the strict (classical or Enlightenment) definition, it is only possible to speak of public opinion and the public
in England at the end of the seventeenth century and in France in the eighteenth century.

Habermas, in *Structural Transformation*, gives Bentham credit for explicating
"for the first time in monographic form the connection between public opinion and the principle of publicity" (Habermas [1962] 1995, 99), in other
words, the principle of publicity as the foundation of public opinion and the
doctrine of the sovereignty of the people. According to Bentham, publicity is a

necessary precondition "for putting the *tribunal of the public* in a condition for forming an *enlightened judgment*" (Bentham [1791] 1994, 590; emphasis added). In his discussion of publicity, which he characterized as "the fittest law for securing the public confidence," Bentham ([1791] 1994) laid a comprehensive foundation for the necessity of constituting the public as the "strongest tribunal." This was accompanied by a detailed analysis of the reasons for the transparent relationship between the parliament and the people or between those who govern and those who are governed:

1. to constrain the members of the assembly to perform their duty;
2. to secure the confidence of the people, and their assent to the measures of the legislature;
3. to enable the governors to know the wishes of the governed;
4. to enable the electors to act from knowledge;
5. to provide the assembly with the means of profiting by the information of the public;
6. to generate the amusement that by itself increases the happiness of the people. (Bentham [1791] 1994, 581–86)

The public workings of the parliament ought to be guaranteed through four methods: (1) authentic publication of the transactions of the assembly, (2) keeping the minutes of all speeches, questions, and answers, (3) toleration of nonauthentic publications (e.g., unofficial journals), and (4) admission of strangers to the sittings in the assembly—with the exclusion of women. Indeed, the male character is as important a characteristic of the public as its foundation on the freedom of the press. Although Bentham did not directly relate the formation of enlightened judgment to a general rational (critical) discussion in the public, such an idea is to some degree implied by his polemic against the hypothetical objection that generally "the public is an incompetent judge of the proceedings of a political assembly, in consequence of the ignorance and passions of the majority of those who compose it" (Bentham [1791] 1994, 586). However, similarly to Edmund Burke, who argued that among 8 million people in Great Britain in the last quarter of the eighteenth century, only 400,000 citizens—affluent, informed adults who had time to discuss and debate—represented the "British public" (Hoffman and Levack [1949] 1967, xxii), Bentham did not proclaim the view that all individuals have the (equal) ability to use reason. He distinguished three segments of the public: (1) the most numerous class is formed by those who can hardly occupy themselves with public affairs because they "have not time to read, nor leisure for reasoning," (2) those who borrow judgments from others because they are not able to form opinions on their own, and (3) the elite, that is, those who judge for themselves. His key argument against any opposing belief about the publicity was that "the public do judge and will always judge." The increase in publicity can only help those who make "ill judgments" to make "more correct opinions" on the basis of accurate information. Obviously, it is the third segment that directly gains from publicity; however, their more informed opinions will also direct the opinions of the other two segments and make them more correct.

At the same time, Bentham clearly related the principle of publicity to a "system of distrust" and argued that "every good political institution is founded upon this base." That is why a Foucaultian reading of Bentham focusing on "distrustful surveillance" is perhaps more accurate than a Habermasian emphasis on rational discourse. As Gaonkar and McCarthy (1994, 559) suggest, Bentham's ideas on publicity and disciplinary technology for regulating legislators are "remarkably similar to the disciplinary technology elaborated in *Panopticon* for regulating the body of the prisoner." In Bentham's understanding of publicity, the aspects of general visibility and accessibility are emphasized, which make possible the establishment of efficient control over power elites. The aspect of rational debate has only secondary importance (which is in sharp contrast to later thematizations, such as Habermas's) and the critical character of publicity is entirely absent.

This first prehistorical period concluded with William A. MacKinnon's comprehensive book (published in 1828), the first work to be entirely devoted to the "rise, progress, and present state of public opinion," as the author indicated in the subtitle. Like Bentham, MacKinnon made distinctions between three social classes that, in his case, were entirely based on wealth because "where freedom and civilization exist, wealth is so entirely the only power either to individuals or to government, that no other means or choice is left of distinguishing the several classes of society, than by the property of the individuals of which they are formed" (MacKinnon [1828] 1971, 2). Using statistical criteria, MacKinnon divided society into (1) the upper class, consisting of those who "have the means of constantly supporting one hundred, or any greater number of men, fit for labour," (2) the middle class, consisting of individuals who are able to support from two to a hundred working men, and (3) the lower class, which consists of all others. Historically, public opinion itself was seen to be created only when the following four fundamental conditions are met: (1) the increase of the power of machinery, (2) communication (transportation) facilities, (3) proper religious feeling, and (4) the spread of information through society (e.g., improved systems of education, the press). All of these conditions were linked to the development and relative growth of the middle class and, to a lesser degree, of the upper class, the size of which was strictly limited in free countries by the growing middle class. MacKinnon was thus the first to systematically formulate certain sociological assumptions for the (political) functioning of public opinion and to put forward a thesis connecting public opinion with the middle class. He emphasized that the power of public opinion primarily depends on the proportion that the upper and middle classes of society bear to the lower class. The size of the middle- and upper-class population relative to a smaller lower class matches "the quantity of intelligence and wealth that exists in the community" (p. 15). According to MacKinnon, "popular clamour is powerful in proportion as the lower class is ignorant and numerous" and relies on the ignorance and prejudice of the uneducated, but the fundamental characteristic of public opinion is that it is well-informed and intelligent:

> Public opinion may be said to be, that sentiment on any given subject which is entertained by the best informed, most intelligent, and most moral persons in the community, which is gradually spread and adopted by nearly all persons of any education or proper feeling in a civilized state. (MacKinnon [1828] 1971, 15)

The increase in the power of public opinion is, according to MacKinnon, closely related to the development of liberal government: "This seems to prove that public opinion secures a liberal form of government, not that a government secures public opinion" (MacKinnon [1828] 1971, 9). And similar to what Burke had written before him, "Let us give a faithful pledge to the people, that we honor, indeed, the crown, but that we *belong* to them; that we are their auxiliaries, and not their task-masters" ([1769] 1967, 212), MacKinnon emphasized that "to follow, not to force, the public inclination; to give a direction, a form, a technical dress, and a specific sanction to the general sense of the community is the true end of legislature," and that in a civilized country[2] the government is governed by public opinion and must follow its dictates; it would be an error to imagine that the government can command public opinion, apart from shorter periods of despotic governments. Without a valid foundation, Wilson (1962, 34) even generalizes the early liberal belief that public opinion creates an obligation for public servants to follow as "one of the converging ideas in the theory of public opinion." Nevertheless, it must be said that whereas the theories of the rule of public opinion from Burke to MacKinnon attributed sovereignty to public opinion and to the public itself, the public, as the materialized form of the principle of publicity, has always been either implicitly or explicitly limited by the competence of individuals and, as such, was efficiently institutionalized into the political system of the bourgeois legal state that represented the beginning of a gradual disintegration of the classical bourgeois public, or as Habermas says, the principle of publicity based on the public of educated people who reason and enjoy art and the medium of bourgeois press—which, at the beginning, undoubtedly had a critical function against the secret practice of the absolutist state and was consolidated in the *methods of organs* of the legal state—has been refunctioned for demonstrative and manipulative purposes. ([1965] 1980, 10)

The concept of the rule of public opinion would soon become the object of severe criticism. The period of confidence in public opinion, based on the belief in the moral judgment of the common man (middle class) proclaimed in the age of Enlightenment, would be followed by a period of distrust in his capabilities and competence. Doubts were first clearly expressed by Hegel, followed in the mid-1800s by political-philosophical critiques of the tyranny of public opinion, which continued to dominate up to the rise of sociopsychological positivism and empiricism, which emerged in the early 1900s.

The continental tradition: Rousseau, Kant, Hegel and Marx. Rousseau's *Social Contract* (1762) can be considered a sort of constitution of the Enlightenment. As Wilhelm Bauer commented ([1933] 1963, 669), Rousseau with his concept of *volonté générale* expanded Montesquieu's *esprit générale* while both were heirs to Locke's attempts to supply a jurist and ethical orientation for the phenomenon of public opinion, which Locke named "the law of opinion and reputation." All three conceptualizations represent prehistory of the notion of public opinion, which began to emerge in the period before the French Revolution.

The guiding spirit in Rousseau's reflections in *The Social Contract* was how to arrive at a legal and reliable government in which justice and legality would be in harmony. The social contract solved the problem of how to find a form of commonality that would defend and protect the personality and property of every member; at the same time, each individual would be united with all the others, subordinated only to himself and remaining free (Rousseau [1762] 189, 247). The solution was the subordination of each individual to the supreme leadership of the general will, which emerges with the association of individuals into a collective, moral body that also has a political character—as the republic. Only the general will *(la volonté générale)*, Rousseau emphasized, can lead the powers of the country in accordance with the reasonable common welfare because of which it was created. The general will, which exists only when a universal good is looked for, is materialized in the law equally valid for everyone and must be distinguished from the will of everyone *(la volonté de tous)*, which is only the sum of individual desires and expresses private interests—it is a difference between normative and empirical collective will. Only in an ideal situation do these two wills coincide, provided that individuals subject themselves to a general law; then a popular vote becomes identical with the general will.

To the categories of political, citizenship, and penal laws, Rousseau added a fourth type of law, which he considered a guarantee for the execution of other laws rather than a special type of law, and for that reason is the most important of all—"manners and morals, customs, and more than all, of *opinions*"[3] (emphasis added). Rousseau, however, did not make a precise distinction between the general will and public opinion. The general will expresses itself through laws whereas public opinion *(l'opinion publique, jugement publique, l'opinion de peuple)* is the judgment of the people, which is expressed in censorship; it is thus "the kind of law of which the censor is the minister, and which he only causes to be applied to particular cases, after the example of the prince" (Rousseau [1762] 1947, 113; Fr. [1762] 189, 330). The general will is based on the debate and decisions of "appropriately educated people," and it is expressed as general opinion, whereas special opinion (the opinion of special groups) prevails at times when the general will does not exist. The general will is always correct; it is only the capacity of the judgment that guides it that is not always sufficiently enlightened. The people on their own will always want the good, but they will not always see the good and may need to be directed, led—in short, enlightened—sometimes also with the help of censorship.[4] Public opinion as general opinion is based (and here Rousseau resembles Montaigne) on a moral authority and therefore comes close to the role of moral arbiter (Tönnies 1922, 291). In other words, it would have an emphatic function of social control as well as a legislative function (Vreg 1980, 44). Rousseau was convinced that the general will could only be expressed (1) if, in society, there were no special interest groups (which would, of course, concern themselves with their own interests)[5] and (2) if every citizen reasoned with his own mind. Public debate and argument were almost superfluous: the general will is more a consensus of hearts than of arguments presented in a public discussion; publicity is reduced to a discussion of public affairs in public assemblies. There is no specific organ that forms the general will; the government is merely an administrative committee.

Whereas the principle of publicity had an instrumental function for the utilitarians, and even a disciplinarian role for Bentham, Immanuel Kant lifted it to a transcendent principle mediating between politics and morals in public law. Unlike Rousseau, Kant did not believe that man was by nature good (yet he was grateful to Rousseau for helping him to overcome his own blind dismissal of the illiterate masses and set him on the path toward respect for the human being and his rights). Thus Kant did not defend the principle of publicity for the sake of the moral improvement of the people but argued that it is necessary to use this "mechanism of nature" as a means to create a legal maxim that people would obey. In his treatise *To Perpetual Peace,* Kant puts forward "*the transcendental formula* of public justice: 'All actions that affect the rights of other men are wrong if their maxim is not consistent with publicity.' This principle is to be considered not only *ethical . . .* but also *juridical*' (Kant [1795] 1983, 135).[6] Without the possibility of publicity, without the principle of public agency, there would be no justice. The reverse is also true: if a goal can only be achieved with the help of publicity, it means that there is no distrust in the underlying political maxims that are congruent with the goals and rights of all. Publicity alone therefore can guarantee harmony between politics and morals: on the one hand, it guarantees legal order while on the other hand it fulfils an enlightened role. In such a way, publicity can mediate between politics and morals, reconciling them within a republican system of government (the only form that is, according to Kant, appropriate for humankind)[7] founded on the representation of the people. The republican form of government—in contrast to the despotic—emerges from (1) the principle of the freedom of every member of society, (2) the dependence of all (as subjects) on common legislation, and (3) their equality as citizens. Hence the republican form of government represents the standard for judging the correctness and justice of the legislature, and it also forms the basis for a "federation of free countries" that might put an end to the violence of wars (Kant [1795] 1983, 100–102).

Kant's principle of publicity is not directly connected to public opinion but rather to the reconciliation of politics with morals and the achievement of consensus; yet his notion of publicity comes very close to the idea of public opinion when he relates it to the mutual "agreement of all judgments with each other." However, Kant specifically elaborates the concept of opinion, which, in *Critique of Pure Reason,* is defined as the lowest level of "holding for true" *(Fürwahrhalten).* Holding for true is, according to Kant, determined by the subjective and objective validity of judgment and has three levels ([1781] 1952, 241): opining *(Meinen),* believing *(Glauben),* and knowing *(Wissen).* Opinion is both subjectively and objectively insufficient,[8] belief is subjectively sufficient but lacks objectivity; only knowledge is sufficient on both accounts. Subjective sufficiency is termed "conviction" (for myself) and objective sufficiency is termed "certainty" (for everyone). Yet one must never dare to put forth even a mere opinion without some knowledge; thus an opinion is never merely an "arbitrary fiction." One cannot possibly hold opinions in judgments of pure reason. It would be absurd, for example, to have an opinion about pure mathematics— in such a field, one must either *know* or abstain from forming a judgment altogether. According to Kant, the same rule applies to issues of morality.

From this, we can deduce a certain notion about public opinion that suits the propaedeutic character of Kant's notion of publicity. The public use of reason is, in the first place, a matter for scholars who have the simultaneous tasks of guiding and enlightening the people. In his essay *What Is Enlightenment?*

Kant wrote that enlightenment is liberation from the human impossibility of using one's own reason without being guided by someone else. "Have the courage to use your *own* reason is the motto of Enlightenment" (Kant [1784] 1965a, 1). Only freedom of the public use of one's reason (which a person makes use of as a scholar before the reading public) can stimulate enlightenment unhindered by the limitations of the private uses of reason. Liberation from immaturity, which is enlightenment, demands that the individual think with his or her own mind. From the standpoint of humanity as a whole, liberation means objective aspiration and progress toward perfectly just order. Enlightened opinion endowed with publicity and scholarly prudence are, according to Kant, the most reliable sources of progress. In spite of his inclination toward a republican and representative system (though not Rousseauian democracy and revolution and consequently Rousseau's social contract), Kant does not see the driving force of development as the running of things from the bottom up but rather from the top down (Kant [1798] 1965b, 164). Education in all fields could only be successful if it were carried out in accordance with the prudently considered plans of the state.

Hegel's analysis of public opinion, published in the study *Grundlinien einer Philosophie des Rechts* in 1821, emerged from his understanding of the freedom of will, which ran counter to liberal thinking. Human freedom is not arbitrary. It presupposes a rationally organized state with laws and institutions that are respected by the individual in his activities. By doing so, the individual first and foremost responds to the demands put forth by the state in terms of the "substantive and particular interest" of all concerned (Schacht 1972, 322). In contrast to Bentham, for example, who saw in the principle of publicity a safeguard for public confidence in the assembly and an assurance that the assembly would perform its duties, Hegel defended the publicity of the Estates debates in Germany primarily on the grounds of expanding knowledge of public affairs among the general population. Publicizing debates should enable the public opinion to gain insight into problems as well as reliable information needed to make rational judgments. At the same time, public opinion ought to "learn to respect the work, abilities, virtues, and dexterity of ministers and officials." Publicity is, according to Hegel ([1821] 1971, 203–4, §315), an "antidote to the self-conceit of individuals singly and *en masse*" and the "chief means of their education." Such a functional definition of publicity is, to a large degree, indebted to Hegel's definition of the role of Estates as the mediating organ that stands "between the government in general on the one hand and the nation broken up into particulars (people and associations) on the other." In contrast to the liberal belief that the government has to follow public opinion, Hegel ([1821] 1971, 197, §302) considered the Estates to be the mediator and reductor of both the power of the crown and of particular interests of individuals and associations. He also viewed Estates as the bulwark against "an unorganized opinion and volition . . . in opposition to the organized state."

Contrary to the business of state—in which only those with "qualifications and disposition that accord with this end" (above all, knowledge, understanding, and property) can participate—the sphere of public opinion is a field that "is open to everyone to express one's purely personal political opinions and make them count" (Hegel [1821] 1971, 201, §308, 309). "Public opinion is the unorganized way in which a people's opinions and wishes are made known," as Gans summarized Hegel's lecture (Add. §316). Within public opinion, two different strands are ceaselessly interwoven: on the one hand, public usage and the authority of reason and, on the other hand, contingency, ignorance, and faulty reasoning:

> The formal subjective freedom of individuals consists in their having and expressing their own private judgments, opinions, and recommendations on affairs of state. This freedom is collectively manifested as what is called "public opinion," in which what is absolutely universal, the substantive and true, is linked with its opposite, the purely particular and private opinions of the Many. Public opinion as it exists is thus a standing self-contradiction, knowledge as appearance, the essential just as directly present as the inessential. (Hegel [1821] 1971, 204, §316)

For public opinion, both maxims simultaneously apply: that *vox populi, vox dei*[9] and also (here Hegel quotes Italian Renaissance poet Lodovico Ariosto) that it is like an ignorant, vulgar person who reproves everyone and talks most of what he understands least. Because of these contradictions in public opinion, the sciences, insofar as they really are sciences, "do not fall under the category of public opinion." In public opinion, one can find as much truth as error and, precisely for that reason, it deserves to be respected when the truth is found in it, and despised when it is expressed in gossip. In this regard, independence from public opinion is, on the one hand, a fundamental condition for achieving anything that is great and rational in life and science. But, on the other hand, each great achievement is recognized by public opinion and thus must also be viewed as one of its prejudices (Hegel [1821] 1971, 205, 318).

Habermas ([1962] 1995, 119) concluded that Hegel's definition of the ambivalent status of public opinion was the necessary consequence of the "disorganization of civil society." However, it is important to add that it is not only that. Although early liberal understanding of public opinion emerged from the doctrine of sovereignty of the people and Kant, with his transcendental formula of publicity, emphasized the principle of harmony, only with Hegel's conceptualization do we first encounter the inherent contradiction in the character of public opinion. In later developments, this contradictory nature would become even more evident, first with the authors who criticized the tyranny of majority—Alexis de Tocqueville, John Stuart Mill, and James Bryce.

Marx in his systematic *Critique of Hegel's Philosophy of Right* ([1843] 1974)—which was above all a critique of Hegel's theory of Estates in which Marx argued that it is not the state, as Hegel asserted, but rather civil society *(bürgerliche Gesellschaft)* that is the key to the understanding of historical development—did not enter into a polemic with Hegel's concept of public opinion and publicity. Similar to Hegel, Marx argued for publicity and freedom of the press, most explicitly in the article "Die Verhandlungen des 6. rheinischen Landtags,"[10] published in a six-part series in the *Rheinische Zeitung* of May 1842. For Marx, publicity was a precondition for a functioning political assembly because a "truly political assembly only prospers under the great protectorate of *public spirit,* as the living [prospers] only under the protectorate of a *clear air*" (Marx [1842] 1969, 65). Parliamentary freedom, which had been defended by certain representatives of the Estates from the ranks of lower nobility as superior to the press freedom, was, according to Marx, nothing else than either privilege or censorship. Perhaps that had been the freedom of the prerevolutionary French assemblies, emphasized Marx, but today is the time of publicness. Publicness not in the sense of things being truthfully reported to the public but in the sense of being reported to a genuine public; in other words, not to an "imaginary reading public" but to a "living current public" (Marx [1842] 1969, 62). That is why the publication of the debates of the provincial parliament only in the official newspapers—a form of censorship performed by the Estates—was worse than no publication at all. Censorship is the criticism as the monopoly in the hands of authority which, because of its secrecy, loses its rationality. However, the substance of freedom of the press stems precisely from the criticism using the "sharp knife of reason." Therefore, what is needed is not laws regulating censorship but laws regulating the press. With press laws, it is freedom that penalizes, whereas with censorship laws—which are only laws formally because they do not express the vital laws of human activities—it is freedom that is penalized. "*The press law is thus a legal recognition of freedom of the press. It is the law* because it is a positive existence of freedom" (Marx [1842] 1969, 77).

Marx also noticed a new kind of nascent censorship in the large cash deposits that the state required of publishers in order to publish. In the sphere of material censorship, he also placed the sort of press freedom favored by representatives of the bourgeoisie. Marx criticized the economic subordination of the press to capital that was based on the presupposition of the formal-legal freedom of the press. His critique was based on the experiences of the then current

French press, an issue also debated by the Rhineland provincial assembly, which ultimately characterized the French press as being "too free." Marx's opinion was, of course, just the opposite (Splichal 1981, 104). As he demonstrates, the interest of the bourgeoisie is not to eliminate the unfreedom of the press in its entirety but only to replace a certain kind of unfreedom—censorship as a kind of external unfreedom—that limits the free availability of property in the sphere of the press by another, inner unfreedom. For representatives of the bourgeoisie, it is a "classic incongruity" if the sphere of the press is excepted from the general freedom of entrepreneurship (Marx [1842] 1969, 88). Yet if freedom of the press is based on free enterprise, it becomes just another privilege—not the right of a human being or a citizen but merely the right of the owner. Wouldn't it be better to reverse things and treat entrepreneurial freedom as a kind of freedom of the press? Absurdity is present in both examples. A press is, of course, also a business although in this case it is not a matter of writers but of printers and publishers, and that raises yet a completely different set of questions. This is why Marx ([1842] 1969, 92) emphasized in his writing that "the first freedom of the press is that it is not a business."

The liberalist theory of the tyranny of public opinion began to take shape in the middle of the nineteenth century, during a period when democracy was expanding for all social classes. At first glance, this new school of thought did not seem to differ substantially from classical liberal theory. Here too questions about the possibility of rational debate of an educated public took center stage along with the historical limitations of the formation of the public opinion to a specific social category—the bourgeois public, which in America, according to Mill, was composed of the whole white population and in England was represented by the middle class—from which "many foolish individuals" were excluded (Mill [1859] 1985, 81). The essential distinction is to be found in the explicit social limitation of the public to the wisest people that emerged from the critique of utilitarian theory of freedom of the press; it is a consequence of a different conceptualization of the function of public opinion. In contrast to the classic understanding, public opinion was no longer understood as a means of freedom and democracy but rather as tyranny over reason. For John Stuart Mill, the purpose of press freedom was not to guarantee happiness for the greatest number of people, as it was with Bentham, but rather the pursuit of Truth, something that is rarely the same as the opinion of the many or the opinion of the masses, which represents "collective mediocrity" (Mill [1859] 1985, 131). Therefore, such freedom can only be enjoyed by mature society, not by a society in which people are becoming ever more similar and therefore more mediocre—as Tocqueville observed about France—and in which the task of the elite must be to limit the excessive power of public opinion. Public opinion, because of its complete domination, is more than any other factor the cause of general similarity among people because, similarly to Christian morals, it requires, above all, the obedience of individuals and dictates what they are allowed to do and what they must not do. This modified perspective in the conceptualization of public opinion was certainly linked to historical changes, inspiring Mill to say that "the time, it is to be hoped, is gone by, when any defence would be necessary of the 'liberty of the press' as one of the securities against corrupt or tyrannical government" (Mill [1859] 1985, 75).

Tocqueville, in his book about democracy in America, emphasized that the greatest dangers to the American republic proceeded from the omnipotence of the majority. He was convinced that the supremacy of the majority was so strong that "freedom of opinion does not exist in America. The Inquisition has never been able to prevent a vast number of anti-religious books from circulating in Spain. The empire of the majority succeeds much better in the United States, since it actually removes any wish to publish them" (Tocqueville [1840] 1995, vol. 1, chap. 15). The domination of the majority, not unlike a rigid social or caste system, produces silence and the impossibility of change. Thus the most favorable to the "great revolutions of the mind" is a society in which there is neither the complete equality of the entire community nor the absolute separation of social classes.

> Whenever social conditions are equal, public opinion presses with enormous weight upon the minds of each individual; it surrounds, directs, and oppresses him; and this arises from the very constitution of society much more than from its political laws. As men grow more alike, each man feels himself weaker in regard to all the rest; as he discerns nothing by which he is considerably raised above them or distinguished from them, he mistrusts himself as soon as they assail him. Not only does he mistrust his strength, but he even doubts of his right; and he is very near acknowledging that he is in the wrong, when the greater number of his countrymen assert that he is so. The majority do not need to force him; they convince him. (Tocqueville [1840] 1995, vol. 2, sec. 3, chap. 21)

Therefore, according to Tocqueville, for a truly democratic arrangement, it is essential that the legislative power is so constituted as to represent the majority without necessarily being "the slave of its passions." In addition, the legislative, executive, and judiciary powers should be separated and mutually independent. In such circumstances, Tocqueville believed, a government could be formed that would still be democratic and yet not endangered by the tyranny of the majority.

In the aftermath of the bourgeois revolutions of the eighteenth and nineteenth centuries, the actual reduction of the public to the bourgeois class

effectively meant the narrowing of the social category of the public and its clo-
sure to the emerging working class. The theoretical arguments of Tocqueville
([1840] 1995), Mill ([1859] 1985), and Bryce ([1888] 1995) only legitimized
that narrowing. Whereas the liberal-democratic concept of public opinion was
critically oriented against the absolutist authority, the revised theory of public
opinion in the period of the consolidation of the rule of law attempted to legitimize and conserve the economic and political power of the bourgeois class
against the mass. In *Liberty,* Mill even advocated despotism as a legitimate mode
of government in dealing with "barbarians," while at the same time he saw in
public opinion a great danger to modern democracies:

> The modern régime of public opinion is, in an unorganized form, what the Chi-
> nese educational and political systems are in an organized; and unless individual-
> ity shall be able successfully to assert itself against the yoke, Europe, notwith-
> standing its noble antecedents and its professed Christianity, will tend to become
> another China. (Mill [1859] 1985, 138)

Just as the early liberal period, in which the rule of public opinion was
championed, concluded with the comprehensive work of William MacKinnon (1828), so the period of the liberalist critique of the tyranny of the majority and public opinion reached its zenith at the end of the nineteenth century with a thorough discussion about public opinion in *The American
Commonwealth,* written by a British diplomat in the United States—James
Bryce (1888). He discussed the United States as an example of the inexpedi-
ent "government by public opinion" in which, according to Bryce, "the wishes
and views of the people prevail, even before they have been conveyed through
the regular law-appointed organs, and without the need of their being so conveyed" (Bryce [1888] 1995, 925). Public opinion is expressed through four
main organs: (1) the press, (2) public meetings, primarily during election campaigns, (3) elections, and (4) citizen associations. Among them, he considered
newspapers the most important because they—"as narrators, as advocates, and
as weathercocks"—not only report events but also advance arguments and
mirror public opinion. Although none of these instruments can provide a constant, instant, and reliable estimation of public opinion, politicians—who do
not differ from their constituents as regards their virtues and ideas—act as if
such an instrument existed: they "look incessantly for manifestations of current popular opinion, and . . . shape their course in accordance with their reading of those manifestations" (p. 920). An active monitoring of public opinion
would become later, particularly with V. O. Key's definition, the critical point
in conceptualizations of public opinion.

Yet Bryce argued that the absence of a reliable means of ascertaining public opinion, or the will of the majority, was less important than the danger that "minorities may not sufficiently assert themselves" because of the widespread pressure of the majority in all spheres of public life, both inside and outside of the legislation. He was the first to identify, in addition to the tyranny of the majority discussed by Tocqueville,[11] the phenomena of a passive "silent majority" and the "fatalism of the multitude," which, together with the former, make the decisive role of public opinion particularly questionable. On the other hand, Bryce also revealed the paradox that the uneducated, humbler classes differ in opinion from the educated and propertied classes; despite the fact that there is little substance in the beliefs of "the man in the car," he argued that the humbler classes "have often been proved by the event to have been right and their so-called betters wrong" (p. 913). Nevertheless, he clearly took up the position typically expressed by Edmund Burke and later by Tocqueville and Mill who, as Wilson (1962, 213) argued, could not "realize that the minority can be even more tyrannical than the majority":

> The duty, therefore, of a patriotic statesman in a country where public opinion rules, would seem to be rather to *resist* and *correct* than to encourage the dominant sentiment. . . . In a nation with a keen moral sense and a capacity for strong emotions, opinion based on a love of what is deemed just or good will *resist the multitude* when bent on evil. (Bryce [1888] 1995, 921; emphasis added)

"Vigorous individuality" and a "keen moral sense" of citizens brought about by appropriate socialization could be the only safeguards against majority pressure toward undesirable conformity and its potentially destructive consequences. No doubt, Bryce's model of public opinion belongs to those liberal theorizations denoted by Habermas as reactionary because they "reacted to the power of the idea of a critically debating public's self-determination . . . as soon as this public was subverted by the propertyless uneducated masses" ([1962] 1995, 136). Later, when the level of literacy and general education increased, the rising significance of the masses in conceptualizations of public opinion was associated particularly with the mass (popular) press and propaganda. The relationship of the public to the masses took the place of the formerly dominant relationship to the authority as the essential dimension in the public opinion phenomenon; the principle of the tolerance of the majority (the uninformed masses) toward the minority (representative power) replaced the principle of the public controlling the actions of the authorities. Masses were increasingly regarded as "crowds," which, as Le Bon ([1895] 1930, 19) believed, "are only powerful for destruction," mentally inferior, and, essentially, "barbarian."[12] Le Bon's concern with the increased power of the crowd was followed by Gabriel Tarde's (1898) analytical distinction between the crowd and the public. This shift in defining the contrasting side of the public, in relation to which the character of the public was determined, had a crucial import for the social-psychological and sociological understanding of public/ness that began to gain prominence toward the end of the nineteenth century. The tendency to expand the concept of the public to include the masses or the total citizenry without doubt had, on the one side, its democratic character. But on the other hand, with this new perspective, the public lost its original rational-critical and political character. Whereas in pre-twentieth-century normative theories, public opinion was conceived of as the result of the deliberation in the public as a social category or in the public sphere as a public opinion context, the twentieth-century empiricist schools of thought did not relate it to any specific social entity or historical condition. From early sociologization of public opinion studies to the institutionalization of public opinion polling and the spiral of silence model, the entire theoretical development in the twentieth century has a common denominator: it is characterized by controversies over the (non)democratic nature of public opinion.

SOCIOLOGIZATION OF PUBLIC OPINION THEORIES
AND AMERICAN PRAGMATISM

In the late nineteenth and early twentieth centuries, public opinion became a subject of systematic study as a result of the sociological conceptualizations that began to emerge particularly in Germany and the United States. During this time, the critical interest of researchers in problems related to public/ness and public opinion became more and more pronounced in the United States. American theorists would soon gain preeminence not only in asking the key research questions but, even more so, in determining research methods for finding the answers. The newly emerging positivist paradigm treated public opinion as an organic social process and linked it to the social-psychological findings about group interaction—as "developing at the societal level out of communicative reaction to disagreement or ambiguity" (Price and Oshagan 1995, 195)—and thus public opinion was progressively depoliticized, although early sociological theorizations continued to emphasize the political dimension of public opinion. The most prominent sociological theorists of public opinion of the time (e.g., Tönnies and Bauer in Germany and Dewey, Park, and Lippmann in the United States) explicitly referred to psychological research as a source (at least) as valuable as normative political theories of the eighteenth and nineteenth centuries. Blumer's definition of public opinion ([1946] 1966, 46–50), representing the end of the classical (Chicago) sociological period and coinciding with the increasing use of public opinion polling, emphasized the collective, interactive, and rational-discursive (but also manipulatable) characteristics of public opinion. He also stressed the competitiveness of groups that form the public as an "elementary and spontaneous collective grouping" that attempts to shape and set the opinions of relatively disinterested people. The public lost its strictly political character and its rigid reference to a national people. The issue with which the public is confronted is not constituted by its political characteristics but rather by the division of people "in their ideas as to how to meet the issue"; the formation of the public only implies "the presence of a situation which cannot be met on the basis of a cultural rule but which must be met by a collective decision arrived at through the process of discussion."

During the first phase of the sociologization of public opinion theories in the United States, a very important role was played by American pragmatism of which the most important representatives were Charles Horton Cooley, William James, Charles S. Peirce, John Dewey, and George Herbert Mead. The tradition of American pragmatism and symbolic interactionism (Dewey, Mead, Blumer) has, with its concept that society does not exist by way of communication but *in* communication, left an important mark on both theories of public opinion and communication theories. American pragmatism emerged from distinctive features of American society and history as an indigenous though heterogeneous tradition. "It was a break with the absolutism which had dominated academic thought and an attempt to produce a philosophical context for social-scientific inquiries into the twentieth century with the aid of 'biological imagination,' and an emphasis on 'human efforts,' 'collective action' and 'meliorism' " (Hardt 1992, 33). Its most significant common denominator was "a future-oriented instrumentalism that tries to deploy thought as a weapon to enable more effective action" (West 1989, 5). Dewey emphasized the practical and constructive role of reason in human action and defined pragmatism, distinct from the orientation of empiricism toward the past, as having an orientation toward the future

> as an extension of historical empiricism but with this fundamental difference, that it does not insist upon antecedent phenomena but consequent phenomena; not upon the precedents but upon the possibilities of action. And this change in point of view is almost revolutionary in its consequences. (Dewey 1931, 24)

Despite its indigenousness, the paradigm also owed much for its development to the European political-philosophical thought from which it descended;

yet surprisingly—in contrast to earlier English contributions—it had almost no, or, in any case, an extremely limited impact on the prevailing European theories of public opinion, including those of Tönnies and Habermas. This is in sharp contrast to the empirical social-psychological tradition that developed in the United States in the sixties and became the dominant theory in almost all of Europe.

American pragmatism itself, from its beginnings, emphasized the importance of the empirical perspective in social research or sociology as "the embodiment of all descriptive and explanatory social science" (Park [1904] 1972, 23), in contrast to philosophy. Yet the notion of the empirical character of sociology in pragmatists' interpretation fundamentally differed from the kind of empiricism whose protagonists believed that the facts speak for themselves and saw no need for theoretical propositions and explanations.

Pragmatists, particularly Dewey, laid great stress on the close link between the goals of social democratization and the development of knowledge in the process of transformation from the Great Society to the Great Community, the latter being, according to Dewey, nothing less than "an organized articulate Public." In the pragmatists' understanding of public opinion we can find much in common with Tönnies's ideas articulated in his *Critique of Public Opinion*, for example, with his emphasis on the significance of science in general and social sciences in particular, the autonomy of the media and their educational function, and, most of all, the close linkage between true public opinion and *Volksgemeinschaft*, which should be, as a modern form of *Gemeinschaft* or socialism, based on social reforms carried out in the *Gesellschaft* (Tönnies 1922, 573).[13] Dewey ascribed an important role in the transformative process to the dissemination of scientific-research findings and, in particular, those of the social sciences:

> Communication of the results of social inquiry is the same thing as the formation of public opinion. This marks one of the first ideas framed in the growth of political democracy as it will be one of the last to be fulfilled. For public opinion is judgment which is formed and entertained by those who constitute the public and is about public affairs. . . . Opinions and beliefs concerning the public presuppose effective and organized inquiry. (Dewey [1927] 1991, 177)

The pragmatists concluded that industrialization and urbanization decisively contributed to the decline of democratic public. They did not see the key to the deterioration of the public primarily in the new conservatism, workers' struggles, or religious revivalism. Rather, they considered these manifestations to be indicators of the increasing mediation, and increasingly distorted mediation, of reality by newspapers, film, and radio (Aronowitz 1993, 75). Due to these complex developments, society was becoming less and less transparent whereas, in fact, the development of communication should make complexity more transparent. However, communication was seen by the pragmatists not only as the cure but also as a kind of poison. "'Communication' was thus a Janus-faced term. Some saw it as just what was needed to restore democracy on a grand scale and the basic criterion of a just and humane society. Others saw it as a community-devouring monster that trampled traditional borders and orders" (Peters 1989, 248).

Liberalist theorists saw the principal danger of public opinion in its mass character and the subsequent potential for an intolerant majority. Therefore, they called for limitations on its excessive power. Pragmatists not only followed a different approach than the liberalists but they also took a critical distance from the classical liberal theories of James Mill (see Dewey [1927] 1991, 171), arguing instead for the publication of results of sociological research in the daily press, the translation of specialized knowledge into an accessible idiom, and breaking down the ossified structure of the social knowledge whose backwardness "is marked in its division into independent and insulated branches of learning" (Dewey [1927] 1991, 171). Only with the wide application of science and scientific method could a "democratically organized public" develop. Similarly to the early tradition of classical liberal theory of public opinion that emerged from the (utilitarian) theory of freedom of the press, the pragmatists linked their critical understanding of public opinion to a critique of the sensationalism of the press and of the journalistic profession. Like their German contemporary, Tönnies, they emphasized the need for press reform and the complete independence of newspapers. They saw the press as the social sensorium that could potentially fill the great void of all hitherto existing social evolution. "The press for these thinkers was not paper, ink, words, and images; it was a set of social and imaginative relationships that could reconstruct, or further ruin, community life" (Peters 1989, 250). The pragmatists demanded not only freedom of the press and freedom of expression but, even more important, freedom of social inquiry and of the distribution of its findings. Yet Park, in his early studies of the public and the mass, observed an inherently contradictory character of the public and public opinion:

> What is usually called a public is a kind of group which stands for the most part at the same stage of awareness-development as the crowd. Thus, *so-called public opinion* is generally nothing more than a naive collective impulse which can be manipulated by catchwords. Modern journalism, which is supposed to instruct and direct public opinion by reporting and discussing events, usually turns out to be

simply a mechanism for controlling collective attention. . . . while *behavior of the public* which is expressed in public opinion, results from discussion among individuals who assume opposing positions. This discussion is based upon presentation of facts. (Park [1904] 1972, 57; emphasis added)

The pragmatists' understanding of the public and public opinion was based on the Rousseauian assumption "that each individual is himself equipped with the intelligence needed, under the operation of self-interest, to engage in political affairs" (Dewey [1927] 1991, 157). The pragmatists vehemently refuted the critique that democracy systematically produces mediocrity—as advanced by the theories of Tocqueville, Mill, and Le Bon in the nineteenth century and Lippmann in the twentieth—and stressed the importance of democratic forms of consultation and discussion (e.g., popular voting, majority rule), which serve to reveal societal needs. Dewey argued against Tocqueville's accusation that democracy generated mediocrity in its elected rulers and reflected the passions and foolish ideas of ordinary men, claiming that such a criticism, in fact, proves that democratic government is educational, which is not the case with other forms of government.

Yet pragmatism would later be the target of the criticism, particularly sharp in the new social-psychological tradition, that public opinion had been unjustifiably reduced to its political-control function, which was supposed to be exercised by specific institutions and mechanisms, and conceptualized as a sort of "systemic-conformist institution of the veto" (Schmidtchen 1959, 259).[14] The sharpest critic of pragmatists, particularly Dewey's unconditional confidence in public opinion and of the idea of the "omnicompetent individual" was probably Walter Lippmann. He firmly believed that all the troubles of the press, of popular government, and even of industry have a common source: "the failure of self-governing people to transcend their casual experience and their prejudice, by inventing, creating, and organizing a machinery of knowledge" (Lippmann [1922] 1960, 365). They are constantly and effectively exposed to vague, emotion-engaging symbols and stereotypes produced by the authorities and experts who generate public opinion, and thus not able to understand and decide on highly complex social issues; it would be only reasonable, according to Lippmann, that the business of politics be left to the experts.

By the time half of the twentieth century had elapsed, American pragmatism had intellectually run out of steam and gave up its dominant position in the study of public opinion (and no longer of the public as well) to the new social-psychological paradigm. When Dewey published *The Public and Its Problems* in 1927, the book attracted much less attention than Lippmann's ideas both in America and in Europe. The expansion of polling in the 1930s and the establishment of *Public Opinion Quarterly* in 1937 actually marked the end of the fruitful theoretical era of American pragmatism and the beginning of social-psychological approaches to public opinion. The first edition of the *Reader in Public Opinion and Communication,* which was edited by Berelson and Janowitz in 1950, clearly reflected the decline of pragmatism. Nevertheless, the questions raised by pragmatists and the controversy between Lippmann and Dewey that took place in the twenties not only had a strong impact on the era during which it was waged but would also exert its influence in later years—as we shall see in the development of public opinion polling in the 1930s. Indeed it would make a decisive mark on the intellectual history of debates about public opinion, the mass media, and democracy even though after World War II the political and economic ascent of public opinion polling would place critical theories of public opinion on a back burner.

SOCIAL-PSYCHOLOGICAL MODELS OF PUBLIC OPINION

During the latter part of the 1920s, interest in questions of communication and media changed from theoretical considerations and social criticism, based upon the expectation of progressive thought, into practical concerns and specific problems within the scope of emerging research methodologies. It was a period during which the social sciences made orchestrated attempts to restrict social-problem and reform-oriented theory and research and to develop disciplinary knowledge primarily with the help of empirical investigation. The social-psychological study of public opinion was, particularly in its earliest period preceding World War II, predominantly directed toward the empirical and quantitative opinion research. The previously close relationship between public opinion, political democracy, and freedom of the press was replaced with a close empirical linkage between public opinion polling, analysis of (particularly international) propaganda, and the development of public relations.

Only exceptionally, the new paradigm would advance more penetrating psychological theories of the public and public opinion. William McDougall, for example, insisted in his book *The Group Mind* (1920) on the notion of public opinion as the product of collective mental life whose moral power cannot be based on the sum of individual opinions; it is an expression of the attitude of mind prevailing in the nation. Half a century later, Sennett would demonstrate in his work *The Fall of Public Man* (1974) that "psychological imagery . . . was superimposed on things for sale in public. The same sort of process began in the behavior of politicians in front of street crowds, first strikingly manifest in the revolutions of 1848" (Sennett 1978, 25). Sennett argued that "representative publicness" coincided directly with the political victory of the bourgeoisie, long before the so-called refeudalization of the public, and should be considered an integral part of the classical bourgeois public sphere. Habermas reacted to this psychological conceptualization of refeudalization in his 1990 introduction to *Strukturwandel der Öffentlichkeit,* arguing that Sennett did not succeed in seeing fundamental differences between representative (feudal and thus exogenous) publicness established before the inauguration of the bourgeois public and the type of endogenous publicness of the bourgeois public sphere that ascended from its early literary forms through the process of gradual politicization (Habermas 1992a, 426–27).

Holistic psychological approaches were definitely marginalized by mainstream empiricist approaches. If "many of the political theorists of the late nineteenth and twentieth centuries were less concerned with measuring public opinion than with studying the conditions under which it was formed" (Berelson, quoted in Janowitz 1950, 1), the empirical tradition that began in the United States in the 1920s led in the opposite direction. Whereas in the earlier period of American pragmatism, public opinion was conceived of as an organic social process, now it was reconceived as "a measurable quantity that could be tapped by survey research" (Peters 1995, 14). The positivist and even empiricist view was characteristically expressed in the classic publication on public relations—Bernays's book *Crystallizing Public Opinion:*

> Public opinion is a term describing ill-defined, mercurial and changeable groups of individual judgments. Public opinion is the aggregate result of individual opinions—now uniform, now conflicting—of the men and women who make up society or any group of society. In order to understand public opinion, one must go back to the individual who makes up the group. (Bernays [1923] 1961, 61)

This (re)orientation of the dominant paradigm was so rapid and so exclusive that Berelson and Janowitz (1950, 1) were compelled to emphatically assert: "Contrary to popular notions and even to the ideas of some practitioners, the study of public opinion did not spring full-panoplied from the brow of George Gallup in the 1930s."[15] Wilson (1962, 86) associates the new behaviorist approach to public opinion with the belief that a new historical situation appeared "in which there are no longer small 'publics,' but rather mass opinion through the process of education and the modern systems of mass communication"— in short, to the idea of mass society. Yet not only the number of publics has decreased but, primarily, the nature of the public/s has fundamentally changed.

During the period from the Enlightenment to the beginning of the twentieth century, theories of public opinion have focused on phenomena that occur in given social places; theories of public opinion that were confronted with the new (electronic) mass media conceptualized public opinion beyond the boundaries of physical settings. Tönnies was among the first who saw the public as a form of imagined intellectual grouping whose members shared similar ideas and opinions without being in a direct interaction. In contrast to Tönnies and earlier normative conceptualizations, the social-psychological tradition rejected collectiveness, rationality, and morality as constitutive attributes of public opinion. It completely abandoned the idea of a specific social group or collectivity in which public opinion is formed and expressed. The rationality of (public) opinion formation was disavowed already by Lippmann. In addition, not only social-psychological approaches but also the post-Tönniesian sociological tradition (including Blumer and Mills) rejected the idea that public opinion implied a moral dimension on which its validity for the collectivity would be based. Instead, the influence of public opinion was considered to be related to psychological mechanisms, as, for example, to the individual's fear of isolation in the Noelle-Neumann spiral of silence.

Berelson and Janowitz's warning indicates that the new social-psychological tradition was strongly affected by the use of new methodological procedures (sampling, scales for the measuring of attitudes) developed in the early twentieth century. Referring to the empirical verifiability and reliability of research, this empiricist current rejected the traditional normative-theoretical conceptualization of public opinion; during the 1930s it achieved the position of the mainstream paradigm. "The advent of so-called 'scientific polls' during the 1930s has gone far toward solving the problem of ascertaining quickly, economically, and accurately the states and trends of public opinion on a large scale" (Childs 1965, 45). New public opinion research was dominated by public opinion polls providing information and predictions about the opinions of citizens and their voting behavior that was of interest to politicians. Polls also gathered information about the purchasing habits of consumers, about the connection between buying decisions and advertisements, that would become a key element in market research. The public as a subject of public opinion, composed of politically reasoning individuals, was replaced in the new understanding of public opinion with a dispersed mass or even any group composed of two or more communicating individuals: "Theoretically, the number of possible publics is the number of groups of two or more individuals that may be selected. The word 'public' and the word 'group' are for all practical purposes interchangeable" (Childs 1965, 13). Public opinion was thus reduced to nothing else than collections of individual opinions. The subject of research was no longer public opinion itself but rather, in keeping with the ascendant social-psychological tradition, above all, *influence* over public opinion.[16] In contrast to older paradigms, the new understanding of public opinion was liberated from any historical determination or assumption; it became

> the label of a social-psychological analysis of group processes, defining its object as follows: Public opinion refers to people's attitudes on an issue when they are members of the same social group. . . . 'Group' abstracts from the multitude of social and historical conditions, as well as from the institutional means, and certainly from the web of social functions that at one time determined the specific joining of ranks on the part of private people to form a critical debating public in the political realm. 'Opinion' itself is conceived no less abstractly. At first it is still identified with 'expression on a controversial topic,' later with 'expression of an attitude,' then with 'attitude' itself. In the end an opinion no longer even needs to be capable of verbalization. (Habermas [1962] 1995, 241)

The social-psychological models of public opinion represented a scientific revolution that was supposed to eliminate fictions and blind alleys from scientific and popular literature on public opinion. In the introductory article of the first issue of *Public Opinion Quarterly* (which would become the most important journal of this emerging research tradition) Floyd Allport enumerated—without well-founded argumentation—eight main confusions/fallacies/fictions of "nonscientific" discussions about public opinion: the personification of public opinion, the personification of the public, the group fallacy of the public, the fallacy of partial inclusion in the use of the term "public," the fiction of an ideational entity, the fiction of the group-product, the "eulogistic theory," and the confusion of public opinion with the public presentation of opinion that he also named, for obvious reasons, "the journalistic fallacy" (Allport 1937). All these ideas, Allport argued, were "unworkable in scientific methodology." Typically, the origin of Allport's critique was the idea that society or the public are only instances of concerted behavior of individuals. Accordingly,

> the phenomena to be studied under the term public opinion are essentially *instances* of behavior . . . of human individuals. . . . The emergent product must be expressed by some *individuals* or we cannot know it at all; and if it is expressed by some individuals, it becomes difficult to show just how much the influence of integrated discussion has helped to form it. . . . So-called 'group thinking' may have taken place in individuals . . . but in the arena of practical affairs it is individuals who do things and not the integrated product of group thought. (Allport 1937, 13)

To avoid a circular definition of the term "public" that he arbitrarily constructed himself in order to criticize "the fallacy of partial inclusion in the use of the term 'public,'"[17] Allport eliminates the public from the definition of public opinion as "superfluous for the purpose of research" (Allport 1937, 9) and reduces public opinion to a multi-individual situation, as earlier suggested by Bernays. Individuals do not produce (public) opinion because opinions are only "reactions of individuals." Thirty years later, Helmut Bauer radicalized this understanding of public opinion: "if the concept of public opinion is meaningful at all," it should be conceived of as "the sum of all relevant individual opinions, as a cut through the peoples' opinions. It is thus nothing but summing of equal or at least similar opinion expressions of citizens inquired by ballot or opinion polls" (H. Bauer 1965, 121).

Reflecting upon this kind of reductionist reasoning, Wilson pointed out that "there is no suggestion of why, functionally speaking, the public has to be mentioned at all . . . if one says the public is just 'any group'" (Wilson 1962, 83). Bernays's, Allport's, H. Bauer's, and similar notions of public opinion as the collection of individual opinions look, at first glance, like a radical expansion of the opinion-making function of society to the total population, and thus they seemingly democratize public opinion; put another way, they pretend to promote the principle of the sovereignty of the entire people and not only of a certain elite part (i.e., the competent public). As Converse emphasized, "From the very beginning in the 1930s, public opinion polling has been closely wedded to the study of popular democratic politics" (Converse 1987, S12). Moreover, public opinion polls were thought to enable "the people" to directly influence the government, unmediated by institutions, regardless of their status and power. Such an understanding of public opinion by empiricists is diametrically opposed to the entire political-philosophical tradition, which has conceived of public opinion as "no mere aggregate of individual opinions, but a genuine social product, a result of communication and reciprocal influence," in the words of Charles H. Cooley (1909, 121), one of the key figures of the Chicago School.

The radical deviation of the mainstream social-psychological tradition from the political-philosophical paradigms of public opinion was most concisely expressed in Allport's thesis that the public is not an explicitly denotable reality but just a metaphor. Yet even as a metaphor, the public as it relates to public opinion remains unspecific: "A number of writers have discussed the difference between a public and a crowd. They seem in general to agree, however, that the phenomena which we call public opinion can occur in either situation" (Allport 1937, 15).[18] A good ten years later, Herbert Blumer (1948) and Lindsay Rogers (1949) "answered" Allport. In his article in *American Sociological Review,* Blumer defined "obvious and commonplace features . . . which the students of current public opinion polling ignore either wittingly or unwittingly in their whole research procedure" (Blumer 1948, 543). In contrast to the individualism of the empirical researchers, Blumer stressed that the formation of public opinion can only occur as a function of a society in operation, largely through the interaction of groups rather than individuals, which implies that the (study of) formation of public opinion must reflect the functional composition and organization of society.

With the reduction of public opinion to individual opinions and its consequent separation from the social context in which individuals interact, whatever difference there was between the public and the mass (or the crowd) lost any meaning. The science of public opinion was interested in the end result (i.e., individual opinions) rather than the actual social processes from which public opinion stems. Scholarly interest in scientific-methodological issues became the priority, and the most important determinant of social research agendas in which "we have tended to overlook that there is a political content in what we call public opinion" (Berelson 1952, 313). In contrast to Berelson, Blumer stressed that this tendency was much more than the result of an unintentional neglect:

> It may be argued that the isolation of a generic object . . . is a goal rather than an initial point of departure—and that consequently the present inability to identify public opinion as a generic object is not damning to current public opinion polling. . . . However, what impresses me is the apparent absence of effort or sincere interest on the part of students of public opinion polling to move in the direction of identifying the object which they are supposedly seeking to study, to record, and to measure. . . . Their work is largely merely making application of their technique. (Blumer 1948, 542)

Blumer argued for a new research direction—symbolic interactionism—which emerged out of the democratic tradition of the Chicago School and American pragmatism, in particular Robert Park and George Herbert Mead, as an opposition to Parson's functionalism and empiricism in social research. For Blumer, equating empirical opinion research (polling) with research of public opinion was a perfect example of the invalid dismissal of the interaction—the direct reciprocally oriented social action—between groups and individuals with varying amounts of influence, who in their interaction create and express public opinion (Blumer 1948, 545). Like Park, Blumer perceived the public to be an essential component of the democratic process and, in keeping with the pragmatist tradition, he considered the empirical research of the nature and development of public opinion to be, for the most part, a method of stimulating interest and expressing opinions.

Four decades later, in the very first sentence of the introduction to the issue of *Public Opinion Quarterly* celebrating its fiftieth anniversary, Eleanor Singer triumphantly announced: "Blumer was wrong! However partial, misleading, or inconclusive the polls may be as indicators of public opinion, they are better than anything else we've got." Converse, also addressing the changing conceptions of public opinion in the political process in the same issue, tried to prove "that Blumer did not entirely understand the scientific tune" (Converse 1987, S15). Nevertheless, his critique of Blumer could only end with the statement that "Blumer's definition of what public opinion is might better have been taken as an agenda for a few decades of research. And indeed, there is almost no wrinkle in the subject matter mentioned by Blumer . . . that has not been a matter of systematic study at one time or another" (Converse 1987, S16). This comment proves the validity rather than the delusion of Blumer's critique.

Nevertheless, methodological developments in the first half of the twentieth century, worshiped by social psychologists, helped to disenchant some normative illusions about public opinion. For example, normative-political theories largely ignored, as did the early social-psychological approaches until the mid-1930s, the difference between issue attitudes and participation attitudes: individual opinions or attitudes were viewed as "more or less *decisive predispositions toward behavior*" (Lemert 1981, 30; emphasis added). Social-psychological research has proved that there is no one-to-one correspondence between attitude and behavior. As Seemann (1993, 14) suggests, perhaps the most promising idea is to understand attitudes as mediators between individuals' social setting and situational circumstances, and the range of potential behaviors. The idea that opinion expression as a form of behavior is also a function of the situation in which it is expressed goes back to the classics of the nineteenth-century normative-political theories, to American pragmatists (notably Cooley and Mead), and to Tönnies. Social psychologists rediscovered it and in the 1960s this idea was promoted particularly by Erving Goffman and Milton Rokeach (Seeman 1993, 6) with the aim of making normative theories empirically testable. However, the recognition of the importance of the situational component in opinion or attitude expression did not lead yet to significant methodological progress, although some interesting approaches were developed. In practice, the focal point of public opinion research in social-psychological tradition became a highly formalized and restricted form of behavior—voting.

POSTMODERN THEORIZATIONS: THE "DISAPPEARANCE" OF PUBLIC OPINION?

The central points in postmodern theorizations or, rather, (implicit) critiques of the public opinion concept are (1) the refusal of the centrality of consensus in social relationships in general and thus in public opinion process (2) due to the growing complexity and diversification of contemporary "network society" that is characterized by transnationalization and globalization of all vital processes. In *La condition postmoderne* (1979), Lyotard argues against Habermas that there are neither universally valid pragmatic rules in language (which would be the necessary condition to reach "consensus" in a rational discourse) nor consensus is the purpose of dialogue (1979, 106).[19]

Changes brought about by the development and massive use of new information and communication technologies in economy, culture, and politics radically transform former conceptions of publicity, public opinion, and the public sphere. Habermas became aware of the fundamental importance of these changes only much after the publication of *The Structural Transformation,* when he added three revisions to the 1962 original version.[20] He justified the revisions of his views as resulting from developmental changes in the self-regulation of society in the period between the early 1960s and late 1980s, which had significantly affected (1) the private sphere and the social foundations of private autonomy; (2) the structure of the public (sphere) and the composition and behavior of the publics, and (3) the legitimization processes of mass democracies.

Habermas revised his earliest theory of the linear development from a reasoning to a consuming public (what he termed "refeudalization") with an idea of the ambivalence of the public, which he first developed in his theory of communicative action as the idea of the ambivalent—authoritarian and emancipatory—potential of communication (Habermas 1981, 574). This shift was believed to be the consequence of objective, empirical social changes that also transformed the nature of the public and public opinion. Although Habermas stressed that this revision did not mean a withdrawal from the original intentions that guided him in the writing of *Structural Transformation,* he did confess that his revised model was now closer to the liberalist concept of public opinion and the tyranny of the majority found in J. S. Mill and Tocqueville than to the classical liberal theories of the rule of public opinion. With the revision, Habermas also created an ambivalent relation to the research tradition shaped by Lazarsfeld. In his early period, Habermas accepted Lazarsfeld's ideas (not that he knew them well, as he would later admit) as a possible path toward the resolution of the contradictions found in normative theories of public opinion. Later, when he became better acquainted with Lazarsfeld's approach, he "denounced" it. In fact, however, Habermas's newest revision can be seen as a correction of his earlier theory using just the results of the empirical sociological studies advanced by Berelson, Lazarsfeld, and McPhee (1954; see Huckfeldt and Sprague 1995). In light of the results of these studies, individual rationality, one of the key assumptions of classical theories of public opinion, takes on a different meaning and in contemporary society becomes nonproblematic. Individuals selectively and rationally pay attention to what political actors in their environment say and how they act, and search relevant political information. The homogenization of their opinions is not seen as a consequence of manipulation; rather, it originates from rational reconsideration of one's own beliefs, when individuals interactively discover they disagree with others.

Habermas's *Structural Transformation* concludes with a (pessimistic) quote from Mills's *The Power Elite* about the decline of the public and the emergence of a "society of the masses." The pessimism clearly implied Habermas's agreement with Mills, who, unlike Lazarsfeld, critically emphasized the importance of the values that shape, or should shape, the selection of (research) problems and policies. Conversely, Habermas's new introduction concludes with some "reasons for a less pessimistic evaluation, and for a less obstinate and declarative view on the public sphere than before." Specifically, it concludes with Joshua Meyrowitz's ideas (1985, 315–317) about a curious similarity between the information society and the pre-class society of hunters and gatherers expressed in (1) the lack of boundaries and no loyal relationship to territory (specific activities are not fixed to specific physical settings) and (2) egalitarian tendencies in terms of the roles of males and females, children and adults, and leaders and followers. However, his revision is lacking in a more explicit and conclusive validation.

Similarly to Habermas, for example, Zolo (1992) argues that the neoclassical doctrine of democracy remains without satisfactory explanatory power, but he calls for an entire reconstruction of democratic theory. Such a theory must take into account the principal aspects of Habermas's second and third point above but in a more critical way. This needs to be done because, first, the asymmetrical, noninteractive nature of mass-political communication is developed to such a degree that the idea of electronic democracy has definitely become a utopia. As Holston and Appadurai (1996, 202) would add, "cybercitizenship" may well draw some citizens into a more tolerant and easily accessible public sphere, but it drives others "into the recesses of the private and the market." Second, by its further dispersion and primarily as a consequence of the "narcotising disfunction" of the mass media, the public sphere transformed itself into "a reflexive area, a timeless meta-dimension in which the 'real' public passively assists, as if in a sort of permanent television broadcast carried out in real time, in the exploits of an 'electronic' public" (Zolo 1992, 166). These two tendencies are taking on worldwide proportions and are bringing about

a second 'structural transformation of the public sphere' even more radical than the one classically analyzed by Jürgen Habermas. . . . The sovereignty of the political consumer—i.e. the autonomy, rationality and moral responsibility of the citizen called upon to pass sovereign judgment on the competition between parties—can now hardly amount to more than empty verbiage in the context of the massive spectacularisation of teledemocracy to which pluralistic competition between the parties . . . is being reduced. (Zolo 1992, 170)

From American pragmatism onward, all theorizations of the public and public opinion underline their transformation under the influence of mass media. Since quite some time ago, the mass media have not been organized in such a way that "virtually as many people express opinions as receive them," which, for C. W. Mills, was the first condition for the public to exist. In total contradiction to classical ideas of democratic pluralism, however, it has also become clear that the persuasive capacity of the media is even greater in the countries of pluralistic democracy than in totalitarian societies. Relatively early on, Lippmann issued the warning: "The creation of consent is not a new art. It is a very old one which was supposed to have died out with the appearance of democracy. But it has not died out. It has, in fact, improved enormously in technic . . . . Persuasion has become a self-conscious art and a regular organ of popular government" (Lippmann [1922] 1960, 248). As a consequence, the autonomy of public opinion and free public access to the means of communication, which were considered of decisive importance by the theorists of democratic public opinion, have become vulnerable and restricted.

This was also reflected in communication research: "although the old model of the media as a 'hypodermic needle' that could inject ideas into the body politic on command has not been revived, mainstream communication research has now developed a healthy respect for what the media, and the politicians who use it, can accomplish" (Zaller 1992, 311). The significance of the dominant media-effects paradigm for public opinion theories emerged from the Lazarsfeld Bureau of Applied Social Research. Yet early mass communication theories have exaggerated the immediate and simultaneous effects of the media on their audiences. Joseph Klapper (1960) was the first to systematically study this phenomenon in *The Effects of Mass Communication*. Klapper analyzed various media effects studies and, as a result, reduced the importance of media effects on individuals relative to interpersonal interaction. Almost at the same time, Philip Converse (1962) suggested new ways of looking at mass society in response to the challenges of the limited effects paradigm. Similarly, Doris Graber argued that "political communication is very much a transactional process. Mass media messages are not imprinted on the minds of media audiences in the precise manner in which they are offered. Rather, audience members condense the offerings in their own ways, select aspects of interest, and integrate them into their own thinking" (Graber 1984, 209). These (re)conceptualizations of mass communication processes led James R. Beniger to conclude that the limited effects findings might be "an artifact of improper measurement, or of measuring the wrong effects. . . . If most citizens are not politically astute and have no specific policy agenda, then surely they might be mobilized, placated, or suppressed via centralized media as in the mass society writings of Lippmann, Lasswell, Mannheim, or the Frankfurt School" (Beniger 1987, S51). In other words, mass media still are, in one way or another, the most important instrument of public opinion formation, expression, and manipulation.

It might be said that Habermas was, in renouncing his earlier theory of the linear development from a reasoning to a consuming public, either too late—only at the end of the 1980s instead of at the time when he actually wrote *The Structural Transformation,* a time characterized by the overestimation of the effects of the mass media—or too early—because his correction was not yet fully substantiated. With the revision, Habermas radically changed his attitude toward the public, particularly toward the importance of the public-power (state) relationship. In this way, he essentially depoliticized the public, thus approaching the views of the American tradition of empirical public opinion research. In his earlier conception of the theory of public opinion, Habermas did not consider (or did not know?) the contributions of the American pragmatists to the debate about the public and public opinion. In *Structural Transformation,* he turns a blind eye to a segment of the older generation of public opinion theorists—Dewey, Lippmann, and Park—and also to the younger scholars—Lasswell, Blumer, and Mills. Nevertheless, Habermas comes out of the same tradition of Anglo-American political philosophy that American pragmatism did before him, although he was not linked to it, but rather critically reconstructed the Anglo-American tradition while bypassing American pragmatism. Essentially, his reconstruction was founded on the same values and understanding of the public and on the criticism of the psychologization or individualization of public opinion that were characteristic of American pragmatism. Habermas's revision, therefore, meant also a shift away from the ideas and values of the American pragmatists. With his *Structural Transformation* Habermas has "returned a gift to Anglo-American thought," as Peters (1993) claimed he did—and as I have shown he did, at least to a degree. However, for his revision of his own theory of the public sphere, it may be said, in analogy with his early interpretation of Lazarsfeld's endeavors to link empirical research with the (critical) theory, that the price for the reduction of idealization or (scientific) utopianism of normative theory of public opinion was too high: it demanded the elimination of essential critical engagement.

Recent theorizations of public/ness and public opinion[21] emphasize the many-sided narrowness of rationalistic conceptions of public opinion. They are blamed for the historically incorrect neglect of the actual exclusion of large social groupings (e.g., women, workers) from the public. In addition, they putatively do not realize that the contemporary developments of communication technologies and publicity changed communication and political processes to such a degree that the general accessibility and active participation of citizens in the formation and expression of public opinion have been invalidated even as normative ideals. Supposedly they have been replaced by the "mediatization of politics" (Thompson 1990) and the "rhetoric of presentation" (Mayhew 1997).

Mayhew (1997, 271) restates Aristotle's typology of arts of persuasion not only as the analytical typology of the social organization of influence, but also— with considerable hesitation, though—as its historical phases: (1) *ethos* or reliance on the character and social status of the speaker may be considered characteristic of traditional societies, (2) *logos* or persuasion by rational argument brought about by the Enlightenment of modernity, and (3) *pathos* or appeal to the emotions of the audience seems to become dominant in the era of the *New Public*. However, Mayhew's restatement of Aristotle's typology omits the *hierarchy* among the constituents of the art of rhetoric in which the primacy was given to persuasion through reason *(logos)* and only a secondary status to *pathos* and *ethos* (Sutton 1993, 80). Mayhew argues that more than a simplistic conception of the dominant mode of persuasion and Aristotle's general categories, new rhetorical modes—rhetoric of *spectacle* and rhetoric of *presentation*—may help understand (the rhetoric of) the New Public. Similarly, as we have seen earlier, Thompson (1990, 1993) argues against Habermas's "refeudalization" theory that new communication technologies, primarily television, increase the visibility of political leaders and limit their control of information flow, which moves the audiences away from the role of passive consumers. We may agree with the critique that Habermas's term "refeudalization" is more a "rhetorical gesture" then a scientific explanation because important differences exist between the staging of political spectacle in a contemporary democratic state and the public representation of the feudal nobility. Yet, what Mayhew says about "prominent postmodern theoreticians"—that they "are prone to exaggerate . . . the novelty of contemporary rhetoric" (p. 280)—may well apply to Thompson and his own negligence to relate "new rhetorics" to Aristotle's differentiation between the essential and inessential rhetoric or political and judicial rhetoric (e.g., reason vs. imagination, literal vs. figurative, public vs. individual).

In spite of the changed circumstances, public opinion still is much more than a "fiction" (Habermas) or a "mystery" (Lippmann). As Peters (1995) argues, public opinion since its eighteenth-century origins always had a significant "symbolically constructed component" and never existed apart from mediated representations in the sense of Benedict Anderson's "imagined community" whose most representative case is "the nation."[22] A typical process in which imagined communities originate is the ceremony of "almost precisely simultaneous consumption ('imagining') of the newspaper-as-fiction," which individuals perform in privacy. But they are aware that the same ceremony is performed simultaneously by thousands of other anonymous, private persons (Anderson [1983] 1991, 35). One could find the roots of Anderson's idea in Tönnies's conception of "the large public" consisting of only "spiritually connected" members, although Tönnies understood the public as an essentially political and moral phenomenon in contrast to postmodern depoliticized conceptualizations. For Peters, public opinion is generated by a sort of "imagined public" formed by symbols. Instead of a direct interaction among individuals, symbolic representations of the social whole are circulated before them, primarily through the media, that may stimulate them to act as a social entity. The formation of a postmodern or—as Mayhew names it—"new" public is much more affected by mass media, television in particular, than by contiguous interactions among members of the public. Yet the "imagined public" is nonetheless as "real" as any other "imagined community" in the sense that "in acting upon symbolic representations of 'the public' the public can come to exist as a real actor. . . . Fictions, if persuasive, become material, political reality. In the region of politics, facts and fictions intermingle, often begetting one another" (Peters 1995, 18–19). The deviation from classical conceptions of public opinion based on the principle of publicity is clearly present in diverse procedures of mediatization and representation, and in their social consequences disclosed in postmodern societies, e.g., by Thompson, Peters, or Mayhew. Yet this turn is so radical that the question is in place as to whether all these procedures still help form and express public opinion. The answer to this question is essentially determined by the definition of public opinion—and clearly negative if public opinion is conceptualized as opinion of the public, which makes political claims that authoritative institutions must take into account (in the chapters to follow I intend to provide evidence that such a conceptualization is certainly not utopian). The core of the problem is in the question of what constitutes the material substance of the postmodern imagined public; paradoxically, it is not the public but in the mass.

CONVERGENCE OF CONFLICTING APPROACHES?

It may be true that theories of public opinion and normative claims for the materialization of the idea of public opinion in democratic society usually were not directly influenced by, nor did they influence, the social environment. Nevertheless, different understandings and theories of the public/ness and public opinion are historically determined and, precisely because of this fact, any generalization becomes problematic. From the very beginning, public/ness and public opinion have been not only politically relevant, because they have always included in a certain way the relationship to power, but also politically problematic, because the relationship has always been determined in a historically biased (ideological) way.

In theory, the public and public opinion are mainly not defined as generic concepts that would allow a historically specific operationalization and empirical identification of these concepts. There is much significant history and theory, for example, in the attempts to restrict the meaning of "the public" to certain groups of individuals able to form and express public opinion and to exclude those who are not sufficiently educated or are politically incompetent, or simply not rational enough. The two concepts often imply the exclusion of a universal claim of all segments of society to participate in the process of communication through the organization and control of media practices. Paradoxically, whereas the theories lack a universal concept of the public and public opinion, empirical public opinion research *seems* to provide one with little difficulty. In empirical research, the public and particularly public opinion are conceived of as universal operational concepts. These concepts, however, do not allow for the identification of the public, or of public opinion, as specific objects (political agents or activities) that are distinct from segments of society or practices that fall outside the two. Rather, public opinion is often simply equated with what opinion polls measure, and the public with the population from which a (representative) sample of respondents is drawn. One may ironically say that such an empiricist understanding is less politically problematic because it evades any systematic bias (in sampling perhaps, but certainly not in the selection of questions!) by excluding any procedure that may cause bias, that is, theory in general.

Throughout the history of public opinion theories, several mutually competing and conflicting streams of thought developed, as we have seen above. From among key dualisms in the twentieth century, two major streams can be discerned that differ primarily in the dominant questions they are endeavoring to answer, in methods (or even methodology) of the research of the communication processes, and in the specific results that are achieved and explained by the researchers and are verified by the users in society. One of the two streams is usually named empirical or administrative; it denotes a research orientation into specific, measurable, short-term, individual, attitudinal, and behavioral characteristics. Lazarsfeld is believed to be (at least in the eyes of the other side) the prototype of the investigators who "see their tasks as technical and themselves as scientific investigators who need not be concerned with the values that generated the problem or with the societal implications of the results, as long as the problem is intellectually exciting" (Coleman 1978, 691), and also of "scientific" survey market investigators.[23]

The second main stream is usually referred to as critical orientation and is linked primarily to the Frankfurt Circle in the period between the two world wars and thus only indirectly to public opinion theories and research in the strict sense. Contrary to the administrative researchers who are concerned neither with the values that generated the research problem nor with the social consequences of their research endeavors, for critical scholars the key question became the values and political positions of the researcher and the research activity itself. The proposition that absence of an explicit attention to values in the selection of "important" or "significant" problems for researching leads implicitly or explicitly to the support of the social status quo could be taken as a common denominator of the critical orientation.

The reduction of all dualisms to one single dichotomy is a grave simplification and, even more, an attempt to find the lowest common denominator—usually in the use versus rejection of quantitative research and data analysis methods. The orientation of Lazarsfeld's circle to research directly or indirectly measurable characteristics and effects of communication (especially by content analysis and attitude measurement) into the application of quantitative research methods at first glance seems an inseparable constituent part of the administrative research, and perhaps even its essential characteristic. It is not only a logical error that is at stake in such a conclusion but also a misunderstanding of the relations between the qualitative and the quantitative research methods, which in fact are complementary rather than exclusive. As Siegfried Kracauer pointed out, notions of qualitative analysis and quantitative analysis do not refer to radically different approaches:

> Quantitative analysis includes qualitative aspects, for it both originates and culminates in qualitative considerations. On the other hand, qualitative analysis proper often requires quantification in the interest of exhaustive treatment. Far from being strict alternatives the two approaches actually overlap, and have in fact complemented and interpenetrated each other in several investigations. (Kracauer 1952, 637)

A similar request for a simultaneous application of both qualitative and quantitative methods in empirical sociology was earlier expressed by Ferdinand Tönnies in his *Introduction to Sociology* (1931), in which he referred to Laplace, who pleaded for the use of both observation and measurement in the political and moral sciences. The radicalism of the critical paradigm, which often intermingled empirical research with empiricism, does not surpass Adorno's idea of "mediation between the administrative and the critical research" but turns it upside down. It is true that empirical social science can succumb to manipulating goals; however, the authentic sense of empirical research methods is their critical impulse against ideologized abstract social science (Adorno and Horkheimer [1956] 1980, 119–21). My objections against the exclusivism of some new representatives of the critical paradigm by no means deny particularistic consciousness and partialities of administrative research. They were thoroughly analyzed by numerous scholars from Adorno on, including partly even Lazarsfeld himself. But if these critical analyses of administrative research were to contribute to a more fruitful assertion and development of the critical research (they cannot assure it, as its realization depends considerably also on the social position of the critical science), then the discussions on dominant paradigms should (again) clarify the relation between theory and empirical research, and particularly the meaning of different research methods.

The relation between critical theory and empirical (but not empiricist!) research could hypothetically be of three kinds. First, all methods of empirical research developed so far are antagonistic (even hostile) toward theoretical concepts of the Critical School and as such are completely inappropriate for studying the fundamental issues as they are defined within critical theory. Second, critical theory does not consider at all whether the assumptions and the logic of concrete quantitative methods are compatible with or correspond to the given theoretical framework, simply because they are outside its reflexive range. Third, empirical research and critical theory do not exclude each other, but—under certain preconditions—complement and interpenetrate each other. As I argued elsewhere (Splichal 1987), there is no justification to reject the second and third hypotheses, although a number of authors argue that either empiricists do not accept theoretical critique (Wilson 1962) or theoreticians are not likely to consider seriously empirical critiques and challenges (Katz 1987). On the one hand, empiricism by the very definition implies an aversion to *any* theory. On the other hand, for two key reasons, some critical scholars are not likely to accept the idea of a potential merger between positive (empirical) and critical research: (1) a misapprehension of the true relationship between qualitative and quantitative methods, and the logic and assumptions of the statistical analysis of data (few, if any, among the critical prophets who disprove empirical research are sufficiently acquainted with the methodology of empirical research) and (2) the intermingling of administrative research with the development and use of quantitative research methods. As a result, invalidation of empirical research is ideologically grounded, rather than on a critique of the administrative ideology that is displayed in particularistic research aims and (e.g., political, commercial) interests of researchers.

Yet the main critiques of polling, which begun with William Albig (1939), Herbert Blumer (1948), and Lindsay Rogers (1949), were not ideological by their very nature but questioned the validity of polling. Nevertheless, these critiques were not accepted as justified and well-intentioned among pollsters and empirical scholars. Particularly Blumer's radical critique of empiricist public opinion research—"a most celebrated attack on the young industry of public opinion polling," according to Converse (1987, S13)—and "some feeling of disappointment" expressed by Julian Woodward and Theodore M. Newcomb in their response to Blumer in the same issue of *American Sociological Review* of 1948 indicated that there was not much hope of combining or reconciling the two paradigms. Only a decade later Lazarsfeld, in his much-quoted article "Public Opinion and the Classical Tradition," searched for a solution that would link the theoretical and empirical procedures in the debate about public opinion rather than further divide them:

> Modern research techniques can confirm and develop notions advanced by classical writers, while authors such as Dicey and Bryce can help direct present-day researchers to significant problems and suggest new ways of analysing empirical data. Merging of the two approaches will hasten the development of a more adequate theory of public opinion. . . . The essence of progress . . . consists in leaving the ashes and taking the flames from the altars of one's forebears. (Lazarsfeld 1957, 39, 53)

Habermas in his *Structural Transformation* excessively characterized Lazarsfeld's efforts in the sense that he "has pointedly insisted that the price to be paid for the social-psychological concept of public opinion is too high if it is held at the expense of eliminating all essential sociological and politological elements" (Habermas [1962] 1995, 242). Lazarsfeld, in principle, did not oppose Blumer and Roger's criticism of public opinion polling that "when the pollsters use the term public opinion, they do not know and cannot say what they mean." Yet he did object to the critiques because they were themselves unable to propose their own definition. Even more generally, according to Lazarsfeld, "earlier writers overflow with comments about the mysterious and intangible character of public opinion" (Lazarsfeld 1957, 41). Habermas later corrected his unfounded "commitment" to Lazarsfeld's research tradition and accepted the interpretation that Lazarsfeld was unable to forge his critical research perspective into a major theoretical statement (Habermas 1992a, 439). According to Zolo (1992,

155), "Lazarsfeld applied to media research the most rigid criteria of neo-positivist sociology, while Berelson exalted the American democratic system for its (alleged) ability to function democratically without the need for the presence of the 'democratic citizen.'" In any case, Lazarsfeld was anything but favorably disposed toward the tradition that he called (in contrast to science) "social analysis," the most prominent representative of which was, in Lazarsfeld's opinion, C. Wright Mills.

This criticism may be well founded, as may be the placement of Lazarsfeld among those who see their tasks as technical. Nevertheless it cannot be overlooked that, in the development of empirical research, Lazarsfeld has been among the rare advocates for transcending the paradigmatic separation of critical theory and empirical, mainly quantitative research—which has, in fact, contrary to Lazarsfeld expectations, grown even more radical (Splichal 1987). As Katz wrote, Lazarsfeld in his Bureau of Applied Social Research "kept trying to explain to others how work in public opinion and mass communication can contribute directly, or through interaction, to disciplines such as history, journalism, political science, and, of course, critical theory" (Katz 1987, S30n). Lazarsfeld clearly took seriously criticism of empirical research such as Blumer's and attempted to advance the validity of empirical research. "His answer to the type of objection Blumer raised was contextual analysis, design of observation which . . . proposes to characterize the individuals sampled in surveys, not only by personal variables such as age or number of years of formal education, but by variables characterizing their social context as well, for example, the proportion of churchgoers or the median income in the neighborhood, state, or country where they live" (Boudon 1993, 24). Lazarsfeld, in his landmark study of voting behavior in Erie County, Ohio, constructed the index of political predisposition (IPP), in which he combined three variables, social-economic status of the respondent, residential environment (rural-urban) and dominant religion (Protestant-Catholic), "that rank the people according to how strongly their demographic location predisposes them to receive social influences or otherwise be inclined to vote for one or the other of the major parties" (Berelson, Lazarsfeld, and McPhee 1954, 126). Lazarsfeld with Berelson and McPhee for the first time faced the problem of social determinism, or the influence of the social and political environment on opinion formation. Although the authors of this work did not explicitly treat the problem as the problem of multilevel observation and analysis, and the research was still reduced to survey response data gathering, they attributed a great explanatory power to the difference between an individual and the social aggregate as the individual's context. V. O. Key (1949) was the first to discuss interdependence between individuals and their social context, the idea being to explain the individual's political behavior via the structural characteristics of the individual's context. In *Southern Politics,* for example, he demonstrated that the intensity of racial intolerance of whites appeared to be dependent upon the concentration of the black population. Lazarsfeld and his team from the bureau, using individual data, drew conclusions about the social process and, on this basis, about the interdependence between the individual and a specific aggregate environment with which the individual constantly interacts. Decades later, these two approaches, at first completely marginalized by public opinion polling, reemerged in coorientation research, which represents perhaps the most important departure from reductionist social-psychological conceptualization of public opinion processes and reveals the possibility of reconciling the theoretical and empirical conceptions of public opinion.

The realization of Lazarsfeld's (1957, 52) modest yet "somewhat utopian" expectations, as he himself characterized them, about the "convergence of two trends, i.e. a careful analysis in the classical tradition supported by modern empirical data," might have been deferred to a distant future when, only five years after the jubilee issue of *Public Opinion Quarterly* (1957) devoted to twenty years of public opinion research, two fundamental theoretical works were published: Habermas's *Structural Transformation* and Wilson's *Theory of Public Opinion* (1962). Before that, "at the level of fundamental theory nothing has been added. The basic concepts of the 'public' and 'opinion' were as adequate in the leading scholarly writings of the nineteenth century as they have been in the twentieth" (Lasswell 1957, 34–35). After Lazarsfeld and Lasswell, many authors emphasized the expedience of the synthesis of the classical (liberal) normative concepts of the public and public opinion, and the social-psychological definitions of public opinion—though with little success. Because the synthesis was anticipated during the period of supremacy of empirical opinion research, it should have meant above all a politically enlightened concept of public opinion, a return to a wider political meaning or, put another way, a renewed (and transformed) thematization of the relationship between public opinion and the institutions of (political) power. In the judgment of Ulla Otto, these efforts were not fruitful, responsibility for the failure falling on the side of (critical) theory: "If they did not become the victims of their own, totally unreal, democratic idealization of the rational 'homo politicus'—as Hennis, Lippmann and Wilson did—they were finally lost, despite adequate set-ins, in the network of excessively differentiated social-political aspirations for power, as for example Habermas and Lenz" (Otto 1966, 112).

What about the empirical social-psychological tradition? In the early 1950s, Berelson tried to link "democratic theory and public opinion," recognizing that significant contributions to the development of public opinion research have been made not only by psychologists, sociologists, market researchers, and statisticians but also by political scientists who developed "a helpful framework for the organization and conduct of opinion studies." Berelson's concept of a synthesis was that the tools that were developed by survey researchers should be used to operationalize and measure "the extent to which the practice of politics by the citizens of a democratic state conforms to the requirements and assumptions of the theory of democratic politics" (Berelson 1952, 313). These would include, for example, the suitability of personality structure, interest, and participation in public affairs, the possession of information and knowledge and stable moral standards, accurate observation of political realities, communication and discussion, rationality of political decisions, regard for community interest. Empirical research should be used, on the one hand, to improve the picture about the actual process of democratic decision making; in other words, to document and validate theory, and to stimulate its development and explanatory reach. On the other hand, it "can help a democracy not only to know itself in a topical and immediate way but also to evaluate its achievement and its progress in more general terms. In this framework, the study of public opinion can make a telling contribution in the basic, continuous struggle to bring democratic practice more and more into harmony with the requirements and the assumptions—that is, with the ideals—of democratic theory" (Berelson 1952, 330).

Perhaps Berelson's expectations can—at least in principle—be seen as the same as Habermas's later demands, which he articulated in the discussion of the cleavage between the "legal-state-fiction" of public opinion and the "social-psychological analysis" of the meaning of public opinion: "The *criteria by which opinions may be empirically gauged* as to their degree of publicness are therefore to be developed in reference to this dimension of the evolution of state and society; indeed, such an empirical specification of public opinion in a comparative sense is today the most reliable means for attaining valid and comparable statements about the extent of democratic integration characterizing a specific constitutional reality" (Habermas [1962] 1995, 244–45; emphasis added). Yet the essential difference between Berelson's and Habermas's demands was that Habermas saw the possibility for the realization of his demand only in the sociological theoretical explanation of the structural transformation of the public sphere, whereas Berelson's problem was easier to resolve—on the basis of the operationalization of key social-psychological concepts, which could be deduced from the normative theory of public opinion. Peters is convinced that with Berelson's article in the 1987 celebratory issue of *Public Opinion Quarterly* "the *resistance* of public opinion research to the classic philosophical ideas of democracy reached an apex" (Peters 1995, 21). This judgment seems too harsh, since Berelson, in terms of the relationship between theory and empirical research, not only concluded that a large part of the requirements of democratic theory were not met in practice (and thus not identified in the world of empirical observations) but also defined the basic functions of empirical research in relation to theory (1) to document theoretical assumptions with facts about the actual behavior of citizens, (2) to clarify theoretical concepts of democratic theory (primarily by "insisting upon researchable formulations"), and (3) to differentiate and reformulate general theoretical propositions "in more exact terms" (Berelson 1957, 330). Clearly, Berelson's functions of empirical research typically reflected positivist thinking, which saw the key problems and deficiencies only in theory whereas empirical research, as largely unproblematic, was given a too large and significant role in the understanding and explanation of processes of public opinion formation. Nevertheless, the starting point for a (empirical) validation of theoretical assumptions was grounded precisely in the classic philosophical ideas of democracy.

The authors of empirical solutions, Berelson among others, did not become, to use Otto's words, "the victims of their own unreal, democratic idealization." They did "not lose themselves in the network of excessively differentiated social-political aspirations for power," but they did lose themselves in the complexity of the problem. Although the modern public sphere expanded—with contradictory consequences—into all spheres of society, the social-psychological meaning of public opinion as operationalized in empirical research remained restricted to the "multi-individual situation" (Allport 1937, 23) and even to individual private opinions. Decades ago, Wilson had argued that "indications of a reconciliation" certainly existed between what he called the "classical and speculative mode of study" and the "statistical and survey techniques." However, these indications did not mean that it would be possible to achieve a perfect reconciliation between the two streams of thought. "The unfortunate aspect of the situation is that the speculative and philosophical mind can accept the use of empirical techniques more easily than the empirical technician can accept the idea of the legitimacy of philosophical inquiry" (Wilson 1962, 16–17).

Despite the numerous controversies between the normative-critical and the empirical-psychological understanding of public opinion, it is nevertheless possible to see their convergence in at least one dimension, namely, in the belief that "public opinion creates an obligation for public servants to follow" (Wilson 1962, 34). This belief is based on different principles, interests, and methods of government adapting to public opinion—so that either public opinion actually supervises government and its policies or government supervises public opinion and monitors whether it enjoys the trust of the citizens. But in either case, government must take into consideration public opinion. It is also possible to agree with Katz's conclusion that the narrowing of the gap between the critical paradigm and the dominant empirical school (the limited effects model) is "attributable in some measure to the fact that critical theorists are now conducting empirical research." Yet in contrast to Wilson, Katz was convinced that "not everybody is pleased when gaps are narrowed, least of all critical theorists."

Can we conclude, then, that the hope of a convergence between the dominant traditions of studying public opinion in the twentieth century is by the end of the century less utopian than it was fifty years ago? This question remains to be answered in the next century.

3

+

Public Opinion as a Form of Social Will: Tönnies's *Critique of Public Opinion*

Opinion of the public is clearly a modern phenomenon: its origin and development are connected with the spirit of the Enlightenment, which, in a reciprocal influence with the development of natural sciences but also historical political thought in parallel with the present state and civil society on which it is founded in a permanent struggle with once ruling but now weaker and weaker religious-theological mental world, up till now has never been fully materialized and, under the influence of deeply moving events, experiences ever new blows that hamper and sometimes destructively influence public opinion formation.

—Ferdinand Tönnies,
"Die öffentliche Meinung in unserer Klassik"

One of the most significant classical social-theoretical contributions to the field represents Ferdinand Tönnies's critical theory of public opinion, in which he gave preference to the complex processes in culture and society over their institutionalized forms in politics and the state. Unfortunately, theories originating at the beginning of the twentieth century seem to be much less influential at present than more practical-minded and empirical approaches that developed after the 1930s; some have even been completely forgotten. This chapter strives for the rehabilitation of Tönnies's largely forgotten theory, which represents the most comprehensive effort to conceptualize public opinion as a form of social will that has normative validity as moral judgment; it is not enforced by physical force or external means (e.g., money) but through ideas and thoughts that lead to enlightenment. In his dynamic conceptualization of the opinion of the public as a form of social will, which represents his most important idea, Tönnies recognized the mutual influence of public opinion and other forms of social will. Opinion of the public, with "the public" as its subject, differs from other forms of social will in that the unanimous will is a result of knowledge and is formed by a rational judgment; it competes in *Gesellschaft* with two other forms of the complex social will—convention and legislation. In his comprehensive book *Critique of Public Opinion,* Tönnies pursues a theoretical and historical analysis of differences between published opinion, public opinion, and opinion of the public, theorizes the relationship between religion and public opinion, analyzes three "aggregate states" of the opinion of the public (gaseous, fluid, and solid), and conceptualizes the role of the press as a means of expression of public opinion. The press and parliament may be considered the most important "organs of opinion of the public," but even they, as Tönnies critically observed, are more often instruments of influencing public opinion than expressing it.

Unlike earlier theorists who focused on phenomena that occur in given social places, Tönnies conceptualized public opinion beyond the boundaries of physical settings: he saw the public as a form of imagined intellectual grouping whose members shared similar ideas and opinions without being in a direct interaction. On the one hand, his theory is an attempt to integrate the ideas of rationality, interactivity, and morality of public opinion postulated by normative-philosophical and early psychological approaches to public opinion; on the other hand, it is a sharp contrast to the social-psychological tradition that developed in the 1930s and completely abandoned the idea of a specific group or collectivity in (by) which public opinion is formed and expressed. The rationality of (public) opinion formation was disavowed already by Tönnies's contemporary Lippmann. In addition, both social-psychological approaches and the post-Tönniesian sociological tradition rejected the idea that public opinion made up a moral dimension on which its validity for the collectivity would be based; instead, the influence of public opinion was considered to be related to primary psychological mechanisms, for example, the individual's fear of social isolation, or to the numerical majority, as in the conceptualizations of public opinion as the statistical aggregation of individual opinions.

Although Tönnies acknowledged the importance of conformity pressure in public opinion process, which makes public opinion similar to religion, he vigorously defended the importance of citizens' independent reasoning as the basis of the opinion of the public. Tönnies understood opinion of the public as a "common way of thought, the corporate spirit of any group or association, in so far as its opinion formation is built upon reasoning and knowledge, rather than on unproved impressions, beliefs, or authority" (1922, 78). In this sense, opinion of the public may be considered a rationalized form of religion, as reflexive will in general is a rationalized form of organic will. However, his holistic theory also emphasized the unity of will and emotions that are expressed in reason, and the foundation of reason in human life processes: the rationality of opinion always implies the volitional and affective dimensions of opinion formation.

The dominant social-theoretical approaches of the twentieth century, and particularly empirical research, are generally indifferent to earlier normative-theoretical conceptualizations of the public and public opinion, or they even explicitly renounce them. The most significant departures from this mainstream are represented by American pragmatism and, most notably, Ferdinand Tönnies (1855–1936), the German sociologist whose theory of public opinion has been unjustly ignored by twentieth-century discussions of public opinion.[1] Tönnies embarks on investigating public opinion in his first major and best-known work, *Gemeinschaft und Gesellschaft* ([1887] 1991, 202–4, 214) and proceeded to develop his findings into a coherent theory in an extensive treatise, *Kritik der öffentlichen Meinung*. It was published in 1922 and remains one of the most coherent analyses of public opinion; yet, it is practically absent from any academic or nonacademic discourse on public opinion.[2]

There are several reasons why Tönnies's epochal work has been so totally forgotten, in contrast to his American contemporaries Dewey and Lippmann and even his German "rival," Wilhelm Bauer. With the rise of Nazism, the human sciences in Germany faced the hardship of other enemies of the Reich. Paradoxically, although Tönnies was a straightforward critic of Nazism and German *Zeitungswissenschaft* (science of the press), which at that time was very submissive, his idea of *Volksgemeinschaft* was considered at least compatible with the national-socialist ideology. During the 1920s, the affirmation of empirical research in the United States brought about a radical turn in the humanities. Until that time European empirical sociology and the humanities, in general, understood empirical research most of all as historical facts, whereas American empiricism introduced an empirical world that became above all the world of observation and data collection. Thus, for political and intellectual reasons, German academic journalistic research faded away and surrendered its investigative leadership to academic institutions in the United States, the home of many exiled European scientists, and Tönnies unduly shared the fate of a blind spot. Communication and public opinion research advanced most rapidly during and after World War II in the United States when this research had nearly vanished from Europe. It was only during the postwar era that continental social studies began to advance again, but now distinctly under the influence of U.S. developments.

Tönnies's theory of public opinion is significantly different from any American mainstream approach at that time; it is typically German, according to Wilson, because it primarily addresses the traditional religious and cultural circumstances under which public opinion is formed, rather than the ways and the means with which public opinion effectively influences representative government. The latter is characteristic of an Anglo-Saxon tradition, one that Wilson also adopted (1962, 111). In this sense, Tönnies represents a continuation of a tradition that was not only endorsed in Germany. Prior to sociologizing public opinion research in the twentieth century, most analysts regarded public opinion in relation to religion, middle-class or bourgeois existence, and considered the public in the sense of a social category that generates public opinion. The exception was the United States rather than an Anglo-Saxon tradition. For instance, William MacKinnon's book on public opinion, published in 1828 in London, actually laid the foundation for a European tradition that, without doubt, gives preference to culture over politics, and society over the state. Unlike earlier theories that have focused on phenomena that occur in given social places, Tönnies conceptualized public opinion beyond the boundaries of physical settings: he saw the public as a form of imagined intellectual grouping whose members shared similar ideas and opinions without being in a direct interaction. Tönnies's theory is an attempt to integrate the ideas of rationality, interactivity (and coorientation) and morality of public opinion postulated by normative-philosophical and early social-psychological approaches to public opinion. His theory offers grounds for critique of institutional arrangements (which dominated at that time but still exist) and for emancipatory actions, particularly in the sphere of the press. Thus it is in sharp contrast to the post-Tönniesian behavioral tradition—which completely abandoned the idea that public opinion would be formed and expressed by a specific reference group or collectivity and that it would be rational and moral by its very nature—as well as to the dominant streams of political and sociological thinking of his own time in Europe and, particularly, in the United States. Because of his radical departure from the dominant paradigms and his empirical interest in the past rather than in the present (or future) time, he looked backward; his long-winded style further strengthened such an impression.

However, an unfair disregard of Tönnies's theory of public opinion is not the only or even the main reason for advocating a more thorough analysis of his work. It is no exaggeration to state that Tönnies has created the most complex theory of public opinion since MacKinnon, whose 1828 book was the first study entirely focused on public opinion. Compared to any of the earlier and subsequent theories of public opinion, Tönnies's inquiry into public opinion remains among the most comprehensive and thorough ones, in spite of his occasionally unclear systematic; by extensively introducing ideas of his predecessors, Tönnies gives his *Critique* a nearly encyclopedic quality. The entire first part of the book is assigned to an etymology and genealogy of public opinion and related concepts, whereas the second part contains observations and applications, that is, a historical documentation that in its framework resembles MacKinnon's interest in public opinion in other parts of the world. Tönnies does not succeed in setting up indicators for an empirical analysis of public opinion. Nevertheless, his discussion of public opinion is also important from the perspective of an interconnectedness between theory—for Tönnies, pure and applied sociology—and empirical sociology, although his discussion of public opinion most of all indicates how pure theoretical concepts can be applied to historical examples. Tönnies was the first scholar to outline the central position of public opinion within empirical sociology; particularly problems of empirical analysis remained central to public opinion research and have persisted as the main reasons for disputes to this day. On the other hand, methodological distinctions of his sociology, advanced by his theory of public opinion, constitute another reason for the neglect of his theory during a time in which logical, or methodological, positivism dominated. Thus it is paradoxical that even critics of a positivistic understanding of public opinion did not seek an alliance with Tönnies. In spite of the aforementioned circumstances it is altogether difficult to clarify why his theory of public opinion, contrary to his social theory, remains practically anonymous, especially since public opinion research and public opinion polling advanced faster than any other field of social science research since the 1920s and became dominant also in (empirical) sociology.

CRITIQUE OF PUBLIC OPINION
IN THE *GEMEINSCHAFT-GESELLSCHAFT* MODEL

Tönnies first established a sociological understanding of public opinion as a form of a social will in his celebrated book *Gemeinschaft und Gesellschaft* (1887) and presented it in a fully developed form only thirty-five years later in *Critique of Public Opinion*.[3] He treats the opinion of the public as one of the basic forms of the complex social will that establishes itself in society *(Gesellschaft)* and per-forms the role religion does in traditional community *(Gemeinschaft)*. His the-ory of public opinion represents a basis of his rational critique of religion and, inversely, the relationship between religion and public opinion is also the foun-dation of his theory of public opinion (Tönnies 1922, VII).[4]

The significance of Tönnies's social theory and his theory of public opinion arises from his attempts to interrelate empirical and rationalistic procedures in the development of scientific knowledge, as well as to restore the unity of hu-man being and nature. The unity is reflected in his fundamental assumption that human thought arises from a natural matrix and can never be separated from it, whereas, on the other hand, all social phenomena are construed by hu-man thought and will. Sociality stems from human willing: the will is the spirit *(Geist)* in which individual wanting *(Wollen)* has its roots, and wanting stands for the all readiness to act (1922, 17). As Park argued earlier, "Since the general will exists as a historic structure in society, it would have to be viewed as a prod-uct and *formative element in the empirical process of society*" (Park [1904] 1972, 74; emphasis added). Tönnies's understanding of the concept of will is based on the psychological conceptualizations of his time, but it can also be related to earlier philosophical conceptualizations of will by Rousseau and Hegel. Like Rousseau's "general will" or Hegel's "substantial will," Tönnies's forms of social will are normative constructs that cannot be equated with any of their empiri-cal manifestations.

Central to Tönnies's social theory is an opposition between two types of will—organic will *(Wesenwille)* and reflexive will *(Kürwille)*, which condition the two ways in which men form social groups—community *(Gemeinschaft)* or society *(Gesellschaft)*. The two types of will and the two forms of social groups represent the fundamental ideas of normal concepts *(Normalbegriffe)*, which are "things of thought," according to Tönnies, or pure abstractions existing only in "pure sociology" and, by definition, cannot be verified. Pure sociology is con-structive—it does not describe positive and variable social reality; it is static and universal and, therefore, always represents the point of departure that enables historical application or deduction (applied sociology) and inductive empirical research (empirical sociology). Normal concepts are created as tools to illumi-nate reality and to conceptualize it (Tönnies 1922, 18). The centrality of nor-mal concepts and ideal types as their objects makes Tönnies's theory entirely compatible with normative theories of public opinion. Indeed, Tönnies's soci-ological approach to public opinion is unique in that it bridges differences be-tween two distinct paradigms commonly believed to be incompatible. His the-ory is based on the opinion of the public *(die öffentliche Meinung)* that has a counterfactual normative character; it is a concept that is a "pure" abstraction and used by Tönnies as an intellectual "tool" to inquire into specific historical manifestations of public opinion but cannot itself be realized in practice. It is equally important for his theory—and specifically for its compatibility with normative political theories—that opinion of the public also denotes the moral behavior of the public in which relations in society are grounded.

Idiosyncratic methods of inquiry and interpretation are characteristics of Tönnies's *Critique of Public Opinion,* which summarizes not only the basic features of his social theory from already published works but also extensively introduces the ideas of other authors (including Wilhelm Bauer, another important contemporary German theoretician of public opinion). He never directly accepts or rejects their theses and presents his own ideas as complementary rather than alternative. Contrary to the methodology of logical positivism, it is pointless and by definition even impossible to verify his basic concepts and their abstract objects (the "ideal types") because they are only reflected "objects." For Tönnies, ideas approximate reality; they are tools the researcher produces and uses to recognize reality and investigate the experiential world. Since the starting point is always a general thesis with which to reach specific findings, the beginning rests in pure sociology and is followed by applied sociology (in which "firm," static ideas are applied to dynamic historical developments) and by the empirical (such as his sociographic analysis of suicides, crimes, elections, and strikes). Individual, concrete facts are a goal of inquiry by themselves, and not, as their status within logical positivism suggests, a means to discover more general principles. Empirical research is inductive; it is not intended to test hypotheses but rather to elucidate and explain general ideas by specific examples (Cahnman 1973, 8, 15). Nevertheless, compared to other areas of his sociological research, Tönnies distinctly neglects precisely the empirical level of public opinion inquiry. Consequently, the connection between pure theoretical ideas and their application to concrete historical cases is not always clear—as the example of relations between the opinion of the public and public opinion will demonstrate. This relation becomes specifically obscured in the case of his large historical exegesis.

Fundamental for Tönnies's understanding of public opinion is the distinction between community and society. Community is a traditional and inarticulate form of social organization based on personal relationships, customs, and faith. The concept of society[5] signifies an urban and industrial, that is, a rational social organization (in large cities and states), based on nonpersonal relations, special interests, conventions, law, and public opinion, respectively. In many ways this understanding is a reminder of the concept of civil society: unlike community, which is based on similarities among groups and individuals in terms of beliefs and actions, society is concerned with economic

("convention"), political ("legislation"), and moral ("public opinion") relationships among diverse groups. Society is also characterized by the central position
of the middle class. For Tönnies, community and society are ideal types that
never exist in their pure form; rather, various forms of communal and societal
organizations may appear, in different degrees, simultaneously within the same
social structure. Tönnies stresses the universal and purely theoretical character
of community and society beyond the historical; at the same time, however,
they may be applied to any concrete and historically determined form of life.
Also, one should not overlook—as several Tönnies interpreters have done—
that Gesellschaft does not represent the last stage of development, neither in its
purely theoretical nor in its historical-practical sense. The fact that the features
of community are slowly disappearing while the attributes of society are
prevailing does not mean that historical development is inclined toward
Gesellschaft; both of them are only ideal types that do not exist in pure forms.
Instead, Tönnies sees the next stage of development in a "people's" or "new"
community, which he calls *Volksgemeinschaft* or *neue Gemeinschaft* as a synthe-
sizing third stage of historical development; he has never discussed it as thoroughly as the first two categories precisely because it does not represent an ideal
type or, rather, it does not have a normative meaning. Gemeinschaft is for Tönnies not just a specific historical structure from which Gesellschaft develops but
also a model of the future transformation of the latter. In fact, people's community is a synonym for socialism. Constituted as reality and moral necessity,
or as a matter of consciousness, for the first time during World War I, its nu-
cleus is in a "healthy family life, the hearth of real morality that even the best
of public education can only complete and refine, but it cannot replace it"
(Tönnies 1922, 573). The opinion of the public can greatly contribute to the
rise of a people's community as long as it emanates from this core and is em-
powered to link various worldviews and different parties and direct them toward mass social reforms. Thus the opinion of the public could become a social conscience *(soziales Gewissen)* in the future as religion had been in the past[6];
according to Tönnies, its likelihood depends primarily on the development of
science—an idea we may also find in Dewey's work on the public.

Tönnies's theory posits two basic kinds of human relations that are subjectively grounded and, being a product of human nature, expressed in diverse
forms of social structure (see table 3.1). Differences between Gemeinschaft and
Gesellschaft correspond to differences between organic and reflexive wills: people create either community grounded in organic will or society founded in reflexive will. Both, the essential or organic will *(Wesenwille)* and the arbitrary or
reflexive will *(Kürwille)*, represent the two faces of the totality of human nature
that is expressed in social relations; their relationship is the same as the rela-

Table 3.1: Tönnies's Forms of Social Will

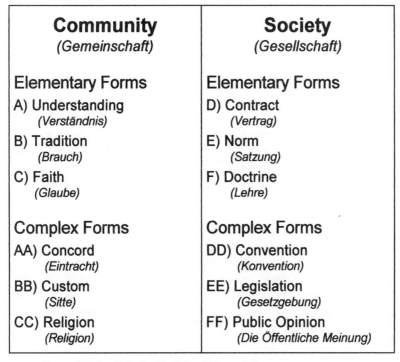

Community *(Gemeinschaft)*	Society *(Gesellschaft)*
Elementary Forms A) Understanding *(Verständnis)* B) Tradition *(Brauch)* C) Faith *(Glaube)*	**Elementary Forms** D) Contract *(Vertrag)* E) Norm *(Satzung)* F) Doctrine *(Lehre)*
Complex Forms AA) Concord *(Eintracht)* BB) Custom *(Sitte)* CC) Religion *(Religion)*	**Complex Forms** DD) Convention *(Konvention)* EE) Legislation *(Gesetzgebung)* FF) Public Opinion *(Die Öffentliche Meinung)*

Source: Tönnies, *Kritik der öffentlichen Meinung*, 219.

tionship between believing and opining. "Just as there is no water that is hydrogen, and another that is oxygen, there is no one will that is organic will, and another that is reflexive; rather, all the wills consist of, and are linked by the organic and reflexive will" (Tönnies 1922, 18). Since neither exists in pure form in the experiential world, any differentiation between two ideal types is possible exclusively in abstraction or on the level of pure ideas. The prevailing form of will determines the pattern of human relations.

Will is closely connected to reflection. Although the will is metaphysically understood as the form in which sentiments and mental moods are manifested, reflection exhibits the rationalistic capability of the intellect. The organic will determines reflection (i.e., the will includes reflection), whereas the opposite is true for the reflexive will: consciousness is liberated so that it is reflection that determines the will (i.e., reflection includes the will). Organic will is characterized by the transrational elements in human nature and the reflexive will by the priority of reason. In organic will the stress is on the traditional, the emotional, and the absolute. Its opposite, the reflexive will, emphasizes instrumentalism and distinctions between goal and means. Since the forms of reflexive will are nothing but rationalized or reflected forms of organic will, the former always somehow depend on the latter. In community, forms of common will spring mainly from common emotions, whereas in society they derive from common thoughts. Moving from organic to reflexive forms of will represents a process of fortifying and formalizing that becomes prominent, at least in simple forms of social will, with the development of writing (Tönnies 1922, 220).[7]

Tönnies's theory represents a realization that the unity of will and emotions is expressed in reason and that reason is grounded in human life processes; therefore, physical and cultural domains cannot be separated. Like American pragmatists, particularly Dewey, Tönnies strives for an integral approach of academic inquiry into human beings and nature, separated by increasingly scientistic specialization and fragmentation. On the macrosociological level, Tönnies advocates evolution and materialist, or realist, interpretations of history: reason, reflection, and institutions are products of material, historical processes and interests, but these processes and interests in return (dialectically) also influence the former (Cahnman 1973, 7). His holistic and humanist views about human beings and society are present also in his efforts to link rationalism and empiricism, two traditions that had been considered mutually exclusive.

OPINION OF THE PUBLIC AS A FORM OF SOCIAL WILL

Tönnies devotes half of the first book of *Critique* to a systematic, comparative, etymological analysis of terms like opinion, reflection, determination, will, or faith. He provides proof for an interconnectedness between ideas, thoughts, convictions, opinions, beliefs, and will. Basically, his understanding of opinion rests on Immanual Kant's conceptualization of three levels of holding for true *(Fürwahrhalten)* in his *Critique of Pure Reason,* which are determined by the subjective and objective validity of judgments. According to Kant ([1781] 1952), opinion is both subjectively and objectively insufficient, belief is sufficient subjectively but lacks objectivity, whereas only knowledge is sufficient on both accounts. Opinions are never merely arbitrary fiction, but it is also not possible to hold opinions in judgments of pure reason; it would be absurd, according to Kant, to have an opinion about pure mathematics—in such a field, one must either know or abstain from forming a judgment altogether. Yet Tönnies rationalized Kant's opinion and defined it as a matter of reason in contrast to belief, which is, according to Tönnies, "a matter of heart." In fact, it could be said that belief is more characteristic of Gemeinschaft whereas opinion belongs to Gesellschaft.

Beginning with his understanding of opinion as will, he outlines the opinion of the public as a form of social will in society, that is, as a form of reflexive will.[8] Social will is articulated as communal and societal will, according to (1) its relation to social behavior and social activity; (2) within this framework, according to its relation to specific actions and to the dissolution of, primarily, common activities and a unified organized collectivity; and (3) how it is revealed in thought and in the recognition of reality, that is, in beliefs or in the ways opinions of individuals are formed (Tönnies 1922, 56). Although forms of societal will represent a negation of the communal will, they also emerge from it. Each complex form of the will has also a forerunner in a simpler form and a specific relationship with similar forms, as, for example, faith in tradition and understanding. Tönnies explains the difference between organic and reflexive will by relying on his model that distinguishes between Gemeinschaft and Gesellschaft (Tönnies 1922, VII) and helps to install the "opinion of the public" concept in his general social theory.

According to his forms of social will (see table 3.1), opinion of the public is determined in three ways (Tönnies 1922, 77–78, 229–30), first, by relation to *religion* as a corresponding/opposite form of communal will; opinion of the public is a rationalized form of religion. Both represent a form of spiritual and moral collective will, and opinion of the public performs in society the role religion does in traditional community.

Second, a relation to *doctrine* as a corresponding elementary form of societal will: just as faith and religion form a totality, so do opinion of the public and doctrine.

Third, relation (difference) to the subjects of other *forms of the complex societal will—law and convention:* the subject of convention is society, the subject of legislation is the state, the subject of opinion of the public is the public or public, and the republic of the learned *(Gelehrtenrepublik)* is at its core.

In his introduction to the *Critique*, Tönnies emphasizes that his understanding of opinion of the public as a form of social will represents his most important idea. This concept connects his theory of public opinion with his model of differentiation between community and society. Opinion of the public is a form of societal will *(gesellschaftlicher Wille)*, more precisely, it is one of its higher or complex forms—whereas religion, for example, is a form of communal will. Tönnies presents the primary tasks of the critical theory of public opinion by explicitly relying on his predecessors, among the most distinguished being Christoph Martin Wieland and Christian Garve (Tönnies 1916; 1928).

These tasks involve determining five differences to help establish a more precise meaning of his concept of opinion of the public (Tönnies 1922, VI):

1. the difference between *public opinion* and *opinion of the public*, partly taken from Emil Löbl[9]: the first is a conglomerate of various controversial views, desires, and intentions, whereas the second one is a unified force, an expression of a common will;

2. the difference between opinion of the public in its historical and politically decisive sense (opinion of the public has an immense influence in politics) and ephemeral public opinions, which are, although unified, present throughout social life in their limited, partly local and partly nonpolitical sense;

3. the difference between three basic aggregate states of opinion of the public with which Tönnies wishes to specify the properties of opinion of the public on an applied level;

4. the difference between public opinion (and opinion of the public), popular beliefs *(Volksstimmung),* and popular feelings *(Volksgefühle);* and

5. the difference between opinion of the public and religion, which are similar and related as well as incompatible and divergent.

Since his early works, Tönnies considers public opinion enlightened and rational, that is, a form of social will based on rational will and an agreement between individual (private) and public opinions. Indeed, only for this reason can reasonable individuals act according to their opinions (see Gollin and Gollin 1973, 185). Opinion of the public is a form of a complex collective will associated with the ethical and aesthetic dimensions of collective life, whereas convention is associated mainly with the general and the economic, and the legislature with political life. In other words, according to Tönnies (1922, 228), convention is, in fact, a regulation *(Vorschrift),* that is, a recommendation or directive; legislation is an order *(Befehl),* that is, a mandate or interdiction, whereas an opinion of the public is a judgment *(Urteil).* In *Gemeinschaft and Gesellschaft,* Tönnies for the first time defines public opinion as a form of social will and power that is not enforced by the physical force or external means (e.g., money) but through ideas and thoughts:

> Public opinion claims to set up general and valid norms, but not on the basis of a blind belief, but rather of a clear insight into the correctness of the acknowledged and adopted doctrines. According to its tendency and form, it is a scientific and enlightened opinion. ([1887] 1991, 202)

This early definition of public opinion is not based on the fundamental differentiation between public opinion and opinion of the public, which Tönnies later establishes in the *Critique,* distinguishing between three different meanings of public opinion (1922, 129–30). These differences are crucial for his theory because they do not produce equivalent concepts that differ only in their objective meanings; instead, they are mostly about differentiating between pure, applied, and empirical understandings of public opinion. Unfortunately, Tönnies chooses terms that are rather unsuitable, even in German, for contributing to a clear terminology and cause annoying problems for translations. For example, Tönnies expresses the difference between the three main meanings (in German) by using definite, indefinite, and no articles, e.g., *die Öffentliche Meinung, eine öffentliche Meinung,* and *öffentliche Meinung;* these terms are regularly translated into English as The Public Opinion and (a) public opinion. Furthermore, Tönnies was inconsistent and also used *die öffentliche Meinung* and *eine Öffentliche Meinung* without specifying differences in their meanings.[10] Moreover, he translated the English term "public opinion" (and not "Public Opinion" or, at least, the public opinion as *die Öffentliche Meinung,* although he specifically studied semantic differences between *opinion* and *Meinung* (Tönnies 1922, 262).[11] Finally, marking essential semantic differences only by using upper or lower case initials is inappropriate because the differentiation is obvious only in writing and not in pronunciation; many languages (failing to have definite and indefinite articles) cannot clearly express this differentiation. For these reasons I decided to use the following terms: "opinion of the public" for *die Öffentliche Meinung,* "public opinion" for *eine öffentliche Meinung,* and "the/a published opinion" for *öffentliche Meinung.*[12]

"Published opinion" *(öffentliche Meinung)* represents an individual's publicly expressed opinion, that is, an opinion meant for recipients in general and different from an individual's internal, that is, private, opinion, as well as from an intimate opinion meant for a confidential, preappointed, select group of individuals; in this sense, it is possible to speak about public opinion as a "totality of all appearances of mental life, especially in a state of a unified nation," or, in other words, a "unity of a container in which very different ingredients are mixed." This reminds one of public opinion polls, but the latter does not fulfil the conditions of intentionality and public representation. According to Tönnies, publicly expressed opinion has to be strictly differentiated from opinion expression in general, and both from the same opinion of two or more individuals.

Public opinion *(eine öffentliche Meinung)* appears when published opinion becomes an opinion of many, of a majority of an open or closed circle, particularly if it clearly expresses support or opposition. This means that in its basic elements published opinion becomes in fact an agreed upon opinion or at least is understood as such. In this sense, public opinion represents "a transition from a published opinion to opinion of the public" (1923, 82 n.). The public attribute here means publicity and not—as in the case of the public—universality *(das Allgemeine)* of opinion (1928, 49).

Opinion of the public *(die Öffentliche Meinung)* is, according to Tönnies, the only purely theoretical conception. It is the real *(die eigene)*, articulated public opinion in a strict sense. Its formation and expression are related to a (large) public that appears in various "aggregate states," determined by the degree to which the public "is harmonious with itself." The subject of opinion of the public is, therefore, the public, a transitory social formation, like the mass or dispersed crowd *(getrennter Haufen)* and present crowd *(versammelter Haufen)*. A physical bond is not essentially typical for the public (although possible for a short time); rather, it is a spiritual connection on the level of ideas. What distinguishes the public from an incidentally connected, dispersed, or present crowd is its capability to clearly articulate opinions.[13]

Opinion of the public is a concept of pure theory and constitutes, as an ideal (normative) type, one of the forms of social will, whereas public opinion and publicly expressed opinion belong to an experiential (applied and empirical) world. The character of the public determines that opinion of the public belongs to a specific form of social will and social structure, that is, to the reflexive (and not organic) will and to society (rather than community). Nevertheless, opinion processes, characteristic for the opinion of the public, also emerge in community, in which they are determined by the organic will. Tönnies understands opinion of the public as a "common way of thought, the corporate spirit of any group or association, in so far as its opinion formation and expression *[Meinen]* is built upon *reasoning* and *knowledge,* rather than on unproven impressions, beliefs, or authority" (Tönnies 1922, 78).

The opinion of the public is an agreement, that is, the unanimous opinion of citizens reached by their own independent reasoning. Agreement is always a result of an acceptance among all, or of a majority of citizens, although this accord may be a passive and silent acceptance of an opinion considered reasonable by this majority. Only an educated elite actively participates in forming and expressing opinions. Complete agreement is unattainable, although it exists as a permanent tendency to overcome the fluid state of the opinion of the public. However, Tönnies nowhere explicitly defines the opinion of the public, which corroborates his principled belief that it is possible to reveal forms of appearance of public opinion and (mis)perceptions of it—this is why his fundamental work is entitled the *critique* of public opinion—but it is very difficult to determine what really is the opinion of the public (1923, 72).[14] Nevertheless, we can conclude from his articles (1916; 1928) that, for all practical purposes, he entirely accepts Christian Garve's rationalistic definition, formulated at the end of the eighteenth century. Tönnies writes:

Public opinion . . . is an agreement of many, or of a majority of citizens of a state about judgments that would be acceptable for every individual according to his own reasoning or experiences. . . . Opinion of the public cannot be equated with a habit (Herkommen), a custom (Gewohnheit), or with effects of learning. It cannot mean an agreement which could change a legislature, or an established religion into a way of thinking for a nation, or create an influence of a strong and articulate individual in a political party. Where only one man thinks and evaluates, while the rest blindly believes him or merely repeats his words, . . . there is no public opinion—which always presupposes that a man who treasures it, follows his own nature and impressions in his judgments. (Tönnies 1916, 415)

Opinion of the public is an agreement in opinion of many people achieved by the "nature of thing" rather than discussion, which essentially influences the support given to actions and changes in state and church that are compatible with these opinions (Tönnies 1928, 45). According to Tönnies, only Garve's words "of many, or of a majority" in his definition need to be replaced with the term "all citizens" in order to obtain "a concept that will probably never correspond to reality, but would, for this very reason, become a strictly scientific, mathematical concept, or, as Kant says, an idea" (1916, 415). In this sense, opinion of the public is closely linked to education, that is, to enlightenment *(Aufklärung)*. Both Garve and Tönnies emphasize that the prospects of participating in the formation of an opinion of the public depend on an individual's education. Consequently, the development of public education is definitely important for the progress of an opinion of the public. Despite such a development, however, only a minority has the degree of higher education needed for an independent formation of opinion, unprejudiced judgments, and a critical evaluation independent of external pressures. Nevertheless, a complete independence in forming opinion, as postulated by Garve, is still an ideal approached rarely in reality.

Opinion of the public differs from other forms of social will by the manner in which the unanimous will is formed. The unanimous common will can be a result of knowledge and is formed by a rational decision reached by an individual or accepted by many people. The latter case expresses a desire for action and expectations of everyone to conform to this common aspiration. A new collective body, a unit capable of making decisions (e.g., a society, a club, a cooperative, a political party, a committee) may be established by such a decision. Accepted and agreed upon by an individual or a group in advance (e.g., according to a group's regulations and by a majority vote), such a decision becomes the decree of this organization and is, therefore, obligatory for all members. The topic of such a decree may even be the *expression of* opinion, which concerns aspirations but not the formation *of* opinion, which concerns reasoning.

OPINION OF THE PUBLIC AND PUBLIC OPINION:
PURE THEORY AND APPLICATION

Tönnies's theory of opinion of the public is a critique of public opinion; it is primarily directed against popular views about public opinion and toward establishing a scientific understanding. In popular conceptions, public opinion is—in contrast to an opinion of the public—understood as publicly expressed opinions:

> The published opinion, in this sense, has only this essential property that it is uttered or communicated, and this, moreover, 'in general' ways. Namely, it is transmitted to any listener or reader, in contrast to 1. an opinion that is by nature internal and personal (intimate), and also in contrast to 2. an opinion that is confidentially conveyed to specific, known persons. If an opinion, thus transmitted, becomes an opinion and a judgment of the many, even a majority, i.e.,—if its weight is judged by the weight of a majority of a meeting—if it is a judgment of a unity, a circle, or a unity that is united into a community or society, then we could call it a public opinion. (Tönnies 1922, 129–130)

Any closed or open circle can generate an indefinite or arbitrary public opinion if its members assign a specific weight to it (e.g., opinions of a town, profession, stratum, or class) and act accordingly. As soon as members of different strata gain freedom of speech and press, a host of various, even opposing and publicly expressed, opinions rise directly from this collective freedom of expression. In this sense, public opinion is far from unanimous (Tönnies 1922, 129). The public nature of public opinion is by itself limitless; however, many practical barriers obstruct the reception of published opinion, such as the language of communication; the relevant political area in which the issue of opinion is meaningful; the level of education among readers and listeners; the strength of the spiritual and moral voice; the opinion circles of recipients; and the external media of communication, especially the largesse of the public in the periodical press (1922, 135–36).

Nevertheless, Tönnies's concept of public opinion does not correspond to what pollsters want to measure in public opinion polls (cf. Gollin and Gollin 1973, 196). Indeed, Tönnies treats public opinion as a collective and public phenomenon, even when it appears as a phenomenological unity of different and opposing opinions that can easily find their way into the press, and not merely as an aggregate of (quasi-private) opinions that can be expressed by various means. Media in which public opinion can be expressed share the fact that they are natural or artificial, that is, they are only used or misused. Besides the most frequent medium of expression of public opinion, the press (in which mis-

use is represented, for example, by deceptive news), Tönnies also lists formation of associations, meetings, street and town square demonstrations, festivi-
ties, or social occasions at which followers gather. All of these means of expressing public opinion most prominently expose their common features,
namely, praising people and respectfully addressing and inviting them to join
in or to express their opinion. The newspaper is the most common and general
medium of expression for all of them. However, the tendency among newspapers to praise is mostly concealed, yet it is present. Newspapers also flatter their
readers and tempt them to accept agreement, not as a matter of course but validated by reasoning.

Newspapers both express an opinion of the public and influence public opinion. Equalizing popular public opinion and opinion of the public would be
misleading, since newspapers are neither organs of opinion of the public nor
are they identical with it (Tönnies 1923, 78). In reality, newspapers are, most
of all, organs of political parties; only metropolitan newspapers, read by an educated public, yield information about the opinion of the public. Specifically,
even if these newspapers are not organs of opinion of the public, they can influence such an opinion at least indirectly.[15] If anything, parliament may be
called an "organ of opinion of the public," and even this is not always justified
(Tönnies 1923, 77). Although insignificant places may have their public opinion, opinion of the public has necessarily a national or even an international
and transnational character. Public opinion appears in various ways, but most
strongly and efficiently in newspapers, in which it can actually proceed into an
opinion of the public. This occurs, for example, when the most reasonable and
substantiated opinions about public affairs are published in the most important
newspapers, although rarely, when published in only one of them. We can talk
about opinion of the public when the same opinion is rephrased by several
newspapers and approached beyond partisan bias.

Tönnies's genuine interest is not in inarticulate public opinion; only opinion of the public, in which a (large) audience, the public, acts to form and express an opinion, is worthy of scientific inquiry and theoretical analysis. Opinion of the public substantially differs from public opinion precisely in its
subject. Whereas public opinion does not have any specifically defined subject,

the subject of opinion of the public is a fundamentally connected totality
[Gesamtheit], politically in particular, that has been united by reflection and judgment, and that is precisely why it belongs to the public, to public life. . . . Opinion of the public is in essence one will, the will in and through judgment—and
the judgment is an act of unity—; thus a conscious and expressed form of the will
in a form of a resolution, adopted by a court or any other quorum on what it

agrees—an expression of a will of totality, which, however, is not assembled as a
public or as a subject of opinion of the public, except in spirit—and is normally
much too large to be conceived as an assembly. (Tönnies 1922, 131–32)

Thus both concepts of public opinion are characterized by a publicly communicated opinion and deal with public, mostly political affairs. Although a
general and colloquial connotation of public opinion is, of course, not totally
irrelevant for a scientific conception, it is still more important to understand
what has been established by the "called upon thinkers" (Tönnies 1916, 420
n.).[16] Tönnies determines the fundamental difference between colloquial understanding (i.e., public opinion) and scientific conception (i.e., opinion of
the public) by the subject; the subject of an opinion of the public is spiritually
connected, or gathered, individuals, who debate and reach a conclusion,
whereas public opinion has no evident subject. Opinion of the public is a "general, common opinion of the people or the public, in other words, a form of
social will which is in all its forms expressed as a unified will, as a will of one
person." Tönnies approaches the public as "the judge that judges as opinion
of the public"; the judge must know the truth and judge morally (Tönnies
1923, 83, 92).

A large part of his *Critique* is devoted to a detailed historical description and
a (much less elaborate) theoretical analysis of public(s). Opinion of the public
in recent centuries presupposes a large public, which is the only proper public
("das" Publikum); it is composed of a "limitless mass of people who, in spite of
being dispersed and infinitely diverse, may reflect and judge similarly" (Tönnies 1922, 84).[17] The large public is never spatially joined, that is, gathered in
one place at a certain time, as publics in the past (e.g., a theater audience) were
still able to do. A large public functions within many circles in which it becomes
audible. A public is formed by certain kind of events, for example, in politics,
science, arts, or connected with outstanding personalities, by people who are
capable and willing to pass judgments about such events and have "appropriate
skills and education—members of an educated world," according to Tönnies
(1922, 84). Thus a large public constitutes unity, spatially limited by a nation
(at least in Tönnies's time), determined by attention to a public issue, and,
therefore, temporary and internally divided according to the firmness of a
formed opinion. Thus publics (plural) are never really public, as Arato and Cohen noticed much later (1996, 136). Tönnies speaks of publics only at an ap-
plied-historical level, at which publics act only as carriers of public opinion (and
not of an opinion of the public). It was characteristic of (narrow) publics to
limit access, and they did not attract public attention, did not have a "real public" (Tönnies 1922, 103).

Only a (large) public—consisting of spatially dispersed yet spiritually connected individuals who are distinguished by their education, political impartiality, and support of general public interest—can (as a *Gelehrtenrepublik*) act as subject in the formation of an opinion of the public. The latter is characterized by political nonpartisanship, absence of special interests, and support of the general good. Most of all, a genuine opinion of the public, as a prudent worldview, remains above political parties and their goals. Lippmann (1925, 112) writes almost identically about the properties of public opinion later, stressing that the true public has to purge itself of groups with particular interests who become mistaken for it.[18] Dewey ([1927] 1991) also agreed that "American party politics seem at times to be a device for preventing issues which may excite popular feeling and involve bitter controversies from being put up to the American people" (p. 121) and stressed "the pre-eminence of the claims of the organized public" (organized "in and through those officers who act on behalf of its interests") over other interests (pp. 27–28). Because of these assumptions, the elaboration of a large public and an opinion of the public are predominantly associated with urbanization.

According to Tönnies, the struggle of opinions that is taking its turn in the public arena (e.g., the media) is not so much a struggle inside the formation of public opinion, in which only the chosen can participate. Rather, it is a struggle *for* a (primarily "gaseous") opinion of the public, that is, for individuals who will embrace the expressed or published opinion as their own and/or will present it as their own opinion. Since the struggle over opinion is carried on primarily among political parties, it manifests and perpetuates the eternal antagonisms between government and opposition, conservatism and reformism, and orthodox and heterodox orientations. The public watches these fights over opinions like theatergoers who are able to see only one side of a scene from an elevated box because a newspaper presentation is as one-sided as the presentation by parties is partial. Newspapers are not the organs of (opinion of) the public but rather of political parties that systematically influence them. The "solution" proposed by Lippmann ([1922] 1960, 32) was to replace political parties by expert insiders to rationalize public opinion: "public opinions must be organized for the press if they are to be sound, not by the press, as is the case today." Later, Habermas lists such an inverted relationship between the press and public opinion among basic elements of a refeudalization of the public.

Tönnies's conception of the public ("large public") as a social category that is a basis for an opinion of the public seems to be more valid than, for instance, the conceptualization in Habermas's theory (both in its earlier version developed in *The Structural Transformation of the Public Sphere* or in his later theory of communicative competence) based on the "hyper-intellectualist" (Beaud

1999) assumption of dialogical competence of individuals. "Citizens behave as a public when they confer in an unrestricted fashion—that is, with the guarantee of freedom of assembly and association and the freedom to express and publish their opinions—about matters of general interest" (Habermas [1964] 1979, 198). For Habermas, meaning and essence of the public reside in the participation of equal citizens in free public discussion, freed from any conflict of interest (because they left their private interests in the private sphere) and, therefore, leading to agreement. The function of newspapers in public discussion should, in principle, involve interpersonal interaction, which was characteristic of the golden age of democracy during antiquity but totally utopian at the time of Tönnies's *Critique* and quite naive sounding today. Habermas regards new communication and information technologies that have revolutionized communication relations since the middle of the nineteenth century mostly from their negative consequences rather than positive emancipatory potential.[19] Thus, according to Habermas, a public exists already (or merely) when within it a critical discussion takes place—as opposed to the presentation of public status before some type of court, which means the decay of the genuine public. No mediation exists between the two types of the public/ness, according to Habermas, because they historically exclude each other.

Tönnies, in contrast to Habermas, proceeds in his theory from the process of forming and expressing public opinion as a fundamental form of a complex social will in society and not from the public as a (specific) social category. "The first condition [of an opinion of the public] is a vitality of communication," which is a source of developing reflection and judgment (Tönnies 1922, 316). He stresses the constitutive role of the form of communication in differentiating between community and society. Community is identified by opinion heritage *(Überlieferung)*, expressed as passing knowledge from generation to generation (i.e., from older to younger generations) and from higher (predominantly clergy) to lower strata of society. In contrast, tradition and authority from upside down are losing power and give way to verifiable reason and critique in society. Therefore, written communication and subsequently the press became more important than oral communication. In difference to speech, which is always only aimed at and limited by those who are present, the press addresses an unknown and unidentified mass of people. For Tönnies ([1922, 220), the difference between community and society is first and foremost constituted by writing, as it is writing that marks the transition from a primeval, classless human community to civilization and class society for Marx and Engels in their *Manifesto*. At the beginning, books were still characterized by an intimate association between author and specific reader and by the exalted position of the author of literary and scientific texts alike (expressed by a reader's trust, admiration, and gratitude for a writer). Later, the newspaper and its reader meet on the same level. The newspaper is meant for a large public, and its influence is not based on an individual point of view or respect. Rather, it influences as "a thing that speaks to the unknown about unknown" and persuades most effectively by periodic repetition. For this reason, it soon becomes outdated and forgotten. All of this demonstrates the anonymity of the publisher at best and makes us believe that the author is not a concrete person but the newspaper itself. In addition to political and economic news that give a newspaper its name, the reader's own newspaper mainly confirms a reader's views, or rather the views of friends and those who share a reader's interests and party affiliation, thus strengthening and encouraging existing views. Before the appearance of newspapers there were many channels for communicating news; however, the space in which opinions were exchanged and struggled over was limited by a physical presence of individuals.

The role Tönnies attributes to the press, or rather to publicity, is to "set the public into motion and to draw it to its side," a process that regularly happens during turbulent times. In order to achieve this condition, publicity presents its contents as public opinion, so that even critics frequently equate the products of publicity with public opinion. Thus the essence of publicity (in contrast to science) is not a pursuit of the truth but rather influence. This does not mean that occasionally some products of publicity cannot be even closer to the truth than a scientific statement, according to Tönnies's summary of Wilhelm Bauer's ideas.[20] Since the beginning, newspapers were not only intended to supplement privately mediated news (i.e., letters) but mostly to spread news that was intended for the public or had escaped censorship. Following Bauer, Tönnies also differentiates between two kinds of publicity, corresponding to "what kind of relationship the publicist has with his own products *(Werke)*." The relationship is natural if a publicist represents his views only out of an internal need created by his own conviction.[21] The other type of publicity follows entirely external motives and impulses. However, newspapers are, in reality, principally "a large capitalist business whose direct and main goal is to create profit," and even journalists must conform to this objective (Tönnies 1922, 179–80). Corruption and corporate control cause an evident partiality of newspapers, so that independent newspapers are an absolute illusion; Tönnies, therefore, considers newspapers to be merely (potential) mediators, and by no means subjects of an opinion of the public. Daily newspapers influence the gaseous opinion of the public and vice versa; the narrower and the more solid forms of an opinion of the public are "in a similar relationship of reciprocal influence with a different, more *reliable* literature" all the way to "the republic of the learned which is the highest instance of opinion of the public in a state or in the 'world,'" whose members regularly read books (Tönnies 1922, 187). Thus the direction from a "gaseous state" to the intellectual core is a direction in which an opinion achieves greater reliability and solidity.

Tönnies stresses—in opposition to what Habermas asserts later—that opinions are particular and determined by interests because "the recognizing subjects have their 'human flaws'" (Tönnies 1922, 187). Identical opinions often indicate identical benefits and interests, and opinion struggles largely demonstrate fights among social strata and classes. Only in science can human recognition, and the opinion it establishes, have a universal quality and a quality of necessity, or at least the latter (as an individual and specific truth). Thus the idea that opinions only depend on a human aspiration for knowledge cannot be accepted as a valid general assumption regarding public opinion or an opinion of the public. To a certain extent, differences in opinions are also the result of a different quality of organs and means of perception; this is the reason why, for example, less educated masses often achieve agreement more easily than better educated elites, whose members compete for power and therefore disagree more often. To an even greater extent, differences in opinion result from differences in a subjective life situation (Tönnies 1922, 107). Usual differences in opinion between the city, which is progressive, and the countryside, which is predominantly conservative, can be explained by differences in activities, way of life, and community. Whereas life in the country is calm, stable, and dictated by nature, city life is in constant movement and is conditioned by reflection and purpose; population density in urban accumulations by itself stimulates interaction and reflection.

Tönnies attributes the diversity of interests and needs primarily to the inequality of those who participate in the process of opinion formation; the differences originate from specific conditions of life, education, and particular social groups and classes (1922, 225–26). Similar life conditions activate similar opinions and vice versa: the more the conditions of life differ, the more differentiated opinions become.[22] Tönnies (1922, 46) stresses the fact that ways of speaking and thinking are determined by education and knowledge and are influenced by many people with whom we share life, age, gender, rank, profession, religion, and political party. He also mentions social-demographic and psychic distinctions (age, gender, development of personality) that regularly determine opinion differences and, in addition to them, social strata and classes. There are always disagreements among opinions of competing groups of political leaders; however, the deepest divisions exist between ruling and subordinate classes, between higher and lower ranks, rich and poor, educated and uneducated. Thus the basic antagonism that is brought forward most notably by (opinion) differences among political parties exists between owners and non-owners, rich and poor, capital and work; city and countryside; and the educated and the people (Tönnies 1922, 118). This is the reason why the opinion of the public can also be wrong: it judges issues according to their image rather than reality, and it can never make use of procedures that a real court or judge uses, according to Tönnies (1922, 75).

Opinion formation is too crucial to be open to everyone's participation, according to Tönnies. However, an individual who cannot participate in the formation of opinion should not be prevented from expressing an opinion instead of merely accepting it (Tönnies 1922, 35). Differentiation between opinion formation and opinion expression is established by the fact that opinion formation belongs to the organic will, whereas opinion expression belongs to the reflexive will, according to Tönnies (1922, 27). The latter is independent from the former, even opposed to it, which can be manifest in the formation of opinion itself as a consequence of different motives of individuals.

OPINION OF THE PUBLIC VERSUS RELIGION

The central point of Tönnies's critique of public opinion is the dialectical relationship between opinion of the public and religion; it occupies an important position in his rational critique of religion as a conservative force and an instrument of social conservatism. The idea of considering public opinion in opposition to religion could be implicitly found already in Rousseau's *Social Contract*, in which he differentiates between (particularistic) civil religion as positive divine law and (general) religion of man as natural divine law. However, Tönnies's idea is much more than just a reminiscence of Roussseau's idea of religion of man. His theory of public opinion represents a basis of his rational critique of religion and, inversely, the relationship between religion and public opinion is also the foundation of his theory of public opinion. Religion is "a general and public belief which presupposes a communal interconnectedness, which it constitutes and forms respectively" (Tönnies 1922, 231). In the relationship between an opinion of the public and religion, the relationship between "to opine" and "to believe" is expressed: One always believes someone (or something), which implies a relation that cannot occur with reasoning. In contrast to Kant, who argued that opinion *(Meinen)* is subjectively and objectively insufficient, whereas belief *(Glauben)* is insufficient only objectively, and thus belief is a higher form of "holding for true" than opinion, Tönnies relates opinion to reason. From the standpoint of objective reasons (although insufficient for the conscience) to opine means regarding something as true, whereas to believe is always subjectively grounded in firm feeling and trust, so that to believe means to be convinced. "To believe is a matter of the heart while to opine [is a matter] of the head. In this way, the religious meaning of faith can be directly understood" (Tönnies 1922, 13). Faith that represents one of the forms of *organic will* excludes doubt, which is a property of opinion formation. Earlier, Bluntschli stressed in his *Staatswörterbuch* (1862) that religion and public opinion are basically opposites, since public opinion does not exist without thought and judgment (Wilson 1962, 77). The evolution of democracy isolated and excluded religion from the "sphere of urgent unanimity" (Wirth 1948, 9) because agreement about faith can only be achieved by force, whereas striving for agreement (in public opinion) should build on reason, compatibility, and reconciliation of interests.

Opinion of the public unites and obliges individuals who produce and accept it, as religion unites and binds believers. Opinion of the public not only directs individuals to a certain opinion but also encourages, even demands, a certain kind of behavior and action, for example, membership in a political party or reading a specific newspaper. Similarly, religion requires believers to fulfil the requirements of their religious organization. Resemblance between these two forms of social will is most explicit when opinion of the public takes the form of a patriotic dogma, particularly in the form of revanchism: according to opinion of the public, love for country equals duty, just as love for God is a religious obligation (Tönnies 1923, 85–86). Nevertheless, the powers of religion and opinion of the public do not manifest themselves only as an internally oriented connection and unity but most of all externally in the relationship with the state. Both religion and opinion of the public struggle for the status of a supreme moral instance and corresponding recognition from the government: every religious denomination wants to become a (state) religion, and every public opinion wants to become an opinion of the public (Tönnies 1923, 87). Opinion of the public often takes paths paved by religion. Moreover, opinion of the public adopted its "means of expression" from religion: at the beginning different kinds of artistic expressions, primarily public speech (sermon) and, later, primarily media connected with writing and the press, such as books, posters, journals, and, finally, newspapers (Tönnies 1922, 202). This is equally true of public manifestations (proceeding from religious processions), as well as of propaganda. Furthermore, opinion of the public inherited intolerance and even fanaticism from religion: both of these forms of social will characteristically argue that an opposing opinion should be "cursed as a sin" (Tönnies 1922, 205; 1923, 87).

Even though religion and opinion of the public are really moral judges, they emphasize different subjects. Opinion of the public judges people for their actions and not for their reasoning or belief; the basis for judgments is the code of law. Religion, in contrast, evaluates convictions of people according to their morals. Religion wants to control souls and engage with the most secret beliefs;

an opinion of the public sticks to the visible and apparent and, consequently, can be misled by the image. The most significant difference between religion and opinion of the public was established with the economic and political emancipation of the bourgeoisie, which at the end of the seventeenth century and during the eighteenth century found its expression in the first "institutions of the public," according to Habermas ([1962] 1995, 31–43).

> Important differences between religion and opinion of the public become apparent when, on the one hand, we imagine a silent meeting of believers where faith and piety are really at home, and, on the other hand, those social places that are exceptionally important in everyday life for the formation of an opinion of the public: "the salon" and "the pub;" both of them sites for meetings of a reflecting, discussing, cleverly chatting, and politicising "world." (Tönnies 1922, 202)

Tönnies associates the decline of religion and (like Dewey for the public) an ever greater role for the opinion of the public with the development of science. "The progress of opinion formation and expression [*des Meinens*] is primarily a consequence of the influence of advances in scientific knowledge" (1922, 121). Already in his introduction to *Critique,* in which he discusses basic terminology, Tönnies stresses the difference between belief and opinion. Whereas a belief is a matter of mood and heart, an opinion is a matter of thought and reason: "Belief is often about the most unbelievable and even 'impossible,' while an opinion, if it cannot reach the truth, at least attempts to achieve a probable, a more probable, and the most probable" (Tönnies 1922, 19). Belief excludes every doubt; it is solid and perfect, whereas an opinion is individual and can be erroneous but can also be changed and revised. The scientific quality makes opinion of the public different from religion and also turns it into its opposite, since religion builds on (blind) belief in an absolute truth. This is the reason why the time of opinion of the public represents a new era, that is, the time that affirms scientific and critical ways of thinking.

The next important difference between religion and opinion of the public lies in social classes, or strata, according to Tönnies. Religion is historically rooted in lower social strata and its development is upward toward higher social layers, including priests, artists, and the educated, who give religion its more refined form. In contrast, participation in the formation of an opinion of the public is determined principally by an individual's knowledge, reasoning, education, and political interests. Thus subjects and carriers of public opinion are mostly the bourgeoisie and individuals of rank, men more than women, older people more than younger ones, and those who are personally affected by interests and certain problems more than those who are not (e.g., in economic matters businesspeople more than intellectuals, whereas the reverse is true in spiritual matters). In general, opinion of the public can be defined as an opinion of the educated, in contrast to a "large mass of people" (Tönnies 1923, 91). With the expansion of general and, in particular, political education to lower social strata, the latter become cocreators of opinion of the public, so that opinion of the public, in effect, becomes common and general *(allgemein);* however, a potential reality of a unified opinion of the public or agreement is thus actually diminished (Tönnies 1922, 229).

Differences and conflicts between religion and public opinion have, of course, the character of an ideal type; in the experiential world religion and public opinion coexist and are intertwined—as are organic and reflexive wills. This is true for society and community, although historically opinion of the public is gaining power with the affirmation of society, whereas religion is losing it, as Tönnies stresses on several occasions. This does not preclude temporary regressions, that is, abandoning the vision of enlightenment connected with natural-scientific and historiographic knowledge and returning to Christian (Roman Catholic) morals, a "tragic event," according to Tönnies (1922, 571). Still, such regressions are only short-lived experiences of a long-term historical trend in which the opinion of the public will prevail over religious belief. Tönnies's expectations of the decline of the cohesive importance of religion compared to opinion of the public proved to be well justified in later decades, especially with the development of television; his predictions concerning the consequences of an expanding public into lower social strata proved to be true as well.

THE "AGGREGATE STATES" OF THE OPINION OF THE PUBLIC

Tönnies exemplifies changing forms of opinion of the public with a metaphor of aggregate states of matter borrowed from physics.[23] The change of aggregate states indicates a change in social consciousness that Tönnies named the "spirit of the time" *(Zeitgeist).* In its character, the spirit of the time is distinctly international and essentially connected with doctrines that represent the form of a simple social will in Gesellschaft. Solidity of opinion of the public depends primarily on how unified (politically, or at least mentally and morally) the public is as a carrier of the spirit of the time: the more it constitutes an actual unity, the more its common view and conviction approach the solid opinion of the public (Tönnies 1922, 231). The degree of solidity of opinion of the public is determined by the degree of unanimity of the public; thus, an aggregate state is actually determined by solidity of opinion and not by a changeable character of the public. In its solid form, opinion of the public is "a general, firm conviction of the public which, being a carrier of such convictions, represents the whole nation, or even a wider circle of 'civilized humanity'" (Tönnies 1922, 137). The daily public opinion is always under the influence of solid and fluid opinions of the public, which nevertheless does not exclude discord and contradiction among them (Tönnies 1922, 249).

Tönnies distinguishes three aggregate states of opinion of the public: solid, fluid, and gaseous. He examines their characteristic contents and empirical (historical) examples in three different areas—social and economic, political and legal, and mental and ethical. As Wilson comments (1962, 95), public opinion (for Tönnies, opinion of the public) is inevitably durable and fluid at the same time.[24] Tönnies defines solid opinion of the public as a kind of agreement over general values, as it is "freedom." Since solid opinion is characterized by reason, tolerance, and the rejection of superstition, it is primarily shaped by intellectuals. Opinion of the public is fluid when, in time, changes occur about controversial issues. A fluid opinion of the public expresses primarily its impartiality, namely, changes can occur because an opinion of the public is unbiased and always stands for what is undeniably expressed in a spirit of common good. A gaseous or ephemeral opinion of the public is superficial and changes rapidly; however, at the same time, it depends on the fluid and, particularly, on the solid opinion of the public. Yet the historical process, finally manifested in a solid opinion of the public, always starts with the gaseous state. The gaseous opinion of the public represents a form of opinion of the public because of its congruence with more solid forms, even though it is not clearly differentiated from an inarticulate public opinion in the area of politics. Still, it is exactly the gaseous opinion of the public that most clearly illustrates the dynamics of opinion change and, therefore, everyone notices it. Nevertheless, the power of an opinion of the public is determined primarily by the solid opinion of the public, which is effective precisely because of its solidity or agreement. Tönnies, again, borrows a metaphor from physics to state that the momentum of the opinion of the public is determined by mass and speed: the power of opinion of the public depends on the degree of its solidity and energy that sets an opinion into motion, hence on the degree of its unanimity and intensity of the will.

Tönnies's "normal" concept of the opinion of the public is, in contrast to the static normative political theories, a dynamic category. The dialectical character of the opinion of the public is undeniable not only because it appears in different aggregate states, but also because it can develop from public opinion. Agitation and propaganda[25] disseminate and strengthen opinions, and in favorable circumstances they can accomplish the development of collective opinion *(Gesamtmeinung)* from a partial one *(Teilmeinung),* that is, an opinion of the public can develop from a partisan public opinion and a dominant opinion from a subordinate one

(Tönnies 1922, 200). In general, opinions tend to strengthen with time, gain power, and can even become self-evident; this applies to an individual as well as to a nation or a group of nations. With age, opinion approaches faith. On the other hand, with time, respect diminishes and critique becomes stronger: "the young are always inclined to laugh at old age, and this inclination offsets an otherwise more efficient inclination to respect it" (Tönnies 1922, 200). Consequently, with time even the most solid opinion fades away, mostly because of insufficient action.

Although opinion of the public is not a historical category, it also represents the point of departure for a historical analysis (or "application" in Tönnies's words), which is exemplified in the second and third parts of his *Critique*. However, his discussions of the ephemeral or the daily opinion of the public reveal that in its lowest aggregate state, opinion of the public has been practically devoid of what essentially defined it as a normative concept. It is like a "not very polite child," Tönnies wrote, characterized by rapid variability, inconsistency, superficiality, lack of criticism, burden of prejudices, consistent return to the original state, and vitality of prejudices about people (more than about objects). According to Tönnies, we should still recognize an opinion of the public even in its gaseous state, since even though it rarely corresponds to the idea of a mental form of a reflexive social will, a gaseous opinion of the public nevertheless perceives emotions to which it submits as being alien; even the gaseous opinion of the public expresses ideas that can be found also in its fluid and solid states, especially in the moral sphere. A certain education and intellect (albeit only average) are characteristic even for the gaseous opinion of the public. Yet in spite of these features, Tönnies suggests that in the "daily opinion of the public," or rather, in the "daily public opinion,"[26] which is always the most visible because it is expressed in newspapers, it is impossible to detect its state as (only) a public opinion or (already) an opinion of the public. On the empirical level, this would imply that it is quite impossible to determine whether the principle of publicity is materialized, in a concrete historical situation, in public opinion or merely in published opinions. In other words, similar to other sociological conceptualizations of public opinion in the early twentieth century, Tönnies did not solve the problem of empirical nonidentifiability and immeasurability of public opinion.

THE FUTURE OF THE OPINION OF THE PUBLIC
AND THE NEED FOR REFORMS OF THE PRESS

Like MacKinnon (1828) and other earlier theorists of public opinion, Tönnies also firmly emphasizes the role of the bourgeois class in the processes of forming the public, public opinion, and opinion of the public. Gillian and Albert Gollin (1973, 202) suggest that in Tönnies's efforts at "equalizing opinion of the public with the interests and values of the educated middle class, and in the meaning he assigned to intellectuals in formation of agreement" we must see an expression of the "social-political system that existed in his time in Germany." Tönnies's understanding, in general, was supposed to be burdened with a certain degree of elitism and Plato's understanding of republicanism—presumably a common feature among left-oriented intellectuals, among them Tönnies, without doubt. Although this critique is incorrect from a historical perspective, Tönnies's theory of public opinion could not be discussed polemically.

On the applied level (contrary to the purely theoretical one), Tönnies has very strongly stressed the problem of particularity in the "new-bourgeois government" in relation to the working class; he critically identifies the struggle for freedom of thought and press and the fight for other rights of citizens as "in its essence an expression of the fight of the new-bourgeois, the national-bourgeois class that positions itself as a 'public'—and very often as the 'people,' or the 'nation'—for *power*, that is, first for participation in the power of old classes and the monarchy which it restrains, and later increasingly for *independent* power" (Tönnies 1922, 128). This does not diminish the importance of the fact that by strengthening the power of the bourgeois class, its opinions are also strengthened and become a universal good of the political public; consequently, the ruling class cannot deny the subordinate class those political and citizens' rights it obtained by fighting for itself "without hitting itself into the face." In Tönnies's theory, freedom of thought, speech, and press, which have been enacted by the bourgeois revolution, represent the basic assumption for the formation of the opinion of the public as a specific form of social will. From a historical perspective, that is, on the applied level, the enactment of this assumption is directly connected to the revolutionary activity of the bourgeois class, which has no implication whatsoever for the pure theory of opinion of the public. However, Tönnies was neither a radical nor even a revolutionary critic of capitalism, and even less its advocate. Nevertheless, he was convinced that the problems and dangers of capitalism are greater and more menacing than difficulties and problems facing a transition to socialism; for Tönnies there was no doubt about the need for this transition (Rudolph 1995, 103).

The last chapter of *Critique* (1922, 569–75) Tönnies devotes to possible scenarios regarding the future development of the opinion of the public. Under all circumstances, "the future of the opinion of the public [should be] the future of culture" (1922, 569); the power of the opinion of the public would continue to increase, mainly by extending its solidity through focusing on moral questions. This seemingly makes the opinion of the public look like religion, but its power in public life extends, comparatively speaking, in the inverse proportion: religion has lost what the opinion of the public has gained in the last centuries.

The opinion of the public represents a form of "mental life of a nation" and, therefore, all elements of this life influence it, most among them science and "true art." Since these elements of mental life are nowadays mediated by the press, reform and the future of the opinion of the public are closely linked to the reform and future of newspapers. This reform should be directed toward socializing the press and should not avoid legislative means. On numerous occasions, Tönnies criticized the press and mainstream German *Zeitungswissenschaft*, which avoided radical questions, and demanded the reform of the press (Hardt 1979, 154–55). According to Tönnies, the reform should enact ideas and suggestions taken from German-American Ferdinand Hansen:

- in every city the best instructed and educated men should found a completely independent newspaper;
- all recognized political parties would retain space to introduce and explain events;
- the newspaper should be independent of advertisers; this would be secured by large circulation, since there would be no need for a party press;
- only trustworthy firms would receive space for advertising;
- voices of people would find their direct expression in the newspaper;
- sensationalism would be excluded;
- major articles would be unbiased, without passion, and objective so that introduced opinions would be accepted with attention and trust;
- the newspaper should have its own network of correspondents, independent from "the lying wires and poisoned international sources of agencies Reuters, Havas, Northcliffe and the yellow financial-imperialist press"; these are common enemies of humankind and should be destroyed. (Tönnies 1922, 575)

In 1920s America, Edward C. Hayes also demanded that newspapers give priority to ideas that emerge in free discussion and not to money: newspapers should be forced by law to assign equal space to each of the four parties that were the most powerful in last elections (Wilson 1962, 81). Essentially, Tönnies considered these suggestions significant for Germany, too, similar to Bauer's appeals to stop sensationalism and the violation of the "sanctity of private life." Nevertheless, as much as these goals seem significant, they also seem unrealizable. The proposals are valuable, however, because they are counterfactual and educative, that is, they call critical attention to the negative facts in the press, which, according to Tönnies, can only be reformed from the inside: "The necessity of such a reform itself must spring up as *public opinion,* and it would be an effective, possibly the most effective means of self-education for *the opinion of the public,"* as Tönnies ends his *Critique of Public Opinion* (1922, 575).

To summarize, for Tönnies, the public and the opinion of the public are, in the first place, normative concepts, that is, ideal abstractions, and, at the same time, ideals that can be largely enacted in a "human community" of the future. The ethical opinion of the public has to be able to recognize the truth first and then judge each case by the basic law. "It would be foolish to expect an enactment of such an idea, or to suppose that it could be accomplished by rules or preachers," Tönnies admits. At the same time, he emphasizes that "setting up a goal is always necessary in order to give rational endeavor its direction. If we do not have an ideal of the opinion of the public in our hearts, every effort to *bring up* a true opinion of the public will be in vain" (1923, 97). In contrast to Habermas's theory, Tönnies's opinion of the public as a pure theoretical concept is not a counterfactual ideal, that is, an ideal whose essential feature is its deviation from reality. On the contrary, compatible with Tönnies's theory as a whole, the opinion of the public as a specific form of social will exists in every society, at least in its gaseous state, and progress in science, education, and guidance of a (large) public contribute primarily to a fortification of the opinion of the public—in spite of an abuse (or its insufficient control) of such an important medium of expression as the periodical press.

In his dynamic conceptualization of the opinion of the public, Ferdinand Tönnies recognized the mutual influence of public opinion and other forms of social will. His understanding of opinion of the public as a form of social will represents his most important idea. Whereas he acknowledged the importance of conformity pressure in public opinion process, which makes public opinion similar to religion, he vigorously defended the importance of citizens' independent reasoning as the basis of the opinion of the public. Tönnies understood opinion of the public as a "common way of thought, the corporate spirit of any group or association, in so far as its opinion formation is built upon reasoning and knowledge, rather than on unproved impressions, beliefs, or authority" (1922, 78). In this sense, according to Tönnies, opinion of the public may be considered a rationalized or reflected form of religion, as reflexive will in general is a rationalized form of organic will. However, his holistic theory also emphasized the unity of will and emotions that are expressed in reason, and the foundation of reason in human life processes; thus the rationality of opinion always implies the volitional and affective dimensions of opinion formation.

Opinion of the public differs from other forms of social will in that the unanimous will is a result of knowledge and is formed by a rational decision, and it "competes" in Gesellschaft with two other forms of the complex social will—

convention and legislation. The subject of opinion of the public is "the public," with the "republic of the learned" at its core. It makes judgments concerning the ethical and aesthetic dimensions of communal life. The subject of convention is society regulating with recommendations and directives the general and the economic life; the subject of legislation is the state giving orders (through mandate and interdiction) in political life. The press and parliament may be considered the most important organs of opinion of the public, but even they, as Tönnies critically observed, are more often instruments of influencing public opinion instead of expressing it. Tönnies's differentiation among the state, society, and the public actually represents the roots of the productive idea, which can be later found with Gramsci in the exclusion of the sphere of economy from civil society, which are both opposed to the state.

As a social and political power, opinion of the public is genuinely related to the press, Tönnies suggested. Newspapers play a major role not only in the process of public opinion formation, as the transmitter of information to the public, but also as the main expression means of the public by which the virtual public is constituted. Like many other authors at that time, Tönnies recognized the need for radical reform of the press, which had become politically and commercially dependent. To improve the quality and ethical standards of journalism and to make newspapers a genuine organ of opinion of the public, he suggested the separation of newspapers from political parties and advertising agencies. The development of the press as a moral and cultural power presupposes its autonomy from political actions of the state and economic actions of society in the first place.

Ferdinand Tönnies's critical theory of public opinion, in which he gave preference to the complex processes in culture and society over their institutionalized forms in politics and the state, represents one of the most significant classical social-theoretical contributions to the field. Unfortunately, theories that originated at the beginning of the twentieth century seem to be much less influential at present than more practical-minded and empirical approaches developed after the 1930s. Some have even been forgotten. This oblivion is certainly not brought about by any intellectual or conceptual inferiority. On the contrary, Tönnies's and other early sociological conceptualizations of public opinion actually demonstrate that "leaving aside the abundance of data gathered during more than six decades of empirical communication research, the notion of a continuous progress in theory is apparently not very appropriate" (Pöttker 1993, 213). Similarly, in the late 1950s, Harold Lasswell (1957, 34–35) admitted that since the nineteenth century, no progress in public opinion research was achieved at the theoretical level; rather, it was only instrumental. Four decades later, Lasswell's (self-)critical assessment still holds true.

Its validity can be perhaps best exemplified by Tönnies's systematic analysis of public opinion in relation to other forms of (complex) social will that still, even seventy-five years after the appearance of his *Critique of Public Opinion,* represents a valuable critical challenge to public opinion theory and research.

4

✚

Public Opinion and Participation: The Dewey-Lippmann Controversy

The private citizen today has come to feel rather like a deaf spectator in the back row, who ought to keep his mind on the mystery off there, but cannot quite manage to keep awake.
—Walter Lippmann, *The Phantom Public*

Until secrecy, prejudice, bias, misrepresentation, and propaganda as well as sheer ignorance are replaced by inquiry and publicity, we have no way of telling how apt for judgment of social policies the existing intelligence of the masses may be.
—John Dewey, *The Public and Its Problems*

This chapter is focused on the relationship between public opinion and popular government in pluralist democracies. The connection between them was at the core of the controversy between Walter Lippmann and John Dewey in the 1920s. As many public opinion theorists and critics of individualistic behavioral approach to public opinion argue, the notion that individuals act singly and separately was never congruent with the reality of social relations. On the contrary, the basic fact with which the chapter starts is, as Blumer emphasized,

133

that the formation of public opinion can only occur as a function of a society in operation, largely through the interaction of groups rather than individuals, which implies that the study of formation and expression of public opinion must reflect the functional composition and organization of society.

This close relationship is particularly important if public opinion is conceptualized in terms of its functions for democratic political process, which is certainly the basic idea that has been connected with public opinion since the Enlightenment: it is participation of the public in political process that ensures legitimacy to democracy. In this perspective, public opinion denotes a mandate from the people to the (representative) government, particularly when direct democracy by the people is impossible. V. O. Key related the fundamental political function of public opinion with democratic ideology and the practical necessity that governments obtain support by (influential actors in) society. Key defined public opinion as the ethical imperative that government must heed. In contrast, to the conservative stream, from Edmund Burke to Walter Lippmann, heeding public opinion meant the tyranny of majority opinion in the first place. Since political leaders should be responsible to the true and general public interest rather than to any particularistic interest, which they are able to discern because of their expert knowledge, the government should not follow the dictates of the public.

The differences that will be discussed as the Lippmann-Dewey controversy are primarily related to their understanding of democracy and attitudes toward popular participation in politics. Dewey considered an actively involved public an essential element of democracy. If as many as possible individuals present as many as possible different ideas and facts, and discuss them with arguments, the probability increases that a collectivity will rationally decide. Lippmann's objection to this ideal was based on the belief that it is better to leave decision making to selected best-qualified individuals, who should decide without people's participation; the role of public opinion should only be that of observers. Their controversy about the nature of public opinion, which was related to the fundamental questions of democratic theory, significantly (certainly much more than Tönnies's theory) influenced much of later theoretical discourse on public opinion, but both Dewey's and Lippmann's ideas and thus public opinion theory in general were finally shoved aside by the triumphant rise of public opinion polling.

The controversy between John Dewey and Walter Lippmann visibly marked conceptualizations of public opinion of the time, although their contributions are less innovative than Tönnies's elaborated theory of public opinion, which remained in the shadow of his own more observable sociological treatises and, particularly other primarily American sociological and social psychological de-bates. Dewey's and Lippmann's theories are closely connected with their gen-eral interest in social issues and, primarily, conceptualizations of democratic progress. Dewey and particularly Lippmann devoted much more attention to critical considerations of the underlying normative-political questions con-cerning public opinion than their European contemporary Tönnies. A much wider responsiveness of Dewey's and Lippmann's theories may be related to at least three favorable historical circumstances. Neither Dewey nor Lippmann was a lone rider, as Tönnies was; rather, they represented continuities in two significant historical currents of American pragmatism and long lasting liberal doubt about the virtues of public opinion, perhaps most markedly expressed in J. S. Mill's *On Liberty* (1859). They published their contributions in a time of rapidly growing interest in public opinion incited by the development of (straw) polls. It was also the period of the first steps toward the academic insti-tutionalization of communication research in the United States, although com-munication research, when finally institutionalized, did not follow Lippmann's, and even less Dewey's, ideas. Neither of them was ranked by Schramm (1997) among the forefathers of the forefathers of communication studies in the United States, along with Cooley, Park, and Sapir. Apparently, in the develop-ment dominated by behavioral sciences, Dewey was "the path not taken by American mass communication research" (Peters 1989, 201). If Dewey did not significantly influence further development of academic communication the-ory and research, it seems that Schramm's exclusion of Lippmann is less justi-fied: Carey (1982) argues that Lippmann's work denotes the foundation of American media studies and, as Lasch (1995, 85) suggests, his books on the press and public opinion published in the 1920s "provided a founding charter for modern journalism [and] standards by which the press is still judged."

Controversies over value and function of public opinion for democratic po-litical processes are as old as the idea of public opinion itself, and they represent an enduring issue in theorizing public opinion and democratic government. The notion of public opinion is closely related to both participatory and rep-resentative democracy. Representative government (democracy) was created from above; from the very beginning it was not a means of a direct reproduc-tion of majority opinions and decisions. It was rather an attempt to secure gov-ernment from any simple majority: as Burke insisted, the representative had to be accountable to his or her conscience rather than loyal to his or her con-stituents. Representative democracy excludes "the people" from direct influence on national power. At the same time, it ensures that citizens give their consent, loyalty, and obedience (even under the threat of their exclusion), which legit-imize the government. If direct democracy is the ideal model of democracy, then representative democracy seems to be a form of "antidemocracy" because of its elitist roots. But once recognized and supported as a form of government, people can identify with and feel themselves to be represented by exactly those who exclude them from direct influence. Although it may be true that (due to insurmountable difficulties in the implementation of direct democracy) the idea of representation saved democracy as the guiding ideology of the modern state, it is also true that the implementation of the representative principle caused a great many citizens to become (structurally) excluded from participation in day-to-day decision making. The question of structural exclusion is particularly important because it is in the core of the formation of the bourgeois public sphere.

Lippmann ([1922] 1960, 31) emphasized as a fundamental problem of democracy "that democracy in its original form never seriously faced the problem which arises because the picture inside people's heads [their public opinions] do not automatically correspond with the world outside." Controversial questions should be decided by experts who have access to reliable information and thus, according to Lippmann, they are not mislead by "stereotypes" that commonly rule public debates. In contrast, ordinary citizens are not competent enough (and even not interested enough) to govern themselves. To make democracy workable, there is no need for the people to be directly involved in the process of government; rather, they are willing to leave government to experts as long as (1) democratic rules are legally sanctioned and (2) the experts provide citizens with goods and services they aspire after. Dewey's understanding of the fundamental problems of democracy and public opinion very much differs from Lippmann's judgment.[1] Unlike Lippmann, and in congruence with his own epistemological orientation toward the future and possible actions to achieve it,[2] Dewey insisted on the fundamental importance of citizens' education and their participation in deliberation and decision making for any democratic system—not for the sake of its efficiency but for reasons similar to Kant's conceptualization of the principle of publicity as a means to achieve individuals' independent reasoning and social justice. In other words, Dewey pleaded for a genuine participatory democracy "not as the most efficient but as the most educational form of government" (Lasch 1995, 89), in contrast to Lippmann, who was primarily interested in the internal economy of the public.

Lippmann and Dewey are close to Tönnies in their enchantment with the fascinating scientific and technological progress, confidence in the development of social sciences following the example of natural sciences, firm belief in the use of knowledge for the benefit of humanity, and scientific-utopian conceptions of societal progress. Yet beyond these commonalities, they differ substantially. On the surface, the differences could be seen already in their conceptualizations of future societies—Tönnies's as the "people's" or "new community," Dewey's as the Great Community, and Lippmann as a negative utopia, the "phantom public." However, the differences go much deeper and pertain both to the general understanding of the nature of society and specific questions about the role of public opinion in (democratic) society. It is these differences that are prevailing in the controversy between Lippmann and Dewey.

In the 1920s, when Lippmann and Dewey published their major works on public opinion, the differences between them did not represent a novelty; rather, they could be denoted as the key problems of democratic theory in general that have marked discussions on public opinion ever since the Enlightenment. Lippmann and Dewey argued for opposing alternatives when, in the theorizations of democracy and public opinion, they chose between (1) a large-scale dissemination of information versus face-to-face dialogue, (2) self-discipline and even self-sacrifice of citizens versus personal fulfillment and self-satisfaction; (3) a pure rationality of politics versus its connectedness with people's attachment and affection; (4) strict scientific realism in democratic discourse versus the inclusion of forms of art and culture; and (5) the disappearance of the substance of participatory democracy versus the attempt to reconstruct its practical foundations (Peters 1997a). The first set of alternatives contained in the preceding dichotomies would be selected by Lippmann and the second by Dewey. Dewey was a fervent advocate of "new liberalism" and a zealous critic of individualism. He rejected the reduction of human freedom to a negatively defined freedom (freedom from) and emphasized the substantiality of positive freedom (freedom for), which enables the self-realization of the individual in cooperation with others. Lippmann blamed liberals for misunderstanding the nature of the public to which they appealed; in his view, liberalism was a revolutionary theory that defended and liberated the underdog but lacked the ability to guide him when he was free. Lippmann particularly blamed liberalism for the attempt to eliminate entirely the individual hero when emphasizing the equality of all citizens.

Lippmann and Dewey most explicitly disagree when the substance of democratic ideas is at stake. Their opposing choices relate to the fundamental question posed in theories of democracy and public opinion theories—the question of citizen participation in public and political life. Is it more likely that a group will decide rationally if as many individuals as possible present as many different ideas and facts as possible, and discuss them? Or it is more rational to leave the task of decision making to a rather small group of best-educated and qualified experts, excluding the population at large? By orthodox definitions, an actively involved public (or population or *demos*) is considered an essential element of democracy. Without participation of the public in the political process, democracy lacks its legitimacy. "The development of the means of political participation becomes in effect the keystone in the history of the public," Wilson (1962, 84) argues. Participation in public opinion process is, as Lemert defines it, the act of expressing issue-related attitudes, either by voting[3] in the election framework or by a great variety of acts in the influence framework (Lemert 1981, 19–20). For Dewey, democracy could not exist without participation, and conversation is fundamental to participation. It appears to be congruent with the general principles of democracy that every individual, every group, every organization, and so on, has the right and possibility to express opinions, to make them visible to decision makers who ought to pay heed to them when making decisions. Yet at the same time, it is also clear that such unlimited participation scarcely exists; besides, that many individuals and groups do not care even if such a possibility does exist, and they do not participate even in the most rudimentary forms of democratic procedures (for example, they abstain from parliamentary elections). Thus, taking the opportunity to participate does not necessarily correlate with the rationality of decision making. These findings would lead Lippmann to conclude that the rule of well-qualified minority is simply a necessity and in the best interest of citizens. For Dewey, however, such a judgment would imply a complete demission to democracy.

Marx's famous sentence, what I cannot be for the others, I am not, and I cannot be, for myself ([1842] 1974, 73), speaks of participation in collective life as the determining factor of the individual's identity. Participation is also determinative for the relationship among individuals in a group, community, and society. This is not limited to political participation in the sense of raising citizen initiatives and individual participation in the processes of political decision making, for example, public expressions of opinion and participation in voting and elections. Although political dimensions of participation are most widely seen and most often discussed, participation extends deeper into the existence of human beings and beyond politics: *Through participation the individual enters from privacy into the publicness.*

Yet participation in group interactions and organizational communication always gives rise to individual resistance to group pressures. The involvement of the individual in group interactions not only stimulates the mobilization of his or her abilities and talents but also limits his or her sovereignty because it forces the subordination to group norms, in extreme cases even the dead loss of any individuality, and consequently leads to passiveness. The passiveness (of the majority) may well relieve the process of decision making (by the minority), but the price to be paid is high: the loss of social energy and free initiative of individuals, which in the long run makes devastating effects in all domains from politics to economy. There is no need for laboratory experiments to prove these effects; one need only consider the consequences of a range of totalitarian systems and systems of limited democracy in the twentieth century that trod down all fundamental human rights and freedoms. Thus, as Moscovici and Doise emphasize, "Participation has plainly only meaning if the *plurality* of group members is respected, and *freedom* of *action* and *speech* are guaranteed" (1994, 50; emphasis added). In short, be it participation in the domain of politics or in any group situation, it makes sense only if it is grounded on freedom and equality of individuals.

Since the Enlightenment onward, the concept of a political active public as the generator of public opinion implies at least a vague idea of its participation in decision making (even if only in specific phases or only as a critical observer) or some definite relationship between the insiders actually making decisions and outsiders without such endowment. It is a never ending controversy as to how to regulate the relationship between the opinion of the public and institutional decision making, or else to "realize opinion in action," as C. W. Mills put it. The problem of a "political organization of the public," as defined by Dewey, also gives rise to a number of questions related to the role of other actors involved in decision making—political parties, pressure groups, lobbies, legislative, executive and judicial institutions, economic corporations, and the media—and, more generally, the relationship between (decision-making) elites and the masses, which is the beloved subject of Lippmann's writing.

DEWEY'S CONCEPTION OF "THE PUBLIC" AS THE SITE OF EDUCATION, SOCIAL INQUIRY, AND PUBLIC DELIBERATION

Dewey's conceptualization of public opinion is the most representative case of a substantive public opinion theory; even more, his theory is primarily about *The Public and Its Problems*, i.e., the subject or creator of public opinion rather than the process of opining. Dewey defines the public as *a large body of persons having a common interest in controlling the consequences of social transactions* ([1927] 1991, 137, 126) and relates it (in contrast to the long tradition of normative theory) directly to the state.[4] The conceptualization of public is derived from Dewey's differentiation between the private and the public. He defines as public those human actions that affect others who are not directly involved in the action, provided that these consequences are recognized and some efforts are made to regulate them. In contrast to public transactions, the private ones only have consequences for those directly participating. The fundamental distinction between public and private may help explain the essence of distinguishing between private houses and public buildings, private and public schools, private paths and public roads, private property and public funds, or private persons and public officials.[5] The public thus consists of "all those who are affected by the indirect consequences of transactions to such an extent that it is deemed necessary to have those consequences systematically cared for" (pp. 15–16).[6] Like other pragmatists, Dewey ascribes the increase in indirect consequences to the rapid industrialization and urbanization of the United States, typical of the machine age. At the same time, the formation of the public includes a moment of subjectivity: the consequences have to be recognized and some effort must be made to control them. The recognition of consequences together with actions to regulate them lead to "something having the traits of a state" (p. 12), which is another mark of Dewey's peculiar conceptualization of the transformation of the public into a state:

> The lasting, extensive and serious consequences of associated activity bring into existence a public. In itself it is unorganized and formless. By means of officials and their special powers it becomes a state. A public articulated and operating through representative officers is the state; there is no state without a government, but also there is none without the public. (Dewey [1927] 1991, 67)

The difference between private and public is not equivalent to the difference between individual and social (which actually means socially good to Dewey). Many private actions are social because their outcomes contribute to the welfare of community; essentially, any transaction between two individuals is social by its very nature. A case in point is economic activity: a private business serves the community because it meets the needs of many individuals. Nor can public be considered equal to socially useful. As an action is not asocial just because it is private, its social usefulness is not warranted by the fact that "behavior is carried on in the name of the public by public agents" (p. 15).[7] As Dewey states, the most recurrent actions performed by "politically organized communities" (i.e., the states) were wars, and there can be no doubt about their damaging consequences. In fact, every public discussion is engaged in the issue of whether a public action is socially useful or detrimental in the first place.

The state is, according to Dewey, the politically organized public: The public becomes "the Populus" by means of officials and material agencies to care for the extensive and enduring indirect consequences of transactions between persons (p. 16). The public and the government together constitute the state. Since the public is not constituted by physically present individuals, it can only organize itself when "deep issues or those which can be made to appear such" exist (p. 140) because they delineate a common denominator among all the shifting and unstable relationships. The "deepness" of issues is related to the "attachment" and not merely to the affections they may provoke; without abiding attachments associational forms would be too shaky and could not assure the self-identification of the public.

Dewey's idea of the public politically organized into the state may be contrasted with the dominant theories of public opinion of the time, including Dewey's contemporaries Tönnies and Lippmann, which from the outset regarded public opinion as being opposite to the government (although constantly in relation to it) and emphasized the existence of the public as the subject of public opinion critical to government. Dewey, in contrast to both Tönnies and Lippmann, considered the connection between the state and society the fundamental condition for the existence of the public, rather than a threat to its existence. According to Dewey, the regulations and laws of the state are not commands; rather, they "formulate remote and long-run consequences" that help to channel human action. In other words, the public confines actions within prescribed limits that make their consequences more predictable. No individual could take into account all possible consequences of his or her actions; he or she must focus attention on the most important issues: "Any one who looked too far abroad with regard to the outcome of what he is proposing to do would, if there were no general rules in existence, soon be lost in a hopelessly complicated muddle of considerations" (p. 52). Dewey's conceptualization of the role of laws substantially differs from Tönnies's comprehension of how the state (legislation) relates to public opinion. For Dewey, law is a means in the hand of the public that makes consequences of a transaction more predictable, whereas for Tönnies it is an order that must be obeyed. Dewey locates the public, together with its political organization (the state) in the sphere of politics, whereas Tönnies strictly delineates legislation as a form of social will that belongs to the sphere of politics from the opinion of the public, whose judgments always refer to the ethical and aesthetic domain of collective life.

Although Tönnies's theory also proceeds from the difference between community life and a (large) public, the problem of participation, and influence on the political process, his solution is quite different, since he considers the political state opposite to public opinion. Opinion of the public is not expressed by a spatially gathered public but only by an imagined or virtual public. This is why the press plays, as Tönnies suggests, an important role—not only because it delivers information to the public and thus is an important element in the process of public opinion formation but also because it represents the main "expression means" of the public and thus constitutes the virtual public. Here Tönnies is in complete agreement with Dewey, who considers the press in modern society functionally equivalent to genuine interpersonal discussions in a small community, recreated on a larger scale. Similarly to Tönnies, who located public opinion in modern large cities as a manifestation of Gesellschaft (in contrast to traditional rural environments representing Gemeinschaft), Dewey claims that a public could not develop in primary groups, that is, in community life. The basic definition of the public proceeds from the fact that

> all modes of associated behavior may have extensive and enduring consequences which involve others beyond those directly engaged in them. When these consequences are in turn realized in thought and sentiment, recognition of them reacts to remake the conditions out of which they arose. . . . This supervision and regulation cannot be effected by the primary groupings themselves. For the essence of the consequences which call a public into being is the fact that they expand beyond those directly engaged in producing them. (Dewey [1927] 1991, 27)

Yet Dewey concludes, contrary to Tönnies, that a public must also be formally organized to be actually effective. The formal organization of the public is the political state based on the principle of representation, with the government consisting of officers and agencies with special duties and authorizations to act on behalf of the interests of the public.

Dewey's conceptualization of public/ness is close to Kant's transcendental principle of publicity: they both ascribe to publicity a propaedeutic character. As Dewey writes, "There can be no public without full publicity in respect to all consequences which concern it. Whatever obstructs and restricts publicity, limits and distorts public opinion and checks and distorts thinking on social affairs" (p. 167). As we have seen, according to Kant, publicity harmonizes the relationship between politics and morals because it guarantees legal order and justice, and it has an enlightened role for the people. This view is clearly congruent with Dewey's trust in state actions to care for indirect consequences of transactions in which individuals do not participate directly, although his theory substantiates the relativity of the states, in contrast to idealistic (e.g., Kant's and Hegel's) theories that attribute to the state the absoluteness. The reason for Dewey's theoretical position can also be looked for in the specific historical conditions of the United States that substantially differed from those in Europe. In Europe society has been polarized by class struggles, and the bourgeois public has not universalized itself by the incorporation of nonbourgeois classes but rather publicity has become refeudalized. In the United States, by contrast, during the time of pragmatism (i.e., before the Great Depression) there grew up the (utopian) idea of the development of Great Society and, in Dewey's conception, Great Community that ought to be based on the participation of everyone. The state in the United States did not have the tradition of repression (with the exception of the foreign British crown) that was typical for Europe, where the ideas of public/ness, press freedom, and public opinion had largely been directed against the (absolutist) state ever since the Enlightenment.

Forms of political organization of the public vary extremely; the only thing they actually have in common is "the function of caring for and regulating the interests which accrue as the result of the complex indirect expansion and radiation of conjoint behavior" (p. 47). Dewey's pragmatic understanding of general will counters Rousseau's idealization of general will, which he denotes as "a dogma of mystic and transcendent absolute will." The public is constituted as the public and forms the general will because of general and durable (indirect) consequences of human actions, and perception of such consequences. The recognition of the extent and scope of these consequences stimulates the rise of a common interest and a need to create and employ specific means to regulate transactions and their consequences—a need for political organization of the public or political state. As human actions and forms of control change over time and differ in space, so does the public with its political institutions. Dewey discusses four specific dimensions of political organization of the public, or four arguments for the hypothesis for the relativity of states.

First, the *temporal and local diversification of political organization.* Dewey argues for the (nation-) state as the most appropriate modern political form that makes possible the establishment of agencies responsible for the regulation of indirect and lasting consequences of human transactions. However, this does not mean that any form of the state in whichever historical period represents the best possible form of political organization of the public. History clearly reveals that diversity rather than uniformity of political forms is the rule, which demonstrates that the nature of consequences and the ability to perceive them and act upon them varies with time and space. "In no two ages or places is there the same public. Conditions make the consequences of associated action and the knowledge of them different. In addition the means by which a public can determine the government to serve its interests vary" (Dewey [1927] 1991, 88).

Second, *dependence of the public on the quantitative scope of results of collective behavior.* Transactions may have no indirect consequences for nonparticipants at the beginning, but in the course of time such consequences may appear. In other words, a process of transition from the private to the public takes place. Such changes can typically be observed in the development of law, which covers different spheres of human actions: in the course of time, different types of transactions became subject to legal regulations. Similar is the case of economy, in which modes of private business become "affected with a public interest" because of quantitative expansion. Opposite is the case of religion in democratic societies: when the consequences of irreligion became irrelevant for the broader community, religion was relegated from the public to the private domain. In short, the broader the domain of consequences, the more state regulation is needed; with the changes in the extent of consequences, the nature of regulation would also change.

Third, *the state is concerned with modes of behavior that are relatively old, well established, highly standardized, and uniform.* In contrast, discoveries and novelties are always a matter of personal, individual, and (in Dewey's sense) private initiative. For his own historical period Dewey believed that "innovation itself has become a custom." Yet throughout history, innovation was more often accompanied by resistance and doubts that considered innovation primarily an interruption of the "natural course" of things, rather than by general approval. It is certainly not possible to imagine innovations and discoveries as resulting from state actions—with one obvious exception: the state always stimulated innovations in the production of arms. Generally, however, "(a) measure of goodness of a state is the degree in which it relieves individuals from the waste of negative struggle and needless conflict and confers upon him positive assurance and reinforcement in what he undertakes" (p. 72). The most one can (and should) expect from the state is its lowest possible intervention into the production of private individuals, for this makes possible the development of new ideas. For Dewey, *the creation of new ideas is typically a private enterprise.* He based this hypothesis on his basically conservative attitude that "it is absurd to expect the public . . . to rise *above the intellectual level of its average constituents*" (Dewey [1927] 1991, 60; emphasis added), which actually conflicts with his general trust in collective actions.

Fourth, *each individual community member should have an equal share in the consequences of associated actions.* Equality does not mean that all individuals (should) have the same qualities, but rather that their distinctive needs and interests should be effectively regarded, irrespective of physical and psychological inequalities, and not sacrificed to the superior interests of others. The public must care for and (through the state) legally regulate the conditions of transactions between individuals when it becomes obvious that status inequalities of participants (may) cause a permanent, irreparable infliction of interests among the (groups of) individuals with lower status. Thus the state assumed responsibility for the education of children, although children are primarily in the care of family. Similarly, public regulation deals with safety and health care, and minimum wages.

All these cases indicate that the public intervenes by its political organization when transactions between individuals and groups begin to produce important consequences for those not directly involved. Obviously, not all individuals can actively participate in all transactions with social consequences. Therefore, as Dewey argues, it is even more important that individuals have access to different forms of control and regulation of indirect consequences. Only through co-operation with others can the individual achieve self-realization, and different forms of self-realization make up his or her individual ego. "Liberty is that secure release and fulfillment of personal potentialities which take place only in rich and manifold association with others" (1925, 150); if liberty would imply a complete independence of all social bounds, it would come to social disorganization and anarchy. To avoid such an undesirable development, Dewey pleads for the equality of citizens in the process of (public) opinion[8] formation, in contrast to the then prevalent belief that "the majority is permanently incapable of self-government," as Lippmann (1925, 19) suggested with a citation from Robert Michels's *Political Parties*.

Dewey ([1927] 1991, 157) endorses two fundamental constituents of the classic theory of democracy: (1) that each individual is personally equipped with the intelligence needed to participate in political affairs (what Lippmann called the erroneous idea of the omnicompetent individual) and (2) that general suffrage, frequent elections of officials, and majority rule reliably secure the accountability of elected officers. Although he disagrees with Lippmann in many respects, he agrees that the idea of the omnicompetent individual involves an illusion, which could also make doubtful the second assumption. Dewey admits that the kind of knowledge needed for a public to organize itself democratically does not yet exist. He warns against a too submissive endorsement of public opinion that is not based on knowledge provided by continous social research. Dewey is skeptical about public opinion, for opinion may often be wrong because of the lack of knowledge; those who have something at stake in having a lie believed, and who manipulate with "public" opinion, trade on the ignorance of public opinion. Opinion formed in this way can be public only in name, not in its substance, but calling it by this name increases the chance to lead action in the wrong direction. Thus Dewey pleads for an increase in what we would call predictive use value of information: if accurate and reliable information is acquired in time, which presupposes a systematic and well-organized social inquiry, even (public) opinion may become objectively more certain, if we borrow Kant's term. Yet, like Tönnies (and in contrast to Lippmann), Dewey emphasizes that public opinion cannot be reduced to knowledge because it also involves judgments, evaluations, and anticipations, which, even if informed by knowledge, are subjected to various interests and thus contingencies and errors.

Dewey's notion of democracy denotes neither the liberal democracy of free press and elections nor the representative democracy of delegation to officials. He does not reduce people's government to government for the people; rather, he treats it in a more direct sense of participation in government that is a form of human self-realization. With his understanding of democracy as the chance for each person to achieve "fullness of integrated personality" in a community of others, Dewey is close to the most radical visions of participatory democracy. His solution to the controversy on the nature of democratic government differs from that of Lippmann, who, as a neo-Platonian, trusted in the impartiality of expert intellectuals. In contrast to Lippmann's idea of an *independent* "intelligence bureau," Dewey sees only two kinds of *dependence:* Intellectuals can only rule as a means in the hands of capital; otherwise, they have to affiliate themselves with the masses and help them to participate in power.

> If the masses are as intellectually irredeemable as its premise implies, they at all events have both too many desires and too much power to permit rule by experts to obtain. The very ignorance, bias, frivolity, jealousy, instability, which are alleged to incapacitate them from share in political affairs, unfit them still more for passive submission to rule by intellectuals. (Dewey [1927] 1991, 205)

Dewey finds an even more important argument against the ideas of independent intellectuals in the fact that an expertness can be achieved in matters of technology, provided that a general direction of action is determined in society, but certainly not in the social sciences. He objects to an a priori assumption that experts are "wise and benevolent" and that they serve the interests of society. On the contrary, Dewey argues, to the degree that experts become a specialized class, they become alienated from those whose interests they are supposed to enforce—either a class with its own private interests or a tool of big economic interests.

Even the most rudimentary forms of political democracy (e.g., general elections and the principle of majority rule) at least to some degree enable and involve consultation and discussion that reveal social needs and problems. Despite his vehement critique of the tyranny of majority, even Tocqueville had to admit that popular government is educative whereas other forms of political regulation are not, and that it stimulates the recognition of common interests. In an allusion to Lippmann's argument that elections are nothing but a civilized version of war ("a ballot is a substitute for a bullet" [Lippmann 1925, 59]), Dewey claims that although bullets actually can be a substitute for ballots, one should not forget that before any democratic elections, discussions, deliberations and persuasion take place. Majority rule as one of the fundamental democratic norms is not an aim in itself; its meaning can only come true in the specific discursive way in which the majority is established. It is not the rule of majority itself that is contestable; rather, the rule may seem questionable because methods of majority formation are not properly developed.

The main threat to democracy is represented by the tendency of politics to become just another business, and the most important problem of the public is how to emancipate itself from such political domination. This is the essence of Dewey's idea of the "eclipse of the public." In contrast to Lippmann, who did not see any realistic possibility that the Great Society could become the Great Community, Dewey believed that this was indeed possible, even though the Great Community could never represent a copy of local community, and he devoted himself to the search for conditions under which the transformation would be conceivable. "Till the Great Society is converted into a Great Community, the Public will remain in eclipse. *Communication can alone create a great community.* Our Babel is not one of tongues but of signs and symbols without which shared experience is impossible" (p. 142; emphasis added). Dewey was specifically thinking of the reconstruction of interpersonal communication; even the media he considered a kind of extension of interpersonal communication and (in contrast to Tönnies and particularly Lippmann) he was not occupied with the specificities of the press and its reforms. Dewey's enchantment with community can be traced back to the origin of the United States, when it was considered the basis of all American government. As Bryce ([1887] 1995, 1553) stated, "It is here [in the "commune"] that the bulk of the work of administration is done, here that the citizens learn how to use and love freedom, here that the wonderful activity they display in public affairs finds its chief sphere and its constant stimulus."

Dewey's conceptualization of the nature and social meaning of communication resumes the thought expressed by Marx in *Periods of Economic Formation of Society.* Marx emphasized the fundamental difference between the primary conditions of production as natural existential conditions of the producer, which do not result from human production, and language, which is a self-evident form of the existence of community. Thus the individual's relation to his or her language is directly determined by his or her membership in community (i.e., the relation of a "natural" member of human community), but at the same time it is also a product of community (see Splichal 1981, 87–88). The development and division of labor made the existence of language and the ability to speak insufficient for an individual's participation in various activities. Dewey ([1927] 1991, 154) resumes this idea: "We are born organic beings associated with others, but we are not born members of a community.[9] . . . Everything which is distinctly human is *learned, not native.* . . . To learn to be human is to develop through the *give-and-take communication* an effective sense of being an individually distinctive member of a community" (emphasis added).

The only way out from the eclipse of the public is, as Dewey believes, to cease treating the individual as a spatially and intellectually isolated unit, since "singular things act, but they act together" ([1927] 1991, 22). The doctrine of individualism that demands a minimum interference in the sphere of economy has had a progressive character in the nascent stage, but in the industrial society it became an intellectual bastion of reactionary interests. At the beginning, being "liberal" denoted political progressiveness and the advocacy of liberation from authoritarian power, but the new liberal parties became conservative inasmuch as they represented and defended the ruling financial and commercial interests against governmental regulation. "The irony of the history is nowhere more evident than in the reversal of the practical meaning of the term 'liberalism' in spite of a literal continuity of theory" (p. 134). The reversal is obvious when issues of freedom of thought, communication, and intellectual freedom are discussed: in contrast to liberal doctrine, they cannot become true merely through the abolition of all legal restrictions put on the individual's actions. The abolition of formal or legal restraints is only the negative condition to be fulfilled, but positive freedom also requires methods and instruments for the control of general social conditions that have long-term consequences for the individual's life, and not only those by which she or he is directly affected.

The most important conditions that limit free communication and circulation of facts and ideas are, according to Dewey, "emotional habituations and intellectual habitudes on the part of the mass of men [which] create the conditions of which the exploiters of sentiment and opinion only take advantage," for example, an almost religious idealization of state institutions, particularly those connected with the nationalistic state, and the general backwardness of social (in contrast to technical) knowledge ([1927] 1991, 169). These limitations are more serious than those imposed by "overt obstructive forces" that manipulate social relations, for example, publicity agents. For Dewey, the first condition of a positive freedom is the development of knowledge and science, which ought to become accessible to everyone in the most appropriate way. The public can be democratically organized only if three conditions are fulfilled: (1) public education, (2) freedom of social inquiry and of distribution of its outcomes, and (3) a complete publicity in respect to all issues concerning the public and freedom of expression. The first key to the question of the public and its problems lies in the spread, acquisition, and use of knowledge; and the next in the interpersonal communication in local community. The development of science and knowledge ought to enable a scientific control and regulation of societies that constantly grow in complexity; at the same time, the development of interpersonal communication ought to breathe a spirit of local community and human contiguity into the scientifically managed society. In contrast to Lippmann's (at that time dominant) belief that human knowledge develops in isolated contacts of subjects (preferably scientific observers) with objects, as a copy of reality existing independently of the observer, Dewey argued that knowledge is primarily a function of association and communication rather than individual talents, intelligence, and character. Inequality and inferiority complexes are socially acquired. "The notion that intelligence is a personal endowment or personal attainment is the great conceit of the intellectual class, as that of the commercial class is that wealth is something which they personally have wrought and possess" (p. 211). Intelligence is public rather than private because it is a consequence of possibilities of reasoning and communicating provided by a community. Even if intelligence were native, which was doubtful to Dewey, the actuality of mind or "effective intelligence" depends on the education that social conditions induce (p. 209).

In principle at least, Dewey would agree with Lippmann ([1922] 1960, 408) that generally "education is the supreme remedy" but he would add that democracy demands "a more thoroughgoing education than the education of officials, administrators and directors of industry" that Lippmann had in mind (Dewey 1922, 288). Knowledge implies both communication and understanding. Knowledge of social phenomena particularly depends upon its distribution because (1) this is the only way to obtain and to test it and (2) it equals the formation of public opinion (Dewey [1927] 1991, 177). Since, according to Dewey, public opinion is judgment formed and expressed by the public, and the public is constituted by a large number of individuals and groups who have a common interest in controlling the consequences of social transactions, then the public and public opinion can only come into existence if facts and ideas are effectively disseminated. Systematic social inquiry is only the first step in the formation of knowledge, which has to be followed by the spread of its results through the press to stimulate, and extend the scope of, dialogue. Only if the principle of publicity is enacted, and freedom of expression assured, can the press perform this function. The actual importance of Dewey's claims is perhaps best seen if they are applied to circumstances in formerly socialist countries that heavily restricted freedoms of social inquiry and public expression in the first place.

In contrast to social inquiry, which is a matter of scientific merit, dissemination and presentation of news is considered by Dewey a question of art. "The *freeing of the artist in literary presentation* . . . is as much a precondition of the desirable creation of adequate opinion on public matters as is the *freeing of social inquiry*" (p. 183, emphasis added).[10] By "adequate" Dewey certainly does not mean correct or objectively certain opinion; adequate opinions still imply differences of judgment, but they should not be formed in the absence of evidence. Clearly, Dewey realized that a scientific presentation could not attract the attention of and stimulate action from members of the public, with the

exception of a few intellectuals, but he did not consider the possibility that social inquiry could be as partial as publications or experts who, by Dewey's definition, can never act autonomously.[11]

Dewey considered communication, and particularly interpersonal communication, exceptionally important for the constitution of the public; he believed
that the development of new forms of communication would solve all the problems of dislocated public life, which would then bring an end to the eclipse of
the public. He emphasized the fundamental significance and necessity of a reaffirmation and development of interpersonal communication and understanding, which the industrial revolution brought to a standstill. He believed that the
Great Community would bring about free and full intercommunication, although it still would not possess all the qualities characteristic of a local community and would remain a sort of local metacommunity: its role is "in ordering the relations and enriching the experience of local associations" (p. 211) and
thus preventing the isolation of local communities. The press may help to develop the public with transmission of knowledge, but publications are always
partial—as public opinion would be if social intelligence were not distributed
by word of mouth. Transterritorial and functional (e.g., occupational) associations do not present an alternative solution because nothing could substitute
for the vitality and depth of face-to-face communication and dialogue: democracy must begin at home, in local community, Dewey was convinced, but he
did not define the ways to revitalize (institutionally or otherwise) public discussion in local settings. He simply believed that the press should resume the
oral tradition of interpersonal communication and develop as an almost linear
extrapolation of the town meeting.

BETWEEN "FACTS" AND "STEREOTYPES": LIPPMANN'S CRITIQUE OF THE PHANTOM PUBLIC

Tönnies summed up his extensive and generally very favorable review of Lippmann's book *Public Opinion* (1922) in a critical conclusion that Lippmann missed
emphasizing "the great historical power of opinion of the public, its relationship
to the dominant religion as public belief." Tönnies explained this deficit by suggesting that Lippmann was not much interested in theoretical issues but rather
limited his discussion to the present-day United States (Tönnies 1927, 10**). Indeed, as a professional journalist, Lippmann came as an "outsider" (the term he
used in his conceptualization of public opinion) into the domain of social theory,
but the appearance of his *Public Opinion* in 1922 demonstrated, as Schramm
(1997, 110) put it, "that some journalists were thinking like scholars." Lippmann's

discussion of public opinion fundamentally differs from Tönnies's theory, although the two approaches are not without commonalities (which Tönnies enthusiastically emphasized in his review of Lippmann's book);[12] it shares with Dewey the orientation toward the same "empirical present time" but strongly differs from it in the interpretation of the empirical world, although Dewey's position does not always contradict Lippmann so much as it may seem at first glance.

In contrast to Dewey, who was a typical Aristotelian in his advocacy of public opinion as a political process in which all citizens could participate, Lippmann's position was similar in spirit to Plato's critique of the limitations of democracy: "The orthodox democrats answered Aristotle's question [how to make congruent individuals' limited political capacity with their complex environment] by assuming that a limitless political capacity resides in public opinion. A century of experience compels us to deny this assumption" (Lippmann 1925, 79). Lippmann rejected the notion that the authority of the people could approach rational authority and attempted to prove that both the body politic and the citizenry itself would be better off if the business of politics were left to the experts. In *Public Opinion* ([1922] 1965, 18), he states that objective reality differs sharply from the "pictures in our heads [which] often mislead(s) men in their dealings with the world outside." He often reproached Dewey's liberalism for adopting, without any justification, the hypothesis that "there exists in the hearts of men knowledge of the world beyond their reach" (Lippmann [1922] 1960, 31). But this was not a sound objection against Dewey, who did not blindly trust human intelligence and knowledge. In contrast to Lippmann's rigid differentiation between "the world outside" and "the pictures inside people's heads," Dewey strongly emphasized their mutual inseparability, intertwinement, and mediation, since an active individual simultaneously creates the world outside and the pictures inside. According to Dewey, the greatest possible fallacy of social science, and actually the source of its potential transformation into a pseudoscience, would be the neglect of the fundamental distinction "between facts which are what they are independent of human desire and endeavor and facts which are to some extent what they are because of human interest and purpose" (Dewey [1927] 1991, 7)—a fundamental difference between physical science and social science. This ontological and epistemological difference clearly reflects the core of the controversy between Dewey and Lippmann. It also determines the differences between the two when they define the substance of public opinion and democracy, and look for solutions of practical problems. Whereas Dewey emphasized the importance of the plurality of communication forms originating from interpersonal communication, in which subjective and objective are inseparable, Lippmann believed in the reliability of scientific information about the objective world provided by independent experts.

Lippmann and Dewey diverged markedly regarding how to conceptualize the public as the subject of public opinion. Dewey defines it as a specific (large) body of persons that in itself is unorganized but may become articulated and organized with more elaborate methods of public communication (in the future) and through representative officers (i.e., the state). Lippmann, however, considers the public basically incompetent, external to the issues that are discussed, and dependent on experts—almost a mere phantom, as the title of his second book (1925) suggests. Lippmann does not define the public as an autonomous entity but as a correlative to the opinion, formed and expressed by expert individuals, which is frequently formed by anonymous, uneducated, passive observers. Unlike Tönnies's or Dewey's (large) public, Lippmann's public cannot be a singular phenomenon; there always exist many publics.[13] "The public is not . . . a fixed body of individuals. It is merely those persons who are interested in an affair and can affect it only by supporting or opposing actors" (Lippmann 1925, 77). Although Lippmann considers public opinion, according to its form, a judgment or opinion of the public (as conceptualized both by Dewey and Tönnies), he substantially redefined the nature of the public as its subject, and thus the substance of public opinion.

Whereas in Dewey's theorization the need to regulate the indirect consequences of transactions brings about the rise of the public, Lippmann puts his trust primarily in effective actions by those individuals who are directly affected by and concerned with an issue because "they initiate, they administer, they settle." The less they are disturbed by "ignorant and meddlesome outsiders" who constitute the public, the better they will settle the matter. Based on his insistence that the masses are ineffective in dealing with the unseen environment, Lippmann developed a theory that "economizes the attention of men as members of the public, and asks them to do as little as possible in matters where they can do nothing very well" (1925, 199). Whereas Dewey's public organizes itself—through representative officers—into the state, Lippmann claims that "the intricate business of framing laws and administering them through several hundred thousand public officials is in no sense the act of the voters nor a translation of their will" (1925, 71). Yet Lippmann's analysis failed to realize that the effectiveness of groups derives from the fact that their members participate and become increasingly involved in the solution of vital tasks. Accordingly, "the masses are ineffective" primarily because they do not have the opportunity to participate, which was exactly Dewey's argument.

Lippmann's relation to the public is markedly ambivalent. On the one hand, he would agree with Dewey that the public develops "when people seek to *control the behavior of others,* if not by positive law than at least by persuasion" (Lippmann 1925, 55; emphasis added). In other words, when individuals take a position in respect to the purposes of others, they act as a public. On the other hand, unlike Dewey, he emphasizes that the interest of a public is restricted to two issues only: (1) that "there shall be rules, which means that the rules which prevail shall be enforced," and (2) that "unenforceable rules shall be changed according to a settled rule" (1925, 104)—which is eventually reduced to only one common interest, namely, that all special interests shall act according to the settled rule. Public opinion is not concerned with specific issues, issues that lack opposition and open criticism, or with unproblematic rules, contracts, and customs themselves, but with "the maintenance of a régime of rule, contract and custom," that is, with formal rules that ought to be obeyed by the actors in a controversy. It intervenes only when there is a crisis of maladjustment, when validity of rules becomes questionable, when an opposition appears that does not conform.[14] Yet public opinion can exist only when there is an open opposition, namely, in a democratic society: "When power, however absolute and unaccountable, reigns without provoking a crisis, public opinion does not challenge it. Somebody most challenge arbitrary force first. The public can only come to his assistance" (1925, 70). Without such an external stimulus, the public cannot act.

Like Dewey, Lippmann considers the growing indirectedness caused by the increase in "removed and long delayed consequences" and "the lengthening of the interval between conduct and experience, between cause and effect" (1925, 182) the dominant problem of the public. However, in contrast to Dewey, who emphasizes indirect consequences of human transactions as those that require regulation and thus bring the public into existence, Lippmann concludes that they prevent individuals from ascertaining the validity of their opinions and thus from influencing the course of events in the "world outside." Unlike Dewey, who grounded the need for regulation on the indirect consequences of human transactions, Lippmann related it to "conflicting purposes of men." As he argued, he did not look for the "identity of purpose" of all but rather for an accommodation of different purposes, for a modus vivendi of conflicting interests.

Differences between Lippmann's and Dewey's conceptualizations of the public also influence the differences between their concepts of public opinion. It is actually not possible to speak of differences in a strict sense because Dewey did not pay much attention specifically to public opinion (but rather to the organization and articulation of the public), whereas Lippmann in his critique of liberal democratic ideals focused on the concept of public opinion in which he hypostatized, as Tönnies remarked, "psychological reflexes." Lippmann constructed a dichotomous concept of public opinion that is based on the ontological difference between the world "outside the heads of human beings" and "the pictures inside their heads." Independently of human beings, according to

Lippmann, "features of the world" exist; if they somehow relate to human beings, they become public affairs. Individuals' perceptions of outside world, "of themselves, of others, of their needs, purposes, and relationship," constitute their public opinions. Finally, "Public Opinion" refers to those pictures upon which groups and their representatives act and confront.[15] Since people's direct access to the facts (public affairs) is hindered by a number of obstacles, they can only organize their thinking if they rely upon culturally and personally based stereotypes, which nonetheless often lead to blind spots, errors, and contradictions. Credit should certainly be given to Lippmann for introducing the concept of stereotype into the social sciences, which remains a topical subject to this day.[16] As "pictures in our heads," stereotypes are considered by Lippmann primarily as a cognitive phenomenon, but not without affective admixtures. Yet his preoccupation with the role of stereotypes in the formation of public opinions led Lippmann to an excessive division of human rational and affective abilities and actions.

Lippmann's answer to the question of "whether it is possible for men to find a way of acting effectively upon highly complex affairs by very simple means" (Lippmann 1925, 79) was uncompromising and clearly negative. He declared it a false ideal to imagine that the voters were inherently competent to direct public affairs. Rather, they are exposed to vague, emotion-engaging symbols produced by hierarchical authorities that generate public opinion. Hence, "if the voter cannot grasp the details of the problems of the day because he has not the time, the interest or the knowledge, he will not have a better public opinion because he is asked to express his opinion more often" (Lippmann 1925, 20, 36–37). Critical and much more pessimistic pictures of public opinion heightened interest in "the engineering of consent" by pressure groups, political parties, government and capital, and transformed public opinion into the target of professional manipulation, which was supposed to "crystallize" it.

> The orthodox theory holds that a public opinion constitutes a moral judgment on a group of facts. The theory I am suggesting is that, in the present state of education, a public opinion is primarily a *moralized and codified version of the facts*. I am arguing that the pattern of stereotypes at the center of our codes largely determines what group of facts we shall see, and in what light we shall see them. (Lippmann [1922] 1960, 125; emphasis added)

Whereas Dewey considers knowledge primarily a result of human symbolic interaction (because the individual is not believed to be in a position to satisfy the need of opinion validation alone; she or he has to consult other people who have their own specific observations and opinions), Lippmann sees its foundation in the identification of facts that exist in physical reality independently of human beings or social reality (as far as it does not constitute "the world outside" for an individual). For Dewey, there is no social reality that would not be communicative at the same time; for Lippmann, however, individuals are supposed to be dealing with reference to physical reality as "solipsistic reality" because they do not need any other person in order to identify it or to have "access to the facts." For Lippmann, then, the "outside" reality exists, which the individual alone is able to make correct judgments about in order to act—provided that she or he disposes of technical skills and expert knowledge. In that case, "the pictures in people's heads [would] correspond with the world outside" (p. 31). Yet, as Lippmann warns us, this can only be achieved by expert organizations or by insiders. Without expert knowledge, an individual can only "piece together" his or her opinion from "what others have reported and what [she or he] can imagine" (p. 79). Instead of persons, she or he can only see types—patterns, formulae, or stereotypes, which not only economize our efforts but also have the function of defending our position in society.

Since the formation of public opinions in the heads of ordinary people is characterized by the absence of rational efforts and subjection to emotions, Lippmann's main preoccupation is to find an antidote against propaganda that produces a massive consent. Public Opinion should be free of emotions because "at the end knowledge must come not from the conscience but from the environment with which that conscience deals. When men act on the principle of intelligence they go out to find the facts and to make their wisdom. When they ignore it, they go inside themselves and find only what is there—primarily prejudices which limit people's knowledge" ([1922] 1960, 397). The uncovering of facts is the task of science, which alone can induce the rationalization of public opinions, that is, supplement "personal representations" by a scientifically produced "representation of the unseen facts" (unseen, of course, for the majority of citizens but not for experts). The more an individual's emotions are excluded and methods of "uncovering facts" are developed, according to Lippmann, the easier public opinions would be formed. Lippmann allows no doubt about the claim that experts and scientists alone can rationalize public opinions because only they are capable of "generalization based on analysis" and of the invention of accurate instruments for the analysis. To make the model feasible, Lippmann adds that Public Opinion should be restricted to a few public issues.

Lippmann's unfounded absolutization of differences between "facts outside" and "pictures inside the heads" does not contribute to a clear definition of public opinion(s). Tönnies justifiably pointed to Lippmann's vague definition of public opinion because, according to Lippmann, both individuals and a/the public may have public opinions. On the one hand, public opinions are "the pictures of public affairs inside the heads"[17] of individuals ([1922] 1960, 29) and thus are only moralized and codified forms of objective facts existing independently of the human will. On the other hand, public opinions (in the plural again) are opinions of individuals "as to how others ought to behave" (1925, 55), that is, they imply or emphasize the volitive component of the individual's opinion. In addition, public opinion (Public Opinion) is opinion of the public. When Lippmann discusses the principles of public opinion, he refers to the "*public's* judgment," which implies the existence of the public. But the nature of Lippmann's public is itself ambiguous. Consequently, his concept of Public Opinion remains vague. It has a general meaning of "those pictures which are acted upon by groups of people, or by individuals acting in the name of groups" ([1922] 1960, 29). On the other hand, Public Opinion has a more specific meaning of an unexamined element in political theories, "a mystery made out of public opinion," which Lippmann identifies primarily in the democratic theories of the eighteenth century, or "a mystical force [to be created by the press] that will take up the slack in public institutions" ([1922] 1960, 254, 362).

Because of his radical distrust for the public's rational capacities and the reliability of public opinion, Lippmann severely limits the competencies of public opinion. Individuals have only limited access to information, their comprehension is controlled by stereotypes, the evidence is often illusionary, and simple time sequences are seen as being equivalent to the relationship between cause and effect ([1922] 1960, 154). These limitations on the rationality of public opinion substantially restrict its scope: "Executive action is not for the public. The public acts only by aligning itself as the partisan of some one in a position to act executively," is the first principle of public opinion ([1925, 144). The main function of discussion is not to provide the public with the truth about the controversy but, rather, to identify the "partisans" and "advocates" in order to enable the members of a public to take sides. The public actually does not express opinion but only aligns itself for or against a proposal. Consequently, the people cannot rule, nor can a democratic government be an expression of the people's will.[18] The people have neither the time and interest nor the knowledge necessary to understand problems about which decisions have to be made. Because of their limited knowledge, the majority of people are not able to see the difference between the truth and untruth or lie; thus they are forced to make decisions on the ground of their confidence in information sources. They are not able to identify controversial issues, propose alternative solutions to a problem, or make adherents. Only occasionally (but never all of them, or permanently) do they get mobilized by public issues, and they support or oppose the ruling individuals. "The public will arrive in the middle of the third act and will leave before the last curtain, having stayed just long enough perhaps to decide who is the hero and who the villain of the piece" (1925, 65). Lippmann criticizes "mystical democrats" because of their belief that the general will would become rational by public deliberation in which consensus on common interests is formed on the basis of arguments. Similarly, he claims, the voter would not have "a better public opinion" if he were asked to express opinion more often. In either case, as Lippmann argues similarly to Dewey ([1927] 1991, 609), the compounding of individual ignorances cannot produce a rational outcome:

> For what reason is there to think that subjecting so many more affairs to the method of the vote will reveal hitherto undiscovered wisdom and technical competence and reservoirs of public interest in men? The socialist scheme has at its root the mystical fallacy of democracy, that the people, all of them, are competent. (1925, 38)

The "false ideal of the omnicompetent citizen" would, according to Lippmann, further complicate political processes (that are already much too complicated) because it is not possible to act effectively upon highly complex affairs by very simple means that a public can use. Like Dewey, Lippmann is aware of the fact that citizens' nonparticipation in public life is mainly caused by their lack of knowledge about public affairs; but for Lippmann, the only way to solve this problem is to admit, in the first place, that citizens' capabilities and knowledge are limited because the members of the public do not, and never will, possess an insider's knowledge of events. They do not have opinions on all public affairs, and it would be absurd to expect that they will ever have.

The principle of publicity declared by the Enlightenment is not contestable to Lippmann; yet it is the idea that the purpose of the publication can possibly be to inform every citizen. Human information capacity is limited, and it does not allow that any individual would be informed about all public issues and would rationally form an opinion of or at least consent to it. The only solution to this problem is, according to Lippmann, to distinguish between specific and general opinions. This distinction is based on his second "principle of public opinion" claiming that "the intrinsic merits of a question are not for the public. The public intervenes from the outside upon the work of the insiders" (1925, 144). The two kinds of opinion are usually intervolved in practice, but this does not reduce the importance of the difference. Specific opinions give rise to immediate and concrete executive acts and decisions, whereas general opinions only express general will, which results essentially from "the use of symbols which assemble emotions after they have been detached from their ideas" (1925, 47). General opinions can be expressed only in general forms, for example, in elections, but they can never result in an executive action as do specific opinions. The public cannot start, direct, or administer any concrete actions; it can only accept or reject their outcomes, that is, clearly formulated alternatives. "The anticipation, the analysis and the solution of a question are not for the public. The public's judgment rests on a small sample of the facts at issue"; thus Lippmann expresses his third principle of public opinion (1925, 144).

For Lippmann, the fundamental difference that matters is the one between the few insiders who have expert knowledge on a problem and the many outsiders who have only superficial knowledge. Insiders relate to a problem in a way that differs radically from outsiders: the former are actors who decisively influence the course of political affairs, and the latter are more or less passive spectators. "Only the insider can make decisions . . . because he is so placed that he can understand and can act. The outsider is necessarily ignorant, usually irrelevant and often meddlesome, because he is trying to navigate the ship from the dry land" (1925, 150). On this dichotomy, Lippmann lays down the fourth and fifth principle of public opinion: "The specific, technical, intimate criteria required in the handling of a question are not for the public. The public's criteria are generalized for many problems; they turn essentially on procedure and the overt, external forms of behavior." And "what is left for the public is a judgment as to whether the actors in the controversy are following a settled rule of behavior or their own arbitrary desires. This judgment must be made by sampling an external aspect of the behavior of the insiders" (1925, 144–45).

It is normal, according to Lippmann, to expect that the *opinions* of the insiders are substantially different from those of the outsiders.[19] They also differ in the kind of *action* they are able to undertake. They have different functions and, consequently, they should also differ in *methods* they use in controversies. Thus confusing insiders and outsiders may have dangerous consequences. For example, a centralized society dominated by the fiction that the governors represent a common will tends not only to degrade individuals' initiatives but also to reduce the role of public opinion to insignificance (1925, 185). Public opinion "is not able to master the problem intellectually, nor to deal with it except by wholesale impact" (1925, 71). If it nevertheless attempted to participate in political decision making, that would cause a failure or a tyranny. Lippmann thus agrees with the nineteenth-century critique of the "tyranny of public opinion."[20] On the whole, these principles remind Noam Chomsky (1991) of the Leninist concept of a vanguard party that leads the masses to a better life that they cannot conceive or construct on their own. Yet, on the other hand, Lippmann's dichotomy (without its pejorative connotation) may not just be confronted with Dewey's differentiation between the public (i.e., outsiders) and government (i.e., insiders) but may also be paralleled with the generally postulated relationship between public opinion and authoritative power.

With the "principles of public opinion," Lippmann reduces the role of the public in decision making to giving its judgment on whether or not formal rules are heeded; the actual decision ought to be made by the "executive actors," and the public may only observe their decisions. This was perhaps a very accurate description of the actual situation (in the United States, and perhaps elsewhere) in Lippmann's time, which Dewey would probably endorse too. The description can even be generalized, and Lippmann is probably right when he reproaches democratic theories with their underestimating of the significance of people's nonparticipation in the simplest democratic procedures intended for the expression of opinions, for example, in elections. Yet despite all of these empirical hindrances, democracy can only be based on the assumption that individuals and groups do participate in decision making. Without this assumption, as Wilson (1962, 82) maintains, public opinion would rest "a purely negative principle, for it is then merely the recognition of the fact that people must submit to government." Thus, unlike Lippmann, Dewey tries to answer the question of what conditions are needed to make the public *effective*. In essence, he sees the importance of social research in its attempts to increase the possibilities of the development of appropriate societal conditions that would make possible and would stimulate citizen participation in decision making. This substantial difference between Dewey and Lippmann is also expressed in their conceptualization of *the public* as a social category: Dewey markedly emphasizes the political nature of the public, whereas Lippmann considers it no more than an unstable and rapidly changeable and therefore marginal phenomenon.

Whereas Dewey makes a relative difference between the public and executive actors (governmental officials), which both constitute a political state, Lippmann draws a sharp boundary between the two (see table 4.1). Dewey defines specific tasks of the public and its officers on the temporal continuum (in the past vs. the future). Lippmann ensues a more static approach so that the differences between the two types of actors are defined with simple dichotomies (i.e., an action is/is not appropriate to be taken by an actor). For Dewey, all citizens are to some degree "officers," since they represent the Public; they express their will as representatives of the public interest as much as do state officials. Besides, every officer of the public, whether he represents it as a voter or as a state official, has a *dual capacity:* he has political aims and acts accordingly, as well as the aims he possesses in his nonpolitical roles (1925, 74, 76). Lippmann, however, strongly objects to such a "dangerous confusion." His rigid dichotomous mode of thinking had already been questioned by

Table 4.1: Key Dimensions of Lippmann's Differentiation between Executive
Actors or Insiders and the Public or Outsiders (Based on Lippmann,
The Phantom Public)

CHARACTERISTIC ACTIONS AND CAPACITIES OF	
EXECUTIVE ACTORS (INSIDERS)	**THE PUBLIC (OUTSIDERS)**
Executive action	Alignment to those in position to act executively
Experience and intrinsic knowledge about the problem; acting from inside	Outsiders' experience; intervention from outside
Anticipation, analysis and solution of a problem	Judgment based on a small number of facts
Use of specific, intimate, technical criteria	Generalized criteria to ascertain as to whether the actors in the controversy follow a settled rule

The discovery of criteria to distinguish between reasonable and arbitrary
behavior is the task of political scientists. Educational institutions should
"train the public" how to use them.

Tönnies (1927, 9**), who was dissatisfied with Lippmann's disregard for different aggregate states in public opinion. The logic of dichotomous exclusiveness or antinomies is one of the fairly general characteristics of Lippmann's writing; for example, public opinion is not compatible with an executive action; reason is separated from emotions; science, from ethics; facts and public affairs are outside whereas symbols and public opinions are inside the head; science finds and reports truth whereas the press reports only news; and executive actors are separated from observers.

Dewey believed in an enlightening power of education and even predicted that "sometime methods of instruction will be devised which will enable laymen to read and hear scientific material with comprehension" (Dewey [1927] 1991, 163). For Lippmann, however, the appeal to equal education as the remedy for the incompetence of individuals and the means to improve democracy by assuring equal opportunities for participation to all was sterile because schoolteachers cannot teach people how to govern. Liberal theorists' assumption that all people desire to participate in government (the assumption on which the idea of equal education for everyone is grounded) is mistaken itself. Even if people formally participate, there is no guarantee that they actually influence the course of events, since the main power is always, according to Lippmann, in the hands of political bureaucracies. Thus great expectations about civic education can only cause disenchantment. Nevertheless, Lippmann agreed with Dewey that "'education' is the supreme remedy" and that "the value of this education will depend upon the evolution of knowledge" (Lippmann [1922] 1960, 408). Yet Dewey and Lippmann had different types of education in mind. Dewey did not propose a system of education that would produce highly capable experts but rather an education in social sciences that would be based on the experience of the community. In contrast, Lippmann had in mind the development of an expert system in which the task of political science should be to collect and generalize information into a "conceptual picture of the world" for the schools that would help civic education to become "a preparation for dealing with an unseen environment."

Lippmann argues for differentiating among various types of functional education whose specificity relates to the differences between the public and the "executive actors." Education for citizenship—for membership in the public— ought to be different from education for executive actors because the two categories of actors have a radically different relation to public affairs, requiring different intellectual habits and different methods of action. Lippmann defines public opinion as "the voice of interested spectators of action." Ideally its key function is to "align men during the crisis of a problem in such a way as to favor the action of those individuals who may be able to compose the crisis" (1925, 66). The main task of political science is, according to Lippmann, to discover the methods of identifying these individuals and to define the criteria of judgment, and the job of the educational system to develop the capacity of public opinion to use these methods.

Lippmann was not the first one to stress huge differences between the ideas of participation that individuals should be able to pursue and that institutions should provide for in democratic societies—which were advocated by normative democratic theories of Enlightenment—and the actual feasibility of participation in a developed and complex industrial society, as was American society at that time. Similar admonitions were voiced by J. S. Mill, Tocqueville, and Bryce in the nineteenth century; yet Lippmann's warning perhaps met with a wider response because of his more luminous and persuasive writing, as well as concrete proposals for radical changes not only in the conceptualization of public opinion but also regarding the public regulation of public opinion processes. Despite these serious controversies, Dewey and Lippmann agreed that the forms of discussion that prevailed in the ancient city-states of

Greece and Rome, not to mention the public discussions of the Enlightenment, could not perform the same function in twentieth-century democracies
that they did in the past, that is, to ensure rational public discourse. The pragmatists also concluded that assuming the competence of each individual had
often proved to be problematic in the past; and with the ongoing processes of
consumerism, privatization, and fragmentation of knowledge about public affairs, the competence of the public to decide issues of concern to the public
has become even more problematized. Yet, for the pragmatists, questions regarding the survival and development of the public were the key questions of
democracy: "For if one could not presuppose, even in theory, the existence of
a public capable of grasping both large (national and international) and local
public issues, then the institutions of democracy were fated to wither"
(Aronowitz 1993, 76). But because human "knowledge is a function of association and communication," it is possible to dismiss this "illusion" over the
long haul, as even Lippmann believed: "Re-education will help to bring our
public opinions into grip with the environment. That is the way the enormous
censoring, stereotyping, and dramatizing apparatus can be liquidated" (Lippmann [1922] 1960, 407).

However, Dewey disagreed with Lippmann's answer to the question of how
to "save" the public, emphasizing in addition to (social) sciences the importance
of nontechnocratic instruments like art and human interaction. How it would
be possible to utilize these "resources" not only in the local but also in the national and even global arenas was a question to which the pragmatists ultimately
could find no answer. Unlike Dewey, who believed that improved communications and education can transform the Great Society into the Great Community,
Lippmann believed that what indeed could be done to improve modern public
opinion was the founding of independent, expert investigating agencies, a network of "intelligence bureaux" that ought to be, "as absolutely as it is possible,"
separated from the executive staff and have almost unrestricted mandates
([1922] 1960, 384–89). Unlike advocates of the press as the "fourth power" (see
Sparks 1995), Lippmann (who shared with Dewey a critical view of newspapers
and, even more, press agents on which newspapers depend) argued for the idea
that the people can increase their control over the acts of public officials and industrial directors only by "insisting that all of them shall be plainly recorded, and
their results objectively measured," rather than by relying on the press. The press
should play a major role in this process by providing news as commodity:

> Universally it is admitted that the press is the chief means of contact with the un-
> seen environment and . . . assumed that the press should do spontaneously for us
> what in primitive democracy imagined each of us could do spontaneously for him-

self, that every day and twice a day it will present us with a true picture of all the outer world in which we are interested. This insistent and ancient belief that truth is not earned, but inspired, revealed, supplied gratis, comes out very plainly in our economic prejudices as readers of newspapers. (Lippmann [1922] 1960, 320)

The press may try best to reveal the *truth*, in addition to publishing *news*, but the two endeavors are not necessarily in consonance, and they may even contradict each other. Nor is the press capable of bringing the hidden facts to light, setting them into relation to each other, and generating a reliable picture of reality that would enable people to act. The problem of "making public opinions" is not a problem to be treated in civil liberties, as "democrats" did, and not in Dewey's sense of positive liberties, but rather "the problem of how to make the invisible world visible to the citizens of a modern state" (Lippmann [1922] 1960, 318, 320). For Lippmann, thus, the fundamental question is, where and how can individuals, or newspapers, get the information they need, who is supposed to provide it, and, eventually, who is supposed to pay for it.[21] Citizen freedoms do not suffice to form public opinion because such an expectation implies an obviously invalid assumption, "either that truth is spontaneous, or that the means of ensuring truth exist when there is no external interference" ([1922] 1960, 319). For Lippmann, the key to the formation of a sound public opinion is the creation of "organized intelligence" or "a good machinery of record." Neither the press nor any other institution, governmental or commercial—schools, governments, or churches—in which people trust and to which they willingly subordinate themselves can solve the problem of "the failure of self-governing people to transcend their casual experience and their prejudice, by inventing, creating, and organizing a machinery of knowledge" ([1922] 1960, 365). The belief that this might actually be possible is, according to Lippmann, the fundamental fault of the idea of popular government. Only a specialized, expert, and independent "intelligence bureau" could assure a continuous flow of reliable information, as in that time was already organized for stock exchange and elections.

Lippmann's idea could be exemplified by the institution of public auditing and, as Dewey (1922) suggested, compared with "the concept of intelligence staff of the army." Yet the materialization of Lippmann's idea would imply an enormous increase in authority of such "auditing institutions," which could even lead to the establishment of a new, in addition to traditional powers of legislative, executive, and judiciary, fourth branch of power (or, including the mass media, the fifth one). The three traditional powers in principle constitute the realm of the state, whereas the press (responsible for "news," according to Lippmann) and public auditors (responsible for "truth") ought to be an instrument of civil society over traditional state powers. Yet, is the idea of *omnipotent* investigating bureaux (which ought also to be a check on the press) any less utopian than the idea of *omnicompetent* individuals? Why should the "new power" be any more competent and independent than other of the three or four traditional powers in the same societies? In principle, Lippmann's idea of independent and politically neutral social scientists (an idea criticized already by Dewey) in a "system of intelligence" is no less utopian than Dewey's idea of the public organized in a Great Community, criticized by Lippmann. Lippmann actually realized that a substantial proportion of social sciences are apologetic rather than constructively critical, but he (naively?) presupposed that this was a consequence of underdeveloped and unreliable research methods: when social scientists catch up with physical scientists, who "achieved their freedom from clericalism by working out a method that produced conclusions of a sort that could not be suppressed or ignored," they will likewise achieve autonomy and impartiality ([1922] 1960, 373). Lippmann's expectation is utopian because it implies two invalid assumptions: (1) that social "facts" by themselves are spontaneously accessible to scientists (provided that appropriate methods exist) and thus facts only have to be registered and (2) that, in contrast to what pragmatists and Dewey believed, social sciences are not burdened by moral questions. In contrast, as we have seen earlier, Dewey argued that the modeling of social science upon physical science would invert the former into pseudoscience.

Lippmann's attitudes suggest that his understanding of the role of the press substantially differs from Dewey's. Lippmann compares majority rule with war and denotes elections as "sublimated warfare" when attempting to prove that the public is not able to express opinion but only to consent or not to consent with a proposal. In analogy, his conception of the press could also be compared with sublimation, not of the primary communication forms but *entrepreneurship*. For Dewey, in contrast, the mass nature of the press did not represent a substantial departure from other forms of communication. In his critique of the press, Dewey ([1927] 1991, 180) argued for the reconciliation of the intellectual form of the press with remarkable development of "swift reduplication of material at low cost," which he saw primarily in the possibility that "a genuine social science would manifest its reality in the daily press," which, of course, revealed his understanding of public opinion formation as identical to "communication of results of social inquiry" (Dewey [1927] 1991, 177). Like Lippmann, Dewey grounded his plea for the reconstruction of interpersonal communication and dialogue in local community—"that and that only gives reality to public opinion"—on a parable from economy: the absence of dialogue is as if material wealth is generated by associated endeavor of people, but it is subordinated to private interests in its distribution. Thus local community, which alone can assure that ideas are shared, should become the most important medium of communication.

Dewey's idea of a global network of local communities is utopian not only because of the absence of feasible technological solution—despite the contemporary development of computer mediated communication—but also because of his idealistic concept of dialogue. As Peters (1997a) claims, dialogue organically limits the number of participants (which is also the problem with forms of direct democracy),[22] and it does not necessarily imply equality of participants because the reciprocity of dialogue can be as violent as one-way (mass) communication. Even the most intimate interpersonal relations in families or among friends can be both one-way and interactive, generous as well as violent. Why, then, would one expect a different situation in the world of politics? As Schudson (1997, 306) argues, democratic conversation provides no magic solution to democracy because democratic deliberation is not based on spontaneity (as it is in a community); it is "a facility of public communication under norms of public reasonableness, not simply a facility of social interaction." The norms may even require withdrawal from conversation on some issues; constitutional efforts to keep religion out of political discussions, to which Schudson refers, were emphasized already by Dewey. Even more, democracy may require "withdrawal from civility itself," as in the case of demonstrations in which "conversation is itself an impediment to democracy's fulfillment" (Schudson 1997, 308).

In Lippmann's understanding of democracy, in contrast to Dewey's, mass media do not function as mediators of dialogue. Rather, Lippmann emphasizes that the mass character of the media fundamentally changes the quality of communication. The public that buys news sprang up, but it does not exhibit any loyalty to the newspaper it buys; the nature of news has changed (e.g., the relationship between reporting facts and opinions, and news selection); and, most important, *news* and *truth* are (should be) separated because they have completely different functions: "The function of news is to signalize an event, the function of truth is to bring to light the hidden facts, to set them into relation with each other, and make a picture of reality on which men can act" ([1922] 1960, 358). Lippmann's function of truth is close to Dewey's view of genuine social science; however, whereas Dewey argues for the closest possible relationship between science and the daily press, Lippmann emphasizes that science has no place in the newspapers, except if it monitors and supervises them in the capacity of an "auditing bureau."

MORE IS LESS, AND LESS IS MORE

Despite all differences, many of Lippmann's and Dewey's ideas are similar in their *utopian*[23] character and thus (although they seem to be exclusive at first glance) are complementary. As Peters (1997a) concludes, Dewey tried, with his attempts directed toward the reconstruction of the practical foundations of democracy, "to find the promised land, refusing to think of the wilderness as a permanent dwelling." On the other hand, Lippmann argued that the idea of self-governing people who ought to transcend their partial knowledge and particularistic interests was an inherent defect in popular government, but he wanted to find an alternative to the tragedy of democracy he was revealing. During the 1920s, when Lippmann and Dewey discussed questions of democracy and public opinion, and both grounded their theories on the extremely rapid progress in science, technology and communications, actual social development seemed to be more congruent with Lippmann's views than with Dewey's. The latter proved utopian because the development of communications—fundamental to Dewey's conceptualization of the public and Great Community—did not take the path Dewey hoped to see. Even in the 1960s, when similar differences reappeared between Key and Wilson, the development seemed to speak in favor of Lippmann and Key rather than Dewey and Wilson; Habermas—despairing of the possibility of a radical democratic transformation—set up the idea of refeudalization of publicness. Does the information revolution at the end of the twentieth century offer a more realistic base to Dewey's ideas than the outcomes of the industrial revolution in the beginning of the century? Does the development of computer-mediated communication draw near the solution to the problems Dewey was only able to observe but not feasibly resolve? The development of information activities and technologies reduces (even as it decisively amplifies) an excessive social complexity. New communication technologies, which solve many problems, also bring about new kinds of problems. We are constantly facing the growth of indirect long-term consequences—the issue discussed from entirely different perspectives by Dewey and Lippmann. In a way, the immense potential of new communication technologies would certainly be to Dewey's advantage because they may help to develop Great Community on the basis of widespread interactive communication with almost no spatial limitations. Nowadays it is not difficult to imagine Great Community, or a modern Tönniesian Gemeinschaft, as a virtual community of hundreds and thousands of individuals, groups, and organizations interconnected electronically. New communication technologies not only make long-distance voice communication easier but also make possible interaction in writing and, incidentally, the merger of oral and print cultures. These developments may help to solve Dewey's basic problem, namely, that "*vision* is spectator; *hearing* is a participator. *Publication* is partial and the public which results is partially informed and formed until the meanings it purveys pass from mouth to mouth" (Dewey [1927] 1991, 219; emphasis added). Scott Aikens renovates Dewey's idea by arguing that, with the help of computer-mediated communication technology, "instead of the information at the heart of the democratic process being collected by reporters working for privately owned organizations, the information at the heart of the democratic process will be the subject of community debate as well as subjected to community debate" (Aikens 1996, 8). However, without answering the question of *who* will have the interest and ability to participate in such debates, the problem remains pending. It was the failure to find an answer to this very question that convinced Lippmann to reject the thesis of the participatory public and to replace "participation of all" by an expert "machinery of record." Even today, it would be difficult to use the growing electronic communicative interconnectedness (not only on the national but also on the global scale) as an argument against the development of and need for reliable intelligence bureaux, as suggested by Lippmann.

Another reason to remain skeptical about the feasibility of Dewey's ideas is related to the softening of technological determinism in the search for Great Community. As fast and as revolutionary as technological development may be, it cannot expand dialogue from a relatively small number of active individuals because the participating minority is not determined only by limited capacities and unfriendliness of communication tools (which, of course, is constantly improving) but to an even higher degree by the limited human capacity to listen and read, which no technological revolution whatsoever can reverse.

If the tasks of recording facts and distributing information cannot be pursued by the media or any other governmental or commercial organization, as both Dewey and Lippmann believed, how then can information activity ever become socially responsible? For Lippmann, the solution was "registration machinery"; for Dewey, the remedy was systematic publication of results of social inquiries in the daily press in combination with the development of interpersonal communication in community. Once clearly alternative and mutually exclusive solutions are now becoming, due to technological mergers, realistically compatible. Consequently, Aikens (1996, 8) suggests a possible (in his opinion a Deweyan) solution—the founding of "a democratized system of public opinion formation in which the *new public,* the *information elite,* participates in an open system of social inquiry. The knowledge that results from this process will then be what is distributed to the *passive mass public* by reporters" (emphasis added). However, the new public[24] or information elite is more a substitute for Lippmann's "registration machinery" and the passive mass public for his "outsiders" than a redefinition of Dewey's conceptualization of the public. Thus the solution is actually more in line with Lippmann than Dewey.

Similar conclusions about surmounting traditionally exclusive solutions can be derived from a series of empirical inquiries into the sources and nature of political participation in the developed capitalist democracies. As they show, citizens are frequently involved in politics directly as individuals, and they make political decisions on the ground of their own judgments, whereas they are less dependent on executive actors—party elites, reference groups, or opinion leaders. In reviewing contemporary patterns of political changes, Russell J. Dalton (1996) concludes that an "eclectic and egocentric pattern of citizen action" is developing, which refers to different methods of direct democracy citizens are using in the framework of local communities and social movements. The "eclecticity" of these patterns is clearly in the surprising compatibility of Dewey's and Lippmann's plans of societal organization.

The core of the perplexity caused by Dewey's and Lippmann's visions of the development of the public lies in the fact that the growth of complexity—which is brought about by the very same technological development that reduces complexity—still implies that more and more, the "world that we have to deal with politically is out of reach, out of sight, out of mind. It has to be explored, reported, and imagined" (Lippmann [1922] 1960, 29). The development of computer-mediated communication does not lead by itself to Great Community but rather enables the development of those nonpolitical forms of community life and scientific, religious, artistic, educational, industrial, and commercial groupings that should be, according to Dewey ([1927] 1991, 26), strictly demarcated from the organized public. The greater the number of transactions among people, the smaller the proportion of transactions in which an individual can participate either directly or indirectly in the regulation of indirect consequences. The amount of information available is growing, information access is becoming easier; but at the same time, the gap between the amounts of produced and "consumed" information is deepening. The media supply is also growing, but it often does not imply a greater diversity; rather, homogenization of the supply seems to be a natural consequence of media concentration and competition for the audiences.[25] More and more (access to) information and more possibilities to interact globally in the absolute sense, which speaks for Dewey's Great Community, so much the less of both in the relative (pragmatic) sense, which speaks for the need of Lippmann's "public accounting." After almost a century of discussion, the Dewey-Lippmann controversy over the nature of public opinion and democracy is no less exciting than it was at the beginning.

5

✛

Public Opinion as Panopticon:
A Critique of the Spiral of Silence

According to the Reichminister *Dr Goebbels, public opinion "is largely the result of a willful influence." From this recognition a duty derives for German publicists and their intellectual head office,* Propagandaministerium, *to establish a close contact with the whole of the people as the holder of public opinion in order to control the effectiveness of different influences on the formation of opinions, to recognize in time an abuse of the formability of public opinion, and to determine the limits of the formability.*

—Elisabeth Noelle, *Amerikanische Massenbefragungen
über Politik und Presse*

The French say "cherchez la femme;" social psychologists say "look for the dependence, and everything will be explained."

—Serge Moscovici, *Social Influence and Social Change*

The individual's tendency to reduce cognitive dissonance, ensuring consensus in the society, the role of the media as a coherent public eye, and public opinion's simultaneous control over citizens and governments represent four cornerstones of Elisabeth Noelle-Neumann's spiral of silence theory. Her model represents the first integrated model of opinion formation in the empirical sociological tradition, despite the fact that many of the ideas embodied in the model are not new. Even her idea to equate public opinion with the "public eye" is reminiscent of Bentham's (and Foucault's) idea of Panopticon: to bring large numbers of people under permanent surveillance or, in Bentham's words, to make them "not only suspect, but be assured, that whatever they do is known, even though that should not be the case."

This chapter discusses basic assumptions in the spiral of silence model from two perspectives: (1) as the key points of an empirical critique, such as the individual's fear of isolation, perception of trends in public opinion, portrayals of public opinion in the media, and methods of investigation of the spiral of silence; (2) since the spiral of silence was called by Noelle-Neumann a "theory of public opinion," its theoretical status and reference to public opinion are examined, particularly the ideas related to the power of public opinion, consensus on the community's values and goals, and to the meaning of the concepts such as public and opinion. Noelle-Neumann has solved the problem of contradictions, inherent in the concept of public opinion, in a very simple way. To resolve the internal contradiction between public and opinion, the concept of publicness is reduced to only one dimension, that of visibility (what can be seen or heard by everybody), so that the widest possible range of empirically observable phenomena may be referred to. At the same time, the widest possible observational understanding of the concept of opinion as any, not only verbal(ized) "visible expression of a value-related opinion" is taken, and all the problems of rationality, consensuality, objectivity, and truthfulness disappear. In summary, it is argued that Noelle-Neumann's theory generalizes a marginal case of individuals who are relatively isolated socially and do not talk readily about some subjects of (public) discussion (e.g., political issues). The generalization tacitly presupposes a nondemocratic polity that spurs the spiral of silence.

THE NAMES FORGOTTEN: THE INTELLECTUAL ORIGINS OF THE "SPIRAL OF SILENCE"

The spiral of silence theory formulated by Elisabeth Noelle-Neumann in the early 1970s represents the first integrated model of opinion formation in the behavioral tradition of public opinion research. It was based on a challenging idea—to apply social psychological research on conformity to public opinion process. Her theory was frequently criticized and defended with severity. Since its first publication in English in 1984, *The Spiral of Silence,* in which her theory was integrally presented, appeared on the "must read" list of any social scientist interested in public opinion, as predicted by a reviewer in the *American Political Science Review.* By showing its precursors in older theories and, to some extent, its derivation from them, its attempt to resolve the internal and external contradictions in the concept of public opinion, its empirical dubiousness and methodological flaws, and the nondemocratic context in which the model is validated, I come across almost all fundamental questions pertinent to contemporary thinking on public opinion. Despite my obvious dissatisfaction with the level of validity of most of Noelle-Neumann's hypotheses, her model, due to its integrative character, represents a useful basis for outlining the junctions of traditional and more recent theoretical perspectives and behavioral traditions, which may open new prospects for their potential merger.

The spiral of silence does not consider public opinion to be opinion of the public in Tönniesian terms; hence, it is closer to an adjective theory of public opinion, as Wilson would put it. Still more, Noelle-Neumann (1991, 257) insists that "we will make no progress toward a theory of public opinion if we do not adopt a completely different concept of public opinion [from those relating it to the processes of government]." On the other hand, the spiral of silence model had a significant advantage over "competing" simple empirical models because it was based, though only implicitly, on the *coorientation* approach to communication. According to Noelle-Neumann, public opinion develops as a result of *interaction between individuals and the environment* (in which the environment is actually restricted to individuals' beliefs that others are reacting in the same way); thus, it indeed represents a *process* rather than a situation. In the model, the concept of public opinion is correlated with sanction and punishment (1979, 172); individuals' interaction with the environment is determined by their fear of isolating themselves. The model is operationalized with the following dimensions or assumptions, which are presumably testable through empirical investigation:

1. Society threatens deviant individuals with isolation.
2. Individuals continuously experience fear of isolation, which usually makes people willing to heed the opinions of others and to suppress expressions of their own opinions.
3. Because of this fear of isolation, individuals are constantly trying to assess the climate of opinion. They are able to realize what opinions are held by others and when public opinions grow in strength or weaken with a sort of "quasi-statistical organ."
4. The results of this estimate affect people's behavior in public, leading them to more confident speech or to silence: public opinion serves as an important source of social orientation of individuals.
5. Mass media present a consonant portrayal of trends in the climate of opinion, which has powerful effects over opinion formation: media are

consonant because all journalists share the same values, which limits the possibility of a selective perception of media contents and, consequently, an autonomous opinion formation. (Noelle-Neumann [1980] 1993, 62, 202)

The cornerstones of the spiral of silence theory are the individual's tendency to reduce cognitive dissonance, ensuring consensus in the society, the role of the media as a coherent "public eye" and the source of information about dominant social norms, and public opinion's simultaneous control over both citizens and governments. Most of the ideas embodied in the model are not new. For example, V. O. Key discussed in brief the relationship between public opinion, *conformity* induced by majority opinion, and the tendency of the minority toward *silence* in his *Public Opinion and American Democracy* ([1961] 1967) along the same lines, but he also saw limitations to the disposition to accept or to tolerate the majority view. What is usually considered new in the Noelle-Neumann model, however, is an attempt to interrelate these ideas and articulate them more clearly as *dimensions of public opinion process,*[1] and to *test them empirically.* As Elihu Katz ([1981] 1983, 89) emphasized in his critique of her model (one of the earliest), Noelle-Neumann should be credited for her attempt to bring together public opinion research, mass communication research, and public opinion theory that have become disconnected.

Yet the idea of integrating into a public opinion model individuals' tendency to conform and their fear of sanctions, which condition their behavior in public, is perhaps wrongly attributed to Noelle-Neumann. It was Tom Harrisson, an English anthropologist and the founder of the British Institute of Public Opinion, who has first defined the "spiral of silence" in his article "What is Public Opinion?" published in 1940. The following fragment provides a sufficient account of Harrisson's merit for the model named after Noelle-Neumann:

> At all ordinary times and places, there is a tendency for most ordinary people to follow what they believe to be the majority, to voice in public mainly those sentiments and opinions which are generally acceptable and respectable. . . . Public opinion is only a part of private opinion[2] and only that part which, so to speak, dare show itself at any moment. (Harrisson 1940, 370, 373)

> Public opinion is what you will say out loud to anyone. . . . It is only when opinions have reached this level that they are freely discussed and gain mass currency, an upward impact. Many things which agitate many minds never reach this level at all. And generally opinions can only reach this level if they receive social sanc-

tion—that is, evidence of external, authoritative, and preferably numerous, support. (Harrisson 1940, 374)

As we will see shortly, Harrisson's ideas, on which Lindsay Rogers in his book *Pollsters* nine years later founded his critique of polling, are remarkably similar to the model Noelle-Neumann developed more than thirty years later (without crediting T. Harrisson, L. Rogers, or V. O. Key). In one of her early elaborations of the spiral of silence, Noelle-Neumann proceeds from Floyd H. Allport's definition of public opinion as

> a multi-individual situation in which individuals are expressing themselves, or can be called upon to express themselves, as favoring or supporting (or else disfavoring or opposing) some definite condition, person, or proposal of widespread importance, in such a proportion of number, intensity, and constancy, as to give rise to the probability of affecting action, directly or indirectly, toward the object concerned. (Allport 1937, 23)

She criticizes Allport's effort to define public opinion as a simplistic attempt to validate the results of polling as the expression of public opinion. She reproaches him for not having included in the definition elements that she finds "most important": there is no word of the fights for public opinion; "how public opinion comes into being, how the thing starts" (in Allport's definition it is already there and "constant"); the power of public opinion is reduced to "giving rise to the probability of affecting action" (Noelle-Neumann 1979, 170–71). On the other hand, she finds in Allport's article three interesting "hints" that she uses as the cornerstones of her model: (1) that public opinion should be understood as a process with a time dimension (thus not as a "situation," as in Allport's definition), (2) that public opinion implies an awareness that others are reacting to the same situations in a similar manner, and (3) that it relates not only to political questions but also to common issues in the sphere of social control. But again, Noelle-Neumann actually owes her spiral of silence idea also to Floyd Allport. He confirmed on many occasions the inclination of individuals to compromise in a group situation (although without any reference to public opinion) and also considered the expression of "atypical" attitudes by individuals who are more (primarily emotionally) confident in what they think. In 1924 he wrote that there is

> a basic human tendency to temper one's opinions and conduct by deference to the opinions and conduct of others. Early training and social contact have bred in us the avoidance of extremes of all sorts, whether of clothing, of manners, or of

beliefs. This tendency is so fundamental that we are seldom conscious of it, yet we are seldom if ever without it. (Quoted in Moscovici and Doise 1994, 27)

The fundamental and the only explicit assumption related to the societal rather than the individual level in the model of the spiral of silence is that "society threatens deviant individuals with isolation" (Noelle-Neumann [1980] 1993, 202). However, this assumption was never submitted to theoretical validation or empirical verification. In answering the more specific questions of how the spiral of silence is shaping *public opinion,* Noelle-Neumann actually eliminates public opinion by reducing it to the "climate of opinion," which is, theoretically speaking, opposite rather than synonymous to public opinion: "In the manipulated public sphere an acclamation-prone mood comes to predominate, an opinion climate *instead of* a public opinion" (Habermas [1962] 1995, 217; emphasis added). She tries to test the measurability of the threat of isolation itself in a situation that does not correspond to the public either as a collective subject of public opinion or as a virtual network of individuals. In fact, when testing her hypotheses, she assumes that the individual is an isolated person out of any interaction in his or her reference groups. Noelle-Neumann's public opinion is "public" primarily in the sense of social control or "pressure to conform," as "public eye" to which individuals are exposed and by which they are forced to conform (1977, 144; 1991, 256). More concretely, public opinion is defined as "controversial opinions that one is *able* to express in public without becoming isolated" or, in the case of "definite principles and customs," as constituted by "attitudes and modes of behavior one *has* to express in public if one does not want to become isolated" (Noelle-Neumann 1977, 145). In both senses, despite stressing its controversial nature, her understanding of public opinion is closer to Tönnies's notion of *expressed* or *published opinions* and Habermas's *representative publicness* than to a *genuine* opinion of the public. She formally draws a distinction between "the climate of opinion" and "public opinion," but eventually she conceives the latter as directly determined by the former. As Peters argues, the key mechanism of the spiral of silence is "public opinion as a stage image before the eyes of the people, not as a latent sociological or psychological entity" (Peters 1995, 22): public opinion seems to be influenced by media representations of public opinion, not by the media or other controlling powers.

On the one hand, Noelle-Neumann sees public opinion as the individual's public expression of opinion or even only the willingness to speak out. On the other hand, she defines public opinion as the "public eye," as media representation of public opinion to which individuals are *exposed* and by which they are forced to *conform* (Noelle-Neumann [1980] 1993, 194–95, 230; 1985, 70).

Positive sanctions, she argues, may play a role in conformist behavior only for "ambitious persons" (which "many people are not"), but they would not suffice "to make most members of a community (i.e., all of them, leaving aside the outsiders, the marginal groups) strive for conformity." In both senses, "public opinion is not just a matter for those who feel a calling, or for talented critics—the 'politically functioning public' of Habermas. Everyone is involved." To exemplify her notion of public opinion as something of everyone's concern, she took the example presented by Allport to distinguish between public opinion and "long-standing behaviors, namely, those which constitute laws, customs, and traditions"—the pressure brought to bear on householders in a neighborhood to shovel the snow from their sidewalks (Allport 1937, 18; Noelle-Neumann 1974, 43).

Noelle-Neumann's idea of equating public opinion with the "public eye" and defining fear of isolation as the *basic motive* of most members of a community in the process of their opinion formation and expression is reminiscent of Bentham's (and after him Foucault's) idea of Panopticon (all-seeing): to bring prisoners under permanent surveillance or, in Foucault's words, "to induce in the inmate a state of conscious and permanent visibility that assures the automatic functioning of power" (Foucault 1977, 201). In congruence with the idea of Panopticon as a technique for controlling large numbers of people in an institution, public opinion is defined by Noelle-Neumann (1974, 44) as "the opinion which can be voiced in public without fear of sanctions and upon which action in public can be based; . . . the dominating opinion which compels compliance of attitude and behavior in that it threatens the dissenting individual with isolation, the politician with loss of popular support." It clearly resembles Bentham's Inspection House, in which the *inspection principle* is materialized to perfection: "The object of the inspection principle is . . . to make them [i.e., prisoners] not only *suspect,* but be *assured,* that whatever they do is known, even though that should not be the case" (Bentham [1787] 1995, 94). Bentham himself extended the strategy of distrustful surveillance to the political assembly and incorporated it in the principle of publicity; consequently, he argued that every good political institution was founded upon the system of distrust (Bentham [1791] 1994, 589). As Poster argues, in his contemporary application of Bentham's idea, Foucault actually did not realize that information and communication technologies extended Panopticon monitoring considerably, "not simply to massed groups but to *the isolated individual.* The normalized individual is not only the one at work, in an asylum, in jail, in school, in the military, as Foucault observes, but also the individual in his or her home, at play, in all the mundane activities of *everyday life*" (Poster 1984, 103; emphasis added).[3] Indeed, such an extension of Panopticon in the information age brings it very close to Noelle-Neumann's concept of public opinion as social control based on individuals' fear of social isolation.

Theorization of public opinion as Panopticon represents an ill-defined concept for three main reasons. First, as it was made clear, it actually does not refer to the process of public opinion but to the general process of an individual's opinion formation and expression under external control. To paraphrase V. O. Key, *if everyone is controlled, there is no need to think about public opinion* (cf. Key [1961] 1967, 543). Second, the model unduly hypostatizes the fear of isolation as the only motive influencing human public behavior. Even if other avoidance and affiliative motives (efforts to avoid different kinds of discomfort and to affiliate with others) are added, they still represent only a part of the individual's total motivational structure.[4] Thus even if all other relevant motives (e.g., achievement and power motives) were included in the Noelle-Neumann behavioral model (which, of course, is practically impossible), it would still fail to explain public opinion because motives alone cannot fully explain behavior or, in other words, a particular type of behavior (i.e., conformity) cannot be considered the consequence of the individual's motives only, let alone one single motive (McClelland [1985] 1995, 33). Third, the question of what public opinion *means* and how it *influences* individuals grasps only one component of public opinion. The second (in fact, the principal) component any theory of public opinion is supposed to explain relates to the *formation* and *expression* of public opinion in society. Or should we believe it is simply always there? Paradoxically, Noelle-Neumann criticized Allport's definition of public opinion for assuming the preexistence of public opinion and not explaining "how public opinion comes into being, how the thing starts." But she did not present any indication of "how the thing *starts*" either. Rather, she admitted that "to the question, 'How does the new begin?' we can provide no answer" (Noelle-Neumann [1980] 1993, 142). In Wilson's words, for example, any attempt at a definition of public opinion should clarify (1) the nature of the public as an organ of *political* society and (2) formal and philosophical conditions of a *free* public opinion (Wilson 1962, 276). The existence of the (great) public as the subject of public opinion and freedom of opinion expression are the cornerstones of many other theorizations, including Tönnies's. Thus *here* "the thing" may start.

Yet the behaviorist consideration of public opinion disregards both theory and history. It clearly ignores the evidence of the historical development of public opinion, both in theory and practice, through the extension of suffrage, the organization of political propaganda groups, the establishment of pressure groups and political parties, the eligibility of ever wider circles of public officials, and eventually the installation of several forms of direct democracy. All these inventions "increased the participation and power of public opinion," although in the democratic state one may note also "the emergence of a civil service relatively independent of the legislative body" (Wilson 1962, 66, 68). Still, both tendencies indicate close relationship between public opinion and government and/or administrative organization of the state—but this is "out of sight and out of mind" of the behaviorist conviction.

Neither behaviorist position seems to need any theoretical foundation. Justification of polls and representative surveys as public opinion institutions does not refer to, let alone confront, any theory of public opinion and/or the basic dimensions of public opinion formation. Tom Smith (1987, S107), for example, argues that public opinion polls indeed measure public opinion because (1) "they are samplings of general adult population, the American public," (2) "are mostly conducted for the mass media . . . or by the mass media . . . and thus the results of the polls are routinely made public," and (3) "deal mostly with public matters, what people want government to do (or not do)." However, Noelle-Neumann (1979, 169) ascribes a "surprising naiveté" to the use of the term "public opinion" in connection with results of opinion polls—presumably because, as Robert Lynd argued in his critique (1940, 219), "polls take over naively the assumption of the Founding Fathers . . . that men are rational, free, and equal." According to her judgment, polls neither represent any evidence of the power of public opinion nor influence it; published polling results have no effect on opinion formation—shifts in opinion are "due to other causes, for example, to the observation of other parts in the social environment" (1977, 150). This obviously implies that individuals' "quasi-statistical organs" are more accurate instruments for detecting (changes of) the climate of opinion than scientific polls, but empirical studies certainly do not prove that these organs are more accurate than measuring instruments used by social scientists.[5] Noelle-Neumann's negative attitude toward public opinion polls rose in the World War II period, when she linked the need for polls to the alienation of U.S. political leaders from the people, whereas the "people's leaders" in Nazi Germany sought to be so closely linked to the people that they easily knew its opinions and, consequently, there was no need for opinion polls (Noelle 1940, 1)—similarly to the early period of communism in Eastern Europe.

On the other hand, Noelle-Neumann is surprised that the term "public opinion" was never used by the researchers in the field of group dynamics who measured the fear of isolation and embarrassment. And she disagrees with Sydney Verba, who, at the conference of the American Association for Public Opinion Research in 1970, recapitulated Blumer's (1948) critique that "political science was making no progress toward a theory of public opinion because it 'usually focuses on the individual as a unit of analysis'" (Noelle-Neumann [1980] 1993, 218, 198). Noelle-Neumann replies with an argument similar to the one

Lazarsfeld used in the 1940s to respond to Blumer's criticism: instead of (or in addition to) survey questions that inquire about an individual's opinion, knowledge, and behavior, questions should be asked that are oriented toward an individual's social setting and his or her social nature—questions asking individuals about "the climate of opinion" in society, for example, "What do most people think? Who is winning? What is IN, OUT?" (Noelle-Neumann [1980] 1993, 218–219, 231; 1991, 279). The representation of public opinion in the climate of opinion is taken for granted. If questions in representative surveys address value-laden opinions and modes of behavior "by which the individual isolates or may isolate himself in public," this is a valid observation of public opinion process, argues Noelle-Neumann ([1980] 1993, 231). Since all members of society participate in the process of public opinion as social control, "it is possible to observe this process with the tools of representative surveys."

In her discussion of "public opinion as social control," Noelle-Neumann ([1980] 1993, 228) only refers to Lazarsfeld's explanation of what he called the "bandwagon effect," which is congruent with the spiral of silence, but she does not seriously confront her theory with competing studies of pluralistic ignorance with evidence that the people often have a wrong idea about what is the majority opinion ([1980] 1993, 124, 169; 1991, 269). She maintains that both the bandwagon mechanism and the spiral of silence theory rest on the assumption that "individuals monitor signals in their environment with regard to the strength and weakness of the various camps." The difference between the two conceptualizations, according to Noelle-Neumann, lies (1) in the *motive* for such observations: for the bandwagon mechanism, the dominant motive for individuals is "to *be on* the winning side," whereas for the spiral of silence, it is "to *avoid* the threat of isolation," that is, it is a difference between pull and push motivations; and (2) in the span of time: the spiral of silence theory emphasizes "gradual, incremental changes that result from an ongoing social process," whereas the bandwagon effect suggests "a more sudden jump from one position to another based on new information as to who's ahead." The two models are congruent in the prediction that individuals will behave (e.g., vote, express opinions) according to their expectations of who or what will be the winning option. The temporal dimension of the difference is difficult to define precisely; in her introductory discussion of public opinion in *The Spiral of Silence,* Noelle-Neumann ([1980] 1993, 2) herself explains the power of public opinion in terms of bandwagon effect, "At the last minute they [voters] had gone along with the crowd." Essentially, then, the two models mainly differ in the nature of individual's motivation for opinion changes.

From the perspective of a public opinion theory, however, a much more important question is whether both the bandwagon effect and the spiral of silence result from a form of communication monopoly (see McQuail and Windahl 1981, 69), or only the bandwagon effect. As I will argue, the spiral of silence tacitly assumes precisely such nondemocratic circumstances.

THEORETICAL CRITIQUE: PUBLIC OPINION AS RATIONAL PROCESS VERSUS PUBLIC OPINION AS SOCIAL CONTROL

The spiral of silence was called by Noelle-Neumann a "theory of public opinion," but both its *theoretical status* and *reference to public opinion* deserve some skepticism (which she admitted in 1985, 67). The spiral of silence is lacking in elaborated theorization that would justify it as a theory of public opinion, primarily because it does not distinguish between the individual's (published) opinion and public opinion (opinion of the public). Nevertheless, it may be beneficial to contemporary dissertations on public opinion to take a closer look at some theses put forward by Noelle-Neumann in order to elucidate some controversies on public opinion between the theoretical and empirical schools of thought.

Noelle-Neumann ([1980] 1993, 229–34) reintroduced the (pre-) Enlightenment dichotomy of *public* opinion and *popular* opinion, which she labeled as a difference between rationalist and social control function of public opinion. The former concept denotes a *rational* human activity instrumental in the process of opinion formation and decision making in democracy. However, according to Noelle-Neumann, a more realistic concept is that denoting a form of social control with the main function to promote social integration and to insure a sufficient level of consent on which actions and decisions may be based and thus legitimized. She draws a parallel between these two concepts and Robert Merton's distinction between manifest and latent functions; a rational process of opinion formation represents the manifest function of public opinion, whereas social control represents its latent function (Noelle-Neumann [1980] 1993, 220). It should be noted, however, that the distinction between manifest and latent functions in Merton's terms implies not only the distinction between the functions "referring to those objective consequences for a specified unit (person, subgroup, social or cultural system) which contribute to its adjustment or adaptation and were so intended" (manifest functions) and those "referring to unintended and unrecognized consequences of the same order" (Merton [1949] 1993, 330). The two functions also differ in validity:

It is precisely the latent functions of a practice or belief which are not common knowledge, for these are unintended and generally unrecognized social and psychological

consequences. As a result, findings concerning latent functions represent a greater in-
crement in knowledge than findings concerning manifest functions. They represent,
also, greater departures from "common-sense" knowledge about social life. Inasmuch
as the latent functions depart, more or less, from the avowed manifest functions, the
research which uncovers latent functions very often produces "paradoxical" results.
(Merton [1949] 1993, 333)

In other words, Merton helped Noelle-Neumann prove that the function of
social control, because it is a latent function, represents the potentially more
fruitful object of study than the classical commonsense function of public opinion. According to Noelle-Neumann, the rational concept of public opinion
"does not explain the pressure that public opinion must exert if it is to have any
influence on the government and the citizens. *Raisonnement* is enlightening,
stimulating, and interesting, but it is not able to exert the kind of pressure from
which—as John Locke said—not one in ten thousand remains invulnerable"
(Noelle-Neumann [1980] 1993, 227). However, she believes that the power of
public opinion is easy to explain if public opinion is conceptualized as social
control. Noelle-Neumann refers here to her spiral of silence theory, which predicts that individuals will tend to avoid isolation and negative sanctions; consequently, they will tend to not deviate from the majority opinion. By doing so,
they generate integration and cohesion in a society, which is exactly the latent
function of public opinion.

> According to this hypothesis, the individual members of a society constantly ob-
> serve their environment, in order to see which opinions and modes of behavior
> will win the approval of society and which will lead to their isolation. When one
> side in political or social controversy is highly visible in public, other individuals
> adopt that position as well, displaying their convictions in public and thus rein-
> forcing the impression that everyone else thinks that way too. When there is only
> low public visibility, there is a tendency for people to conceal their position in pub-
> lic, making this position appear even weaker than it really is and prompting oth-
> ers to fall silent as well. (Noelle-Neumann 1995, 42)

What is even more problematic than a simplified dichomotization of definitions of public opinion (which actualizes only the aspects that may be found
already in Bentham's work but neglects the bulk of later developments, particularly of the Enlightenment tradition) is Noelle-Neumann's leveling of public
opinion with the *dominant opinion* in her model of the spiral of silence. Thus
public opinion is reduced to "the opinion that can be publicly expressed without fear of sanction and according to which it is possible to act visibly in public, while at the same time, the expression of an opposing opinion, or visible ac-

tion in public according to an opposing opinion, is burdened with the risk of isolation" (Noelle-Neumann 1979, 173). Basically, this is an adoption of Festinger's model of cognitive dissonance, which predicts "*a priori* self-protective behavior," that is, that a fear of dissonance leads to a reluctance to take action or commit oneself in order to avoid potential dissonance in the future (Festinger [1957] 1962, 31). The arguments presented by Noelle-Neumann are neither new nor inaccurate. The same sort of problems were discussed both in the framework of normative models of public (expression of) opinion and in the social-psychological research of cognitive consistency in communication processes. The question, however, remains the same as the one already posed by Blumer: What determines the validity of a research procedure like "public opinion" polling or the conceptualization of public opinion as "social control"? It is not that this kind of phenomena "must appear completely inexplicable to rationalists like Herbert Blumer or Bourdieu," as Noelle-Neumann (1995, 45) believes. Although they clearly recognize these processes in society, rationalists would rather not equate them with public opinion.

Noelle-Neumann characterized Blumer's theory as "masterfully outlining the concept of a rational public opinion with its manifest function of informing politicians in a democracy about the attitudes of the functional groups that constitute a society's organizations" ([1980] 1993, 226). Although Blumer convincingly displayed, according to Noelle-Neumann, the importance of interest groups in the process of opinion formation, he "does not say why these interest groups, and the pressure they exert on the politicians, may be termed 'public opinion.'" In other words, if there is no justification for simply equating public opinion with the results of opinion polls, why should one believe that interactions among interest groups constitute what is called public opinion? It is true that public opinion polls cannot record and measure public opinion conceptualized on the assumption that opinion formation is a rational process. However, they can validly record and measure public opinion as social control, which is "a matter of cohesion and a consensus on values in a society. This can only involve moral values—good and bad—or aesthetic values—beautiful and ugly—as only these have the emotional component capable of triggering the threat of isolation and the fear of isolation" (p. 229).

Comparing two fundamental and exclusive[6] concepts of public opinion, Noelle-Neumann only attempts to define positively public opinion as social control or "the integrative concept of public opinion" (i.e., what public opinion *is*), whereas public opinion as a rational process or the elite concept of public opinion is primarily considered a liberal democratic *ideal* or even a *myth* lacking any empirical referent. Without a clear reference to any concrete definition of the elite concept of public opinion,[7] it is merely taken to demonstrate its deficiencies in comparison to the social control concept. Noelle-Neumann briefly discusses four fundamental assumptions about the differences between the two concepts related to

1. the source of power of public opinion,
2. consensus on the community's values and goals,
3. the meaning of the concept of opinion,
4. and the meaning of the concept of public.

First, regarding the source of power of public opinion, Noelle-Neumann asserts that "public opinion as social control is centered on ensuring a sufficient level of consensus within society on the community's values and goals. According to this concept, the *power of public opinion* is so great that it cannot be ignored by either the government or the individual members of society. *This power stems from the threat of isolation.* . . . [The interaction between the individual and society] lends power to the common consciousness, common values and common goals, along with the accompanying threats directed at those who deviate from these values and goals" ([1980] 1993, 229; emphasis added).

The Noelle-Neumann model of public opinion formation incorporates all principal features characteristic of the social-psychological tradition. The *isolated individual* is in the center, whereas *group interactions* and the *rationality of discourse* as well as the *moral value* of public opinion as its "source of power" are out of focus. The power of public opinion is understood as the origin of its influence on both government and individuals, and the origin of power is attributed to the threat of isolation, which, however, can only exist if individuals have been previously influenced! The Noelle-Neumann model is a rather representative example of the erroneous (implicit) assumption widespread in social psychology that different aspects of power are closely associated with influence (or that there is even no difference between power and influence) and that conformity increases influence. Since Asch onward, it has been characteristic of this perspective to think that "the degree of conformity corresponds to an individual's social status, and that dependence on the authority of the group or the majority was the principal source of influence," although neither the connection between status and conformity nor between dependence and conformity was empirically verified (Moscovici 1976, 58). On the contrary, experiments evidently show that both conformity and nonconformity may affect influence attainment. It was already Robert E. Park who, with reference to Spencer, pointed out that the individual finds his position in the collectivity "through (1) *imitation* of his fellow men and (2) *competition* with them" (Park [1904] 1972, 56; emphasis added).

Noelle-Neumann equates the power of public opinion with its function of one-way social control; the fulfillment of this function denotes ensuring a sufficient level of consensus within society. However, power is something that people exercise over each other in a complex interplay, and it encompasses the entire range from absolute power to the weakest forms of threats; it is not simply present or absent. It is not possible to associate any actor or agent, including public opinion (or "the common consciousness, common values and common goals") with only the highest possible level of power, since situations and relations in which power is immanent are constantly changing and power is always confronted with resistance (not only in forms of dissent). Power can never be taken for granted; it requires constant exercise, fostering, and reproduction. Even if "power of public opinion" may be related to the threat of isolation, it is not simply the effect of such a threat because the reverse is also the case: *the threat of isolation is generated by power relations.* In this sense, power relationships may imply relations of domination, that is, power over another or others, the securing of compliance by means that may range from violence and force through manipulation to authority and rational persuasion. Thus power relations may also be understood as essentially cooperative and not necessarily related to the command-obedience relationship.

Like "power" and "influence," the words "power" and "control" are commonly used interchangeably, and Noelle-Neumann does not draw a clear distinction between them. Yet closer analysis reveals some significant differences. In contrast to power and similar to influence, control carries with it the sense of an informational environment, of a system of influences, commands, and feedback. Whereas power often (although incorrectly) seems to be a static concept, control is clearly situated in time (Mulgan 1991, 52). Control includes a sense of feedback and points to the fact that control is impossible without communication so that effects can be monitored and actions adjusted. In its most general sense, control is a purposive influence toward a predetermined goal; it is always purposive in the sense that it is directed toward some prior goal of the controlling agent (Beniger 1986, 7). In other words, the subject of action is in control of the external environment; it exercises control to bring the environment into line with what is desired (cf. Masuda [1980] 1983, 131). As a general concept, control ranges from absolute control to the weakest and most probabilistic forms, that is, any kind of purposive influence on behavior, however insignificant. For example, television advertising is said to control specific demands, direct mail campaigns control voting on a specific issue, or, as Park ([1904] 1972, 46) suggested, modern advertising technology "consists of controlling the mechanism for directing attention," although in each case only a very narrow segment of the intended audience may be influenced. In other words, *any form of coorientation implies a degree of control.* The crucial question is whether the relations among those included in coorientation are symmetrical or not, or who is in power of control?

Contrary to Noelle-Neumann's understanding of differences between "the concept of public opinion shaped by rationality" and "public opinion as social control," power and influence as multidimensional concepts attributed to specific situations (which do not necessarily imply hierarchical relations) are central to *both* concepts. As long as public opinion as a form of social will (irrespective of any specific understanding or definition of it) is related to other types of social relationship and assumes attempts at influencing opinions, normative power is immanent in it, regardless of whether we accept a more or less decentered definition of power. Power in a broader sense cannot be reduced to coercive power, since it also includes normative power (influence), which is based on expert knowledge. This type of power is typical of opinion leaders, whose expert authority is willingly accepted by outsiders who usually go beyond passively accepting the opinion of their opinion leader and also agree with it. However, as Tönnies argued, opinion formation should be related to reasoning. Not all citizens can participate in initiating the process of opinion formation, only the most educated and intelligent. Yet, in the opinion of the public, citizens may reach consensus by accepting silently an opinion they recognize as a correct one. Thus we may argue that exposure to public discussion affects individuals without strong or prior opinions about an issue at least as much as those seeing their position falling into decline, the former obviously not out of fear of isolation but because of a lack of (prior) information.

One of the fundamental questions we may find among rationalists is, as Wilson (1962, 39) formulated it, "under which conditions public opinion creates obligations for a government to follow," in other words, in what social circumstances does public opinion generate influence or enough power to be politically effective? This was exactly the question already raised by Tönnies (1922, 154), namely, under what conditions, on what grounds, the opinion formed by *Gelehrtenrepublik* (because it is it whose opinion is firm or "solid" enough) may become effective. Such an important condition is the *subject* or *actor* that initiates the process of public opinion formation through its status and competence. Although at the final stage of the process it seems that public opinion disposes of power that was somehow generated by itself, it is rather a specific situation that enables a group or collectivity to generate power and influence. This certainly implies that all social actors (from the government to individual members of society) can never have the same relation to public opinion because they have different status and competence and thus different power and influence—

regardless of whether public opinion is conceptualized primarily as social control or discursive process.

Of course, the main difference between the two conceptualizations is the perspective we use: is public opinion a phenomenon in which coercive or normative power (which is influence) manifests itself, or is it a form of what Buckley (1967) named "authority"? In Buckley's distinction between power and authority, power is related to private goals and the lack of ascertainable consensus, whereas authority promotes collective goals based on consensus and implies "informed voluntary compliance which is a definite psychological state and a coordination or identity of the goal orientations of controller and controlled." Thus, in Buckley's terms, authority rather than power should be considered the basis of public opinion. Similarly (and unlike Noelle-Neumann, who connects the power of public opinion with individuals' conformity to the majority), Tönnies relates it to the level of its articulation and strength (of consensus).

The difference between authority and power reflects a more universal opposition between the general will (or *normative* collective will that is morally valid for the collectivity) and the will of everyone (*empirical* collective will, that is, interests and ideas actually prevailing in the collectivity in a given moment) as formulated by Rousseau and his followers. To argue that the power of public opinion stems from the individual's fear of isolation misses completely the fundamental argument of normative and early sociological theories that saw public opinion as both rational and moral process and power. As the normative collective will must not be equated with the empirical will, public opinion must not be equated with the opinion of everyone or the majority at a given moment. As Park argues, "It is incorrect to think that the collective consciousness which judges immoral actions is determined only by personal and individual interests. . . . The ability to empathize at all with others *assumes* that something *in common* exists" (Park [1904] 1972, 77; emphasis added). The general will cannot be considered the will of the majority; rather, it assumes the existence of a collective spirit or purpose. Park asserts that the general will is "first expressed as a collective force overpowering and assimilating all individual drives. Existing at times as a norm, it opposes the transient individual feelings and drives of the collectivity" (p. 77) and thus becomes a general characteristic of any social collectivity.

The difference between rational public opinion and public opinion as social control is not between rationality and controllability (influence) but rather in the *origin* and *aim* of control, since both concepts imply a specific form of control. In the former, it is the need for coorientation; in the latter, as in Panopticon, it is the fear of authority of tradition, power, or isolation. They also imply a specific form of rationality (either prevalently "formal" or "instrumental," or "substantive" in Weberian dichotomy).[8] If the fear of isolation is the main mechanism of opinion expression (as in public opinion as social control), it cannot be only an idiosyncratic trait of the individual; it must be also characteristic of the social structure and social will. The difference between the two concepts of public opinion is essentially a consequence of two different approaches to public opinion; the instrumental approach is focused on the forces in the modern world that shape and restrain opinions and actions of individuals, whereas the substantive conceptualization is focused on the ways and forms of action individuals are using to get control over their environment. In the first approach, social control represents "a property of the external social structure that acts upon persons within," whereas the second approach "consists of the models and forms of conduct devised by persons in action" (Kreiling and Sims 1981, 9). The former concentrates on different forms of group control over its members to reduce divergences among them; the latter stresses originality, the recognition of individuality, and social change. The latter approach is characteristic of Tönnies's theorization of the opinion of the public and symbolic interactionism of Mead and Dewey, on which the coorientational approach to public opinion is based. The differences between the two conceptualizations clearly reflect the controversy between positive and critical science.

Second, regarding the nature and importance of society's consensus, Noelle-Neumann argues that in contrast to "rational public opinion," the power of public opinion as social control is based on a sufficient level of consensus within society on the community's values and goals ([1980] 1993, 229). She equalizes consensus and the pressure to conform, to which both rulers and ordinary people have to pay attention, the former because "they feel that they will lose power otherwise" and the latter because "their social nature makes them suffer from isolation" (Noelle-Neumann 1985, 69). The pressure to conform because of the fear of losing power and of isolation results in integration and cohesion, which enables a community to make decisions and take actions. This, according to Noelle-Neumann, is the basis of the integrative concept of public opinion, in contrast to the elitist concept based on the idea of critical judgment of informed and responsible members of society.

Generally, the concept of public opinion as social control implies the existence of either consensus or coercion, or both of them, whereas the concept of rational public opinion refers only to consensus in the strict sense. Noelle-Neumann justly argues that without a certain level of consensus it would be impossible for community to exist, but she believes that *conformity is the necessary condition to achieve consensus.* Yet conformity is not the only way in which social influence generates consensus. As Coser (1994, 107) claims, "Consensus does not involve clinging forever to fixed standards that guide conduct." Consensus among some *always* implies dissensus among others; and what is a matter of agreement at a certain point of time may become an area of disagreement at the next point, or vice versa—which is the principal mover of public opinion process. In other words, in a democratic society, consensus is achieved from dissensus through a reflective or rational discussion of controversial issues.

In Noelle-Neumann's theory, the power of public opinion is actually not based on a sufficient level of consensus within society but rather on a sufficient level of social *coordination,* or any form of Tönnies's *Einigung* (i.e., producing agreement). Coordination is made possible either by consensus (which, in turn, is made possible by communication) or by coercion and conformity. *Consensus* represents that specific situation in which motivation for coordination is high and intrinsic. Consensus cannot be imposed by coercion; it can only result from intercommunication, debate, negotiation, compromise, and toleration. In contrast to consensus, coordination can be also based on threat of punishment and thus achieved in a situation in which motivation for agreement is very low or even completely absent (Scheff 1967, 35).

A seeming unanimity obtained by coercion "does not truly give us consensus." Rather, it is "pseudoconsensus" or *Gleichschaltung,* as it was called by the Nazis (Wirth 1948, 8). In contrast to consensus, the submission or pseudoconsensus is forcefully imposed: it is the result of coercion that forces individuals to accept and follow a norm of behavior or decision because they fear possible reprisal or because they fear isolation, as in the spiral of silence model of opinion expression. In Noelle-Neumann's theory, consensus within society does not necessarily imply a process of discussion but may imply coercion, since "the concepts of public opinion, sanction, and punishment are closely linked with one another" (Noelle-Neumann 1974, 43). In either case, the power of public opinion as social control *is not* based on attempts by individuals and social groups to achieve rational agreements; therefore, it indeed excludes consensus in the strict sense. For Noelle-Neumann, the most important condition of sufficient integration that enables life in human society is the individual's need not to isolate himself (Noelle-Neumann 1974, 43), whereas for Coser, only a measure of consensus, at least within a fraction of population, can provide a sufficient foundation for a social order (coercion alone cannot provide it). Tönnies's position in his discussion of "binding opinions" would be, not surprisingly, closer to Coser and Wirth than Noelle-Neumann, namely, that

> the content of the will of a group—a union, an association—is a valid law for the members of the group, provided that it is *thought* of as grounded on the *consensual* will of all, and *decided* and *published* in the forms appropriate to the *consensual* will. (Tönnies 1922, 43–44; emphasis added)

The Noelle-Neumann model represents a typical example of the "conformity bias" that dominated social psychology as a whole and theories of social influence in particular for decades. As a critique of this bias, Moscovici developed a radically different and more complex model of the influence process. In addition to conformity, he discusses how opinion can be changed by a (deviant) minority on the basis of a reciprocal influence between minorities and majorities in the multilevel processes of normalization and innovation as typical modes of influence (Moscovici 1976, 166–97; 1991, 301–7). In the first place, according to Moscovici, even conformity does not necessarily prevent deviance. A kind of conformity can be also used "in order to allow for the possibility of *reciprocal* influence, permitting the *modification* of existing relations, opinions and behaviors" (Moscovici 1976, 39; emphasis added). Thus conformity may also serve as a means to achieve innovation. In contrast to the dialectical conceptualization of conformity, nonconformity, and influence, Noelle-Neumann considers only the traditionally conceptualized "first phase" of conformity process relevant for public opinion.[9]

There is already substantial evidence to support Hollander's theory (developed in early 1970s) that higher status, once attained, allows and even requests greater nonconformity, which enhances influence (Ridgeway 1981). In the leadership process, the individual in the first phase of conformity process acquires authority over the group by adhering to the norms and values of the group. In the next phase, the individual can (and is even expected to) modify and innovate norms and values of the group because he or she represents the group as its leader, and the others will follow because they place their confidence in him or her.[10] As Moscovici emphasizes, in both phases "nobody is ever deviant in the last analysis except, perhaps, the group." Experiments conducted by Cecilia Ridgeway (1981) indicate that this dialectical relationship extends beyond the situation of enhanced status. Even in the first phase of leadership process, when members of a group strive for status and influence, nonconformity rather than conformity may increase influence. This is basically related to the fact that conformity is not a reliable indicator of the individual's true motivation; it is at least ambiguous because it may be also interpreted in terms of hiding the true motivation to belong to the group, and thus individuals' conformity is not necessarily positively sanctioned.

Public opinion, according to Noelle-Neumann, implies what V. O. Key named "consensus on fundamentals." In contrast to Key's concept, however, "consensus" has no democratic implications for Noelle-Neumann. This clearly reflects the fundamental difference between the idea of public opinion as only a generalized form of collective will and social control in modern societies, and public opinion as opinion of the public (in contrast to custom) about public issues, which governments must heed or may find it prudent to heed; the importance of public opinion in the latter (democratic) sense is that it may condition the behavior of those in positions of public authority (Key [1961] 1967). Obviously, the latter understanding assumes a form of democratic government, whereas the former does not. Contrary to Noelle-Neumann's belief, consensus is one of the key elements of public opinion process also in the normative and interactionist theories of public opinion, and in Tönnies's critique of public opinion. The latter are even able to provide the answer to the critical question Noelle-Neumann even does not ask, Where does (or can) such a consensus come from? It always arises from substantial disagreement, discussion of controversial issues, and coorientation. To come to a consensus from a disagreement, an informed, rational discussion is needed; it always implies coorientation ("I know that you know . . .") because without it discussion is not possible. And this is exactly what the idea of public opinion as a rational process is about.

Third, regarding the meaning of the concept of opinion, Noelle-Neumann writes that "according to the democratic-theoretical concept, *opinion* is primarily a matter of individual views and arguments, whereas the concept of public opinion as social control applies it to much greater area, in fact to everything that visibly expresses a value-related opinion in public, which may be directly in the form of buttons and badges, flags, gestures, hairstyles and beards, publicly visible symbols, and publicly visible, morally loaded behavior" (Noelle-Neumann [1980] 1993, 230).

Public opinion is, according to Noelle-Neumann ([1980] 1993, 64), typically spread by the *spiral of silence,* which is "a reaction to openly visible approval or disapproval among shifting constellations of values." It has no relevance for the spiral of silence process whether a person isolates himself or herself through an opinion or through his or her behavior. Consequently, "opinion" should be understood as a synonym for the expression of anything, or any kind of behavior that might be regarded as acceptable or unacceptable; it refers not only to verbal behavior but to all forms of behavior in public. Public opinion thus includes all forms of collective will—as Tönnies names them—*beyond opinion formation and expression* such as, for example, *conventions* or even *religion.*

In Noelle-Neumann's view, part of the controversy related to different meanings and understandings of (public) opinion is caused by linguistic differences. Supposedly, her broad meaning of the concept of opinion is more common in English and French, in contrast to German *Meinung,* which is "preoccupied with the value or lack of value." It supposedly implies an element of commonness and agreement and is not necessarily limited to the consensus of opinion but may deal "with concurrent behavior—wearing or not wearing a badge, offering one's seat to an old person or remaining seated in a public vehicle." Thus opinion should be understood "as a synonym for the expression of something regarded as acceptable, thereby hinting at the element of consensus or agreement found in the English and French usage" (Noelle-Neumann [1980] 1993, 60).

Regarding the specificity of the German notion of opinion, Noelle-Neumann is perhaps right. According to Tönnies (1922, 8–9), "at least in German," opining (*Meinen*) does not mean only to form and/or to have opinion but also to express opinion. Opinion of the public denotes "common way of thought, the corporate spirit of any group or association, in so far as its opining (*Meinen*) is built upon *reasoning* and *knowledge,* rather than on unproved impressions, beliefs or authority" (Tönnies 1922, 78; emphasis added). Opining (either individual or collective, e.g., public) is closely connected with human reasoning[11] (*Denken*), and both are related to wishing and wanting, and feeling; opining is always a combination of rationality, volition, and affection. The rational, even intellectual component is particularly important for public opinion and separates it from popular beliefs: public friendship or public mourning must not be equated with the opinion of the public! Yet Tönnies's interpretation of the meaning of the concept of opinion in German contradicts Noelle-Neumann's belief that the German concept is preoccupied with the evaluative dimension—unless reasoning and knowledge were considered evaluative.

Still, Noelle-Neumann's belief that the element of consensus is characteristic of the English or French concept of opinion rather than the German concept remains contradictory. Quite to the contrary, Albig argues that "we may logically distinguish between consensus and opinion." In modern life, awareness of different and conflicting beliefs has made for relativism; areas of certainty were narrowed whereas areas of divergent beliefs, codes, and standards expanded. Accordingly, "*the field of opinion widens,* and *the sphere of consensus diminishes. . . .* Public opinion . . . deals with those topics which are controversial and discussible in the publics concerned, and not with those aspects of mind-life which are comparatively fixed" (Albig 1956, 9; emphasis added). With reference to Tönnies, Albig emphasizes that the realm of opinion includes neither popular beliefs nor ethical consensus (the mores), which is a state of agreement.

In contrast to Noelle-Neumann, who does not see the element of consensus in the German use of the term *Meinung,* and in contrast to Albig's clear separation of opinion from consensus, Tönnies did stress the consensual nature of the opinion of the public (as a pure theoretical concept) in which citizens participate either actively (i.e., they form and express opinions) or passively (i.e., they accept opinions). Opinion of the public differs from the other forms of social will according to the way in which common will is generated; in the opinion of the public, the typical way is consensus. When comparing opinion of the public as a form of reflexive social will with religion, which is the equivalent form in organic will, Tönnies sees one of the major differences between the two in the degree of seriousness and rigor to enforce and sanction their rules in the fields of order, legality, and morals. In all these fields, and particularly in the field of morals, religion is more rigorous than public opinion. In contrast to Noelle-Neumann's belief, however, this would not imply that the rationalistic concept of public opinion excludes value-related opinions and morally loaded behavior. On the contrary, "The politics of sentiments (*Gefühlspolitik*) is the playground of public opinion. It can often perfectly correspond with a planned politics of reason (*Verstandespolitik*)" (Tönnies 1922, 253). But of course, in such a perspective public opinion is reduced to formation and expression of opinions, to people's concern with an object or an issue toward which their attention is directed (despite differences in their opinions). Park ([1904] 1972) would argue that it is directed to those forms of interaction that are beyond primitive forms of reciprocity observed in the animal herd or suggest imitation of surrounding social forms (which Park considers a form of learning rather than fear) exemplified by the crowd.[12]

Fourth, regarding the meaning of the concept of public, Noelle-Neumann asserts that "according to democratic-theoretical concept of public opinion as the product of *raisonnement*, 'public' is viewed in terms of the content of the themes of public opinion, which are political contents. The concept of public opinion as social control interprets 'public' in the sense of the 'public eye.' . . . Its relevance extends from all rules of moral nature ('political correctness') to taboos, areas of severe, unresolved conflict that may not be addressed in public, lest social cohesion be threatened" ([1980] 1993, 230).

Noelle-Neumann differentiates among three meanings of "public." First, in the legal sense, it means openness to everyone, like a public place, a public path, or a public trial, in contrast to the private. Second, another meaning can be found in the concepts of public rights or public force; here "public" denotes public interest and implies some involvement of the state, or a ruling character, as in the case of public opinion (i.e., ruling opinion). Third, and most specifically, a meaning actually constructed by Noelle-Neumann ([1980] 1993, 61), is the social-psychological or behavioral. Because of their fear of isolation, disrespect, or unpopularity, individuals are willingly exposed to the demands of society—to their "social skin." Accordingly, public opinion as social control refers to "the approval and disapproval of publicly observable positions and behavior," whereas public opinion "as the product of raisonnement" is related to "public interest" (Noelle-Neumann [1980] 1993, 64).

I have already pointed out that not only the democratic-theoretical concept of public opinion but also what Blumer would call a "narrow operationalist concept of public opinion" suggests that public opinion is related to "public matters, what people want government to do (or not do)," that is, to political contents. On the other hand, in the rationalistic concept of public opinion, visibility or accessibility of an opinion or behavior to many or all is also one—but only one—important dimension of the (concept of) publicness. Visibility of an opinion does not constitute public opinion by itself; an opinion does not transform into public opinion just by its visibility alone. Tönnies, for example, argued that "public opinion does not mean only the expressed opinion but the opinion expressed and intended toward the public [*die Öffentlichkeit, das Publikum*], toward the generality" (Tönnies 1922, 131), which means that every one has access to it, physically and intellectually. In Tönnies's differentiation between the articulate and inarticulate public opinion, even the latter is more than just any visible opinion; it is intended toward the public. This does not necessarily imply a sort of elitism, according to Joseph Moseley, another significant but neglected author from the mid-1800s. The term "public" in principle includes all members of the community, and in that sense public opinion is, even in the elite conception, the opinion of all. All may be present in public meetings, join associations and clubs, and participate in elections; they constitute "One Great Public." The question is whether or not they may significantly influence the government (Wilson 1962, 76).

Reducing the concept of public to visibility, and thus public opinion to visible opinion (or publicly expressed opinion, or behavior), connotes what Habermas calls "representative publicness," that is, a public representation of secular or clerical authority before common people—a very effective form of social control characteristic of feudal society. In contemporary democratic societies, this reduction is related to a "new staging of the political public" as "demonstratively and manipulatively developed public sphere" that, according to Habermas ([1962] 1995, 215), manifests itself as a form of decay of the bourgeois public and could better fit with a form of enlightened absolutism than a democratic state.

Even if we accepted Noelle-Neumann's broad understanding of opinion that includes both verbal(ized) and nonverbal forms of behavior, sharing the same opinion in either sense does not yet make it public (nor does any form of expression). Sharing of opinion(s) is one thing; public opinion is another. Any theorization of public opinion would agree, as Binkley and Wilson believe, that "things of the mind, whether rational or not, are shared; it is the sharing of opinion *under certain conditions* that makes it public. . . . Public opinion, and more particularly the public, is a *mode* or a *specific means of sharing*" (Wilson 1962, 93). The sharing of opinions and values, and so on, is constitutive for any community or society and thus is a fundamental prerequisite for public opinion to develop; it may be considered a *genus proximum* for a number of societal phenomena. *Differentia specifica* of public opinion, however, rest upon a specific means of sharing opinions, for Wilson, both in opinion expression and in action leading to decisions.

Nevertheless, Noelle-Neumann's emphasis on the behavioral component of public opinion ("an opinion that can be voiced in public") brings to the front of the discussion an important difference between individuals' issue-centered attitudes and attitudes toward behavior, which results in the difference between private beliefs and public behavior, as Festinger put it. Normative theories of public opinion focus on (controversial) public issues that are discussed by the public and, eventually, resolved into a consensus that has the potential to influence decision makers, whereas they usually ignore the problem of attitudes toward behavior. As James B. Lemert argues for earlier social-psychological approaches, "one of the major justifications for focusing on issue attitudes was the presumption that if one knew about attitudes, one knew about behavior" (1981, 30). Noelle-Neumann reversed the direction of the presumption. It is not that issue-centered attitudes predict individuals' behavior and form public opinion but rather that public opinion controls individuals' behavior and "ensures the formation and maintenance of consensus in value-laden areas" (1991, 282–83). Yet both assumptions are reductionist; neither variable can be used as the predictor of the other one.

EXCURSUS: THE SPIRAL OF SILENCE AND TÖNNIES'S CRITIQUE OF PUBLIC OPINION

Noelle-Neumann's (1979; [1980] 1993; Noelle 1940, 29) references to Tönnies's theory of public opinion give the impression that the spiral of silence is congruent with his theory or even founded on it, despite the fact that she also claimed that both Bauer's and Tönnies's "standard German works of the first decade of the twentieth century . . . seem to fail" (Noelle-Neumann [1980] 1993, 92). Tönnies should certainly be acknowledged for having informed Noelle-Neumann, through her reading of his *Critique,* with Tocqueville's ideas. His assumption that French king Louis XVI "obeyed public opinion which guided or pulled him daily; which he constantly considered, feared, and to which he continually flattered" (Tönnies 1922, 394) is particularly important for the spiral of silence (Noelle-Neumann [1980] 1993, 183). It is much more important than Tocqueville's and Tönnies's ascertainment that "the French nation in its *upper classes* was the most *enlightened* and *free* on the continent," that is, that in the prerevolutionary period public opinion was formed by the educated and wealthy elite. Precisely the assumption that public opinion concerns every-body—both those in power and common citizens—in the same way is one of the central ideas of the spiral of silence, so that the spiral of silence seems to be even more democratic than elitist-rationalist theories (Noelle-Neumann specifically mentions Habermas) that relate public opinion to rational discourse.

Noelle-Neumann's and Tönnies's theories are similar in that both link public opinion to human conformity, which originates in the fear of social isolation. Tönnies discusses conformity both on the most abstract level, that is, in the process of formation and expression of opinion in general, and specifically in defining the concept of opinion of the public:

> On a difficult question, when the majority "agree," a person can form a judgment and truly entertain the view whose grounds s/he knows; but the others only express it when they faithfully repeat it. People follow and subordinate themselves to the "authorities." The objection is suppressed either because it is considered irrelevant to the judgment or because of the fear of disapproval and unfavourable *consequences;* particularly when we are not confronted with the individual's opinion that is widely unknown, but rather with an unanimous and published opinion of the many.... *With silence one demonstrates consent.* (Tönnies 1922, 27; emphasis added)

Tönnies's opinion of the public, particularly in its "solid state," includes a high degree of consensus and thus (which makes it comparable to religion) exerts pressure on individuals to conform, although they intimately do not agree with it:

> The opinion of the public always appears with a claim to be deciding, it demands consent and obliges at least to the silence, to the omission of a resistance. With greater or smaller success; the more perfect the success, the more it proves to be the opinion of the public, despite the resistance that is more or less compelled to silence. This is most clearly indicated by the questions linked with religion. (Tönnies 1922, 138)

Tönnies's ideas on conformity of human behavior may appear to be congruent with Noelle-Neumann's model of public opinion, but the framework and scope of the two theories are totally different, and so are the understandings and evaluations of conformity. Contrary to the seeming congruity with the spiral of silence, Tönnies's theory represents a basis to falsify the spiral of silence theory. His discussion of conformity centers on the formation of common opinions, which are characteristic of all forms of common will (of which "opinion of the public" is a specific case) rather than specifically on public opinion or even opinion of the public. Among all forms of complex will, opinion of the public is, by Tönnies's definition, the form of social will least jeopardized by the silencing of dissenting voices. "The new, the modern, the enlightened way of thinking" is, according to Tönnies, the strongest in the public and has an irresistible power. Changes in the opinion of the public about controversial issues, which denote its fluid state, express primarily its impartiality; fluidity of the opinion of the public is a consequence of the fact that it is always impartial and unbiased; it supports what is "undeniably in a spirit of common good and what guarantees a better future. This is how it justifies the changes to itself and to the world; its frequently abrupt turn reminds of the changes in fashion, like clothing, furniture, etc." (Tönnies 1922, 273). When individuals exhibit conformity, it by necessity implies that "in every group, in every circle a 'public' opinion is formed and expressed outward and inward." Thus there is a plurality of reference groups and situations in which individuals are exposed to the group pressure. However, the individual's personal "firmness" has a decisive importance.

Noelle-Neumann considers conformity the basis of public opinion formation (also) in the empirical sense as a universal phenomenon, a sort of common or natural law. " 'Howling in chorus' is just as common among dogs as among wolves, and chimpanzees too will sometimes howl in chorus" (Noelle-Neumann [1980] 1993, 98). Conformity is also the basic principle of social behavior of human beings. According to Noelle-Neumann, "the attention individuals pay to group judgments" was "unfairly defamed with the label of 'conformity,' " instead of being recognized as "the *social nature* of human beings" (p. 41). Even if we declare freedom and autonomy in opinion formation to be the fundamental values, individuals' behavior is "objectively" determined by other norms:

> Freedom, sincerity, individualism—all these are adopted consciously as expressions of the values we feel in our own beings, but they simply do not fit the *ways we must assume people behave,* given our description of the spiral of silence. . . . Must we create a *fiction of public opinion based on critical judgment* because to acknowledge the real forces that keep human society together would not be compatible with our ego ideal? (Noelle-Neumann [1980] 1993, 43, 100; emphasis added)

In contrast to the biological universalism of Noelle-Neumann, Tönnies's opinion of the public represents a socially and historically determined phenomenon: as a purely theoretical concept, opinion of the public is a universal and transhistoric category that, however, is closely linked with the human will and reason, and both with freedom. On the applied level, public opinion is always historically specific, socially and culturally determined. In a historically concrete sense, it never exists as a pure, ideal category; rather, it is full of contradictions because it always includes admixtures of other forms of social will, even organic will (which in its pure form, as religion, represents an absolute opposition to the opinion of the public). Last but not least, his opinion of the public was actually a part of Tönnies's central idea of the development of a new social order—a "popular" or "new community" *(Volksgemeinschaft)*—emancipated from the control of political parties and, particularly, the church, with a free and socialized press as the key means of free opinion expression. His theory rises from a principal differentiation among published opinion, public opinion, and the opinion of the public, whereas Noelle-Neumann is firmly convinced that "*published* opinion and *public* opinion are basically the same thing" (p. 150).

In opposition to the apparent value neutralism in Noelle-Neumann, who does not consider the relevance of human freedom for public opinion, Tönnies explicitly stresses the moral (and aesthetic) foundation of an opinion of the public: it is always closely connected with humanism. His applied analysis of the "solid opinion of the public" is focused on the idea of personal freedom as a typical issue in the social and economic realm: "The idea of social life in which opinion of the public is deeply anchored, is the idea of personal *freedom;* it was set as an ideal" (Tönnies 1922, 258). Tönnies emphasizes the attachment of opinion of the public to rationality as a result of a general endeavor for knowledge and freedom in the spiritual and ethical sphere, whereas "rare solid components" of an opinion of the public in the political sphere are mainly exhibited by the opinion that the substance of the state is in that it acts for citizens' benefit, and thus—similarly to Kant—by the support to the *republic* as the only environment in which a political opinion of the public can exist in its "firm form."

Paradoxically, Noelle-Neumann incorporates in public opinion customs and traditions but explicitly excludes "the solid" and "the gaseous" states of public opinion as defined by Tönnies. "If one uses Tönnies' analogy, *the spiral of silence appears only during the fluid state*" (Noelle-Neumann [1980] 1993, 63; emphasis added). This reduction is significant because, in Tönnies's conceptualization, the opinion of the public is a continuous developmental process from its solid to its gaseous state. Tönnies himself warned against a reduction of the opinion of the public to its most striking manifestation, the "gaseous opinion of the public," because the most important is its "solid" state (Tönnies 1922, 276). Different stages of public opinion primarily reflect individuals' *internal agreement* and *firmness,* or *certainty of opinions,* rather than external (interpersonal or group) consensus. Tönnies even exemplifies fluid opinion with an artistic genius, and gaseous opinion with a mass in which opinions are superficial and poorly grounded.

From Tönnies's perspective, Noelle-Neumann's exclusion of the solid opinion of the public from her model of public opinion as social control is paradoxical because, according to Tönnies, the most effective social control is performed by the solid rather than by the fluid or gaseous opinion of the public. She misinterprets[13] the solid phase of public opinion as if it were the form in which opinions and forms of behavior have not only "gained a firm *majority*" but where they also "become *custom or tradition*," and thus they do not have "an element of *controversy*," neither of rationality (Noelle-Neumann [1980] 1993, 63; emphasis added). For Tönnies, custom (as a complex form) and tradition (as an elementary form) of common will represent specific forms of social will characteristic of the Gemeinschaft-type societies, as opposed to Gesellschaft, in which the opinion of the public develops. Both custom and tradition are generated by transmission of knowledge from the older generation to the younger, or from a higher class (particularly priests) to a lower. In contrast to that, opinion of the public as a complex form of social will in all its stages (solid, fluid, gaseous) exists in the Gesellschaft-type societies in which tradition and authority are losing validity and yielding up to reason and criticism (Tönnies 1922, 219–57). Opinion of the public is not (neither can it become) custom or tradition, in contrast to Noelle-Neumann's favored exemplification of public opinion with fashion.

With his theorization of different aggregate states of the opinion of the public, Tönnies emphasizes a contradictory character of the opinion of the public. The contradiction stems from the fact that, on the one hand, the opinion of the public demands freedom of thought, expression, and the press due to its moral and humane character; on the other hand it is "a power that *unites* its members and *obliges* them; it applies the principle of tolerance to differences in religious opinion, as being of minor importance, and definitely not to others, primarily political differences, where it most of the time acts as being on its own turf" (Tönnies 1922, 285; emphasis added). However, opinion of the public does not demand from those who assume leading positions to obey it, but only to recognize the correct and fair opinions or at least not to oppose them. Furthermore, opinion of the public cannot be equated with habit, custom, or education. "Where only one man thinks and evaluates, while the rest blindly believes him or merely repeats his words . . . there is no public opinion—which always presupposes that a man who treasures it follows his own nature and impressions in his judgments" (Tönnies 1916, 415). Individuals can never achieve the ideal of a complete independence in the process of forming a unanimous opinion; however, the fundamental characteristic of such an agreement is the endeavor to reach it on the basis of human *knowledge* and *rational conclusion* drawn by every individual. The contradictions of the opinion of the public are further related to the fundamental social contradictions between the classes of proprietors and nonproprietors, between the urban and the rural, and between the cultivated layers and the people (Tönnies 1922, 117).

As Tönnies argues, rational and irrational forms of the *common will* are an important dimension of common opinions (*gemeinsame Meinungen)* but not necessarily of the opinion of the public. Common will (*gemeinsame Wille*) and common want (*gemeinsame Wollen*) can be hierarchically conceptualized as (1) a simple agreement of many individuals, (2) an extension of agreement to practical action, (3) an establishment of a formal organization that includes rules of decision making, (4) a generalization of organization to long-term activities of the members, (5) an institutionalization based on statutory regulation of activities, (6) a form of professionalization of activities, and (7) a general determination of what is true and what is not, which opinions are correct and which ones are wrong (Tönnies 1922, 46–51). A higher and more complex form represents a "natural" extension of the lower form and ordinarily presupposes it. In this respect, only the seventh "form" may be an exception; all other forms contribute to the rational unification of the will. Even if the will of those associated is primarily intended for making a truth (or rather belief in it) public, and for preventing any public doubt or even denial of it, such a will is fully realized only when it commands the *thoughts* themselves. Only in that case will it be sure that alternative thoughts will *never* become the dominant and public ones (Tönnies 1922, 50, 52). On the other hand, however, dissenting opinions tend to become widespread and diffused to newcomers and the new generation, and organized. In this way, new factions, parties, or cliques develop within the organization, the state, or the church. These forms of common will may well be part of formation of the opinion of the public and reflexive will in general, provided that they are based on *reason* and *knowledge* and not on beliefs and authority; the latter are characteristic of forms of organic will only (e.g., custom and religion). The difference between Noelle-Neumann's "rational" public opinion and public opinion reduced to "social control" is, then, exactly the difference between Tönnies's reflective (arbitrary) and organic (essential) will. As Tönnies argues throughout his *Kritik* (1922), public opinion or, more exactly, the opinion of the public, only exists in the form of reflective will; otherwise it is a *religion.*

According to Noelle-Neumann's understanding, everyone depends on public opinion in the same way: "it cannot be ignored by either the government or the individual members of society" ([1980] 1993, 229). Tönnies, however, clearly distinguishes between the layers that form and express opinion (wealthy, more educated individuals in urban centers), and those that primarily receive or agree with an already published opinion. Equally significant is the difference in the functions they attribute to the mass media and journalists in the process of public opinion formation. In Noelle-Neumann's model, they have "the privilege of conferring public attention." Individuals assess the climate of opinion on the basis of information received from two sources: from their direct observation of the environment and from the mass media, particularly television. The latter are supposed to be most important—the autonomous and homogeneous creator of public opinion, having the "jaws of a tiger" (p. 155) for millions of recipients. Political and economic elites seem to have no relevance for the social-psychological model of the spiral of silence, which removes all concrete historical circumstances of public opinion processes: "the selection of what the public *must* attend to, of indicating what is urgent, which questions everyone *must* be considered with . . . *all of this is decided by the media.* Moreover, the media influence the individual's perception of what can be said or done without danger of isolation" (p. 156; emphasis added). Unlike Noelle-Neumann, Tönnies considered the newspapers essentially instruments used by the state, political parties, and enterprises to influence public opinion. He proposed a number of reforms needed to reestablish the financial and party-political autonomy of the media, which he considered the fundamental condition for the realization of their authentic function—to be a means of expression of the opinion of the public.

Tönnies's theory of public opinion obviously represents an opposition to the spiral of silence model; whereas Tönnies enforces a humanistic vision of the opinion of the public as a fundamental societal tribunal or institution of reasoned critique, which is also governed by general rules of opinion formation and expression, the Noelle-Neumann model represents a notable example of an "obsession with dependence" characteristic of social-psychological study of influence processes, as Moscovici (1976, 16) put it.

EMPIRICAL CRITIQUE OF THE SPIRAL OF SILENCE: DISAPPEARANCE OF PUBLIC OPINION

The empirical case on which Noelle-Neumann starts to prove the validity of her theory is comparable with that presented by Festinger to explain the process of establishing cognitive consonance. In the introductory chapter to her *Spiral of Silence* (1980), Noelle-Neumann reports that a significant number (3–4 percent) of German voters in 1965, and again in 1972, changed the party they intended to vote for at the last minute and chose the party that actually won the election (but was also in power at the time of the election). "Repeated questioning of the same people before and after the 1972 election revealed to us that those who feel they are relatively isolated from others . . . are the ones most likely to participate in a last-minute election swing. Those with weaker self-confidence and less interest in politics are also likely to make a last-minute switch" (Noelle-Neumann [1980] 1993, 6). What had occurred, she generalizes, "had been recognized and named centuries earlier, but was still not understood, the power of public opinion. . . . At the last minute they had gone along with the crowd" (Noelle-Neumann [1980] 1993, 2). From the above and similar cases of empirical evidence, Noelle-Neumann infers that the *fear of isolation* of those individuals who deviate from the majority opinion is the force that sets in motion the *spiral of silence* as the *generator of public opinion* that leads to a decrease in support for the less discussed opinions and, eventually, to the disappearance of minority opinion:

> If people believe that their opinion is part of a consensus, they have the confidence to speak out in both private and public discussions, displaying their convictions with buttons and car stickers, for example, but also by the clothes they wear and other publicly visible symbols. Conversely, when people feel that they are in minority, they become cautious and silent, thus reinforcing the impression of weakness, until the apparently weaker side disappears completely except for a hard core that holds on to its previous values, or until the opinion becomes taboo. (Noelle-Neumann [1980] 1993, 202)

Despite its theoretical deficiencies, since its publication in 1973 the spiral of silence has gone through dozens of *empirical* replications, tests, and critiques, mostly in Germany, the United States, and Japan.[14] Its wide popularity is the reason for discussing it at length here, although these critiques are not directly related to the theoretical merits of the spiral of silence discussed above. On the other hand, theoretical critique of the spiral of silence as a *theory of public opinion* has no direct implications for the empirical importance of the model. Yet the validity of the empirical model may also be disputed.

Empirical critiques mainly focus on the probability of the spiraling process to exist, specific circumstances and conditions that increase or decrease its validity, and the (lack of) evidence of its universality. They concentrate on the four major dimensions of Noelle-Neumann's model that she emphasized in her publications:

1. the individual's fear of isolation
2. the individual's ability to perceive trends in public opinion
3. the existence of a generalized picture of public opinion as represented in the media
4. validity of research methods used to test empirically the spiral of silence

First, regarding the assumption that fear of isolation is the basic pressure to conform, Noelle-Neumann maintains that "public opinion arises from an interaction of individuals with their social environments. . . . To the individual, not isolating himself is more important than his own judgment. This appears to be a condition of life in human society" (Noelle-Neumann 1974, 43).

In spite of the controversy on the nature of public opinion, I can agree with Noelle-Neumann that the threat of isolation exists and that people can often identify opinions that may "run a high risk of triggering the threat of isolation when publicly expressed" (Noelle-Neumann [1980] 1993, 204). *However,* as McQuail and Windahl (1981, 69) claim, "the process of opinion forming represented by the model almost certainly occurs under *some conditions* and to *some degree,* but the *extent* of its occurrence is still not known" (emphasis added). The key question is not whether silence (as a form of communication) exists (of course it does), but rather *why it exists,* under what *conditions,* and *who generates it.* Perhaps the most straightforward answer to these questions is provided by Adam Jaworski (1993), who argues that "silencing a group (or an individual) through creating and maintaining their ambiguous status is *deliberate* and forms an *inseparable part of every power struggle*" (p. 137; emphasis added). According to Jaworski, silence is caused by a potential or actual threat to a group (e.g., ethnic minority, women) that is made by another power group. A dominant group can suppress the voice of a minority by changing society's perception of the minority's status, for example, by making it ambiguous or even questioning the minority's right to exist; the latter is typical of totalitarian regimes. As Csikszentmihalyi justly insists, societies differ greatly in what they define as deviant as well as in degrees of tolerance, and so they differ in terms of the level of "the threat of isolation" and silence as its consequence (1991, 296).

The foundation of Noelle-Neumann's thesis (that fear of isolation is the key motivating factor in shaping a person's willingness to express a personal opinion) stems primarily from an experiment performed by Solomon Asch.[15] He found that only one-fourth of experimental persons always selected the correct answer in a situation when they were confronted by a group of confederates who were unanimous in their incorrect response. Yet, as we shall see, Noelle-Neumann partially interprets the results of the Asch experiment and uncritically borrows the concept of fear of isolation from psychological experiments on the individual's conformity in a small group and applies it to an entirely different situation, in which an individual receives media messages in his or her primary-group environment. Although (non)conformity is indeed a basic dimension of (small) group behavior, it is most doubtful to extrapolate its effects on influence processes in such complex settings as (contemporary) societies. Noelle-Neumann does not justify her hypothesis of the societal omnipresence of the fear of isolation, which is assumed rather than observed and tested, and actually inferred it from some specific or even marginal occurrences only. It is not explicitly clear if the fear of isolation is a *variable* or a *constant* (Glynn and McLeod 1985, 46), or perhaps a multidimensional *complex situation* differing across societies and cultures, as Foucault would probably hold. As Pöttker (1993, 205) argues, Noelle-Neumann's frequent analogies with physiological phenomena and the world of animals suggests that she considers the fear of isolation as an anthropological (i.e., universal) characteristic of human beings.

In the Asch experiment only 30 percent of experimental persons accepted the (obviously) wrong opinion of the majority in more than half of experimental trials.[16] But Asch also found that very few of them thought they actually yielded to majority opinion. In other words, although the difference between the wrong answer and the correct answer was obvious for those designing the experiment, the experimental persons who conformed were not sure about the difference; because of the lack of confidence in their own estimation they went along with the majority. Thus their reactions were not necessarily motivated by any kind of stress or dissonance in Festinger's terms but rather by expectation to get reliable information as evidence about reality, as Deutsch and Gerard (1955) suggested. Asch (quoted in Moscovici 1976, 14) himself warned against unjustified assumption that "a theory of social influence should be a theory of *submission to social pressures*" (emphasis added). Individuals' *knowledge* about the issue at stake may influence their behavior. And we have to bear in mind that, in contrast to Asch's experiment, in which the correct answer was quite unambiguous, opinions published in the media are less clearly distinguishable. The less an individual is certain about an object or situation, the more she or he will be ready to submit to the influence of others. In addition to the character of stimulus situation, Asch suggested that the *character of group forces* and *personality characteristics* may influence the extent of conformity and (we may add with reference to Noelle-Neumann's studies) the willingness to speak out. He noted that when the experimental person was joined by even a single experimental ally who disagreed with the majority and stated the correct response, conformity rates declined dramatically from the average 33 percent to only 5 percent.

The first empirical critiques of overemphasizing conformity actually preceded the Noelle-Neumann spiral of silence model. Reference groups provide norms and perspectives that are used by an individual to interpret social reality; they may be either actual, empirically existing groups with which an individual interacts or considers important or psychologically constructed or virtual groups as a sort of social category (e.g., liberals or conservatives). The classic literature on conformity shows that individuals tend to conform with opinions in their immediate surroundings or reference groups rather than with opinions in a larger (e.g., national) environment, and that majority opinion induces conformity only in *specific circumstances*.[17] Findings from many subsequent experiments provided a systematic evidence that (1) "anything less than an *unanimous majority* tends to produce dramatically lower rates of conformity and bolsters subjects' willingness to dissent" (Price and Oshagan 1995, 183) and (2) conformity is less likely to occur when *isolated* persons receive (incorrect) choices of confederates (which resembles mass communication circumstances) than when individuals are communicating face to face (Salmon and Kline 1985, 9).

Generally, a number of studies revealed that increased levels of conformity may be expected in situations of group membership and (expected) interaction with group members, extreme group norms, public identification of individuals' judgments, difficulty and ambiguity of the correct response to a situation, and less available information. Obviously, conformity in all these cases reduces the individual's personal responsibility for his or her opinion. The differences in the degree to which individuals conform to social expectations also depend on personality factors like authoritarianism, persuasibility, social self-esteem, and self-confidence.[18] As Noelle-Neumann (1991, 272) remarks herself, "human beings have different levels of sensitivity to the threat of isolation." A number of studies can also be listed that provide comprehensive evidence that the threat of isolation cannot be treated as the ubiquitous factor of conformity in a complex social situation. Findings from many majority pressure studies enabled researchers to identify a large number of factors affecting the individual's social conformity, such as, *political* and *cultural* specificities (Tokinoya 1996), individual *interests*[19] and *needs* that arise from specific life conditions (Tönnies 1922), the individual's membership in *different reference groups* (Merten 1985; Glynn and McLeod 1985), the degree of the individual's *(un)certainty*, that is, how firmly he or she believes that his or her judgment is correct (Moscovici 1976), and the fact that the minority opinion might be shared by hundreds of thousands of individuals and even by elites (Salmon and Kline 1985); so there is really no need for an individual to fear isolation in a democratic setting. As Deutsch and Gerard (1955) argue, there is actually *only one type* of conformity that could be related to the fear of isolation—conformity that is a consequence of *normative* or *group-centered* influence and refers to cohesion of the group and the necessity of *convergence toward identical opinions* (which is a universal situation assumed in Noelle-Neumann's spiral of silence). The other type of conformity stems from *informational* or *task-centered influence* and concerns the relation with the *object* and not relations between individuals.[20] An individual interprets majority opinion as valuable information, as evidence for a certain view of reality, which may be particularly the case when "the 'correct' response to the matter at hand is not at all clear or if the proper course of action is very uncertain" (Price and Allen 1990, 378).

Fear of *political* isolation, which is, at least implicitly, the main concern of Noelle-Neumann's theory, is even less a (or even *the*) key factor of political opinion processes. On the basis of a survey that is conceptualized a bit differently,[21] and similarly to the bandwagon hypothesis, Garth Taylor (1982, 333) argues that the key motivating factor to accept or support the majority opinion or candidate is the *expected benefit arising from political expression* rather than fear of isolation. In other words, people can react in different ways to the majority opinion, and even if they submit to such an opinion, they can do it for different reasons, not only because of their fear of isolation as hypothesized by Noelle-Neumann. Indeed, it would be very difficult to explain recent political changes in former communist countries with the fear of isolation; in a more or less undemocratic environment, minority dissidents were systematically, over decades, gathering support for their dissenting opinions despite the unanimous dominant opinions as presented by the official media—because of the expected (political) benefit. If fear of isolation were the *key* mechanism of public opinion, minority opinions could never dethrone helically spreading majority opinions; neither normalization nor innovation could take place. The pressure to conform is certainly even weaker when individuals express their opinions privately or anonymously, not in front of the "public eye," which is typically the case of voting and, perhaps to a lesser degree, polling. An additional factor that may reduce fear of (political) isolation and conformity is the *diffusion of people's expectations;* the more expectations are diffused, the less stresses they generate, and vice versa. For example, if all expectations center on political sources of fulfillment, the tendency to heed the majority opinion may be expected to be much higher than in the case of expectations dispersed among family, business, trade unions, nonpolitical associations, and so on. In the latter case, "the stakes of the political game might be expected to be more readily kept within those limits that make defeat tolerable" (Key [1961] 1967, 551).

The above arguments were primarily aimed at limiting the validity of the Noelle-Neumann fear of isolation hypothesis to *specific* and presumably marginal situations (e.g., of relatively isolated individuals). However, in experimental studies Moscovici and his colleagues (1976) even found that the minority not only often successfully resists the majority's opinion but may even defeat the majority when the minority is consistent in its opinion.[22] Thus the determining variable is not the size of the group (minority vs. majority) but rather the degree of group unanimity. This is perhaps best empirically substantiated by deliberative polling experiments conducted by Fishkin (1997). In several experiments in the United States and United Kingdom, randomly selected respondents significantly changed their opinions after having had intensive discussions among themselves in small groups and with experts and politicians. A major result in all experiments was that, after the deliberation in groups, "don't know" responses (which are completely ignored in all of Noelle-Neumann's analyses) significantly declined. In addition, participants' definite responses *significantly changed* as a consequence of discussions, but without any tendency to support the fear of isolation hypothesis. The most excessive example clearly falsifies the hypothesis: in three local deliberative polls on electric utility issues in Texas in 1996, the average support for renewable energy (e.g., wind or solar power) as the most important energy option fell from a two-thirds majority before group discussion to less than one-third support after it, a drop of more than 30 percent (Fishkin 1997, 220). In contrast to the spiral of silence, Moscovici's theory and Fishkin's experiments may help us to explain how the minority opinion develops into the majority opinion—a process characteristic not only of public opinion formation but of all social innovations that foster development in general.

Second, regarding the assumption that the individual has the ability to perceive trends in public opinion, Noelle-Neumann asks, "When does one isolate oneself? The individual tries to find this out by means of a 'quasi-statistical organ,' by observing his social environment, by assessing the distribution of opinions for and against his ideas, but above all by evaluating the strength (commitment), the urgency, and the chances of success of certain proposals and viewpoints" (Noelle-Neumann 1974, 44).

Two kinds of studies present evidence that individuals tend to perceive selectively their more remote and mediate environment, such as the mass media, in contrast to perceptions and conformity in their reference groups. Both of them contradict the idea that individuals dispose of a reliable "quasi-statistical organ." Rather, as the models of coorientation propose, a situation of perfect cognitive overlapping and accuracy appears only exceptionally. Pluralistic ignorance, dissensus, and false consensus, which are based on disagreement, inaccurate perceptions, and/or misunderstandings, may appear as often as true consensus.

A number of studies indicated the validity of the theory of *pluralistic ignorance,* which states that when people share false ideas about the majority position on an issue, they are unaware that other members of the same community share their opinions,[23] or they wrongly believe that they disagree with the environment, or they mistakenly perceive their own opinion as corresponding with the majority opinion in their environment even if such a cognitive overlapping does not exist because they want to believe that other people have the same opinion (looking-glass perception or false consensus effect; Scheff 1967; Moscovici 1976; Taylor 1982; Salmon and Kline 1985; Kennamer 1990;

Huckfeldt and Sprague 1995; Shamir and Shamir 1997).[24] In either case, they obviously do not have a reliable "statistical intuition," as Noelle-Neumann believed. An inaccurate perception of others' (or the majority) opinion may even be predicted, according to Festinger's theory of cognitive dissonance, because people tend to avoid dissonance-producing information and selectively pay attention to information that is not contrary to their strongly held attitudes. Some authors contend that "the thoughts and deeds attributed by individuals to others are particularly apt to be distorted if the perceivers define the others as different from them in some important cultural or structural respect" (O'Gorman and Garry 1976, 449).

Noelle-Neumann responds to such criticisms of the unreliability of the "quasi-statistical organ" that the matter at issue is not whether people are accurate in their estimates of the existing majority/minority opinion but whether or not they can accurately perceive *changes* in the form of increasing or decreasing support for their views (Noelle-Neumann 1985, 72). Yet there is no clear empirical support for this claim either—with the only exception of voting behavior and party preferences, due to regular electoral polls and publication of poll results. And even if changes in perceptions of public opinion and changes in voting preference correlate, correlation is not proof that perceptions affect changes in voting. However, election is not a representative case of public opinion, first, as a matter of theory, because voting is a *private* act whereas *public* opinion is not. Second, as a matter of methodology, electoral polls and voting behavior significantly differ from a normal (in statistical terms) distribution of opinions, particularly in countries with an essentially two-party system, such as Germany and the United States. Although in a typical situation of opinion process many different opinions and different levels of (dis)agreement exist, a typical decision expected from an individual in polling or voting is just between two alternatives—for or against a candidate or a party.[25] It is not difficult to imagine that in a multiparty environment it is much more difficult for an individual to estimate which political party has (relative) majority support among citizens; it is even much more difficult when the issue is not as simply identifiable as a political party.

Noelle-Neumann was "amazed about the report" in the United States "that 66% were unable to assess how most people think. We have never found such a high percentage in Germany," which was for her "a sign of weakness" (Noelle-Neumann 1985, 73). But the false consensus effect is likely to occur in a pluralistic, democratic situation in which each party, candidate, or opinion is challenged by *plurality of alternatives*, and it is difficult for an individual to determine which option is preferred by the (relative) majority. In a more authoritarian setting, however, it is more likely that (public) opinion is not about a controversial issue but only about a social issue, for example, "a theme of a public situation" or "some affect- or value-laden question" (Noelle-Neumann 1979, 180; [1980] 1993, 179) because no real alternative or opposite opinions exist. In such a situation it is very likely that individuals' "quasi-statistical instinct" perceives not only changes but even the actual majority/minority opinion. This, however, is not a recurrent situation when political issues are at stake in democratic societies.

The second kinds of studies deal with the ways individuals are *exposed to mass media* and how the exposure is related to participation in interpersonal communication. In his early critique of the spiral of silence model, Katz ([1981] 1983) pointed out that empirical research on mass communication already in the late 1930s falsified the hypothesis of powerful immediate effects of the media on atomized individuals; mass media were found less effective than expected because the media differed in what they offered to their publics; recipients were selectively exposed to the media, and they used the organizations and social groups to which they belonged to test what they received from the media. At

Table 5.1: Possible Explanations of Inacccurate Perception of One's Own Opinion and Majority Opinion

Type of explanation	Individual perceives his/her own opinion as:	Individual perceives majority opinion as:
Pluralistic ignorance*	True person's opinion	Opinion opposite to true majority opinion
Looking-glass perception	True person's opinion	His/her own opinion attributed to others
Conservative bias**	True person's opinion	What it used to be previously
Disowning projection	Perceived majority opinion (as socially desirable opinion)	His/her true opinion (as socially undesirable opinion)
Third-person effect	Not affected by the media	Affected by the media

* In a broader sense, both looking-glass perception and conservative bias may be considered specific forms of pluralistic ignorance.

** Shamir and Shamir (1997) rightly point out that there is no theoretical grounding to interpret conservative bias in the *ideological* sense. Rather, it refers to people's tendency to continue to see others (the majority) at present as they used to be previously, which can be related to the lack of accurate information.

least since Lazarsfeld's studies in the late 1930s it has been largely documented that people tend to expose selectively primarily to media whose content is congruent with their predispositions, and they tend to avoid messages that they suspect will not agree with their frame of reference. Katz and Lazarsfeld emphasized that the whole moral of their research was that "knowledge of an individual's interpersonal environment is basic to an understanding of his exposure and reactions to the mass media" (Katz and Lazarsfeld 1955, 133). Festinger's dissonance theory predicts that individuals tend to avoid dissonance-producing media contents by *selective exposure* (selection of media and messages) and *selective attention* (paying attention only to those parts of messages that will not produce dissonance). Consequently, individual perception of media contents is not a sort of objective (statistical) content analysis but rather is subjective, biased, and partial interpretation motivated by establishing agreement with other members in the reference group as the major way either to reduce dissonance or to produce consonance. Selective exposure and selective perception may thus reinforce existing individual opinions and those of the reference groups regardless of whether they are dominant nationwide or not. In other words, exposure to media contents influences people, but mainly in line with their latent attitudes: "Don't confuse me with the facts—I have already made up my mind." Thus even if the media tended to adopt a homogeneous prevailing attitude, people might not—because of their selective exposure and perception. Figure 5.1 is a cogent argument against the simplistic belief that individuals are able to "detect" and anticipate opinion changes; it clearly demonstrates that "pictures in our heads" are heavily stereotyped, as Lippmann would say.

In his discussion of conflict and influence, Moscovici (1976, 105–6) argues that conceptualizing sources of influence (e.g., other persons, the media) as sheer *mediators of facts* with regard to the environment is not appropriate in an antagonistic situation. Other persons may serve the individual as "a sort of remote sensor or grappler, permitting the subject to extend his resources for dealing with the material world" only if they do not serve any specific (particularistic) interests. If the latter is the case, they are not only mediators of facts but also sources of influence promoting their own interests, "relative strengths, feelings, intentions, sincerity, courage, and so on, all must be taken into account, and they are very easily overlooked when we are dealing with nonpersonal, nonsocial entities." This is not to say that mass media have no (significant) influence on people's opinions and behavior. Rather, the point is that their influence is not as simple, unambiguous, universal, and independent of recipients' idiosyncrasies as hypothesized by Noelle-Neumann. It may well be that the media are becoming the most powerful agents in socialization processes, agenda setting, advertising, and infotainment, but *this does not imply* (1) that *signifi-*

Figure 5.1: Looking-Glass Perception of the Increase and Decrease in Supporters
    (1) **Of Slovenia's affiliation to the European Union (on the left)**
    (2) **Of the right of foreign citizens to buy real estate in Slovenia (on the right) among the supporters, opponents, and undecided respondents (in percents, representative sample of Slovene adult population, N = 456, 1998).**

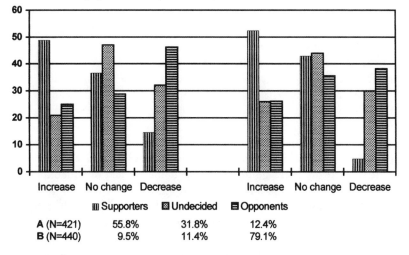

	Supporters	**Undecided**	**Opponents**
A (N=421)	55.8%	31.8%	12.4%
B (N=440)	9.5%	11.4%	79.1%

cant agents of influence no longer exist or (2) that individuals cannot effectively resist direct, short-term influence aimed at their opinions and behavior. Individuals' increasing involvement in computer-mediated communications that foster interactivity is an obvious case in point. Not only the media have not substituted reference groups and interpersonal communication; individuals also effectively create new forms of social interaction.

Third, Noelle-Neumann asserts that the main sources of individuals' perception of majority/minority opinion are the media. However, it is not clear whether the media are believed to primarily create public opinion or simply mirror it. Noelle-Neumann argues that (German) media often adopt a "prevailing attitude" and articulate a certain point of view because journalists share certain values and ideological orientations (Noelle-Neumann 1985, 80). Yet she explicitly excludes "the mere publication of opinion research findings" as a part of public opinion portrayal that may significantly influence individuals' perceptions of trends in public opinion.

In a pluralist society it would be difficult to believe, and to prove, that all the media exhibit systematically and consistently the same "prevailing attitude" (or bias) toward an idea, candidate, opinion, and so on. Their tendency toward cultural homogenization does not imply a complete singleness in terms of presented information and opinions. Noelle-Neumann herself admits that the hard core of minorities "may manage to support their opinions by *selecting out persons and media which confirm their views*" (Noelle-Neumann 1974, 49; emphasis added). In a totalitarian political environment all the media may be in a perfect consonance, but even there, official media are challenged by alternative and underground media, as was clearly demonstrated in the formerly communist countries of Central and Eastern Europe. Of course, it is not enough that individuals or groups are willing to express their opinions; they also must be *able to do so*, that is, communication channels in society must be organized and regulated in a way that enables *access*. Tönnies (1922, 141) argued convincingly that opinion struggles in the arena of public opinion are the *struggles for* public opinion. They are primarily fought under the influence of political parties, which always tend to show only one side of the issues discussed. Since the newspapers are influenced by political parties, they exhibit the same sort of one-sidedness. There are never simply two—one dominant and one subordinate—opinions on a controversial issue, but there are many different and *competing* opinions in different media, each of them biased and partial, and all of them in a constant process of changing until consensus is reached and the problem is solved and/or removed from the agenda. Mass media may have different functions in different environments of a society, but they largely depend on dominant powers. Usually the most *effective* opinions presented in the media are not *majority* opinions; rather, they are (or may become) *dominant* opinions because they have sufficient power and resources to be translated into policy (Salmon and Kline 1985, 24).

Empirical studies show that *conflict reporting*, not homogeneous reporting, is a major stimulator of opinion formation and knowledge. Intense conflict about an issue brings about an increase in the quantity of information published in the media, and media audiences are likely to be better informed about the issue. The more intense the public controversy, the more likely members of the public are to hold and express opinions on the issue (Olien, Donohue, and Tichenor 1995, 320). Studies of the effects of poll results on voting intentions and behavior provide some additional evidence on the controversial relationship between the media and the public. As we saw earlier, Noelle-Neumann admits that it is "possible to observe this process [of public opinion] with the tools of representative surveys" and uses polling techniques throughout her work on public opinion to test her hypotheses; but she explicitly denies, without a clear argument, that the publication of polling results in the media might be an indicator of the climate of opinion that could be detected by the "quasi-statistical organ" of citizens (Noelle-Neumann [1980] 1993, 230). Clearly, opinion polling is a model of elections rather than public opinion, and *elections* are conceptually very different from *public opinion* phenomena. But in opinion *polling* the two concepts are operationalized in the same way. Polling can affect not only the opinions of those who read the poll results published in the media but also (in the first place, even) the opinions of respondents in a subsequent survey. Despite his critical attitudes toward polling, Wilson believes that the use of techniques of public opinion polls gives useful results for several reasons; among others, it enables the individual citizen to judge whether he is following along with his fellow citizens or whether his own opinions are becoming more and more unlike those of the general population. Moreover, all groups in the public want to know the effects of today's opinion on tomorrow's decisions (Wilson 1962, 163). Wilson further argues that when individuals are confronted with results of opinion polls, those among them who like to be part of the majority can act accordingly, whereas those who hold minority opinions may be stimulated to more enthusiastic actions.

Polls are not just another story in the media but are becoming an inseparable part of journalism itself. A large number of media organizations conduct and report on their own polls, news stories focus on the results of polls, poll data are used in the news decision process and in the process of checking accuracy of information from other sources, particularly in "precision journalism," which utilizes a variety of statistical tools to analyze large quantities of data. Pollsters are often very accurate in assessing citizens' voting intentions, but the publication of poll results in different forms has controversial effects that do not exhibit any systematic pattern. Under some conditions, polling results seem to induce the bandwagon effect, whereas in other circumstances they bring about the underdog effect (individuals tend to support the losing side) or have no effect at all. The grounds of such divergent effects is still a matter of research.

In an exhaustive empirical validity testing of the spiral of silence model, Helmut Scherer (1990, 269) comes to the conclusion that the spiral of silence theory actually fails at the vital point—in explaining (great) changes in individuals' opinions. The supposed advantage of the spiral of silence ought to be that it makes it possible to explain changes in individuals' opinions as resulting from the influence of the media to which they are exposed. Yet Scherer's tests proved with great reliability that there was neither a clear connection between mass media and the individual's estimate of the climate of opinion nor between the climate of opinion and the individual's opinion.

Fourth, the central idea behind Noelle-Neumann's article on the spiral of silence is "to substantiate empirically the process of public opinion formation through the individual's observation of his or her social environment" (Noelle-Neumann 1974, 51). She believes that laboratory experiments on the effects of the mass media should be replaced by more valid survey interview methods or, as Noelle-Neumann ([1980] 1993, 42) calls them, field experiments, in order to observe and interview a representative sample of population (not just specific groups, e.g., students, as in experiments) "in their natural setting."

Noelle-Neumann overestimates the validity to be provided by survey interviews with randomly selected respondents in testing her model of public opinion as social control. An interview with the *isolated* respondent in his "natural setting" is not appropriate to test the spiral of silence theory because, as the classic literature on conformity shows, individuals tend to conform with opinions in their immediate surroundings of reference groups rather than with opinions in a larger environment. In addition, intensity and quality of relations that a person has with his or her fellows in the reference groups are of utmost importance. Any approach that reduces the analysis to properties or characteristics of individuals or groups as units (attribute data) and excludes the possibility of analyzing *relations* among individuals in a group, or between groups (relational data), reduces rather than increases research validity. That is why the idea of *coorientation,* which replaced the individual as a unit of analysis with higher-level units (created by comparing two or more individuals or measuring relationship among them) is the foundation of the departure from a reductionist stimulus-response model of communication and attitude change. Just such a reduction to individual-level effects is typical for polling techniques, which are appropriate to study very formalized situations, in which an individual (re)acts semi-privately in response to a clearly formulated question, but not highly informal public or semi-public *interactions* of individuals and, particularly, groups from which public opinion originates. It is true that laboratory experiments may cut out a significant portion of the real life of persons participating in experiments (their relations with family, friends, colleagues, etc.), but this is exactly the part of real life that is out of reach of field experiments with randomly selected respondents too.[26]

The major breakthrough in the behavioral sciences was brought about by the creation of the (equally appearing) interval scales for measuring attitudinal variables (e.g., Thurstone and Likert Scales). From the political viewpoint, as V. O. Key ([1961] 1967, 208) argues, the distribution of intensities of opinions within the population may be related to political action, that is, persons with intense opinions are more disposed to act. If the general patterns of distribution of opinion determine the context for governmental action, the location of intensities (the mode in statistical terms) within the distribution may be important; for example, unimodal, bimodal, and multimodal distributions would probably bring about different consequences in terms of actions. As Key argued, "instead of a yes-no dichotomy, attitudes toward a public issue may be ranged along a scale represented by a series of different ways of dealing with the question" (Key [1961] 1967, 21). That was one of the major points of criticism expressed by William Albig already in 1939. In Albig's opinion, the limited dichotomized (yes/no) response usually generated in polls is "*worthless for any understanding of human attitudes*" (Albig 1939, 157; emphasis added). Since then, it has become commonly accepted that not only the *direction* of attitudes ("for" or "against") but also their *degree, intensity, salience,* and *certainty* represent important attitude dimensions that enhance or limit attitude changes.

Yet all the tests performed by Noelle-Neumann are based on simple dichotomous opinions or "votes"—"for" versus "against," "yes" versus "no"—and on the comparison of only two—"for" versus "against"—groups, with elimination of "don't know" answers that represented in some cases even the relative majority. With the exception of highly formalized voting (e.g., "opinions" in polling), dichotomization of opinions in the model represents a highly improbable situation in everyday life. Although the revision of the model that includes (in addition to the individual's perception of majority opinion in society) the expected tendency of opinion in the future represents an improvement, it does not solve the problem of simplistic dichotomies. A much closer approximation to a usual opinion formation process may be achieved by measuring the *degree* of opinions, which significantly influences the degree of cognitive consonance or dissonance. The degree of opinions about different issues varies within each individual for personal and situational reasons, and a given opinion (for or against) is accepted to a different degree (which usually correlates with the intensity) by different individuals across society. In both individual and societal perspective, extreme, very intense, and firm opinions, which allow a clear-cut dichotomization, are rather exceptional. If the degree of opinions is measured with ordinal or even interval scales, we may rather assume a bimodal or even normal distribution of opinions on both the individual and the societal level. In such a case, opinions are distributed on a continuum from extremely favorable opinions through neutral or indifferent to extremely unfavorable opinions, with few or no large gaps between adjacent degrees. Any categorization, and particularly dichotomization of a continuous distribution, is quite arbitrary. The spiral of silence model could be used validly only for situations in which a true (rather than forced) clear dichotomy exists in opinions, since the model assumes such a clear dichotomy. This applies to all the three types of questions included in the test measuring (1) the respondent's own attitude in terms of *for or against* a proposal, party, and so on, (2) his or her estimation of the majority attitude, and (3) the perception of what will be the majority attitude in the future. From the methodological point of view, then, it is quite obvious that the model tends to generalize a rather specific case of discrete opinions.

An additional methodological fallacy in the Noelle-Neumann model is the prediction of behavior from attitude measures. Nonwillingness to participate in a conversation with strangers (train passengers) holding strong opposite opinions or supporting the opposite political party (which Noelle-Neumann used as the indicator of fear) is only one of several possible (alternative) behavioral indices to which a measure of fear of isolation could be related. In contrast to polling, in which a simple attitude measure is usually a very reliable predictor of actual behavior in elections, the relation between attitude(s) and action(s) is much less reliable when more complex issues are set down for attitude objects, mainly due to situational constraints and influences. Using only one indicator to measure a concept makes any validity test impossible. Even if several retests showed similar results, this is no more than a *reliability* test; but reliability alone is not sufficient to prove *validity*. Harrisson and Rogers interpreted opinion shifts frequently recorded in (election) polling as a consequence of a continuous transformation of *private* opinions into *public* opinions, which *polls are unable to discriminate* (Rogers 1949, 41–44). Thus it would be essential to measure private opinions, but polls can only identify respondents' public opinions, that is, opinions that respondents are willing to disclose in the interview, and they may substantially differ from their true opinions—opinions they hold *privately*. In democratic elections, voters do not change their preferences for candidates as easily as they may on controversial public issues. In both cases private opinions, which are out of reach of polls, may significantly differ from public opinions, which individuals are willing to share with strange interviewers, but the direction of changes might be different. In the case of elections, polls reveal voters' *public opinions*, whereas voters express their *private opinions* in the polling booth. In the case of opinions on public issues, individuals' *private opinions* change over the course of time and, at the same time, the *past private opinions* may be tranformed into *actual public opinions*.

THE DISAVOWAL OF CONTRADICTIONS

In a statistical (re)assessment of the relationships between respondents' own opinions, their perception of majority opinion, and their willingness to speak out found in seventeen surveys, Glynn, Hayes, and Shanahan (1997, 461) conclude that "the literature provides little support . . . for the claim that willingness to express opinions is influenced by perceived support for those opinions."

The work that has been done by Noelle-Neumann and her reviewers suggests that the spiral of silence model generalizes a very specific, even marginal case discussed, for example, already by Harrisson and Festinger—the case of individuals who are relatively isolated socially and do not talk readily about some subjects of (public) discussion (e.g., political issues). According to Festinger, attitudes and opinions of relatively isolated people may heavily depend on media contents. However, for the majority of nonisolated people, exposure to the media primarily creates doubts that are usually tested and often erased in interpersonal discussion. Even in the Asch-type group pressure experiments to which Noelle-Neumann refers in her studies, two-thirds of individuals tested did not completely conform, even to a unanimous majority (Asch 1951, 190). Besides, general characteristics and particularly the effects of small-group communication cannot simply be extrapolated to mass communication. A number of studies, beginning with those by Lazarsfeld and associates on the two-step flow of communication, pointed to significant differences between the two. At least, there is no evidence that people in large collectivities (in a democratic society, of course) can be exposed to the same negative sanctions or threats of isolation as individuals in small groups. Numerous replications of Noelle-Neumann's work do not provide an evidence for the general validity of her model. Although it may account for some specific situations, it certainly fails to explain more complex situations because of the exclusion of a number of hypothetical factors related to the individual, his or her reference groups, and the issue at stake.

It might well be that the ratio between the relatively isolated people who strongly depend on the media and those involved in interactions who "test" opinions from the media in their interactions has changed during the last decades of the twentieth century in favor of the former. But this does not imply that the tendency of a growing fear of social isolation is the dominant tendency regulating the process of opinion formation. In this way, marginal, deviant, and minority opinions could never become majority opinions—but this exactly is happening all the time. Indeed, if group behavior were primarily regulated by conformity only, we should ask ourselves, as Moscovici and Doise suggest (1994, 35), "how natural selection has allowed such a disadvantageous organism to continue to exist, and even multiply." Majority opinions cannot be born as majority opinions; they always start to grow as individual, dissent, specific, or minority opinions. As Dewey ([1927] 1991, 208) put it, "It is true that all valuable as well as new ideas begin with minorities, perhaps a minority of one." Even more, majority opinions themselves are often overthrown—despite social conformity. There is a certain naiveté in the spiral of silence theory that attributes changes in the dominant (public) opinion to the media; they alone are able to transform their own minority opinion into the socially dominant majority opinion.

Since the earliest theorizations, the concept of public opinion has been encumbered with two fundamental contradictions, first, the *internal contradiction*, which is a consequence of connecting two conceptually conflicting concepts—public and opinion—and, second, the *external contradiction* resulting from the relationship between the subjects of public opinion and the subjects opposing it, or between the expression and realization of public opinion. Noelle-Neumann "solved" the problem of the two inherent contradictions in a very simple way. To resolve the *internal contradiction* between public and opinion, she reduced the concept of publicness to only one dimension, so that the widest possible range of empirically observable phenomena may be referred to, that is, to its narrowest meaning of what can be seen or heard by everybody. At the same time, she took the widest possible observational understanding of the concept of opinion as any "visible expression of a value-related opinion," which includes both verbal and nonverbal expressions. The problems of rationality, consensuality, objectivity, and truthfulness disappear. Public opinion is defined by Noelle-Neumann (1974, 44) as (1) "the opinion which can be voiced in public without fear of sanctions and upon which action in public can be based" and (2) the "public eye," that is, media representation of public opinion, which performs the function of social control. This implies the absence of any opinion dissenting from those that may appear in public; the spiral of silence rather than the process of coorientation produces a stable consensus. Noelle-Neumann's theorization of public opinion as social control exemplifies a sociological orientation that Wilson (1962, 109) logically denoted as "the study of *propaganda*" rather than public opinion.[27]

The "solution" to the internal contradiction also "solved" the *external contradiction* between the subjects forming and expressing public opinion, and subjects confronted by public opinion: there is no specific subject of public opinion because everyone is involved (i.e., exposed). When Key ([1961] 1967, 14) defined public opinion as "those opinions held by private persons which governments find it prudent to heed," he recognized that such a "broad, somewhat vague, conception of public opinion" helped to solve some analytical problems[28] but also brought "within the range of the discussion an extremely wide variety of phenomena." Noelle-Neumann went much farther when she declared that everyone is involved in public opinion. Her conceptualization perhaps solves even more analytical problems than Key's "working view on public opinion," but it is certainly disproportionally more vague and, therefore, invalid.

For a *sociological* approach to public opinion to which Noelle-Neumann inclines, the questions of permitted versus forbidden (or even ostracized) publication of opinions, and of similarity/diversity of opinions in relation to life conditions of individuals (who do or do not express opinions) are far from being inventive. Tönnies, for example, devoted his integral theory of public opinion to these problems. If we compare Noelle-Neumann's understanding of public opinion with Tönnies's conceptualization of the opinion of the public as a form of *social will*, we may be "surprised" to find out that social control is not a specific (latent, according to Noelle-Neumann) function of public opinion, but a *general and manifest function of any form of complex social (or common) will*, since they all tend to achieve the highest possible degree of consent among associated individuals and to reduce any form of dissent, and they are all institutionalized. "The existence of institutions commonly yields primary social control. When a sphere of human activity is institutionalized, it means *eo ipso* that it is under social control" (Berger and Luckmann 1969, 59).

As Tönnies argued, all forms of common will are manifestations of *collective opinions;* it is common will that gives to these opinions an obligatory character. Different forms of common will are mutually dependent and they transfer from one form to another. Although the forms may differ also in the degree to which they are actually binding upon the whole community or society (e.g., forms of organic will more than forms of reflective will), they primarily differ in relation to the *spheres of common life* they "represent." According to Tönnies, the opinion of the public refers primarily to the *ethical* and aesthetic domain of common life, and it manifests itself in *judgment* (*Urteil*). Tönnies recognized in his theory, as did Noelle-Neumann in her model, that not every opinion can be voiced in public; however, in contrast to Noelle-Neumann, Tönnies also observed *what* and/or *who* limits public expression of opinions: the most powerful institutions that limit the expression of "dangerous" opinions are the church and the state. As a matter of fact, a person cannot be ordered how to think or not to think, or what opinions she or he may have or have not; however, public expression and dissemination of opinions can be effectively controlled and directed by different forms of censorship and propaganda. "What is more, a negative influence, prevention by prohibition, is always closest at hand when imaginary or actual damages ought to be prevented" (Tönnies 1922, 23).

The spiral of silence assumes a one-way relationship between public opinion and individuals' behavior; the latter is the consequence of the former. It remains hidden that public opinion, even if conceived as a simple aggregate of opinions, must be *created* as a form of *collective opinions* in the first place to become visible and a form of controlling force. As Allport argued in his critique of "blind alleys," even an operational definition of public opinion must define it "as related to actual behavior of individuals" primarily in the sense that it "must be expressed by some individuals or we cannot know it at all" (Allport

1937, 10–11). In other words, any opinion, including public opinion, can only be *formed* by individuals; thus, the individual level and the aggregate level are interdependent, and so are rational discussion and social control. Whereas in the initial process of public opinion *formation* (e.g., within the core of Tönnies's large public) the cognitive or rational component prevails, in the process of its *reception* by individuals the affective component may become more important. Precisely the processes of opinion formation, expression, and reception are essential for an opinion to become public; they determine the difference between a simple sharing of opinion among many individuals and a true opinion of the public.

Normative and informational influences do not exclude each other, but Noelle-Neumann's spiral of silence only assumes the validity of conformity incited by normative influence and of the social-control (i.e., latent) function of public opinion. She explicates even "public opinion as a rational process" in terms of critical concerns (expressed by Habermas, for example) "that the opinion-formation process may be *manipulated* by the power of the state and capital, by the mass media and modern technology" (Noelle-Neumann [1980] 1993, 229; emphasis added), which may suggest the necessity of conforming to the dominant opinions, but she neglects the precedence of informational over normative influence in it. Consequently, "public opinion as social control" seems to have nothing in common with the earlier sociological ideas of Robert Park, Ferdinand Tönnies, or even Floyd Allport, and even less with normative theories. As there is no "informational influence" to which individuals can be exposed, and no need to acquire information, there is no rational opinion formation process. *We may perfectly agree with that—provided that this refers to an undemocratic societal environment.* However, in such a situation, public opinion loses its substantial characteristics and becomes similar to or even identical with religion, as Tönnies would argue. And, *nota bene,* it is not only normative political theories of public opinion that postulate freedom of opinion formation as *the* condition of the existence of public opinion; social psychology (e.g., Kurt Lewin's experiments in the 1940s) suggests that the democratic atmosphere in which group interaction takes place significantly weakens the pressure to conform. On the other hand, the social "climate" of fear that is typical for authoritarian environments fosters a *dual* public opinion: opinions expressed in the media have the function of social control (and they are usually based on self-censorship of journalists who thus indeed produce a monolithic climate as Noelle-Neumann would always expect it), whereas the rational and moral general will cannot be publicly expressed because of the fear of sanctions. Wilson (1962, 147) pointed out that "it is one thing to recognize that rational ideals have not been attained. . . . It is quite another to place the irrational aspects of behavior at the center of politics and to behave as if the truth or falsity of principles is irrelevant." Thus he seemingly anticipated Noelle-Neumann's spurious dichotomy.

Noelle-Neumann's spiral of silence is uncritically based on the mass society model in which individuals are separate from each other and are directly dependent on and influenced by the mass media as the most powerful agents of social control. In the preface to her doctoral dissertation (1940), this model was still explicit:

> The roles the public plays in America and Germany are very different. In the great "democracy" across the ocean it has the position of a share-holding company in which millions of shareholders dictate the policy of company. In the national-socialist Germany it appears as the nation's body [*Volkskörper*] that receives instructions from its head and is the *guarantor of their accomplishment*. . . . In the former case the public rules, in the latter it is directed. (Noelle 1940, 1; emphasis added)[29]

In contrast to the assumptions and visions of democratic theories that attempt, when facing undemocratic practice, to "reconstruct" it, at least theoretically, her theory (by generalizing the tendency to conform found among, in many societies rather numerous, relatively isolated individuals with low self-confidence and less interest in politics) actually legitimizes media manipulation and fear of social isolation as the key mechanisms by which individuals may retain adherence to society. Not only the whole *societal structure* of institutions and social groups, which was strenuously "defended" by Blumer as the genuine arena of public opinion, but also the individual's relationship with other members of his or her *reference groups* is totally absent. The model (still) implies the assumption of a "German comprehension of the essence of public opinion, according to which, as the *Reichminister* Dr Goebbels put it, public opinion 'is largely the result of a willful influence'" (Noelle 1940, 134). As Elihu Katz observed, "Noelle-Neumann wants us to consider the dark side of mass communication" (Katz [1981] 1983, 91), but she forgets about the enlightening and emancipatory influence of publicity and mass media. Noelle-Neumann's worthwhile and much needed effort to conceptualize public opinion beyond (or in contrast to) the nominalistic definitions of public opinion as simple aggregation of individual's response data in public opinion polls nevertheless did not result in an integral understanding and a more valid theory of public opinion.

6

✛

Political Institutionalization
of Public Opinion:
Controversies on Polling

*Unlike measurements in physics, attempted measurements of opinion do
not speak for themselves. Even if they did, the pollsters would chafe at being mensurationists only—that is, counters of yeses and noes. They want
to become evangelists and speeders-up of democracy. Hence they baptize
themselves "public opinion analysts."*
   —Lindsay Rogers, *The Pollsters: Public Opinion, Politics,
         and Democratic Leadership*

*The irony of polling is that the development of scientific means of mea-
suring public opinion had its most negative effect upon precisely those
groups whose political fortunes were historically most closely linked with
mass public opinion.*
   —Benjamin Ginsberg, *How Polling Transforms Public Opinion*

Modern ideas of public opinion are closely related to techniques, instruments, and institutions related to the expression and representation of
opinions, and most notably to the development of polling, which sensitized
everyone involved in political life to shifts in the opinion climate. In a way, the

221

introduction of polls into the public sphere may substantially expand the democratic basis of public opinion, which is typically institutionalized in three distinct nationwide forms: parliament, newspapers, and public opinion polling. Through polling, research practice, politics, and the media became closely linked together. Yet the growing interconnectedness of the three institutions of public opinion may further erode its authentic democratic meaning.

Polling developed during the decline of the critical (reading) public. Public opinion became an object of research after it mostly lost control over its former institutions, that is, parliament and the press. During the last fifty years, polling has become largely institutionalized in Western democracies. One of the first prominent U.S. pollsters, George Gallup, believed that polling ought to compensate for the growing limitations of a parliamentary democracy. However, polling, like the press and the parliament, was soon criticized for its effects on public opinion and democratic life in general and was accused of manipulation and antidemocratic support. Opinion polls certainly cause people who are interested in political life to become more sensitive to shifts in the popular temper and awareness of significant issues. But at the same time they have, as Leo Bogart noted, "a pernicious effect on political candidates who follow the precepts of market research rather than their own considered and conscientiously arrived-at policy choices." This, however, is far from being the only controversy. This chapter systematically analyzes critiques of polling (starting with Albig in the 1930s) in their social and historical contexts and attempts to answer two fundamental questions: What is the relationship between public opinion polling and democracy? Is polling an instrument of monitoring or manufacturing public opinion? If polls became a part of our everyday life, it does not imply that they are a necessary element of a democratic system.

Regardless of whether public opinion is considered as originating from rational discussion or merely as a widespread diffusion of elite opinion, even by coercion, or whether the concept of public opinion presupposes the public either as a corporate social entity or merely a (statistical) aggregation of individuals, or it is conceived without any specific actor, it was always assumed that public opinion is (at least) *publicly expressed* opinion that *represents* the (majority of) people or the citizenry, if there were actually no *government by* public opinion. Since early modern times, public opinion has typically been institutionalized in three distinct nationwide[1] forms, parliament, newspapers, and polling, but none of them genuinely represented an ideally defined public.[2]

If anything, according to Tönnies (1923, 77), parliament may generally be called an "organ of opinion of the public," although even this is not always completely justified. Tönnies's belief reflects a widely held assumption that is advocated by normative political theories and sociological theorizing of public opinion, notably American pragmatism (Park and Dewey). However, representative government has never been a system in which parliamentary representatives had to regard opinions of the electorate; it has never been a direct form of popular sovereignty. Rather, since its foundation, representative government, even if based on the principle of universal suffrage, has been a rule by elites, distinguished from the majority of citizens by their social status, education, particularistic interests, and way of life.

Since its very beginning, the press has played an important role in public opinion processes. It delivered not only information to the public and thus was an important element in the process of public opinion *formation,* but it was also the main means of *expression* or organ of the public, constituting a virtual public. In addition, according to Tönnies, the press was a general medium for more restricted means of expression, like associations, meetings, or demonstrations, whereas the public was always, and nearly exclusively, a newspaper-reading public. However, newspapers not only express the opinion of the public but also influence public opinion. In reality, newspapers are not organs of opinion of the public and are not identical with it; rather, they are primarily organs of political parties and commercial corporations.

Public opinion polling developed during the decline of the critical (reading) public. Public opinion became an object of research after it largely lost control over its former institutions, that is, parliament and particularly the press because of its commercialization. During the last fifty years, polling was largely considered the first scientific mastering of public opinion and generally institutionalized in Western democracies. One of the first prominent U.S. pollsters, George Gallup, believed that polling ought to compensate for the growing limitations of parliamentary democracy; it was thus considered not only a research technique (a scientific instrument) but also a political construct—a new instrument of (political) democracy. Formerly, social sciences made rather unsuccessful attempts at a scientific operationalization of normative concepts of public opinion. But with polling, as its prophets believed, they seemed to have achieved a satisfactory degree of empirical validity. Moreover, media owners and news workers soon became aware of the importance of polling as a competitive form of institutionalization of public opinion; particularly after the *Literary Digest*'s scandalous "defeat" in 1936, media largely adopted scientific polls. They became the main sponsors and disseminators of polling results and developed reporting on polls into a popular journalistic genre. However, similarly to the press and parliament, polling was soon criticized for its negative effects on public opinion and democratic life, and were accused of antidemocratic manipulation and control over public opinion.

In his discussion of the nature of public opinion in *The American Common-wealth* ([1888] 1995), James Bryce distinguished three stages in the evolution of public opinion "from its unconscious and passive into its conscious and active condition." According to his scheme, in the (until then) most developed phase, the sovereign multitude expresses its will at certain intervals—in elections. However, a fourth stage could be reached, Bryce argued, "if the will of the majority of the citizens were to become ascertainable at all times, and without the need of its passing through a body of representatives, possibly even without the need of voting machinery at all." Yet Bryce believed that the fourth stage was utopian because "the machinery for weighing or measuring the popular will from week to week or month to month has not been, and is not likely to be, invented." His prediction obviously proved wrong—the machinery was invented only a few decades later in the form of public opinion polls, almost in the very form predicted a few years earlier by Carl Schmitt ([1928] 1954, 245), who, in a cynical way and alluding to the American "voting machines," anticipated that some day, "without leaving his apartment, every man could continuously express his opinions on political questions through an apparatus, and all these opinions will be automatically recorded in the head office." A recent expression of this phenomenon is the idea of government by instant polling, as advocated by Ross Perot during the 1992 presidential race in the United States.

Public opinion polling as it is known today was born in the 1930s in the United States; its rise is commonly associated with the names of George Gallup (1940) and Elmo Roper (1942). Its scientific justification may be primarily related to the positivist thinking of Walter Lippmann (1922) and Floyd Allport (1937). The polls conducted by Gallup, Roper, and other pollsters differed from the formerly dominant straw polls[3] in that the new scientific polls were based on the random and thus representative small-size sample that ought to provide highly reliable and generalizable data. By the end of World War II, polling in the United States (and after the war in Western Europe also) has secured political legitimization, scientific recognition, and social efficacy for public opinion (Blondiaux 1998, 278). It became closely connected with, and largely used by, at least three types of activities: (political) journalism, party politics, and market research. Whereas straw polls were conducted by journalists and ordinary citizens (since they did not require any expertise), scientific polls (based on sampling and requiring not only statistical expertise but also financial resources) were turned over to professionals. What the two forms of polling had in common, however, was the general election whose outcomes polls predicted.[4]

From the very beginning to the present times, polling provoked enduring and intense controversies regarding its nature and functions in society and particularly in democracy. The conflict between different understandings of the role of polls reflects (1) differences in broader *theorizations* of public opinion (e.g., how well the procedure and results of polling fit in with the "true" public opinion) and (2) differences in *methodological* orientations, primarily related to the application of qualitative and/or quantitative methods in empirical research. When polling became (in spite of theoretical and empirical controversies) largely *institutionalized* and *industrialized,* a third controversy arouse about the role polls play, or ought to play, in political life. The key, though not the only and certainly not homogenous, groups of protagonists in the controversy are "insiders" and "outsiders: those who work inside the public opinion industry and are primarily interested in how to do the work well, and those outside the industry who doubt whether the work should be done at all (Miller 1995, 105).

Two key types of critiques of the institutionalized forms of public opinion research will be discussed in this chapter. The first one primarily questions the validity of interview response data gathering as an instrument of public opinion *research,* and the use of quantitative methods for data analysis. The second stream of criticism derives from the social and political consequences of public opinion polling, and it questions empirical research procedures as an adequate instrument for public opinion *expression.* In addition, we can also identify a third stream of criticism that questions the *political* status of polling as a *democratic instrument* or procedure (regardless of whether it "measures" *public* opinion or *private* attitudes, for example, comparing it with elections or referenda), but the question of normative validity is beyond the scope of my interest here, since I do not discuss democratic theories in general.[5]

A BRIEF HISTORICAL EXCURSUS:
THE (NON)SENSE OF OPINION RESEARCH

The universally applied method of attitude measurement in social research easily obscures substantial differences in research aims. Opinion research (including its most specific form—public opinion polling) may be predominantly used as a means for achieving three distinct goals: (1) producing a model of public opinion, (2) testing hypotheses based on a theoretical model, on the characteristics and rules of the social phenomena objectively measurable on the level of individuals, or (3) simply describing attitudinal characteristics of the population. These three sorts of goals are associated with a wide array of survey organizations interested in different goals and, consequently, specialized in different types of research. Different survey organizations are faced with some similar problems and groups of actors (e.g., subsidies and clients, respondents, [mis]uses of methods and results), and they may be seen as structurally equivalent (they have similar positions in a network of clients and respondents). However, they widely differ in their interests (Miller 1995, 112) and, perhaps even more importantly, only a tiny minority of survey organizations usually exert a disproportionately large amount of influence at different levels and in different spheres of society (Moore 1995, xi). The dominant types of organizations involved in polling are governmental offices (population surveys, censuses, and other surveys usually associated with national statistical bureaux), academic institutes usually based at universities and sponsored by governmental offices, and commercial companies.

Modern methods of interview response data gathering were developed in close relationship with the development of statistics, particularly probability theory and random sampling. Further development brought about the standardization of interviews or questionnaires, thanks to the construction of scales for measuring attitudes. Yet the method of interviewing antedates the origins of modern sociology, and it was developed under the influence of specific social rather than scientific interests. On the other hand, in the 1920s *operationalism,* which insisted on a perfect identity between a concept and operations or procedures of empirical research, was the cause of the *reduction* of the definition of a concept to a set of research operations. Thus human intelligence was reduced to IQ test results, and public opinion to the results of opinion polls.[6] Since the development of empirical research methods is clearly a *historical process,* we should ask ourselves how early research incentives, and specific social and scientific conditions of that period, determine the function and character of modern opinion research, particularly polling. Does the logic (if) hidden in the methods and procedures of opinion research determine the aims of research?

Moral Statistics

The beginnings of empirical (opinion) research belong to the time of progressive bourgeois ideology, to the time of the realization of new capitalist relations in developed societies, when empirical perceiving and recording of the new processes in itself contributed to the abolition of feudal metaphysics and thus to the development of a new bourgeois society. Opinion research grew in close connection with the development of two different sorts of statistics: (1) the so-called *moral statistics* having developed since the eighteenth century and, later on, (2) *mathematical statistics* (statistical science in the modern sense). The predecessors of empirical social research could be looked for at least at the end of the eighteenth century in England in the studies of social questions, in which for the first time a standardized interview was used and out of which developed a systematic gathering of data about the population of specific geographical, cultural, and administrative environments (social surveys).[7] During that period, data were intended primarily for state administration, were mostly of the subjective evaluation type, and were scarcely used in scientific endeavors (Mitchell 1968, 100; Maus 1973, 26). The subject of these studies, which were very often vividly *critical,* was the consequences of early capitalist industrialization on the social structure and especially the proletariat, primarily women and children. For ethnology, nonstandardized interviews remained a chief information source but strong emphasis was laid on *the competence of the respondent.* The main initiative for the development of a scientifically based, standardized interview, other than in ethnology, came from the activities of the British Royal Commissions in the beginning of the nineteenth century and was oriented to reveal the pauperization of the proletariat in the developing industrial housing agglomerations. The work of the Commissions was usually based on reports by different experts but also on interviews with workers and group discussions. Interviews and (standardized) questionnaires became the means for gathering data, which provided the Commissions with more objective insights into the workers' situation than was provided by the owners and managers.

The importance of the development of moral statistics (named also social physics or social statistics) for critical investigation was stressed also by Karl Marx (e.g., in the foreword of the first edition of *Capital*) and was to a great extent used by Engels in his *Lage der arbeitenden Klasse in England* (1845). The significance of Engels's study does not lie so much in the originality of the method, the sources of data, or the data themselves, since a larger part of them had already been published, but primarily in the *aim* and the starting point of the interpretation of the data. It would not be an exaggeration to claim that Engels's study on the working classes in England is the first attempt to apply social statistics in order to reveal and explain the *class* situation of working men, women, and children. As Engels ([1845] 1974, 502) pointed out himself, "To avoid all misunderstandings and from them arising reproaches I'd like to add that I spoke about the bourgeoisie as *a class,* so all the things I mentioned about individuals are mere markings of the reasoning and acting of *the class.*"

The framework for studies of poverty, illiteracy, diseases, and other social questions was the popular census (in England after 1801), itself a kind of social survey. The methodological improvement of this kind of empirical study was especially influenced by already founded statistical associations. At the same time, this research activity started to echo more widely in society due to the development of the (mass) *press.* One of the most severe critics of social conditions of workers in England was journalist Henry Mayhew, one of the founders of *Punch,* who was the first to start using "undirected interview" (as was the whole literary circle around Charles Dickens).

Research into social questions spread in England and the United States at the end of the nineteenth century and predominantly retained its traditional *socially reformistic* orientation. In the foreword to the first volume of *Capital,* Marx denoted the members of the "fact-finding commissions" which acted in England, as "proficient, unbiased and reckless men." At the same time Engels was already revealing the hypocrisy of a part of the middle class in their studies of the social situation of the working class (e.g., Ure). This conservative, explicitly antisocialist research tradition was continued in the second half of the nineteenth century by French engineer Le Play and influenced a wide circle of Catholic researchers in France and elsewhere, though not only (or even not predominantly) by its conservatism but by strict methodological concept of its *sociography.*

A socioreformist orientation for the improvement of the living conditions of the working class generally predominated in social statistics, supported also by reformist tendencies within the developing mass press. Due to their critical dealings with the bottom of the American society, these journalists have been nicknamed muckrakers. They were the authors of the first attempts at investigating public opinion based on the interviews with "representatively" selected (i.e., from specific social classes) but in no way particularly qualified or competent citizens. Their sensational reports about deprivileged classes in U.S. cities also raised interest in empirical research and created a picture of researchers as "societal doctors" or "social engineers" (Scheuch 1973, 73). One of the most prominent representatives of "moral statistics" in Germany was Ferdinand Tönnies, who conducted extensive statistical research into crime, suicide, strikes, and other morally relevant demographic phenomena—not to describe them but primarily to explain them through socioeconomic conditions of human life.

Opinion research is inseparably connected with another form of statistics—the development and application of statistical *methods.* Statistics, which originally denoted a science of state, administration, economy, and population (from Latin *status*), began to develop as a science that discovers, describes, and explains the rules of mass phenomena through quantitative methods in the eighteenth century. In the beginning its only function was descriptively summing up (e.g., with percentages, means, correlation coefficients) large quantities of information in order to make them conceivable (descriptive statistics). Later on, inductive statistics was developed. It enabled researchers, on the basis of probability theory, to make inferences about population from sample results or to generalize on the basis of a limited quantity of information (Blalock 1960, 5). This transformation of statistics largely enabled its breakthrough into numerous natural and social sciences, from physics and biology to demography, economy, and sociology.

In the middle of the nineteenth century, two antagonistic views of the introduction of mathematical statistics into the social sciences were asserted. Among the most severe opponents of statistics was Comte, the founder of observation, experiment, and comparative method in sociology as a "positive social science." The positivist Comte, who had even taught mathematics in his youth, rejected the sociological application of the "awkward, funny calculations of the cheating theory of probability," which he called "a serious social danger to support extremely harmful errors, because it [the theory of probability] surrounds them by an imposing look of intelligence" (Maus 1973, 22; Hacking [1990] 1995, 143–455). Comte's criticism was devoted mainly to Adolphe Quételet's endeavors to develop, by statistical means, "social physics," which would be based on objective observation, measurement, and enumerating the activities and characteristics of individuals in order to find out the basic principles in the conduct of mass phenomena.

Quételet's aspirations for the development of the science of statistics are rooted in political arithmetic, conceived in the seventeenth century by W. Petty as a critique of the former verbalized descriptive statistics that often was no more than a conglomerate of interesting descriptions and reports. The main incentive for the development of modern statistics came, however, from probability calculus and its early applications in astronomy and insurance, which developed into a scientific theory with the works of Bernoulli, Laplace, and Fourier. With the first international congress of statisticians in 1853, modern statistics was internationally institutionalized.

Quételet's endeavors met with strong opposition, especially in conservative circles. Conservatives saw in the study of the principles of human behavior and activity a danger to idealistic conceptions of the freedom of the human will. Similar to contemporary controversies between critical and administrative research, dissertations about the role of statistics in the nineteenth century were not without a political background. In the same way that Marx in his treatises on the freedom of the press in the 1840s often proved Prussian conservatism by means of comparison with the development of the press, for example, in the more advanced France or Belgium, a German statistician, Johannes Fallati, was explaining the opposition to statistics in Germany as a consequence of the *absence of the publicity* that existed in England, France, and Belgium. Using the application of statistical questionnaires in these countries as an example, he was proving that "everywhere where there is no publicity in politics and where there is no freedom of the press, there is no confidence in statistics which also more or less limits its development and influence" (Maus 1973, 33).

The views of Quételet and Fallati have prevailed at last, and by the end of the nineteenth century the development of statistics helped bring sociology as a theoretical discipline and social research, which had always had a clearly empirical character, closer together. As it often happens with innovations, the importance of this achievement was overestimated; it was even believed that the new science would solve the division between natural and social sciences in the form of a "unified science" that had been predicted already by Marx and later expected by Tönnies, but all these expectations finally proved utopian. Nevertheless, it would be difficult to find today a (social) scientist who would agree with Comte's thesis that statistics represents "a serious social danger," although such a danger actually exists in statistics as well as any other science when knowledge is only superficial, unsystematic, and occasional. A consequence of ignorance and misunderstanding is, on the one hand, the mystification of statistics as universal solutions to all research problems and thus the reduction of investigation to the use of those research methods that admit statistical data analysis; on the other hand, it is an almost blind resistance to the use of any statistical techniques.

Developments in the Twentieth Century

The first decades of the twentieth century considerably transformed empirical research. The details of this transformation are beyond the scope of this book, but a brief review of important methodological achievements will provide a context for the discussion of the political instrumentalization of polling.

The year 1915 can be taken as a great turning point in the development of opinion research. For the first time, random samples were used in empirical research, by A. L. Bowley. True, empirical research during this period had already spread widely, particularly in the United States. Statistics was changing from a bare means for more accurate description of mass phenomena into an analytical tool for generalization and explanation of social phenomena. The representative sample finally opened the way to market research and public opinion polling. At the same time, numerous disputes were raised about the role and the meaning of representative sampling and statistical analyses generally in social-scientific research.

The development of statistics has also significantly influenced the standardization of interviews and the development of refined procedures for attitude measurement (e.g., Thurstone's, Likert's, Guttman's, and Osgood's scaling procedures).[8] Rapid progress in the development of attitude measurement helped lead the conceptualizations of public opinion away from alternative possibilities and concepts that were not supported by available measurement devices and significantly contributed to the prevalence of empirical public opinion research. With a growing number of social researchers, a methodological discourse was established among scholars supported by scientific journals that started to publish articles on methodological problems of empirical research methods and statistics.

From periodical and individual research attempts a permanent and organized activity was developed in the framework of universities (with the publishing activity and teaching courses in public opinion),[9] governmental offices (e.g., national statistical bureaus), and commercial companies. Professional institutionalization of survey research not only heightened interest in reliability and (at least partly) validity of the research instruments but, because of its ever higher costs, simultaneously led empirical research into dependence on capital. A generation of social researchers has grown "without ever seeing a modern critic of polls focus on much besides the quality and representativeness of poll projections" (Lemert 1981, 5). The cleft between critical-scientific reflection and empirical research subordinated to commercial interests became ever stronger and raised questions about the social role of opinion research and its scientific (non)productivity, but at the same time, as Lemert noted, "the ranks of competent critics of the underlying simple reductionist model were thinned by age, career changes, and loss of confidence created by their inability to supply an alternative research strategy."

Since 1936, polls have become functionally important in the political process in the United States.[10] As Albig (1956, 178) maintains, "Polls became significant, not in terms of sporadic instances which may be unearthed by exploration in the files of a few crumbling newspapers, but when the polls are really important to leadership and to mass publics. In the 1820s the straw polls were not thus significant; in the 1920s they had become so." The political usefulness of straw polls became evident to many political leaders because it was possible to use polling results for policy decisions and propaganda.

Already before World War I, a new sort of empirical research was born that made use (and misuse) of all existing scientific findings: market research. For a short period of time, the leading role was played by newspaper companies, which created their own research departments. Yet advertisers did not trust the objectivity of their results (since publishers had an interest in convincing advertisers of a wide response to their own magazines among readership), and so they turned increasingly to research performed by advertising agencies, whose interest was more similar to their own (Mayhew 1997, 198).

The new commercial orientation had nothing in common with the former social-scientific empirical studies (which were to a large extent critically oriented) but research methods. Yet it greatly broadened interest in polls, among both subsidizers and audiences. With market research, public opinion polling largely became private, profitable business. In contrast to political polls, whose results were largely published or at least released at a later date (which was usually the practice of governmental and other administrative agencies), only a small part of studies conducted for commercial corporations were made public. In 1956, Albig reported that only a small part of opinion research dealt with political and social issues[11] of interest to the readers of newspapers and magazines, whereas the prevalent part was centered on various fields of commercial research: advertising copy testing, evaluation of advertising appeals, motives for purchasing, media measurement (the relative effectiveness of advertising for a particular product in various types of media), product research (consumer opinion of the product), movement of branded goods and causes for shifts, testing of sales methods, and public relations studies (Albig 1956, 183).

Finally, after World War II, polling stimulated internationalization of empirical research. In 1946 Elmo Roper and Joshua Powers established International Public Opinion Research, Inc., to conduct market research and polling in South America (Albig 1956, 189), which perhaps represents the first transnational research corporation. Internationalization of research (e.g., comparative polls and surveys) was further developed by the growing internationalization of politics and economy.

In contrast to its prehistory in the eighteenth and nineteenth centuries, modern opinion research is becoming ever more sterile in its subordination to capital. On the one hand, the expenses of systematic opinion research affect prohibitively the use of complementary or alternative (and usually less expensive) research methods; on the other hand, the dependence on the ruling interests closes the questions and subjects them to the interests of political and commercial sponsors and subsidizers. As Lynd argued already in 1940, "A major barrier to a socially constructive use of public opinion polls is that these polls are in private hands for private profit" (Lynd 1940, 220). A path similar to the "conservative revolution" in opinion research was taken by the press, formerly the most important instrument of the public. Instead of serving the public as its critical voice, journalism is now submitting to a mass production of publicity for the market and to public opinion manufactured through opinion polling.

Nevertheless, insight into the cultural prehistory of opinion research undoubtedly proves that *the thesis of overdetermination of interview response data gathering by the administrative ideology is false.* It is evident from historical development that opinion research was conceived to a great extent as a critical impulse—not against the ideologized science, as later demanded by Adorno and Horkheimer, but against the ideologized consciousness of the old and new ruling classes in developing capitalist societies of the eighteenth and nineteenth centuries. In fact, a large part of (mostly empirical) social research fell under the general law of capitalist production—as was the case with numerous other human activities, including (mass) communication—when the bourgeois public transforms itself into the subject of the public representation of power. *The bourgeois liberal public disappears as the public but not as the historical subject.* In a way, we may recognize this idea already in Tönnies's *Kritik,* in which he claims that with the rise and strengthening of the middle classes their ideas were also rising and strengthening; the new classes succeeded in turning their ideas into a common good of the political public. The struggle for freedom of thought, freedom of the press, and other civic rights and liberties was substantially an expression of the rise of the new, national bourgeois class that identified itself with "the society," "the people," or "the nation," and its struggle for power—first for participation in the rule of the old estates and then for its own government (Tönnies 1922, 128). This collapse of the public is the real social foundation on which the sociopsychological research of public opinion may have developed.

Empirical research had a different status in the former socialist societies, acting as a critical impulse against ideologized abstract social sciences, against formalism and simplified generalizations, and for investigating differences in interests and social contradictions in the processes of the development of socialism. This was actually the same role it had against feudalism and for capitalism during the revolutionary social changes that occurred almost two centuries before. Socialist societies that originated in the revolutions of the twentieth century were not inclined to the development of critical social research, particularly not toward empirical research. For a long time, sociology was considered a bourgeois science and was excluded from academic life. Later, this anti-Marxist "class character" pertained only to empirical research.

In the former socialist countries, opinion research experienced its first institutionalization in ex-Yugoslavia in the field of market research (in Zagreb in the 1950s). The institutionalization of self-management in 1950 also meant the social affirmation of commodity production as a condition for going beyond state socialism and the actual development of socialist relations. Self-management could not, of course, bring about political decentralization on its own, but it did open up possibilities for greater autonomy of economic and other spheres. However, in the 1950s, individual attempts at (public) opinion research were held back. The first political public opinion polls were done as late as the mid-1960s. After confrontation with the political police, the then prime minister of Slovenia in the autumn of 1966 publicly proposed the need to research the opinions of citizens on political questions. Among the key arguments for the initiation of public opinion polling in a self-management society was (certainly not dominant at that time) the conviction that (1) empirical opinion research is evidence, or at least an expression, of democracy in society and that (2) it is precisely empirical research of politically relevant opinions of citizens that can prevent social situations in which opinions are secretly investigated only by the police.

As in the beginning of empirical research in capitalism, examples of opinion research in former socialist countries undoubtedly falsified the thesis of the *innately conservative,* administrative nature of empirical research. Like its beginnings in the nineteenth century, empirical research in the late socialism of the second half of the twentieth century actually developed as a direct expression of the democratization of society. That period saw frequent friction and conflict between the political and research spheres, since politicians, as those who directly or indirectly ordered and subsidized empirical opinion research, limited research autonomy, so that at times there was even a cessation of public opinion polling. It would be naive to search for the reasons for such antagonisms above all or even solely in the "bourgeois nature" of opinion research, although the political implications of empiricism cannot be excluded.

THE DECLINE OF THE PUBLIC AND THE RISE OF POLLING

The practice of social research changed significantly in the 1920s, with the rising importance of empirical research, its institutionalization at universities, and the development of new techniques for attitude measurement and random sampling methods. The most significant innovation was certainly the application of new research tools in market research whose only subject was individuals' consumption needs and capabilities, and particularly their motivations for specific modes of consumption. The fall of the public caused a transformation of public opinion from the genuine opinion of the public into a fiction—a mask under which the manipulative publicity of privileged opinions can be hidden. In such conditions, the experiences of market research, which achieved a level of objective measurement and a reliable enough prediction of consumers' behavior, became strongly relevant to the authoritative institutions in order to ensure the success of manipulative procurement of support by the masses to the political aims and decisions of the power elites. Empirical public opinion research was the result of the actual equalizing of the consumption and political spheres, the decline of the critical public/ity, and not the opposite. Public opinion thus became an *object of empirical research* after it became the *object of rule* (manipulation).

The construction of a "marketplace of ideas" that transformed the lower classes into mere consumers of opinions advanced by the upper classes was, according to Ginsberg (1986, 37–39), sustained by three key factors: (1) the promotion of mass literacy, (2) the subsidy and encouragement of private media of communication, and (3) the legal protection of freedom of speech and of the press. The organization of the free marketplace of ideas was intended to reduce the adversary relationship between the lower classes and the state, as well as to domesticate public opinion. The new formal channels for the expression of opinions (primarily political representative bodies and elections) that were constructed by the state, together with the education of masses in their use, made "the expression of mass opinion . . . less disruptive" and enabled the state "to reduce the threat that informed expressions of mass opinion often posed to the political order" (Ginsberg 1986, 57, 48). These transformations were perpetuated and strengthened by polling.[12]

During the eighteenth and nineteenth centuries, when democrats truly believed in the existence of the public and public opinion, opinion research in the framework of moral statistics was never related to the idea (or even a model of) public opinion. Paradoxically, in the period of the decline of the (liberal bourgeois) public in the late nineteenth century, newspapers (particularly in the United States) started to publish *numerical crowd estimates* for election campaign rallies as *indicators of public opinion*.[13] Finally, in the 1930s, methodological perfection enabled the transformation of straw polls and other (earlier) forms of *opinion research* into *public opinion polling*. Yet the critics of the use (abuse) of scientific discoveries in the field of empirical social-scientific research for the "antidemocratic vindications of measurement and manufacture of public opinion" (Keane 1984, 148) overlook the fact that such research only increases the reliability and effectiveness of harmonizing mass consciousness with (in reality) alienated social relationships. Empirical research, in and on itself, certainly does not produce such a harmonization, or should I say, it is not its precondition. Rather, the contrary is the case: alienated social relations enable alienated empirical research. As, for example, Borneman argued already in 1947, "to hold the pollsters solely responsible for the decline in radio programming was perhaps somewhat hasty. The pattern of programming was closely linked to the particular pattern of finance that had arisen in the entertainment industry" (Borneman 1947, 32). In fact, there is no "tacitly proposed equivalence between the universe of consumption and that of politics" (Keane 1984, 148) in polling, but a completely explicit use of the same research methods, which also achieve in both spheres the same high level of vindication. Although it is true that "the data reported by opinion polls are actually the product of an interplay between opinion and the survey instrument" (Ginsberg

1989, 273), this is only a specific instance of the general relationship that exists among the subject (researcher), the method or the tool (interview in polling), and the object (respondent's attitudes in polling) in the development of scientific knowledge.

It should be stressed that the concrete *methods* of opinion research do not have an antidemocratic character in themselves but that the *object* of research (i.e., public opinion rather than opinion of the public) is the result of undemocratic historical development; it is precisely to such developments that the *aim* of research is subordinated. Analogously, one could claim that atomic physics is guilty of the nuclear bomb. In the latter case, however, science directly *produced* the possibility of abuse, whereas in the case of administrative public opinion research (polling), science has been abused by *externally produced* undemocratic circumstances. The development of methods of objectivated measurement in the form of interview responses within the nineteenth-century framework of social statistics is undoubtedly sufficient evidence to falsify the equation of empirical (opinion) research with its subordination to the authoritative institutions *in general* and not only under the specific historical conditions of late capitalism. Besides, there was no golden age of public opinion in the sense of its full materialization either: even the democratic political system in ancient Greece or the liberal bourgeois public excluded the majority of population from participation in public opinion formation. But it is also clear that opinion polls do not contribute to a (more) democratic system because they "do not bring within their range elements of the political system basic for the understanding of the role of mass opinion within the system." They underestimate and conceal the role and power of the upper layer of the politically influential (Key [1961] 1967, 536).

This is not to say that opinion polling has no relevant consequences for the conceptualization of public opinion and/or the form of existence of public opinion itself. Beniger (1992) identifies five types of "social and behavioral changes" potentially brought about by the development of opinion polling. These changes occur in (1) the definition of public opinion, (2) what may affect public opinion, (3) the effects that public opinion may have in society, (4) the behavior of individuals because of polling, and (5) the behavior of individuals because of publication of poll results. We may definitely agree with Beniger on the substantial issues of *what constitutes public opinion* and how the spread of opinion polling in the twentieth century has influenced and/or transformed the nature of public opinion. However, Beniger's attempt to answer these questions is controversial and inaccurate because he claims that (in contrast to the "classical conception of public opinion of ancient Athens," public opinion has increasingly become (1) *something* in which not just the elite but everyone might at least potentially participate; (2) an *aggregate* of individual opinions in which all are assumed to be of equal importance and uniformly informed; (3) *something* which might be unconscious in individuals and yet subject to external measurement and manipulation; (4) *something* abstracted and isolated from actual political controversies and discourse; and (5) *something* wholly independent of the uses to which it might be put. (Beniger 1992, 208; emphasis added)

Despite two substantial flaws in Beniger's analysis—denoting public opinion as "something" without specifying how it is *constituted* and misconceiving the first two characteristics of polled opinion as contrasted to the equality of citizens in ancient Athens rather than to the opinion of the liberal bourgeois public—Beniger is right in believing that questions of how polling influences "conceptions of public opinion, and public opinion's role in modern economies, polities and societies" are "crucial to any reasonable conception of a democratic or free society" (Beniger 1992, 218). Bryce ([1888] 1995, 916), and after him Tönnies, argued similarly that the opinion of the public became a *new world power* with eighteenth-century rationalism, when governments became more popular. The development of newspapers as new means of expressing opinions, made possible by developments in economy, technology, and politics (particularly political rights and freedoms, e.g., freedom of expression and the press), was a necessary condition. In other words, a new technology of forming and expressing opinions may commonly be associated with changes in the nature of public opinion.[14]

Although we can agree that "*theory* about the ways that quantitative data are employed in public life is sorely lacking" (Herbst 1993, 41), it is doubtful to expect that more detailed and exhaustive research would support Herbst's hypothesis that "much of the texture and complexity of political attitudes is lost in the polling process, yet *much is gained in the way of public discourse, since poll data are so easily communicated,*" primarily because of "obvious and sometimes critical functions these numbers serve for statesmen, journalists, political activists, *and, occasionally, average citizens*" (Herbst 1993, 39; emphasis added). Changes in (functions of) public opinion caused by the development of polling are not of a quid pro quo kind in which everyone or every social group would partly lose and partly gain or, as Herbst suggests, in which "numerical symbols of public opinion" produced by polls would be utilized differently. *The* substantial question is not how polling data is used and who *uses* (or may possibly use) it, but rather who *produces* it and how it is produced. Explicit or implicit assumptions about the nature of public opinion introduced by polling as a new means of expressing opinions brought about two types of partly interrelated changes: (1) the transformation of traditional or classic understandings and practices of public opinion processes and (2) the development of a new kind of social institution functioning in the political system.

Polling helped transform autonomous public opinions into much more manageable "mass opinions" that could be created and shaped to suit particular interests. Moreover, polling became largely institutionalized[15] in all democratic societies. Controversies over the value and function of opinion polls for democratic political processes are as old as polling itself, and they largely reflect much older efforts at theorizing public opinion and democratic government. The first eminent heralds of fundamental differences in conceptualizing the political function of polling were George Gallup and Lindsay Rogers; their disagreements in the 1940s reflected ideas presented by Dewey and Lippmann during the 1920s. For instance, Gallup (1940) claimed that polling results as a "mandate from the people" to the government, that is, in a society in which direct democracy is impossible, polling ought to compensate for the limitations of electing political representatives. Public opinion revealed through polling was believed to provide a democratic counterweight to the growing independence of political representatives and, therefore, a separation of representation from popular rule. From that perspective, as Albig argued, public opinion polls may be an indication of democratic developments. In predemocratic societies, customs, beliefs, and convictions are subjects of early indoctrination and remain very stable over a person's lifetime so that "periods of limited opinion do not have need for the recorders of opinion, for the straw-vote takers and pollers, for the study of opinions as important phenomena" (Albig 1956, 175). Similarly, V. O. Key related the interest of governments in the distribution of public opinion among their citizenry to "the ethical imperative that government heed the opinion of the public (which) has its origins in democratic ideology as well as in the practical necessity that governments obtain support of influential elements in society" ([1961] 1967, 4). In contrast, Rogers (1949) defended the liberalist criticism of the tyranny of public (i.e., majority) opinion prophesied earlier by Edmund Burke, James Bryce, and Walter Lippmann—that political representatives, who should be responsible to the general rather than any particularistic public, should not follow the dictates of the public. He considered "completely false" Gallup's ideas that, in contemporary societies with representative political systems, polling might help reestablish the town meetings of antique Greece on a national scale because polling prevents the *discussion* and *agreement* that are essential to effective (democratic) government. "*Vox populi* cannot help democratic governments to decide what they ought to do. Political and intellectual leaders must propose alternative policies. They must educate the electorate, and if the leadership and education are effective, then the people will demonstrate their 'essential wisdom'" (Rogers 1949, 235).

EARLY CRITIQUES OF POLLING: WILLIAM ALBIG, HERBERT BLUMER, AND LINDSAY ROGERS

Early critiques of public opinion polls concentrated on problems of *validity*, that is, on the question of whether polls actually measure what they aim and claim to measure—public opinion—and on the political implications of polling. Proceeding from the differentiation he made between *opinion* and *attitude*, Albig maintained that no record of opinions is adequate unless it leads to accurate assumptions regarding the attitudes that underlie opinions (1956, 174). He saw two fundamental problems in attempting to measure public opinion: (1) the development of attitude tests sufficiently comprehensive to include, at least, the more typical attitude patterns of most individuals constituting a public ("of millions of individuals") and (2) the development of sampling methods adequate to the task of reporting on large publics by means of the smallest feasible representative sample.

Whereas the problem of adequate sampling seemed "rather simple" to Albig, Blumer (1948, 546) emphasized that "the inherent deficiency of public opinion polling, certainly as currently done, is contained in its sampling procedure." Both Albig and Blumer were concerned with the validity problem of attitude tests, an enduringly controversial issue. Albig was among the first prophets of polling who nevertheless warned against uncritical massive use of opinion polls that might lead to their invalidity. Public opinion polling may be devaluated on the ground of (1) the reduction of data gathering to interview response data, neglecting alternative methods, and the limitation of data analysis to response counting, and (2) misunderstandings in interaction between the researcher and respondent, and manipulative question wording.

Albig discussed seven crucial issues of polling, which he related to *news reporting* (1939, 229–34), by looking at the problems of validity, social and political implications, and ethics of polling, primarily through newspaper publications of poll results. Albig's first issue was the importance and quality of public opinion. When answering the question of what is and should be the role of the "opinions of members of large publics on public affairs," Albig suggested that pollsters too often fail to assess the quality and quantity of public opinion: they tend to *overemphasize the significance of public opinion* on hundreds of issues on which no really significant opinion exists. Thus reporting the very large number of polls in the media is of dubious interest to the public.

Albig's second issue was the display of public ignorance. One of the most valuable results of polls is, according to Albig, the reporting on broad areas of *popular ignorance* that are abundantly revealed by polling. Although the portrayal of popular ignorance of public affairs is more extensive than systematic, it is, nevertheless, an important public service performed by polls.

The third issue was influence on legislative and administrative decisions. A politically critical question is whether polling tends to distort and degenerate the quality of the decisions made by legislative representatives and administrative leaders. Albig suggested that the absence of polls certainly would not keep politicians from attempting to assess public opinion; they would have to find other ways of polling the opinions of their followers, as they did in the past, although less frequently and unsystematically. However, "if the polls are more accurate than other sources of reporting on opinion, they should be required reading for men in public life" (Albig 1939, 232). As a matter of fact, Albig assumed a considerable influence of the polls on legislative and administrative decisions; although he admitted the difficulty of assessing direct effects, he did not consider "the poller the villain in this drama."

Albig's fourth issue was checking interest claims. Also related to the influence of polling is the matter of controlling otherwise essentially uncontrolled claims of interest groups. Albig accepted Gallup's belief that polls support democracy because they "can limit the claims of pressure groups to the facts, and thus prevent many insupportable demands for special privilege." Polling could provide political representatives and administrators with information about the distribution of opinions to counter the claims of pressure groups, although perhaps not to the extent argued by Gallup.

Albig's fifth main concern was how reporting poll results may influence the opinions of readers, which especially pertains to topics about which the readers do not have (firm) opinions.[16] The publication of poll results in the media may possibly have an agenda setting function and increase adherence to majority positions, that is, produce a bandwagon effect. Since polling greatly oversimplifies complicated issues, it is highly unlikely that the publication of poll results increases reflective thought. However, polls do not bear any crucial responsibility for simplifying the thinking of the public, according to Albig, because such oversimplifications are also characteristic of the mind-set of the majority of those polled, that is, they are not caused by polls.

Albig's sixth issue was ethics. He raised two ethical questions in relation to polls, first, do commercial pollsters correctly inform their publics about the quality and quantity of the opinions of their respondents? Second, is there a danger of corruption in the polling process and, therefore, a need to regulate polling formally or informally? He believed that major commercial and academic pollsters were generally competent and ethical, but these questions became increasingly relevant with the growth of polling organizations and widely differing forms of professional competence, ownership, and control (Albig

1956, 234). Regarding adequate social control, Albig did not see realistic possibilities for voluntary trade association agreements or legal regulation. In both respects Albig was right. Mayhew (1997, 246) recently stated that pollsters are often required to produce the results that clients want; professional pollsters mostly resist these pressures, but they have no control over their clients' use of the results and are bound by no strict rules of conduct comparable to those pertaining to attorneys.

In contrast to Albig, Blumer was concerned with the validity problem in the strict sense, "whether public opinion polling actually deals with public opinion"(1948, 542). He was among the first to severely criticize the transformation of public opinion from a "property of groups" to an "attribute of individuals," explicitly carried out by those who justified polling as an instrument of measuring public opinion and, strictly speaking, made public opinion equal to what public opinion polls polled. Blumer had five major objections to polling. First, the central arguments of Blumer's critique of public opinion polling as a method of recording and measuring public opinion relate to the problem of *(in)adequate sampling.* Blumer was convinced that the operationalistic understanding of public opinion as an aggregate of equally valid opinions by independent individuals was the direct result of random sampling procedure. Due to its demand for the independence of each unit, this procedure advances the notion of society as a mere aggregate of disparate individuals, in contrast to actual public opinion, which is organic and functions as a moving organization of interconnected parts. Compared to "commonsense empirical observations of public opinion," there is no guarantee in polling that those individuals who truly participate in the formation of public opinion are included in the sample.

Second, demographic variables—age, sex, occupation, economic status, educational attainment or class status—are rarely "the marks of significant functional position in the formation of public opinion on a given issue." Since these are the only variables included in public opinion polling, "we know essentially nothing of the individual in the sample with reference to the significance of him or his opinion in the public opinion" (Blumer 1948, 546).

Third, aggregate data. Blumer emphasized that "the collective findings have no assurance of depicting public opinion on a given issue because these findings ignore the framework and the functional operation of the public opinion" (Blumer 1948, 547). An individual who is responsive to public opinion must assess public opinion as it comes to his or her attention in terms of the functional organization of society to which he or she is responsive. Different individuals and groups will certainly find different specific issues most relevant for them. Thus, on the one hand, public opinion polls *must* ignore concrete, specific questions relevant only for specific environments, since they are directed to the aggregate level of society. On the other hand, many questions will remain unanswered by respondents because they lack relevance for specific environments or groups.

Fourth, validity is not transferable. Polling is regarded as intrinsically valid (only) because of its rather spectacular success in predicting elections. However, "the casting of ballots is distinctly an action of separate individuals wherein a ballot cast by one individual has exactly the same weight as a ballot cast by another individual" (Blumer 1948, 547). In other words, the validity of sampling ballots is not proof of the universal validity of random sampling! Polls exhibit a high *predictive* validity when used to predict election results, but (1) the predictive validity of a measuring instrument is only one dimension of validity and does not yet guarantee its validity in general (see Splichal 1990), and (2) the accuracy of a prediction of one type of findings is not transferable to (all) other types of findings. In a more recent study, Robert Huckfeldt and John Sprague (1995) demonstrate that Blumer was actually too generous in his assessment of validity of election studies, basically because predictive validity is only a thin dimension of validity. Even polling with the highest possible predictive validity has no *explanatory* power. For example, the most accurate prediction of the voting turnover provides no answer to the question asked by Huckfeldt and Sprague: "What is the engine that drives the dynamics of . . . political preference during an election campaign?" In other words, the most accurate *prediction* of election results does not yet *explain* how and why the results spring up.

Fifth is the loss of generic subject. In toto, public opinion polling is not able to "isolate 'public opinion' as an abstract or generic concept which could thereby become the focal point for the formation of a system of propositions." Rather, the findings that result from polling "are regarded as constituting the object of study instead of being some contributory addition to knowledge of the object of study" (Blumer 1948, 542, 543). Blumer proved this general observation by arguing (1) that there are *no efforts* to try to identify public opinion as an object of study; (2) that *no specific studies* are used to test a general proposition about public opinion, and (3) that *no generalizations* exist about public opinion despite a large number of polling studies.

Opinion polls tend to extract citizens' attitudes and make them available to subsidizers (governments, parties, or lobbies) who decide on their own what actions (not) to take. But they ignore all other nonsubsidized or subsidized, sources and forms of information about opinion(s) of the public, for example, letters, petitions, resolutions, lobbies, delegations, personal meetings, press conferences, and, perhaps most important, the mass media through which interested individuals and groups can influence those who have to act in response to public opinion. In other words, polling cannot be used as a valid measure of public opinion because

> public opinion which was a mere display, or which was terminal in its very expression, or which never came to the attention of those who have to act on public opinion would be impotent and meaningless as far as affecting the action or operation of society is concerned. (Blumer 1948, 545)

At best, then, opinion polling may serve as only one indicator of public opinion whose validity has to be proven in comparison with other indicators or means of expression. In that case, polling "supplements rather than supplants other *modes of opinion expression,* each with its own limitations" (Miller 1995, 111; emphasis added). It obviously cannot serve as a (universal) procedure to *measure* public opinion or objectify itself to become a neutral means of expressing an individual's' opinion. At worst, it may be used as a means of manufacturing public opinion.

Therefore, according to Blumer, a new model should be constructed to study how public opinion operates in a concrete society. The operationalist understanding of public opinion did not yield, as Blumer argued, an operationalization of any theoretically defined concept of public opinion. A new model should enable such an operationalization, which Blumer saw in his early contribution to the field ([1946] 1966) mainly in the difference between the public and the mass. Blumer conceptualized the formation of public opinion as a function of society in operation through the *interaction of groups* rather than disparate individuals, who share equally in the process of forming and expressing opinions. In his understanding, the public "acquires its particular type of unity and manages to act by arriving at a collective decision or by developing a collective opinion," which could be differentiated from society and from the dispersed mass. Blumer sees the public, in a way that resembles the views of Tönnies, as consisting of two parts: (1) the active part composed primarily of interest groups and (2) "a more detached and disinterested spectator-like body." Public opinion is formed through public discussion and it is always a collective product. Although it does have a certain emotional character, "the very process of controversial discussion forces a certain amount of rational consideration."

> [Public opinion] is not a unanimous opinion with which everyone in the public agrees, nor is it necessarily the opinion of the majority. Being a collective opinion it may be (it usually is) different from the opinion of any of the groups in the public. . . . [It] does represent the entire public as it is being mobilized to act on the

issue, and as such, does enable concerted action which is not necessarily based on consensus, rapport, or chance alignment of individual choices. Public opinion is always moving toward a decision even though it never is unanimous. (Blumer [1946] 1966, 48)

Clearly present in Blumer's conceptualization were the ideas of normative theories of public opinion with an emphasis on rational debate in which not only individuals but also (and primarily) social groups participated. Thus public opinion was in no case the mere sum of individual opinions; moreover, it often differs from the opinions of individual interest groups. Blumer conceived of it as a "central tendency" among separate opinions, which was not necessarily the majority opinion but could also approach the opinion of the minority if it happened to be the most interested and at the same time had the greatest influence.

Although many normative theories and models of public opinion cannot (yet) be verified empirically, this does not mean to Blumer that they must be rejected. He stressed, rather, that we must continue to strive to find empirical verification with which to test them and possibly to reverse them. This applies also to his own conceptualization of public opinion. The essence is, however, that *first* we come up with a consistent definition of public opinion, which Blumer to some extent succeeded in doing. Only based on that can we formulate valid procedures of falsification, including the empirical testing of hypotheses and measurements.

Despite strong arguments against polling presented by Albig and Blumer, "scientific pollsters" continued to discuss and improve, primarily sampling reliability, as if it were the most important factor of an unsatisfactory (predictive) validity of polling. They largely ignored Blumer's theoretical critique, which emphasized a highly problematic operational conceptualization of public opinion in polling, and Albig's questioning of the accuracy of measuring instruments used in polling (e.g., how wording and contextualization of questions influence opinions).

Whereas Albig's and particularly Blumer's critiques were often resumed in the following decades, Lindsay Rogers belongs to the "invisible echelon" of public opinion scholars, although it was he who wrote the *first comprehensive critique* of public opinion polling in 1949. Like Blumer, Rogers went in his critique of polling beyond imperfections in sampling methods and inaccuracy in predicting election results. He did not object to the practice of polling itself; rather, he criticized pollsters' boasting. He accused the Gallup institute of deception:

It had *not* tested reactions; it had *not* measured sentiment and it had *not* charted the mood of the people. About all the polls had done was to tell us the numbers of persons who answered yes or no or who confessed ignorance or indifference when they were asked specific questions. . . . To say that "public opinion" is being "measured" is to make skimmed milk masquerade as cream. (Rogers 1949, 9)

Rogers admitted that polls have become an important feature of journalism. However, he criticized pollsters because they claimed, more importantly, that polling significantly contributed to the development of democracy, but they (1) neither defined what they were actually measuring (2) nor attempted to define "the nature of the political society in which public opinion should be the ruler." Following Lynd's earlier critique (1940), Rogers severely criticized pollsters' wrong premise that public opinion expressed by a majority in polling should be followed by political action in the same way that merchants follow the results of consumer research. Rather, he accepted Bryce's judgment that the duty of "a patriotic statesman in a country where public opinion rules, would seem to be rather to resist and correct than to encourage the dominant sentiment" (Bryce [1888] 1995, 921).

Since Rogers, polls have often been considered a potential threat to rational decision making in politics because of their noxious effect on political representatives who may prefer to follow the results of market research rather than make their own deliberate policy choices. In addition, mass media use polling results to detract public attention from principled political debates to a sort of political entertainment or, as it is now popularly named, infotainment.

Rogers found the most convincing arguments against equating polling with "measuring public opinion" in Walter Lippmann's critique of public opinion theories in his books *Public Opinion* and *The Phantom Public* and in Edmund Burke's belief that the responsibility of the citizens' representative in parliament is not to follow but to *lead* public opinion. The idea that polling might improve democracy is nonsense for Rogers: "I think that even to talk in such a fashion discloses reasoning that is fantastically muddled" (Rogers 1949, 222). Individuals who are interviewed in polls do not have sufficient knowledge to form their own opinions, Rogers claims, because they "read little and think less," and most of them are not capable of appealing to authorities; nevertheless, in polling they "have to give their instantaneous reactions to propositions that they may have considered for the first time" (p. 29). The majority of citizens in any society have no opinion on most of the matters government is dealing with. There are very few questions appropriate for mass answers by yes or no, as practiced in polling or in a referendum, and the electorate is "so intelligent that it is not keen on voting on measures that it imperfectly comprehends, and a large percentage of it refuses to do so" (p. 79). This may be related primarily to the fact that *attitude objects* are much more complex in the case of public opinion ("controversial issues") than in elections (political parties, party candidates), which, in turn, is closely linked with the possibility of attitude object *change* (substitution of one specific attitude object for another in terms of specific characteristics of the object perceived as relevant) and/or semantic *incongruence* (e.g., between the interviewer and respondent in polling).[17]

In modern societies, Rogers argues, direct government by the electorate (in a "permanent referendum") would be a caricature of democracy. Therefore it is misplaced to substantiate the validity of public opinion polling with its resemblance to referendum. In modern democracy, the vital role is with representative assemblies in which political issues are *discussed:* "If there were no Congress, with its clash of personalities, parties, and sections, could questions be asked, for example, about the Taft-Hartley Act or the Marshall Plan? If they were, 'no opinion' would be by far the most frequent reply" (Rogers 1949, 34). The autonomy of political representatives is necessary to enable public discussion and criticism that alone can lead to a reasonable decision. Freedom of public discussion is "the architectonic freedom" because without it, "a people cannot determine whether they are competent judges and whether they want to improve or change the regime under which they live" (p. 235). Yet polling not only does not stimulate public discussion, it prevents and/or substitutes for it. The contribution of polling to the improvement of democratic government is limited to "debunking the claims of a pressure group as to the amount of strength behind it" (p. 188) and inquiring *locally* into "matters of community needs and preferences." Only on questions of *local* (in contrast to national) concern, "while *Vox populi* may not be *Vox dei, Vox pollsteri* may be considered the equivalent of *Vox populi*" (pp. 194, 196).

According to Rogers, those who claim that they are measuring public opinion are offering "vain oblations." There is no justification to call those opinions that individuals are willing (and partly forced) to disclose "in interviews with strangers" public opinion; the individual can easily change them when exposed to public discussion and arguments, or under the pressure of majority opinion. Rogers accepted the pollsters' argument that in polls they got yeses and noes also from part of an *apathetic electorate* and thus extended the basis of involvement in politics. But this raises another question:

> What weight should be given opinions about which men and women care so little that they do not bother to take a small amount of trouble in order to express

them? . . . Some poll might profitably ask this question: "If the issue about which you have just expressed an opinion were put to you on a ballot paper at an election, would you bother to vote?" (Rogers 1949, 83)

According to Rogers's judgment, the measuring procedure itself is problematic because a mere counting of yeses and noes does not pay regard to the *intensity* and *stability* of opinion, to eagerness and enthusiasm of those who agree or disagree with an idea or opinion. Polling is a simulation of *voting,* but voting is neither comparable to the formation and expression of *opinion,* nor it can be taken as an *index* of public opinion. Strictly speaking, in contrast to many economic phenomena, public opinion is not measurable because measurement implies that a relationship exists between a given object and the standard. "In other words," Rogers quotes C. M. Sparrow, "measurability is an intrinsic property of the subject matter; we can measure only that which is measurable" (p. 54). Like Blumer, Rogers argues that pollsters emphasize the power of methods to hide their incapacity to define what they actually do when they pretend to "measure public opinion." Gallup's statement in *The Pulse of Democracy* (1940) that "the limitations and shortcomings of the polls are the limitations and shortcomings of public opinion itself" is a typical pollster's fallacy that Rogers (1949, 162) compares with the delusive belief that "when a thermometer does not work, the fault is not with it, but with the temperature it fails to measure!" But even if polls accurately predict the results of elections and consumer behavior (which are the only instances of true *measuring* in polling), the *reliability of predictions* based on electoral polls and market research[18] does not justify the adaptation of polling to the cultural field, which is the field of public opinion.

Like Albig, Rogers criticized pollsters because they were not concerned with the lack of information and the ignorance of large segments of the electorate, that is, with "no-opinions." For Rogers, that was an unwise practice. Indeed, newspapers might lose interest in polling results if they would only be gathered among the most knowledgeable part of the electorate, and the publication of results is the main goal of polling. However, the hiding of "don't knows" (which was Gallup's usual practice) is not only an important ethical question but also a question of predictive validity: a large proportion of ignorant or undecided respondents indicates that if the question were (further) discussed, it could be answered differently by a decisive margin. Moreover, as Albig suggested earlier, if "pollsters did play up areas of ignorance, they would enable newspaper editors, radio commentators, politicians, teachers, and preachers to know the subjects on which they had real *opportunities to spread light and leading*" (1949, 140; emphasis added). The main purpose of the government's use of polling should be, according to Rogers, to try to change citizen opinions that are not congruent with its course of action: not to heed, but to lead public opinion.

MODERN CRITIQUE: PUBLIC OPINION POLLS AND DEMOCRACY

Contrary to critiques of public opinion polling in the 1930s and 1940s and their primary concern with the question of validity, more recent critiques focus on social and particularly on political implications of polling. James Lemert (1981, 5) was too censorious when arguing that since the late 1940s, modern critics of polling did not seriously question the simple reductionist model of polling, with the exception of the predictive validity and representativeness of polling. In fact, modern critiques go beyond the main validity argument, saying that polls fail to measure public opinion and emphasizing that polling impedes or even prevents the formation and expression of public opinion.

Undoubtedly, the importance of polling is closely related to profound societal and particularly economic changes during the period in which polling was invented. It is another question, however, whether changes in twentieth-century political systems, which brought about the prevalence of opinion polling, denote a democratic development or not. Although polling probably represents a more democratic means of expressing opinions than some alternatives (e.g., demonstrations), it may, at the same time, deprive public opinion of its potential to create an obligation for the authorities to heed. Thanks to polling, public opinion became more predictable and could be managed more easily: instead of promoting the influence of public opinion on governmental policy, polling may help governments adapt public opinion to their interests. The interests of the modern democratic state, managed by professional political elites who seek to minimize electoral and social disruptions from below, may be defined and pursued by various strategies of opinion management. A tendency to marginalize the power of public opinion is typical of a "managerial democracy," which generates a major transformation from an adversary relationship between public opinion and government, typical before the twentieth century, to a managerial one. "We seem to be approaching a state of government by hired promoters of opinion called publicity agents," wrote John Dewey ([1927] 1991, 169). Or, as Walter Lippmann ([1922] 1960, 248) put it, "Within the life of the generation now in control of affairs, persuasion has become a self-conscious art and a regular organ of popular government." According to Mayhew (1997, 236), the dominance of professional institutions of public communication entails the dissociation of public discussion from the genuine issues of public concern and, consequently, "the inflation of influence." The dissociation of public discussion from the structure of social life is brought about mainly by (1) the lack of meaningful policy issues on the public agenda, (2) appeals to vague themes and undercurrent sentiments, (3) one-sided communication that prevents public response (e.g., direct mailing), and (4) the use of strategic rhetorical devices to avoid answering questions or objections directly (Mayhew 1997, 236–40).

Political consultants create campaign issues that work in favor of their political protagonists, without regard to the actual political and social problems. In this way, campaign design tends toward "public discussion on manufactured, dissociated issues" (Mayhew 1997, 240). Polling and pretesting are used as a substantial part of this manufacturing to find out what messages can efficiently appeal to specifically targeted groups of citizens. In general, the rise of opinion polling cannot be connected to a truly democratic development, as Ginsberg argued (1986, 62–85; 1989, 274–93), because polling

1. changes both what is expressed and what is perceived as public opinion "by transforming public opinion from a voluntary to an externally subsidized matter,"
2. transforms public opinion from a behavioral to an attitudinal phenomenon,
3. shifts public opinion from "a property of groups" to an "attribute of individuals," and
4. transforms public opinion from a "spontaneous assertion" to a "constrained response," partially removing the control of individuals over the subject matter of their public expression.

Ginsberg differs from Gallup and Rogers (as well as Albig). His critique of polling tacitly assumes, in contrast to Rogers's, that public opinion should influence governmental policy. But, in contrast to Gallup, he does not see any possibility for polling to perform such a function. The more polling becomes the dominant mode of "measuring public opinion," the more these four transformations result in a "domestication or pacification" of public opinion, according to Ginsberg, and change its relationship to government. Opinion polling is a typical example of (direct) information subsidies: it subsidizes the costs of public presentation of (mass) opinions with which power actors may attempt to influence the actions of others and/or ensure their willingness to occupy themselves with specific themes, primarily through defining public issues, that is, the issues for public discussion. In other words, "clients who provide the essential funds for survey research, therefore, exercise at least *de facto* control over what research gets done and how it is conducted" (Miller 1995, 109). The argument resembles Tönnies's critique of the press, which he considered an organ of political parties, and its dependence on political parties, which prevented the press from being a means of public expression or an organ of the public.

Pacification of public opinion is basically related to the fact that polls assume an equal value of all opinions regardless of their intensity. If the costs of public expressions of opinions are borne by opinion holders themselves, those with more intense or extreme opinions may be more likely to bear the costs of publication. Consequently, more intense opinions are more likely to appear in public. If the costs are subsidized or, as in the case of polling, entirely financed externally rather than by opinion holders, less intense opinions are as likely to be publicly presented as the most extreme opinions. A large proportion of individuals who don't know how to respond to a survey question would never participate in public discussion or actions initiated by citizens themselves. Similar to Lynd's (1940) and Blumer's (1948) criticism, Ginsberg argues that

> the polls, in effect, submerge individuals with strongly held views in a more apathetic mass public. . . . A government wishing to maintain some semblance of responsiveness to public opinion would typically find it less difficult to comply with the preferences reported by the polls than to obey the opinion that might be inferred from letters, strikes, or protests. Indeed, relative to other modes of public expression, polled opinion could be characterized as a collective statement of permission. (Ginsberg 1989, 276)

The concept of a permissive consensus originates in Key's theory of public opinion, in which he defined it as a specific form of consensus that is not directive but only loosely connected with governmental decisions or actions (Key [1961] 1967, 32–35). A simple majority agreement with an opinion or option in an opinion poll may largely arise from persons not strongly attached to the opinion they agreed with. On the other hand, "a 10 per cent dissent may include small pockets of the most determined opposition whose members command controlling points in the governmental mechanism." When such a simple majority agreement exists, a government may be relatively free to act or not to act. Although Key's conception of permissive consensus is clearly related to opinion polling, it is not considered a deficiency in the democratic political process. However, he recognized the need "to go beyond the survey data and make assumptions and estimates about the role of . . . the political elite," when not enough persons from this stratum are included in a random sample to enable a systematic analysis of the "leadership echelon." According to Key, the under-representation of "political influentials"—"the activist subculture"—who significantly affect public opinion is the most important "missing piece of the puzzle" of public opinion ([1961] 1967, 536). Similarly, Key's ideas of multiple consensus and the differentiation between attentive and nonattentive publics also imply a critical attitude toward the conceptualization of public opinion as an agreement among individuals that does not differentiate among the values of individual opinions.

The relations between public opinion and government have been fundamentally changed in the twentieth century, both in terms of how the public is informed and influenced, and how public opinion is expressed. Key related these profound changes to the concentration of power in large corporations and the increasing complexity of government. Before the advent of polling, public opinion was primarily expressed in, and inferred from, different forms of political behavior. Through the nineteenth century, public opinion was often equated with mass behavior, for example, riots, strikes, or demonstrations. In the sociological tradition of the early twentieth century, the expression of public opinion was considered "in the form of direct influence on those who are to act in response to public opinion" (Blumer 1948, 545). Tönnies identified a number of means of expression used by public opinion, like the formation of associations, assemblies, and demonstrations, but he considered newspapers by far the most important means, regardless of their controversial function, because they were also used by political parties to manipulate and deceive the public. With the rise of daily newspapers, previous institutions that organized meaning, identity, and authoritative information for the public, which shaped political preferences of the people and simplified the process of democratic power seeking—political parties, mainstream religion, the nuclear family, the workplace, the neighborhood, and social-class groupings—have all but waned in importance and influence. The press and other mass media developed as power centers, and media-based strategies for shaping public opinion and winning support became increasingly important.

Since the American elections of 1936, scientific opinion polls (which followed earlier straw polls) have occupied a politically most significant position. During that period, newspapers, periodicals, and other commercial actors, in addition to political parties and candidates, became key financial supporters of polling and increasingly subsidized the expression of opinions regarding issues they selected according to their commercial (advertising) or political (propaganda) interests. Whereas before the twentieth century public opinion could often, or even primarily, be inferred from nonverbal behavior, the press and polling largely verbalized and standardized public opinion or, as Ginsberg (1989, 278–79) put it, "polling transformed public opinion *from behavioral to an attitudinal phenomenon.* The polls elicit, organize, and publicize opinion without requiring any action on the part of the opinion-holder" (emphasis added). As any other form of information subsidy, polls may help direct attention, control specific demands, and influence behavior. Poll results do not directly constrain the expression of public opinion through behavior, but they do reduce the probability of behavioral expression, because they provide an opportunity to subsidizers to predict changes in popular opinions and react accordingly. A fundamental dimension of critiques of polling as an antidemocratic process is related to the question of whether public opinion is a mere expression of opinion in the form of *answers* in polls or whether it includes *action.* Arthur Schlesinger Jr. argues (Glynn and McLeod 1984, 65) that polling "elicits essentially an irresponsible expression of opinion. . . . The measure of responsible (in the sense of 'real') opinion is not answers, but acts."

It is obvious that, in modern democratic societies, a growing tendency of the reduction of public opinion from a more complex (behavioral) phenomenon to a merely attitudinal phenomenon exists, but the "theoretical solution" suggested by Schlesinger is rather disputable. The idea to relate a genuine public opinion to the chance that opinion formed by public discussion may be effectively translated into action, even against the authorities, if necessary, goes back to C. W. Mills's (1956) differentiation between "public" and "mass." For Mills, authoritative control over communication channels and over any action to make the opinion effective (i.e., blocking any practical action) was not a consequence of polling but was brought about by industrialization of culture and structural changes in society. In the first place, then, the irresponsibility of opinion expression is not a unique characteristic of polling.

In addition, it is questionable if actions are a more valid instrument of attitude expression than opinions that respondents express anonymously, or if a sharp difference or even opposition may exist between the two. Luis Thurstone already in 1928 denied that attitudes could be more accurately and reliably inferred from overt behavior or actions than from verbally expressed opinions. Similarly, William Albig argued in *Public Opinion* that even anonymity may not modify the subject's tendency to give a conventional answer, which is also typically the case in more public expression of attitudes, or else that individuals' public actions are no less congruent with socially desirable or at least acceptable behavior than are their anonymously expressed opinions. Consequently, "action as well as opinion is a fallible indication of all the attitudes involved in a situation" (Albig 1939, 171).

Since the famous polling contest in 1936, politicians have become increasingly interested in public opinion polling. Such an intense interest in a (new) means of opinion expression is not a phenomenon characteristic of polling; before, political parties and governments were inclined to influence and control public opinion through the contents of newspapers; at the end of the twentieth century they are becoming more sensitive to feedback through new computer-mediated communication channels. Like opinion polls, telephone, telefax, and, increasingly, electronic mail enable politicians to establish contacts with the electorate and measure its pulse. These modern means of expression and control of public opinion—mass media, opinion polls, and computer-mediated communications—spur populism. Broadcasting, in particular, elicits the experiences, views, and priorities of ordinary people and encourages them to discuss social and political problems via various new communication vehicles—call-in programs, electronic town meetings, televised citizen juries, and, especially, talk shows. Polling enables political elites to anticipate and avert the electorate's displeasure, even if they subordinate themselves imprudently and dysfunctionally to popular sentiments by passing dubious laws—not to solve societal problems but to avoid popular irritation and retain the electorate's votes. Electronic mail further stimulates this sort of speculative coorientation: the new democratic rhetoric, emerging both in legislatures and public discourse (or public relations), draws primarily on public sentiment. Yet there is no simple answer to the most simple question: whether these spectacular developments in information and communication technologies in the twentieth century revive direct democracy and open universal possibilities for direct citizen participation in political decision making, or are routinely used to influence and manipulate public opinion. On the one hand, these new means of communication may help the public influence decisions by those in power to respond to its demands, which is perfectly congruent with the democratic idea and reflects optimism among advocates of polling. On the other hand, polling may also help develop a generally "permissive consensus," which may provide a government more freedom to act (or not act) and, thus, opportunities to manipulate ("educate") public opinion.

Undoubtedly, polling has controversial effects. Indeed, the deficiencies of polling are not just an academic matter, or only a question of an (in)appropriate method. Polling may provide a "more representative picture of the public's views than would usually be obtained from group leaders and notables," but the price for such an "antidote to inaccuracy as well as to mendacity" of group representatives and leaders may be rather high. By delegitimizing the claims of group leaders and activists to speak for membership opinions, polling reduces the political effectiveness of public opinion. It seems, then, that in principle both Gallup and Rogers and their followers were right. However, the *specific historical conditions* are decisive for determining the (anti)democratic nature of polling; as I have demonstrated earlier, particularly in the former socialist countries, opinion polling had a clearly antiauthoritarian character. Yet as Ginsberg argued, the introduction of polling was most damaging to the representation of working-class interests in capitalist societies because it "erodes one of the major competitive advantages that has traditionally been available to lower-class groups and parties—a knowledge of mass public opinion superior to that of middle- and upper-class opponents" (Ginsberg 1989, 284).[19] Although polls may be used, in principle, by any commercial or political group, they were particularly useful for non-working-class associations and parties that were more loosely organized and thus had less knowledge of public sentiments and public opinions. In modern democracies, however, no political party—regardless of its political orientation—can avoid the use of polling due to its massive political institutionalization.

Because of the transformations that polls introduced into the formation and expression of (public) opinions, polling became a major power in structuring public issues and providing agendas of public discourse. Similar to media or other carriers of subsidized information, polls reflect content and priority of issues determined primarily by groups that subsidize polling. In fact, since the late 1800s, newspapers have been both major promoters and supporters of the (straw) polls. However, it is probably an overstatement to conclude, as Ginsberg (1989, 287) did, that polling "erodes individuals' control over the agenda of their own expression of opinion." It is one thing for polling to produce a misleading picture of a public agenda; it is another thing to "erode control." Polling results may still create an obligation for authorities and may be considered an expression *of* public opinion, which is one of the central ideas in a theory of public opinion. Most likely, polls create more effects in the other direction, that is, *on* public opinion: the selection of questions (and answers) for questionnaires and, particularly, the reporting of polling results by the media help determine the relative importance of public issues that the public(s) ought to discuss. However, media, political elites, and even the public(s) are autonomous in developing their own agendas; there is no evidence of a causal connection between various agendas in any possible direction. Nevertheless, one may expect that those subsidizing polling will influence the agenda set by polls rather than vice versa—which does not mean that pollsters are merely objective inquirers into public opinion without their own ideologies and particular interests. In other words, polling plays largely an instrumental (or secondary) role in the process of agenda setting; it intensifies rather than establishes the power of political and commercial elites. Ginsberg provided relevant evidence of that himself when he reported that in the late 1960s and early 1970s U.S. polls "took little interest in the issues which aroused so much public concern," thus clearly indicating the existence of different agendas.

An erosion may have occurred, however, when, particularly during the 1940s, some students of U.S. opinion polls considered polling a partial substitute for democratic political procedures, including elections. It implied a constitutional position for polling that equals traditional political procedures and would, indeed, essentially erode the control of individuals over their agenda(s). Wilson argued that in such a case "the public would have no initiative of its own, and there might be some question whether there is any public at all. It has been sarcastically suggested that all we need in modern government is a competent body of civil servants and a United States Polling Authority" (1962, 171).

MONITORING OR MANUFACTURING PUBLIC OPINION?

Setting aside ideological protests from criticisms of public opinion polling, the following major objections against polling remain under review:

1. Opinion polling presupposes that each individual has, or must have, an opinion about everything (Lynd 1940, 219; Bourdieu 1979, 124; Keane 1984, 148; Peer 1992, 231).
2. Opinion polling presupposes that opinions could be statistically sampled, tabulated as results, and mathematically reconstructed (Keane 1984, 148).
3. It is presupposed that all individual opinions have an equal value or realistic importance, respectively (Lynd 1940, 219; Blumer 1948, 543; Rogers 1949, 57; Bourdieu 1979, 124; Lemert 1981, 3).
4. Polling presupposes that opinions extracted from respondents are their true opinions, independent from interactions with those conducting polls, or that their *public opinions* do not differ from the *private* ones (Harrisson 1940, 371–79; Rogers 1949, 40–41).
5. Polling presupposes that there exists in society a consensus about which questions are important and therefore must be put to the respondents (Bourdieu 1979, 124).

The Distribution of Opinions

The thesis that each individual must have an opinion about everything, widely postulated as a necessary although not an explicit presupposition of opinion polling, is simply erroneous. Leemor Peer mentioned two reasons why opinion polling *must assume* that (all) people have opinions. Accordingly, the *theoretical* reason ought to originate from "the democratic principle of self rule . . . that all people have opinions, that they have the same value, and that they should be expressed and acted upon" (Peer 1992, 231). If this were the basic assumption of democracy, to be materialized in opinion polling as an instrument of democratically expressed opinions, how then is one to explain a citizen's right to abstain from *voting?* On the contrary, citizens' participation in politics is not a necessity and they even have "freedom from politics," which represents a substantial element of modern democracies. Bryce ([1888] 1995, 911) has been among the first to point out that the assumption of the "orthodox democratic theory . . . that every citizen has, or ought to have, thought out for himself certain opinions," is simply far from any empirical evidence. As Held (1987, 291) argues, "It is one thing to recognize a right, quite another to say it follows that everyone must, irrespective of choice, actually participate in public life." For classical Greek democracy, the basic principle was liberty, which included, according to Aristotle, two defining elements: "ruling and being ruled in turn" and "to live as you like" (Held 1987, 19). Based on equality, these two elements are noncontroversial only as long as each individual, indeed, has the opportunity of "ruling and being ruled in turn." Otherwise equality may conflict with liberty, which was the case throughout history, including democratic regimes.

In ancient Greece, only men over twenty were eligible for citizenship: women, immigrants, younger men, and, particularly, slaves were politically marginalized. The notion of equality as the basis of liberty was restricted to those with equal status (male and Athenian born), but even they did not really enjoy the equal opportunity of ruling (Held 1987, 23). For instance, the Assembly was too large to organize and propose public decisions; that responsibility was with the Council of Five Hundred. Since the Assembly had a quorum of 6,000 citizens, the majority could abstain from voting and elections. In sum, even in the legendary Athenian democracy, only citizens who represented an exclusive minority of the Athenian populace were expected to have opinions. Citizens had the *right* to speak and be heard by attending a political assembly, but only few of them would, in fact, speak. A characteristic form of the citizens' behavior was *acclamation* (Schmitt [1928] 1954, 243).

Similarly, in contemporary democracies, citizenship rights and freedoms represent key features, particularly *freedom* of expression, *freedom* of association, and the *equal right* to vote (one person, one vote), but there is no assumption that everybody expresses opinions, associates, and votes. Even if democratic theories assume that citizens are well informed and interested in public issues, which enables them to participate in decision making, they do not assume that *all people have or even express opinions on all issues.*

Not every member of society is engaged by every issue, nor is each omni-opinionated. Not every issue is universally deliberated, nor are all modes of consideration and points of view given equal publicity. Large and complex societies of the sort that have or aspire to civil society—to self-regulation independent of the state and in ways that value difference—are composed of a plurality of publics and public spheres. (Hauser 1997, 278)

For Hauser, the question of diversity and plurality is not only a matter of recognizing empirical fact; it should be "the starting place for theorizing about public spheres, the public that emerge there, and the public opinion they express." Consequently, there is no theoretical reason why opinion polling should assume more active citizens than (all the other) traditional democratic institutions. On the contrary, as Albig claimed, the portrayal of popular ignorance of public affairs is one of the most valuable results of polling. Apart from it, it is probably safe to maintain that, despite the increasing disproportion of the number of people who express opinions and the number of those who only receive them, more societies have become more rather than less democratic over time; the institutionalization of public opinion polling in the twentieth century does not change this fact.

Nevertheless, the *practical* reason why opinion polling ought to assume that people have opinions seems related to sampling: its methodology assumes that every unit in the population should have a specific value on the variable to be measured. Accordingly, Peer (1992, 231) believed that opinion polls "are not designed to determine whether opinions exist, but to measure the variation in existing opinions." She wrongly believes that the (non)existence of opinions is a practical question of sampling. It is true that the unit of population (and sampling unit) is always determined with the value of a variable or with a combination of the values of variables; still not with all the variables but only with those by which the unit is constituted and on the basis of which a unit may be included in the sample. In opinion research, this is usually the function of the sociodemographic variables, for example, sex, age, or place of residence. These, and only these, variables must have values different from zero in each unit (i.e., each respondent), because this is the condition for the unit (respondent) to exist. But immediately when we turn to other sociodemographic variables like education, occupation, income, religion, or employment, it becomes clear that for many units the value of these variables is zero (because they are, e.g., unemployed, uneducated, lacking an income, lacking an occupation, or not faithful). The same holds true for respondents' opinions. The difference between *sampling units* and *units of analysis* is much more evident when we are not dealing with the "natural units" (as persons are) but rather with arbitrarily defined population and sampling units, as, for example, in content analysis. Only for sampling units is it required that values of the variables with which a sampling unit is actually defined differ from zero.

As it is true for any variable, what is found in a questionnaire is only an indicator of a variable (concept) that always requires theoretical definition. It is another question, of course, whether such a theoretical definition exists or not. In other words, what the "true values" of a variable are is not (primarily) a practical, but rather a theoretical, issue; it does not change the problem if the variable is a (specific) opinion or an attitude intended to be measured. The respondent's refusal to answer or a "don't know" response are not obvious cases of "nonopinions" and thus simply missing values; they may be considered true values, at least as much as "random responses." Ratio variables with a natural *zero point* (in contrast to interval variables with an arbitrarily defined zero point) are, from the methodological point of view, even the preferable variables, but unfortunately they rarely appear in the social sciences (e.g., in measuring social distance).

Methodological reasoning may also suggest that opinions of a population are spread in the form of a normal distribution, which would imply that *on the majority of issues the majority of people has no opinion* and only small minorities have definite favorable or unfavorable opinions, respectively. According to a critical insider of the public opinion industry, polling assumes that "the public is a population of individuals (often citizens or residents of a geographic region) who *may have* an opinion about the subject matter of the survey" (Miller 1995, 107). Peer contradicted herself when she argued that the analysis of respondents who tend toward a nonresponse "puts them in categories," a clear indication of normalization that assures the perpetuation of the democratic discourse (that all people have opinions and that all opinions count equally). If polls really "are not designed to determine whether opinions exist, but to measure the variation in existing opinions," where does an interest in nonopinions come from? On the other hand, what is the consequence of the same sort of analyses ("putting in categories") of respondents who do express (different) opinions? Is the "act of categorizing people into groups" according to *different opinions* they have expressed an act of power as well?

Yet I am far from believing that no serious theoretical and methodological problems are associated with polling. However, the problems are not caused by a tacit assumption that "people have opinions." Interpretations of polling results ignore most frequently answers such as "I don't know," "I'm not aware," or "I cannot answer," instead of accurately analyzing them, especially since they are not the result of randomness but represent the actual position of the respondent in society and are related to his or her political competence (Bourdieu

[1972] 1979, 125). It is not, therefore, a matter of inability in principle, but a question of why the possibility of analyzing no-answers is not affirmed as an integral part of testing validity in research practices (e.g., Michelat and Simon 1985). As later established by Bourdieu (1985), this is, above all, a question of the *autonomy of the social sciences* in a given society. Because of financial demands, empirical research relatively often succumbs to the influence of those who order and finance it—not only in the selection of "important" questions but also in consenting to descriptive presentations of interview response data and rejecting methods that would allow an explanation of the findings, since those ordering research are usually not interested in them. This position certainly counters Peer's controversial thought that respondents with nonopinions should not be analyzed and categorized because that would help perpetuate the disciplinary discourse; exactly the same would hold true for any analysis or categorization of respondents regardless of whether they do or do not express opinions. The development of polls into a form of social institution did not necessitate the assumption that all people have opinions. In other words, the problem of disciplinary power is associated with polling in general (which became a social institution) rather than with a specific methodological feature within polling procedures.

Empirical research into opinions, interests, needs, and values is undoubtedly a very difficult enterprise if there are no fortuitous historical circumstances in that one can find a clear and fully expressed class or group spirit, but it must be brought to light with the help of interview response data. As important differences exist in everyday life between what people *say* and what they *think* (or just imagine) about themselves and others, so it is necessary to distinguish in empirical research the imagination of individuals and groups from their actual attitudes, opinions, and interests; their ideas from reality. This is *equally true* of published opinions, usually the opinions of the power elites, for example, in the mass media, as well as private, anonymous expressions of respondents in opinion research. Both inevitably have a sociopolitical nature. Both may be adapted, changed, or manipulated by political actors. Politics, in order to be effective, must consider the situation and development of *mass consciousness* and *mass opinions,* whether politics is authoritarian or emancipatory in nature. Empirical opinion research, because of political interest in it, is always also a political activity, even if researchers wish to be liberated in their relation to the ruling power.

The most apparent expressions of political interests in opinion research in contemporary democracies are manifested in many surveys conducted for and sponsored by government agencies and officials; in systematic *monitoring* of public opinion polls by governments, primarily to identify the form and intensity of public support for or opposition to governmental actions; and in the *legal regulation* of public opinion polling, in particular election polls (Lazareff 1984). The legal regulation of election polls and the publication of polling results in the mass media not only pertain to the question of actual press freedom but also contain a warning about the possible intervention of opinion polling in the mass production of opinions, as a critical impulse against dominant industrial (i.e., state and party) actors. The subordination of opinion research and its publication to the ruling legal order demonstrates that public opinion research does not in itself have an inherently administrative character; it may even be opposed to it, like the first social statistics of the nineteenth century that were, to a great extent, directed against the primordial forms of capitalist accumulation.

The Consequences of the "Mathematical Reconstruction" of Opinions

Keane demonstrated on the basis of well-placed arguments the commercialization of forming opinions, but he did not see the difference between the actual process of a disintegrating public and consenting to the results of this process, which is implied by uncritical opinion polling. Keane's reproach of statistical mystifications in opinion polls, which represent "antidemocratic vindications of the measurement and manufacture of public opinion" (1984, 148), is an example of the simplified (and thus mistaken) understanding of the relevant possibilities of statistical analysis of interview response data. Polls are usually very accurate in estimating (or "predicting," as criticized by Keane) voting behaviors of citizens or consumer decisions because they simulate the very concrete *private* act that an individual will practically undertake in a voting booth or a store. As Carl Schmitt argues, the consequently carried out elections "transform the citizen, the *citoyen*, as a specifically democratic, that is, *political* figure, into a private man who expresses a private opinion and votes from the sphere of the *private*—be this his private religion or his economic interest or both together" (Schmitt [1928] 1954, 245; cf. Lippmann 1925, 56).

Interaction during the interview does not represent a significant deviation from individual voting or buying practices, since in both cases the individual privately and anonymously responds to a well-defined stimulus (questions). The accuracy of any estimate is clearly based on the use of sampling procedures and statistical data analyses. However, using the same data-gathering techniques and analyses in *(public)* opinion studies represents an epistemological problem because—as Salmon and Kline (1985, 12) reproduced Blumer's and Roger's argumentation—elections are conceptually very different from public opinion phenomena.[20] Or, as Lemert (1981, 17) put it, there are substantial differences between a *firmly structured* and periodically established "election framework," in which individuals receive and interpret information about elections, and a much *less* structured "influence framework" in which individuals permanently receive, transmit, and interpret information on a variety of (controversial) issues. Public opinion is a complex communication process (rather than a concretely defined situation) in which individuals (1) are confronted with innumerable and constantly changing choices for action, including the possibility of not acting at all, and (2) act publicly in conjunction with other members of their reference or interest groups when taking actions. It is true that opinion polling frequently, although not necessarily, remains on the level of "summing the empirically existing beliefs of individuals," but this is not to say that "statistical sampling," "tabulations of results," and "mathematical reconstruction" of opinions (whatever it should mean) generate an "automatic opinion of all and the considered opinion of none," as Keane (1984, 148) argued. He paradoxically referred to Tönnies as one of those who challenged "these antidemocratic vindications of the measurement and manufacture of public opinion," although Tönnies explicitly pleaded for and practiced the application of qualitative and quantitative methods in empirical sociology and advocated a connection between pure sociology and sociographic research.

In summary, empirical research and statistical data may significantly contribute to adequately understanding a problem, provided that the interpretation of data is based on comprehensive theoretical knowledge. Needless to say, this requirement prevents the researcher from equating public opinion with a simple aggregate or an average of (all) individual opinions. It is true that opinion polling usually does not go beyond the level of "summing the empirically existing beliefs of individuals." Adding descriptivism and manufacturing public opinion through public opinion polling are not consequences of the use of statistical and quantitative methods in polling, that is, a logical deficiency of research method, but rather a consequence of the subordination of polling to the interests of those subsidizing the research.

The "Equal Value" of Opinions

Of all the arguments regarding the (in)validity of operationalizing public opinion through opinion polling, the most justified ones seem to be Blumer's and, thirty years later, Bourdieu's arguments that public opinion research wrongly presupposes an equal validity, or realistic importance, for all individual opinions in society (or, rather, in the sample of respondents). According to Blumer,

the formation of public opinion does not occur through an interaction of disparate individuals who share equally in the process. Instead, the formation of public opinion reflects the functional composition and organization of society. The formation of public opinion occurs in large measure through the interaction of groups. (Blumer 1948, 544)

Similarly, Bourdieu ([1972] 1979, 126–27) claimed that not all opinions have equal importance. There are two general principles involving the formation of opinion that the model of public opinion polling does not take into account: (1) the uneven distribution of political competence, which is based on differences in (political) knowledge and education (which is why the probability of an individual's having any opinion at all is not constant!) and (2) "class ethos," a system of implicit values that the individual internalizes from earliest childhood onward and that forms the basis for generating answers to different questions. According to Bourdieu ([1972] 1979, 128), a considerable difference exists between "the opinion which people produce in an artificial situation such as survey and the opinion they produce in a situation closer to the daily-life situation in which opinions are confronted and confirmed."

The assumption of the equal value of opinions, however, does not prove the administrative character of opinion polling, but only important deficiencies and thus, perhaps, the invalidity of concrete research.[21] I do not see why opinion research, *in principle,* would not make possible an objectivized measurement of "political competence" of respondents as a basis for explaining the distribution of opinions (including "don't knows") in society. Yet surveys can only reveal political competence as a fact without being able to reveal the process of its origination and production. To explain the presence/absence, or perhaps better, the various degrees of political competence among individuals, special research is needed, whose results may also be used sensibly for explaining the findings of public opinion polls, although certainly not in all its details. However, it is important to point out that the actual process of political socialization, which results in an individual's political (in)competence, also remains hidden and beyond discussion in the actual processes of generating opinions. Therefore, *public opinion polling is not more deficient than the actual process of forming opinions.*

Certainly, public opinion polling is usually not interested in what determines opinions held by individuals. Such a reduction of the problem disregards the key questions of *who forms* and *who* only *accepts opinions* and expresses them in private discussions (interview). Thus opinion is defined from the consumption side (in accordance with understanding the public as an opinion market) rather than the production side. Public opinion polling is restricted to studying *results* (i.e., opinions) and is not concerned with their *underlying social processes.* This lack of interest in the causes, or at least the presuppositions, of forming opinions is also expressed in the fact that public opinion polling usually lacks any kind of critical reflection on the dominant problems operationalized in opinion questionnaires. Opinion researchers scarcely scrutinize those *for whom* topics defined in the questionnaires are *dominant political topics* and for whom possible answers in questionnaires are realistic answers in the sense of actually constituting possible ways of solving problems in society. Bourdieu firmly established the notion that dominant topics, as they appear in opinion polling, are problems that essentially interest people who have power and consider themselves well informed on the means of organizing political action.

It is possible, however, to address the criticism of public opinion research concerning the neglect of a different validity of opinions (which means that different individual opinions, with respect to their objective circumstances, have different probabilities of becoming a group or even a common opinion) quite differently. Thus, when public opinion actually does not exist, the opinion of the ruling power elite(s) is legitimated as "public," "common," or even as the "only intelligent" opinion. Bourdieu's criticism ([1972] 1979, 128–29) that opinion research is incapable of generating any kind of sensible prediction of what will happen in a crisis situation—although it is capable of accurately forecasting whether (and how) opinions will change or not in stable situations—may also be understood as a belief that public opinion research should describe and forecast the *actually dominant opinion.* Such a demand is, however, precisely the opposite of a criticism treating public opinion research as administrative research, which is subordinated to authoritative institutions. Dominant opinions are created by *power elites* and the *media,* which also ensure *publicity;* thus, *there is no need for opinion research to ascertain the dominant opinion.* On the other hand, research into the opinions of the masses *reveals the differences* between dominant opinions and opinions that "do not have equal value." Revealing the existence of latent opinions that are not "politically competent" and therefore have no possibility of becoming dominant in a given society is precisely the aim of all (including empirical) critical research.

It often happens that forecasts based on public opinion polls fail. The most famous failure occurred in 1948 in the United States when all of the scientific pollsters, including Gallup, predicted that presidential candidate Thomas Dewey would defeat Harry Truman by at least 5 percentage points, but in fact Truman won the election by almost 5 percent. The difference between respondents' expression of intent as measured by polls and individuals' actual behavior (e.g., citizens' voting behavior) may be considered a difference between politically relevant and irrelevant opinions. From this perspective, Gallup was in a way right when he claimed that "the selection, not the polls, had turned out wrong" (Hogan 1997, 163). This reflected a more general attitude among some "academic enthusiasts," as Lindsay Rogers named them, that the polls "may reflect the wishes of the electorate more faithfully than the elections themselves" (Rogers 1949, 4). In other words, pollsters succeeded in identifying those latent opinions (intended voting behavior) that would not materialize in a manifest form but clearly did not succeed in predicting what would happen in the "true" elections.

However, it would be deceiving to claim that polls represent the least accurate method of human behavior prediction. Serious limitations that exist in opinion poll predictions are *not unique to polling*. Predicting human behavior generally represents a central and unresolved problem in all social sciences, and it relates both to theory and empirical research. Predictive validity is an important dimension of validity, but it is still *only one* dimension; consequently, a low predictive validity does not yet indicate an absolute invalidity of theory or research.

On the Independence of Respondents' Opinions

In his critique of public opinion polling, Ginsberg challenged its validity because "the data reported by opinion polls are actually the product of an interplay between opinion and the survey instrument" (1989, 273). One certainly must agree with Ginsberg's thought, but it should be added that polling represents only a specific instance of the general relationship that always exists among subject (researcher), method (the tool), and object in the development of scientific knowledge; the validity of research cannot be equated with objectivity in the sense of independence from the subject of research, that is, the researcher. William Albig (1939) was among the first who, in a concrete way, warned of the limitations of validity in the use of questionnaires, particularly when respondents' reactions are limited to dichotomous yes or no responses. He saw two major sources of systematic errors that lead to invalid opinion surveys: (1) a prejudiced or even exclusive reduction of data gathering to survey responses and (2) specific language difficulties that may cause misunderstandings in interactions between researchers and respondents.

Attitudes as expressed in opinions are, according to Albig (1939, 157), mistakenly considered as entities or units that may "profitably be handled quantitatively"; in fact, attitudes are always interrelated in a complex way and in varying proportions. An appropriate solution to the problem of "simply counting the responses" is the true measurement of attitudes, that is, an attempt to indicate the relation of answers to some standard. The Thurstone test largely but not completely overcomes technical objections to the construction of the tests, but certain problems remain. Apart from the methodological problems, validity of survey response data could be seriously limited, since the judges' attitudes may significantly affect the attitude scale. The standard in attitude tests is constructed by the experimenter or by a limited group of experts. The latter, however, may not provide a valid scale for respondents because they themselves come from another group, often with varied attitudes. In addition, the time and labor involved in the construction of a Thurstone-type scale are often discouraging or even prohibitive, which may help explain why public opinion polls, and even surveys, usually "simply count responses."

These problems, Albig believed, cannot be resolved by multiple-choice and cross-out tests, rating, ranking, and attitude scales. Unlike public opinion, which represents group *consensus,* opinion polls, as Doris Graber argues, "report *pseudo-opinions* and erroneously . . . label them as 'public opinion.' . . . Pseudo-opinions are the top-of-the-head responses people make with little or no thinking or the responses they make by drawing analogies to the pasts stored in their memories" (Graber 1982, 556; emphasis added). Methods other than survey responses exist and should be used to infer opinions from written essays, letters, case history descriptions, autobiographies, diaries, and oral or written interviews. Although text or discourse analysis and in-depth interview permit the use of extensive, often unstructured, long, and wordy messages and documents, and thus escape the limitations of simple interview response data, they present serious methodological problems in attempts to use statistical data analysis (Albig 1939, 158).

The language difficulty leads to more serious errors in simple questionnaires then in any other form of measurement. Different respondents interpret words differently (or misinterpret them), which may cause even a complete opinion change in the respondent because of a language misunderstanding. In addition to problems of (mis)understanding on the part of respondents to which Albig referred, questions may intentionally be worded in a manipulative way to predetermine the respondents' answers in an effort to achieve supportive or at least permissive consensus to legitimize policy decisions. At any rate, the history of polling abounds with examples of significant question-wording effects, which provide ample evidence that respondents' answers depend not only on variations in question wording but also on the number, character, and order of questions in the questionnaire, and response options to individual questions.[22] Experimental studies also revealed a tendency of people to say yes when asked about unfamiliar topics ("response acquiescence"); or in the absence of the "don't know" response, many respondents would select an answer even on nonexistent policies (Hogan 1997, 169–71). Question and answer orderings and wordings are extensively studied to minimize their influence on respondents in polling, based (though only implicitly) on a simplistic *stimulus-response* communication model. Such methodological efforts largely neglect the fact that these effects are not *caused* by the formulation of questions and answers but rather by idiosyncratic characteristics of respondents (particularly their lack of competence) and their relation to topics or attitude objects referred to. I earlier mentioned Childs's differentiation between various forms of agreement typical of various definitions of public opinion, which also includes *degree* of agreement, the *way* in which opinions are formed, and quality or *excellence* of opinions (Childs 1965, 14–24). Individuals' attitudes differ in terms of *orientation* (favorable vs. unfavorable, for vs. against), but each attitude is also multidimensional and includes, besides orientation, the *degree* of attitude, its *salience* in relation to other individual's attitudes, and *firmness* (unchangeableness). All these dimensions are interrelated and reflect an individual's idiosyncratic response to a verbal stimulus, including his or her tendency to select answers not on the basis of cognition but on account of the formulation of questions and answers. Attempts to neutralize these effects with random rotation of questions and/or answers in a questionnaire, so that no response has a higher initial or random probability to be selected, actually devaluate individuals' idiosyncrasies. In this way, attitudes are, as Albig would say, mistakenly considered as entities or units that may profitably be handled quantitatively—independently of the individuals (respondents) who express them.

The Consensus about Dominant Questions

Finally, I return to the fundamental question concerning social actors, who order public opinion surveys and polls and make use of their findings. They define research aims and the so-called dominant questions, which represent a sort of agenda setting for public opinion. At issue here again is the autonomy of social-scientific research and its critical self-reflection as it endeavors to ask and answer the question of who opinion polls and survey questions are for. Public opinion polling can only be considered a valid instrument of measuring public opinion if, and only if, it is about common issues that are currently being discussed and for which different (alternative) opinions and/or courses of action are being formulated. If, in a given historical period and a particular society, public opinion polling were primarily performed for the carriers of dominant opinions (and dominant questions are selected accordingly), it would still not be possible to derive a general conclusion about the innate administrative nature of public opinion research. Such a conclusion can easily be falsified by a closer examination of the social function of public opinion research in former socialist societies. This does not change the fact, however, that public opinion polling is a *substitute for the opinion of the public*, which is repressed by economic and/or political constraints, and that public opinion polling in such circumstances is itself a form of repression. It is a means for increasing the efficiency of the professional production of the "schemes of thought and the expression of the social world" similarly to public relations and political marketing; its specific importance is that it tends to legitimate politics by "giving it the appearance of scientificity and by treating political questions as matters for specialists which it is the specialists' responsibility to answer in the name of knowledge and not of class interest" (Bourdieu 1991, 177).

However, if we consider both dimensions—repressive and emancipatory—all forms of opinion research cannot be simply reduced to "administrative research," which is subordinated to the interests of commerce and the ruling power. In principle, polling does not inherently manufacture public opinion more than any other method of empirical research. According to Miller, "It is fair to say, however, that survey evidence is often used to manufacture public opinion when the constraints of the measurement process are ignored or hidden, and when the sample public is reified and inferences go beyond the intended survey framework" (1995, 110). This is the same sort of criticism Allport (1937) addressed in the 1930s to the authors of "fictions" and "blind alleys" that were widespread "even in textbooks of political and social science," in order to formulate "a workable, scientific approach" to public opinion, that is, a behavioral definition and research into public opinion. He criticized those nonempirical understandings of public opinion that perceived behind it a collective entity, a "group mind," or even a personalized collective being, rather than an instance of behaviors of individuals. Allport believed that empirical research could demystify such conceptions, but presentations and interpretations of poll results apparently go in the opposite direction, thus producing the same fallacy.

Indubitably, public opinion polling is concerned with opinions that are not the result of free discussions and reasoning and are not publicly expressed in themselves. This enables survey organizations and their clients to make free use (or nonuse) of poll results. In other words, polling is an accurate operationalization of Key's definition of public opinion, according to which public opinion "may simply be taken to mean those opinions held by private persons which governments (or any other client) find it prudent to heed" ([1961] 1967, 14). This certainly raises serious doubts about the first part of Moore's controversial belief that

> Gallup's vision of polling as an instrument for improving the practice of democracy seems largely vindicated. Despite response effects due to question wording and placement and interviewer characteristics . . . polling can, indeed, provide a

continuous *monitoring* of the elusive pulse of democracy. (Moore 1995, 357; emphasis added)

Public opinion polling is concerned with opinions that are private in the sense that they are expressed without being intended to reach the public, and they remain unpublished. In addition, the respondent is guaranteed *anonymity*. Guaranteeing the anonymity of individual private opinions is not a direct consequence of the pressure of administrative research but is a research stimulus (not always effective) to encourage the "free" expression of opinions. The lack of publicity may, however, stimulate the transformation of passive or neutral monitoring into active social control that would further reduce an individual's participation in the formation of public opinion. By definition, this would corrupt rather than improve the practice of democracy.

A possible critical orientation of such research (although it always has a manipulative character too) depends on the real interests of the (empirical) social sciences in revealing the emancipatory potential of the masses or the public. Empirical opinion research, similar to other research methods and means of expressing opinions, has numerous limitations in relation to the problems it has to solve. For example, it cannot measure objectively the structural, relational characteristics of groups, but only the state of individual consciousness. It does not allow for individual expression of opinion and/or individual actions but limits expression to answering questions in the questionnaire. Opinion polling cannot replace the information deficit that is a consequence of nonuse, absence, or nonaccessibility of other sources of scientifically relevant information or other means of expressing opinions. However, after considering the realistic methodological limitations to interpretative possibilities and presuppositions of public opinion polling, we can conclude that it can *neither save nor bury a disappearing public opinion*. Opinion polling as a measuring instrument and/or means of expressing opinions is neither good nor bad by itself. Neither is it neutral, as Michael Hogan (1997, 175) convincingly demonstrates with George Gallup's fifty-year attempts to influence the ideological climate in the United States with the publication of the results of his polls. Because public opinion polling develops from institutional needs, its impact is always structurally determined and mediated through institutional arrangements. The key question for researchers should focus on the social groups for whom research is being done, which is also reflected by how the topic (object) of opinion research is restricted and tailored by the particularistic interests of the client as well as by science and scientists themselves.

Public opinion polling is not the only (institutionalized) form of manipulating or influencing public opinion in contemporary society. Other instruments of organized public persuasion have a similar function: different forms of political consulting, lobbying, and public relations, which are also becoming institutionalized components of the political system. Although public opinion polling has been politically institutionalized in modern democracies, neither its scientific validity nor its democratic character is guaranteed. Polling is, at the same time, a commercial enterprise closely linked with recent trends in journalism to adopt polling results in the form of a special journalistic genre (see Gawiser and Witt 1994). Mass media do not publish polling results primarily to influence policy makers but rather to attract the attention of the public. Scientific validity and political implications of poll results are less relevant for reporting, or not relevant at all; what counts is a simplistic dramatization of a news story that can help to increase the circulation of newspapers and to extend broadcasting audiences. Whereas the first polls were about public issues—issues that had significant social consequences and were subject to regulation (or demanded it)—subsequent development brought about polls that were more similar to guesswork, fortune-telling, and lotteries; polling even became a means of illegal pressure exerted on court decisions. Polling results influenced by question wording would become a substitute for the reflection and debate that properly precede any legislative or executive decision in a democratic political order. Head news in the media is often dedicated to the meaningless answers given to simplistic questions on complex subjects. ("Are you for or against the unification of Europe?" is a recent prototype of this nonsense, which bypasses such fundamental issues as what a constitution is for and how the budget is to be balanced without sacrifices that no one seems willing to make.) The answers to such nonquestions are in turn invoked by politicians to support their already fixed positions. Polling can also manipulate with responses from an unrepresentative self-appointed minority of the public. Typical examples of a deviation from methodological validity are pseudopolls, or "self-selected listener-oriented public opinion surveys" (SLOPS), for example, call-in polls and mail-in polls.[23]

The history of newspapers seems to recur with polling. The more the critiques of the commercialization of the press and other media requested substantial reforms to (re)establish the newspaper (and later especially public service radio and television) as "the organ" of public opinion, the more the media developed in the opposite direction. Similarly, public opinion polling primarily develops as an industry of news events rather than an instrument of democracy, despite all the warnings and critiques, and expectations of early prophets of public opinion polling as a corrective mechanism in democratic political systems.

7

✚

Public Opinion and Mass Media: Questions of Democratization and Regulation

No one pretends that actions should be as free as opinions. On the contrary, even opinions lose their immunity, when the circumstances in which they are expressed are such as to constitute their expression a positive instigation to some mischievous act. An opinion that corn-dealers are starvers of the poor, or that private property is robbery, ought to be unmolested when simply circulated through the press, but may justly incur punishment when delivered orally to an excited mob assembled before the house of a corn-dealer, or when handed about among the same mob in the form of a placard.

—John Stuart Mill, *On Liberty*

Yet the most significant change in our time is the recognition that public opinion is not simply to be obeyed or evaded, but that it may be molded and directed to suit given interests.

—Francis G. Wilson, *A Theory of Public Opinion*

A major goal of democratic societies is citizen participation in the political process aimed at an increase of popular control of political elites; an actively involved public is considered one of the foundations of democracy. Without the public's participation in the political process, democracy lacks legitimacy. Conversely, the development of the *means* of political participation is the keystone in normative conceptualizations of the public. Citizen participation in public discussion is an essential element in the process of defining societal goals that should be carried out, again, through the involvement of citizens in politics. None of these processes can take place without communication, since public opinion processes are not only political but essentially communication processes. Since the mid-nineteenth century the communicative nature of public opinion has been inseparable from the operation of mass media, particularly their functions of making some (controversial) issues more salient and appropriate for (public) discussion than others, as well as determining the limits of legitimate public discussion in society. Mass media are at the very heart of both theorizations of and practical endeavors directed toward the enthronement of public opinion; at the same time, they are also used as the most powerful argument against the rationality of public opinion.

This chapter is devoted to restrictions imposed on the autonomy and freedom of individuals to form and express their opinions in a free discussion, which partly arise from their exposure to the media, as well as to the ideas of democratization of the communication sphere and the media. We often hear critical voices saying that the former principle of publicity characteristic of the early period of the political press has been replaced by manipulative publicity, which is, like the "representative publicness," a means of manipulating the public and legitimizing the political ruling class. Although there are considerable similarities in diagnoses of the public's (political) condition, there is much disagreement in proposals for an effective therapy. Media democratization requires specific forms of regulation with regard to specific aims, for example, to limit the power and control held by commercial and political actors, to protect and foster the political and economic autonomy of the media, to thwart the development of powerful coalitions between the state, capital, and the media, and to encourage citizen access to the media. Media democratization should give all citizens an opportunity for relatively equal access to influencing mass communication: the separation of powers should establish (at least in a normative-ideal sense) a democratic balance between the spheres of politics, economy, and culture as specific sources of societal integration and development.

MASS MEDIA AS A MEANS OF EXPRESSION
AND CONTROL OF PUBLIC OPINION

Modern democracy is usually thought of as a product of the Enlightenment, when the idea of publicity was raised to a fundamental moral principle. In his treatise *To Perpetual Peace,* Kant puts forward the "transcendental formula of public justice," according to which all actions that affect the rights of other men are wrong if they are not public; publicity alone can guarantee *harmony between politics and morals.* Clearly, the principle of publicity and the public use of reason were not subordinated but rather opposed to the sphere of economy and should not be limited by the right of ownership. The conception of the freedom of public expression as a special form of the right of ownership was born later, in the mid-1800s. For the representative of the bourgeois class in Karl Marx's *Debatten über Pressfreiheit und Publikation der landständischen Verhandlungen* ([1842] 1974) it was a "classic inconsistency" if the press were exempted from the general rules of economy. Eighty years later Walter Lippmann called it an "anomaly of our civilization" that "community applies one ethical measure to the press and another to trade or manufacture," instead of treating the press as "a business pure and simple" ([1922] 1960, 321). In contemporary democracies, the idea of publicity primarily refers to the media and the public sphere in which the public use of reason or public discussion can take place.

Mass media are constitutive of any adequate contemporary theory of democracy. It is not possible to propose even the most limited and formal definitions of democracy without recognizing the integral role of the media for the actual functioning of all elements of a democratic system. When Marx ([1842] 1974, 73) wrote his famous assertion that "what I cannot be for others, I am not for myself and cannot be for myself,"[1] he was insisting on the recognition of one's rights in the sphere of the press and communication in general because he considered the press "the common means of individuals to communicate their mental existence." Conventionally it is believed that mass media serve democracy and that they serve it inherently. Mass media as the site at which ideas and interests can be freely presented and discussed also became the precondition for the existence of the public sphere, for which two kinds of human rights have fundamental significance—those related to the integrity, autonomy, and personality of the individual, and those related to freedom of communication. It is also believed that the rapid development of information and communication technologies fosters a global dissemination and exchange of information and ideas in a tolerant spirit and leads to dispersions of power. But are these beliefs truly legitimate?

In theory and practice, democracy is historically closely linked to the development of communication technology, primarily to the invention of printing. Together with schooling, printing stimulated the growth of literacy and newspaper reading that drew individuals away from their traditional communities based on physical presence and proximity, and it enabled the creation of new, intellectual ones—along with industrialization based on the use of new steam engine technology that stimulated migrations from rural communities to large urban agglomerations, that is, from Gemeinschaft- to Gesellschaft-type social structures. Early newspapers helped spread revolutionary ideas that delegitimized the authoritarian political order and extended the arena of public debate essential to representative government. On the other hand, history abounds with examples of the media being abused on behalf of the worst forms of tyrannical suppression of society and the media themselves. The period of communism in Eastern-Central Europe is only one of too many historic examples. The critical publicity characteristic of early political newspapers is often believed to have been displaced by manipulative publicity, which can only serve the manipulation of the public and the legitimization of political authorities before it, similarly to feudal representative publicity; but remedies prescribed for the recovery are quite different.

Since the earliest theorizations, the principle of publicity has also been connected with the idea of public opinion, nowadays it too is inseparable from the most complex communication form—mass communication. In discussions of public opinion by Ferdinand Tönnies, John Dewey, and Walter Lippmann, newspapers already were considered more important than other forms of political organization of society, or "the public." With the development of radio and television, the preferential position of the media became even more obvious. Although for a couple of decades, public opinion polls perhaps took the lead in public opinion debates, with the development of computer-mediated communication primacy was returned to the media. Indeed, newspapers and the media have played and still play the central role in the processes of the institutionalization of public opinion.

The fundamental significance of the mass media for the processes of (public) opinion formation and expression largely arises from the fact that they help to determine and demonstrate the *limits of legitimate public discussion* in society. This function of the media is usually referred to as "agenda setting."[2] In the twentieth century, it became commonly accepted that a congruence exists between the order of importance that the media assign to specific issues (in this way, they legitimize them as public issues), and the order of importance attributed to the same issues by the public: the issues and events that receive a greater degree of media attention become the issues and events that are uppermost in citizens' minds. In other words, mass media largely define attitude objects and situations to be perceived by the masses as relevant or important. As Weaver (1984, 689) argues in his review of empirical agenda-setting studies, "there is likely to be a relationship among media emphasis on an issue, the salience of that issue, and public opinion regarding actors (persons or institutions) associated with the issue." The congruence does not necessarily imply a causal relationship between distinct rank orderings of issues or agendas; they may interact in a much more complex way. However, discussions of the role of the media in the formation and expression of public opinion largely assume that the agendas presented by the mass media do have impact on their recipients. The media seem to be particularly influential in making some issues more salient than others. Attention attracted and directed by the media is a sort of "substitute for the generality that contemporary societies are not able to confirm by summing up particularistic interests" (Bašič-Hrvatin 1996, 147). More recent ideas of public opinion as (primarily) a form of social control are even built upon an assumption of a direct causal connection between media content and individual behavior and attitudes, although there is no justification for asserting that individuals' opinions result from their exposure to the media as public opinion; they are (mass) *pseudo-opinions* because they have no intellectual (reflective) and interactive (discursive) foundation. Nevertheless, mass media have (either as a means of *expressing* public opinion or as an instrument of *influencing* it) a crucial role in public opinion process and public opinion theories regardless of whether they *create* the agendas on their own or merely *reflect* those created in/by other components of society, and that is why they attract regulative efforts in all democratic societies.

Whatever interests policy actors may pursue, they are likely to be more efficient when attempting to influence the actions of others ("outsiders," as Lippmann would call them) by controlling their access to information and opinions disseminated through the media, and the use of information relevant to their actions. In the twentieth century, overt censorship, as the main form of direct control of information gathering and dissemination, was largely replaced by more sophisticated forms of "information subsidies," as Gandy (1982) calls attempts to reduce, either directly or indirectly, the costs of receiving and/or (re)producing information and thus to make information available to other participants in the process at a reduced price or completely free. Direct information subsidy does not hide the close linkup between the subsidizer and the transmitter of information; in indirect subsidy, however, this connection is blurred. Information subsidy presupposes that access to information is limited and thus is a form of censorship. The public's confidence in information gatherers and disseminators became a major factor in (mass) communication processes because of barriers that exist between information and the public. In the public, information from interested sources is usually seen as less credible than that from disinterested sources. Tönnies, Lippmann, and Dewey saw the credibility of information sources and opinions in the public as being based on their political impartiality and their attachment to public and general interests rather than private and particularistic ones. Consequently, some actors may prefer to subsidize information indirectly in order to obscure or conceal their relationship to the information they provide because of their particular(istic) interest. Yet, as Habermas ([1992] 1997, 364) noted, "Public opinions that can acquire visibility only because of an undeclared infusion of *money* or organizational *power* lose their credibility as soon as these sources of social power are made public" (emphasis added). This is an important reason that led V. O. Key ([1961] 1967, 539) to attribute great importance to "broad rules of etiquette governing relations among activists, as well as rules governing the relations of activists with the public." These rules are essential for any practice of politics that has "regard for public opinion." Keys specifically emphasized freedom of speech, freedom of the press, and the right to appeal to the electorate for power.

Mass media are likely to represent the most effective influence system in contemporary society. Mayhew (1997, 109) argues that, like other influence systems, it developed in the process of intensification of the division of labor that extended to information activity. "Since complex modern societies cannot provide clear normative guidance in uncertain situations, people are in particular need of information regarding how to co-ordinate their action and about means and opportunities for attaching themselves to others." However, information media do not just provide (nor the people produce) integrative experience and information that reduce majority-minority relations to *conformity*, contrary to what Mayhew suggests. Apart from conformity, people within a group, or the media in relation to other actors, may seek to compromise on the basis of reciprocal influence and to generate innovations (which often creates conflicts rather than integration). These functions have a fundamental significance for democratic societies. Individual and group recipients need media services to fulfil a variety of needs and interests related both to their immediate, narrow environment of private life and to broad matters of public policy relevant for (public) opinion formation: to increase their certainty (e.g., cognitive consonance), to test social reality (e.g., to compare and supplement information acquired interpersonally), and even to identify the "climate of opinion" in a society (as in Noelle-Neumann's spiral of silence). This, of course, is far from an exhaustive list of services mass media can offer to their audiences; it is merely an indication of why these services may be thought of as services that need *public regulation,* which may eventually help transform the services into the *public services,* and mass media into the *public service media.*

Mass media certainly do not represent the only component that calls for public regulation in democratic processes. The twentieth century may be considered the age of the growth of public law, and one of its basic characteristics is the creation of a variety of statutory regulations and bodies governing and controlling such diverse matters of public concern and policy as, for example, safety in the factory, public health, environmental protection, schooling, sexual and race relations, public services, commercial standards, transportation, communications, and, last but not least, the mass media. The general idea of regulation is also deeply rooted in the working out of a realistic theory of public opinion. Dewey's concept of the public is substantiated by the *need to regulate* remote and long-run consequences of human transactions. Lippmann related the need for regulation to the rules of behavior in controversies aimed at the reconciliation of conflicting purposes of men participating in opinion formation. He suggested a sort of contents regulation when saying that it might be "a good thing if there were competent tribunals, preferably not official ones, where charges of untruthfulness and unfairness in the general news [in the newspapers] could be sifted" (Lippmann [1922] 1960, 330 n.). Apparently the general question of mass media regulation came to the fore of both theoretical and practical-political debates because of their growing (in)direct and long-term consequences for individuals and societies. As it became clear in the early period of press monopolization, media could systematically distort public communication when they moved in the direction of coercive manipulation by marginalizing differences and dissenting voices, and effectively propagating consensus established among the privileged classes as a social norm.

THE CHANGING FUNCTION OF PUBLICITY

In the late nineteenth century, Franz von Holtzendorff was perhaps the first to believe that government and statesmen must provide for the formation of public opinion (Wilson 1962, 80). In the beginning of the twentieth century, Tönnies, Dewey, Lippmann, and Hayes emphasized the fundamental, though often ambiguous and contradictory, role of the press in the process of public opinion formation and expression. They criticized both the fact that its role was often underestimated or even completely overlooked, and the manipulative practice of the press that justified the need for substantial reforms. Tönnies (1922, 196) argued that newspapers were the most influential "means of expression of public opinion." They may either express or influence public opinion, but they cannot be considered the "organ of the public" or be considered identical to opinion of the public. Much to the contrary, they are primarily organs of political parties; only indirectly, through the newspapers in big cities, do they allow observers to "estimate" opinion of the public. Since all the "elements of mental life" are mediated through the press, Tönnies believed that the reform of newspapers is central to the future of public opinion and should bring about the socialization of newspapers and their independence from political parties and commercial organizations.

The main reason for the absence of the development of an articulated public was often seen in the interests of pecuniary profit, which tried to subordinate political decisions. Dewey ([1927] 1991, 182) claimed that, just as commercial companies are led by profit rather than technology development and obviously "industry conducted by engineers on a factual technological basis would be a very different thing from what it actually is," news gathering and reporting would substantially differ from the prevailing commercial mode "if the genuine interests of reporters were permitted to work freely." In his plea for *The Public,* he criticized the intellectual form and level of the newspapers, which, instead of contextualizing news stories and placing them into the course of events, decontextualized them systematically and thus mislead the public in its attempts to identify important public issues as it formed its judgments:

> "News" signifies something which has just happened, and which is new just because it deviates from the old and regular. But its meaning depends upon relation to what it imports, to what its social consequences are. This import cannot be determined unless the new is placed in relation to the old. . . . Hence even if we discount the influence of private interests in procuring suppression, secrecy and misinterpretation, we have here an explanation of the triviality and "sensational" quality of so much of what passes as news.[3] (Dewey [1927] 1991, 180)

Walter Lippmann often contradicted Dewey's therapy as to how to reconstruct and politically organize the public, but he mostly agreed with his diagnoses of the malfunction of the press. In his influential book on *Public Opinion* ([1922] 1960, 319–20), Lippmann claimed that "the problem of how to make the invisible world visible to the citizens of a modern state" should become the central question confronted by political science, which, "until quite recently, . . . was taught in our colleges as if newspapers did not exist." Lippmann argued that civil liberties by themselves could not guarantee public opinion in the modern world, primarily because (1) "the truth about distant and complex matters is not self-evident," and (2) because "the machinery for assembling information [about these matters] is technical and expensive." If public opinion is to deal with such an "invisible environment," the press (or, more generally, the media) becomes the main means by which citizens make contact with it, and for that reason the role of the media is often simplified and overstated. Lippmann disagreed with Dewey ([1927] 1991, 180), who wanted social science to "manifest its reality in the daily press, while learned books and articles supply and polish tools of inquiry." To Lippmann such an idea sounded ridiculous, as Dewey had feared:

> The press . . . has come to be regarded as an organ of direct democracy, charged on a much wider scale, and from day to day, with the function often attributed to the initiative, referendum, and recall. The Court of Public Opinion, open day and night, is to lay down the law of everything all the time. It is not workable. And when you consider the nature of news, it is even not thinkable. . . . The press is no substitute for institutions. (Lippmann [1922] 1960, 363)

Such an unthinkable role was attributed to the press by Habermas in his early work *Structural Transformation of the Public Sphere,* in which he argued that early newspapers "were not only made the object of discussion by the public of coffee houses but were viewed as an integral part of this discussion; this was demonstrated by the flood of letters from which the editor each week published a selection" (Habermas [1962] 1995, 42). In the nineteenth century, the development of the mass press (as well as of radio and television in the twentieth century) helped to substitute the form of sociability characteristic of the bourgeois public:

> On the new model the convivial discussion among individuals gave way to more or less noncommittal group activities. These too assumed fixed forms of informal sociability, yet they lacked that specific institutional power that had once ensured the interconnectedness of sociable contacts as the substratum of public communication—no public was formed around "group activities." . . . The private form of appropriation removed the ground for a communication about what has been appropriated. (Habermas [1962] 1995, 163)

As Habermas argues, rational public debate was confined to specific groupings or even became commercialized; it still may fulfil some social-psychological functions (among them, the narcotic dysfunction—it is a substitute for action), but it definitely loses its publicist function. There are fewer and fewer opinions but more information from press agencies and reporters, and among them less and less politically relevant information. "Critical debate disappears behind the veil of internal decisions concerning the selection and presentation of the material. . . . The world fashioned by the mass media is a public sphere in appearance only" (Habermas [1962] 1995, 169, 171).

The nature of publicity enforced by public communication radically changed in the transition from the nineteenth to the twentieth century. Advertising based on systematic market research, followed by the emergence of public relations, represents one fundamental component of the transition, which fostered commercialization of the press. At the same time, the decline of critical publicity was a consequence of an increasing interpenetration of the state and society through bureaucracy, political parties, and interest associations. Like private enterprises, public bureaucracies also competed for publicity, using techniques similar to the ones employed by private enterprises.

Before the 1850s, advertising had no significant role even in the distribution of products; occasionally it was used by shopkeepers, but not by wholesale dealers and factories. Newspaper advertising was initially conceived of as providing information for the reading public rather than stimulating consumers' desires and needs. Newspapers first sold advertising space by the year at a common price to all advertisers, and later by the agate[4] square system. Agate squares were of equal size (10 to 16 lines of type, depending on the size of the font) and were sold by the number of squares and the number of appearances. In contrast to the former pricing scheme, the new system did not preserve an absolute equality among advertisers, but advertisements retained an informational function, particularly by the restraint of illustration (Mayhew 1997, 192). However, in the second half of the nineteenth century the situation radically changed. The development of advertising brought about the separation of the former single newspaper market into communication or publicistic market, and commercial or economic market; whereas the former is (still) determined by the communication relationship between the journalist (or newspaper) and the reader, the latter is external to the communication process and is determined in the relationship between newspaper owner and advertiser. This was reflected by the new pricing system, which was based on the number of readers (newspaper circulation) rather than the size of advertising space (Splichal 1981, 161–67). Between 1876 and 1890, advertising expenditures in the United States increased seven times, in the next three decades ten times (Baran and Sweezy [1967] 1978, 113). The new system forced monopolization both in the newspaper (publicistic) market (to increase circulation and, consequently, advertising revenues) and in the general economic market (because advertising became prohibitively expensive for small enterprises).

The interpenetration of the political bureaucracies and advertising industry into newspapers transformed the critical publicity characteristic of early political newspapers into manipulative publicity that, like feudal publicity, can only serve the manipulation of the public and legitimization of political authorities before it, as Habermas argues. However, he is not as idealistically conservative as to believe that the only impact of the new communication media is negative and incompatible with the idea of the public sphere, as Thompson (1993, 186–87) suggests. The changing function of publicity is clearly related to the new media, but this is not to say that it is their direct or, even more, necessary consequence. As Habermas believes, the idea of critical publicity can be realized

> as a rationalization . . . of the exercise of societal and political power under the mutual control of rival organizations themselves committed to publicity as regards both their internal structure and their interaction with one another and with the state. Only in proportion to advances in this kind of rationalization can there once again evolve a political public sphere as it once existed in the form of the bourgeois public of private people. (Habermas [1962] 1995, 210)

It is a frequent, and quite valid, criticism of Habermas's original formulation of the classic bourgeois public sphere that it failed fully to recognize the exclusionary social basis of this realm of rational discussion. It can also be argued, however, that the contemporary extension of political democracy and the development of the traditional and new mass media have (far from refeudalizing publicness) extended the public sphere to a much wider layer of society. Thompson is basically right in suggesting that a valid understanding of the nature of public life in modern societies is only possible if it is not linked to a dialogical concept of publicness. Already in early 1900s, Tönnies argued that the public may take either an active or a passive role in the process of opinion *formation* and *expression*. In contrast to the forms of the public that existed before the twentieth century, the modern large public is neither spatially not temporally bound (Tönnies 1922, 84). Meyrowitz (1985) and Thompson (1995) suggest that the *new* media create a new kind of publicness that (in contrast to the "old" publicness) does not refer to the sharing of a common locale but rather is despatialized and nondialogical, and largely linked to the type of visibility produced by television. Likewise, Mayhew (1997) argues that in the postmodern era the traditional or modern public has been replaced by the "New Public."

Although print and broadcast media are, as Thompson suggests, nondialogical, and "the rhetoric of presentation" in the media has replaced the classical forms of argumentative persuasion and influence, as Mayhew argues, the same is not true for computer-mediated forms of communication, which in principle at least enable interactivity. In practice, however, this is not a massive phenomenon, since (1) the so-called virtual communities that are formed in computer-mediated communication do not have a massive membership and (2) the use of noninteractive possibilities of communication is more expanded than interactive possibilities. On the one hand, we must admit that the forms of communication changed profoundly over the last century; on the other hand, however, this does not necessarily imply (neither it is historically true) that each historical period (or each culture)[5] must have its own types of public/ness and public opinion. It is obvious that (1) the concept of publicness (and indeed the public and public opinion) cannot have identical meanings in different cultures and historical periods, and (2) its normative definition has to differ according to specific historical circumstances. But it does not follow that constantly new *types* of publicness are coming into existence. On the contrary, Dewey emphasizes the relative character of the public; *forms of political organization* rather than the nature of the public differ and change because the nature of transactions and the character of their consequences change.

New technological communication possibilities, mainly due to the revolutionary character of the merger of information and communication technologies in the computer-mediated communications, rightly provoke an intellectual excitement. Yet the question about the emancipatory and authoritarian power of communication technologies raised by Raymond Williams is still in place. Mainly because of the development of television, the character of publicity has changed, which entails the rise of the so-called *mediatized politics.*[6] Kant once demanded that all human actions related to other people's rights be subjected to the enlightenment principle of publicity, since only the principle of public action that mediates between politics and morality may assure justice. Today we can speak again of publicity as the *foundation of politics,* which essentially occurs through the media. These changes did not bring about only the representative publicity in the Habermasian sense of the representation of power, but also *visibility* or *transparency* as a fundamental dimension of the publicness. The widest possible publicity is the first condition of publicness as Hannah Arendt ([1958] 1989, 50) argues, although the visibility of an opinion ("published opinion" according to Tönnies) is not a sufficient condition for public opinion to spring up. Yet the *universal visibility* assured by modern *mass* media (television in particular) due to their universal (though only passive) accessibility, can provide a greater democratic power than the *elite* newspapers had in the period of the liberal bourgeois public of the late eighteenth century, when they enabled scarce and thus privileged members of the public to discuss public issues. As Tönnies made clear, the two kinds of publicity should not be conceptualized as mutually exclusive; in the formation and expression of the opinion of the public, they are closely interwoven in the relationship between the "republic of the learned" and the large public. The expanding computer-mediated communications, however, shift the democratic emphasis back to technological possibilities of *in-*

teraction that make possible (although they do not assure) the rise of the virtual public as a materialization of formerly only abstract intellectual connections between individuals denoted by Tönnies as the foundation of the public.

The most obvious consequence of technological development is the internationalization of the public(s). Like Tönnies, we can look for the very beginning of internationalization in the medieval "international theological public"; in the beginning of the twentieth century, when the "large public" was typically a national phenomenon, the "international public" was still an exception more than a rule. However, nowadays it seems that development is directed toward transnationalization or even globalization: transnational movements, groupings, and associations are being formed, with interests, ideas, and opinions not being nationally determined or bound. And mistily at least, we may see an international political organization of the public, as Dewey would argue, for example, in the processes of the European unification. Nevertheless, the current processes of Europeanization with a high degree of bureaucratization and the rule of political elites raise doubts as to whether a nonstate, cosmopolitan, and participatory democracy is truly feasible.

It is now commonplace to talk about an increased visibility and interactivity brought about by new communications technologies (e.g., satellite and digital television and computer-mediated communication), although they are not (yet) directly interconnected. These changes pave the way for an extremely rapid expansion of information and opinions, which can strengthen public opinion processes and citizen initiatives but also propaganda and manipulative manufacturing of public opinion controlled by power elites. Politics and politicians have never been as visible as they are today. Visibility can be instrumentalized for representative publicity. In the past, it was based on censorship and thus was absolutely limited to representative publicity. Nowadays, however, visibility is becoming so all-encompassing that it invades the privacy of those who want to instrumentalize it. This parallelism (and even independence) between an increased visibility and representative rhetoric, on the one hand, and the possibilities of interactive communication, on the other hand, may help explain Mayhew's contradictory aspirations: to substantiate the "New Public" on principles different from those on which the "modern public" was based, while at the same time discussing possibilities to establish institutional public forums that would "allow citizens to confront powerful and influential leaders and demand answers to their questions," and citizen participation in public deliberation (Mayhew 1997, 261 passim).

The modern development of electronic media has challenged, due to specific technological possibilities and needs for regulation, the nature of freedom of the press, which was established with the newspapers of the eighteenth century.

In fact, with the rapid development of radio broadcasting and the growth of its political and commercial power, ideas for reform were redirected from the press to broadcasting. The development of broadcast media was based on the use of the electromagnetic spectrum that (1) had to be (like any traffic) technically regulated and coordinated and (2) was considered a public good. Thus private or public broadcasting companies, which were licensed by governmental or parliamentary institutions, had special obligations to perform public services. A number of principles and guidelines have evolved in the period since the 1920s, but it seems that with rapid technological and social changes, regulative practices faced a crisis in the 1980s. Yet the problem of regulation does not concern only its institutionally arranged forms. Even if a communication organization is not a governmental agency, there are many informal ways in which a government can exert influence over the media, and the media have a variety of possible ways to influence the government. Most important, the media industry, which was supposed to be subject to regulation, became a very powerful partner with political actors, and such a partnership decreased the autonomy of the regulative bodies. For a variety of reasons, mass media are likely to provide support for "the establishment" (i.e., individuals and groups with great economic and political power) in general and the government in particular, as Nicholas Johnson (1994, 14) convincingly demonstrated in the case of the U.S. commercial broadcasters. First, the owners of major media are at least millionaires and thus part of the establishment. It is understandable that they prefer not to criticize their friends and that they support government positions on issues. Second, media owners may fear retribution by federal government agencies with regulatory authority over them and enormous discretion (e.g., reduced postal rates, broadcastering licenses, advertising regulations). Third, when newspapers or broadcasting stations are owned by large corporations with other subsidiaries (conglomerates), they may serve other corporate interests and thus support those (governmental) positions on public issues that would bring them most benefits and influence politicians accordingly. Fourth, government officials may attack the media in speeches (jawboning). Media executives do not like being at the center of controversy, particularly if they are attacked and pressured to change their policies (which would decrease their profits). The increase of mutual influence between the political and economic establishments and the media steadily transformed a once open liberal press market with a diversified supply of newspapers into highly concentrated mass communications systems in terms of products, formats, markets, and firms (Neuman 1991, 133, 139).

However, in the "partnership" between the political and economic establishments, only the former is usually considered responsible for violating individual and corporate rights and freedoms. Although broadcast media are often

treated as being significantly different from the press, the idea of the pure marketplace in broadcasting (without any societal or state intervention and non-
market regulation) became apotheosized as the guarantor of the right of free
speech with no less zeal:

> The broadcasting marketplace is indirect and imperfect, but we know that it gen-
> erally works. The stations and networks that carry programs with the highest view-
> ing ratings can charge the highest rates for advertising. . . . Although the adver-
> tiser, rather than the consumer, pays for the program, market forces still move the
> key resource—time on an exclusive broadcasting frequency—toward its highest
> and best use. (Fowler and Brenner 1983, 671)

It is not difficult to ascertain what is, according to the free marketplace defenders, the "highest and best use" of broadcasting frequencies: *profit maximization*. Radio listeners and TV viewers are not the genuine consumers on the
market of broadcasting stations: "The market that a new station enters com-
prises not simply existing broadcast facilities, but all competitors for *the advertising dollar,* from newspapers to billboards" (Fowler and Brenner 1983, 672;
emphasis added). In this perspective, the "genuine consumers" are those who
seem to pay directly for broadcast programming—the advertisers.[7] Citizens only
observe this process as it takes place in the marketplace; they have "ultimate
control" only in the sense of the take it or leave it principle. As Fowler and Brenner (1983, 667) argue in congruence with the spiral of silence model, such regulation is perfectly in accord with the principles of free inquiry and expression:
"Those who deliver popular, acceptable speech have little reason to fear the re-
buke of the majority. Only words and ideas that trouble or confound need the
special aid of constitutional protection." In sum, then, if a commercial station
wants to maximize profit, it has to provide the service consumers most desire—
no other regulation is needed to satisfy the interests of the people. Thus it is argued that in democracy, public service broadcasting should be only exceptionally, and to a strictly limited extent, retained as a kind of "merit goods," like
public parks, museums and libraries, religious and educational institutions. Yet
this argumentation has substantial flaws: (1) profit maximization is in the interest of the *minority* of owners rather than in common interest, (2) it is based
on *majority* interest in specific contents, (3) it presupposes a *large enough* marketplace for profitable broadcasting or publishing,[8] and (4) it *apotheosizes* free
access to the market. A substantial part of (potential) readers, listeners, and
viewers, who have no leanings toward majority interests and preferences (which
the media tend to meet), may be excluded according to the principle that beg-
gars cannot be choosers. The delivery of only "acceptable speech" by the media

and the avoidance of information aimed at compromising, reciprocal influence, and innovation would eventually lead to a complete stagnation of society, not only in terms of democracy but of development in general.

OLD AND NEW RESTRAINTS ON HUMAN ABILITIES TO COMMUNICATE

From the ancient Greeks onward, the general conception of democracy has been based, inter alia, on at least four assumptions related to the communications sphere, namely, that (1) citizens are well informed, (2) citizens are interested in general politics, (3) citizens have equal rights to speak and participate in decision making, and (4) all decisions are submitted to public discussion. Yet even in the simplest and most exclusive model of democracy, which was developed in the small-scale, transparent, sparsely peopled society that was ancient Greek society, in which communication was based on predominantly oral, interpersonal interactions and was relatively easy, the fundamental assumptions of democratic communication did not fully materialize. Citizen participation in the democratic process was restricted by at least three factors: (1) communicative competence (e.g., oratory skills, literacy) was unevenly distributed as a consequence of externally produced inequalities, i.e., differences in education, socialization, knowledge, and so on; (2) informal or even clandestine communication networks, as opposed to public communication, reduced public discussions to public legitimization of the ruling opinions created by power elites; and (3) uneven access to (institutional) communication channels reduced the opportunities to obtain relevant information and to make information available to others.

The ancient Greek idea of the polis was even less sustainable in modern society, as John Stuart Mill argued, because government by open meetings, however attractive and desirable it may be, is probably completely impracticable for any community exceeding a single small town. Nevertheless, Rousseau still claimed that all citizens should and could be involved in the direct creation of the laws through public meetings and, similarly, Marx believed that the revolutionary, though slow and contradictory, transformation of society would gradually restore a form of direct democracy.

The most pervasive arguments against the feasibility of direct democracy did not substantially change from J. S. Mill to Walter Lippmann and Niklas Luhmann. Basically, all of them argue that forms of direct democracy cannot effectively reduce the complexity in modern social systems. According to these criticisms, the ideas of Rousseau, Marx, or Dewey seem to be appropriate for democracy in nonindustrial Gemeinschaft-type communities but not for postindustrial or information societies in which traditional (until the end of the eighteenth century) community life was structurally and functionally destroyed, although this is firmly against expectations held by Marx, Tönnies, and Dewey that new forms of community life and direct democracy would develop with the economic progression. Contrary to optimistic eighteenth- and nineteenth-century ideas and visions of democracy, conceptions of democracy that developed in the last century from Weber onward are much more restricted by objective and subjective determinations and (im)possibilities, and are even pessimistic. The main restrictions seem to be the growing complexity of society, pluralization of interests, and the sheer expansion of information needed for effective administration and control of both the environment in general and the state in particular—in short, "the Lippmann syndrome." Nowadays it seems practically impossible that large populations of contemporary societies would directly participate in public business, not only because of geographical and physical limits to when and where people can meet together (which are at least partly overcome with the help of computer-mediated communications), but primarily because the problems posed by coordination and regulation in contemporary society are too complex to be dealt with using the "simple tools" of classical or direct democracy, as Lippmann would say, and because "the members of too numerous a group could not know each other and would, therefore, be barred from friendly, familiar, and continued discussion in advance of decisions," as Rogers (1949, 71) paraphrased Aristotle's argument.

The ideal of direct democracy, as, for example, that formulated by Aristotle and Rousseau, involves too many elements that complicate processes of decision making; thus, they may destabilize the system (e.g., because of incompetence or apathy). Direct democracy is effective only in organizations having limited membership and characterized by a relative equality of members; in complex systems (well-trained) bureaucratic administration becomes indispensable despite the development of new communication technologies (or even because of them). The ideas of direct democracy were generally rejected as inappropriate and ineffective in large-scale and complex social systems, and new models of indirect democracy based on the competition between different interests and rival political elites and parties have been developed. The only alternative to direct democracy seems to be a fully developed representative democracy based on the freedom of speech, freedom of assembly, freedom of press, and the *right to communicate,* which, in contemporary societies, can be considered the functional equivalent of ancient Greek democracy. In representative democracy accountability ought to be combined with professionalism and expertise; elements of professionalism and expert knowledge also differentiate mass communication from all other less complex forms of communication. Although *rule* by bureaucratic apparatus is not seen as inevitable, bureaucrats necessarily have considerable power due to their expertise and information. On the other hand, the role of the ordinary citizen became strongly delimited due to his or her low competence, lack of relevant information, and general depoliticization. The picture could have been drawn by Walter Lippmann.

The idea that human communication was a natural human ability possessed equally by every member of a collectivity solely because of his or her adherence to the collectivity disappeared long before the modern bureaucratization of society. It existed only as long as the development of human productive forces did not expose the dependence of communication practice on material conditions of human life and its instrumental nature in social relations. It became apparent that human beings are as alienated from this seemingly natural ability as they are in the process of production in general. The struggle between the authoritarian and emancipatory potentials of communication began already with the transition from the oral tradition to the manuscript age, when the development of writing and human ability not only to speak but also to write made it possible for the communication process to take place without the sender and receiver being physically present. The message can be separated and thus alienated from the sender. Even more important, a radical change in the relationship of an individual to "his" or "her" oral language has been introduced by alphabetical codes; the language ceased to be a natural relationship as it had been in a primitive collectivity. Learning and education became an essential part of social relations, embedded in the primal social division of labor into manual work versus mental work.

With the development of writing, the initial civilizational process of enlarging temporal and spatial horizons through communication, that is, surpassing natural existential conditions that determined human beings' relations to production as well as their relation to language as a form of natural belonging to a collectivity, turned for the first time into its opposite: into the rise of alienation. Writing not only made possible the recording of communication but also divided the previously homogeneous collectivity into those capable of the new form of communication and those being short of it. Like writing, all other kinds of communications technologies developed through centuries reveal that new forms of communication are part of general changes in human actions upon nature and other human beings, and therefore no less significant and/or contradictory as economic and political activities. As Raymond Williams ([1962] 1976, 10) pointed out, all new means of communication that implied a possible expansion of human powers to learn and to exchange ideas and experiences "have been abused, for political control (as in propaganda) or for commercial profit (as in advertising)."

The first institutionalized forms of mass communication (e.g., in religion) limited the autonomy of individuals in the formation and expression of opinions by free discussion to those issues that were not critical of the power elites. Since the very beginnings, institutionalization gave rise to different kinds of *distorted communication* (Mueller 1973, 19); it resulted from "governmental policy to structure language and communication" (directed communication) and/or "successful attempts by private and governmental groups to structure and limit public communication in order that their interests prevail" (constrained communication). The intensity of institutionalization culminated with the mass media. Such terms as "fourth estate," "sixth power," and "watchdog," which are often used as nicknames for the mass media, suggest that the social functions of the mass media have always been related to the exercise of power and control in a society. Before the nineteenth century, the two main policies of most regimes toward public opinion were secrecy and censorship. Power elites effectively tended to "block access to information about governmental plans and operations and to seek, through secrecy, to inhibit the development of potentially hostile opinion on as many matters as possible" (Ginsberg 1989, 290). The most crude form of distortion of communication processes—censorship—existed long before the sophisticated forms of constrained and directed communication through the mass media, already at the beginning of written history. At the time printing was invented, strict censorship was introduced by authorities to prevent serious problems such as "offenses" against the state, the sovereign, and authoritative institutions. This historical process is perhaps best exemplified by the efforts of the Catholic Church to control the public knowledge of societies (Hardt 1983, 300). At the end of the fifteenth century, shortly after Gutenberg printed the first Bible, the Church implemented a licensing system, followed by strict censorship and the Index Librorum Prohibitorum, an official index of prohibited texts that were not allowed to appear in public or to be read in private. The emergence of new intellectual elites—the religious reform movements—as a reaction against abuses by the Church and the new printing technology changed the strategy of the Church in the seventeenth century. It moved away from exercising restrictive control to the far more subtle and efficient strategy of strengthening its position through propaganda disseminated by its central institution, Sacra Congregatio de Propaganda Fide. Generally, during the nineteenth and twentieth centuries, rulers began to discover the value of popular support for their actions (including wars) and tried to influence public opinion: propaganda, public relations, and massive information subsidies became a far more suitable strategy than censorship for pacifying public opinion.

During the last two centuries, censorship was largely abolished and the former preventive systems of direct monitoring became penal in democratic countries. At the same time, however, a new form of secular censorship arose, first, taxation and deposits for publishing newspapers and, later, commercialization of the communication sphere. Heine and Marx ([1842] 1974) denoted deposits as "a special type of nonfreedom that was perhaps even more noxious than censorship." Historically, material censorship (deposits) acted as an equivalent and substitute of mental censorship. Both types of censorship functioned to diminish the flow of provocative, offensive, or upsetting issues. The two forms of censorship essentially differ in that material censorship is an *abstract* and *general* nonfreedom whereas mental censorship is a *concrete* and *individual* nonfreedom. The former is directly subordinated to commercial interests and the economic laws of capitalism whereas the latter serves the judicial laws of the authoritarian and absolutist state. Market regulation of the press certainly represented progress in comparison to the former censoring instructions as a form of legal regulation. As Marx ([1842] 1969, 88) wrote, one may well understand that some individuals portray freedom in the form best known and closest—and for the bourgeoisie that was the freedom of entrepreneurship. Yet imposing the entrepreneurial freedom upon the press in place of freedom of publicity is the same kind of tyranny as subordinating the press to censorship (see Splichal 1981, 100–5). Censorship has never been a law enacted by the state *for* the citizens but rather *against* them; therefore it is not a law at all but a privilege. Accordingly, attempts to generalize, on the basis of that particular form of paralegal regulation, that market regulation is more democratic than *any* form of legal regulation, as the free market ideologues argue, is a non sequitur.

In the beginning (i.e., in the latter days of feudalism) material censorship acted like mental censorship: like the mental censorship that obstructed the principle of publicity to materialize, deposits directly hindered or prevented the realization of entrepreneurial freedom in the communication sphere. The bourgeois revolution eliminated deposits as last remnants of the absolutist restrictions to entrepreneurial freedom, so that material censorship started to act in the manner of the dominant commodity mode of production—as the preventive, direct mental censorship in past systems acted in accord with the dominant mode of the public representation of power. However, this is not to say that mental censorship in commercial systems has been abolished. Rather, forms of censorship have been changed from direct into indirect ones. The advent of propaganda made the old system of direct mental censorship obsolete, but as Lippmann argued, propaganda in the strict sense would be impossible without some form of censorship: "In order to conduct a propaganda there must be some barrier between the public and the event. Access to the real environment must be limited, before anyone can create a pseudo-environment that he thinks wise or desirable" (Lippmann [1922] 1960, 43). Mental censorship started to act behind the back of the market, beyond the visible sphere of circulation, as commodity production generally does.

Commercialization and commodification of the communication sphere are based on the assumption that all people have the right to speak freely; but they force them to speak *profitably* as well. Based on the liberal conception of negative freedom (freedom *from* political authorities), freedom of the press increasingly became a freedom of those who owned communication means rather than citizens. The critique of private commercial interests that are presented as the most (or even only) authentic advocates of the democratization of communication is not new; it is often directly connected with the idea of public communication services. A plurality or multiplicity of media channels would seem to raise the probability that nonsubsidized, nonconformist, and maverick opinions or unwanted facts might break through to public awareness. However, isolated voices of dissent in the massive marketplace are unlikely to find many "consumers." A bare *plurality* of the media is not a reliable indicator of a society's level of freedom, since it may create only the illusion of content *diversity* by hiding the fact that all of the media are restrained by a sort of self-censorship and potential threat by subsidizers. The plurality indicator is even more questionable because the developed media systems are becoming steadily more concentrated in their control by a small number of large (transnational) corporations; and in less developed systems this is an even much more probable development. As Mattelart emphasizes, commercialization and privatization may appear as the leading principles of the pluralization of society only in the absence of a critical elaboration of the concept of plurality: "The plurality of the groups making up civil society and the diversity of their interests demolishes a strictly juridico-political and, more often than not, formal conception of pluralism as the doctrinaire foundation of the public service" (Mattelart, quoted in Piemme 1984, 221).

It is true that the awareness of the importance of market competition, commodity production, and exchange among private individuals was an essential element in the modernization of the classical concept of civil society, but economy in that time was *preindustrial* economy based on loosely structured and almost perfect and *transparent competition* among small propertied worker-entrepreneurs, both in economy in general and particularly in the sphere of the press. In addition, civil society consisted of a great number of diverse *nonentrepreneurial* (and even antibourgeois) groups and associations having in common "the fear of despotism," which stimulated—much more than the love of capitalism—political fights against state despotism (Keane 1988, 64). The rhetoric of privatized economy as the cornerstone of political pluralism and parliamentary democracy simply misses these important accounts of modern civil society.

Traditionally a free market economy was considered the guarantor and the basis of individualism as the key dimension of the autonomy of civil society in relation to the state. But contemporary corporate capitalism (re)produces *economic inequalities* to the degree that they prevent a large part of citizens from participation in, and control of, "democratic" decisions. Already in the second half of the nineteenth century, the press began to be dominated by chain-owning proprietors due to the escalation in publishing costs, which "did not just affect individual access to the public sphere: it debarred access for large sections of the community" (Curran 1991, 41). It shifted citizens away from participation in decision making and control, which became increasingly governed by a bureaucratic organizational imperative and technocratic knowledge, and strengthened their consumer function. As a consequence, "*political* choice was limited to the prescriptions formulated by business and *politicized* in its advertising" (Ewen 1977, 91). Oligopolistic inclinations and forces tend to prevail over those of a "spontaneous" and "free" market and disqualify the traditionally political realms of government and civil society.

The problem with the new market liberalism, which insists that market competition of the media is the most important and sufficient precondition of their freedom, is in the invalid assumption that the basic right to private property—because *everyone* has this right—guarantees both freedom of the media (their independence from the state) and freedom of citizens (free choice between different media and contents). Apparently, this is an "ideal type of free market" of the media, which in practice does not exist due to the processes of capital concentration and centralization. As a consequence, the "free" media market is largely oligopolized, and "free" choice is severely limited by constrained supply. "Commercial media conventionally portray themselves as virtual slaves to the 'market,' and thus as providing people with exactly what they want. They quietly gloss over the power of major advertisers and corporations to define *poor* people's media wants as irrelevant, compared to those of the more affluent sectors of the market. . . . Only the extraordinarily gullible believe in the democratic passions of commercial media executives" (Downing 1984, 5–6). Even for producers, the free market does not ensure free access to the "deregulated" marketplace, due to the levels of investment required to enter the market, the rising program production costs, and/or already existing oligopolies (particularly due to syndicatable entertainment programming). In Blumler's words, the "gathering momentum" of organizational concentration and conglomeration in mass communications tends to limit the opportunities of independent producers to offer profitably something different from mainstream supply and fosters standardization of program supply across the entire media (particularly television) industry. At the same time, it jeopardizes media pluralism because it creates a risk that the main channels of access to the public may eventually be controlled by a small number of strategically placed and minimally accountable gatekeepers (Blumler 1991, 9).

The role of political parties, whose organs are often the media, has changed in ways that are similar to changes in the nature of the marketplace. According to Norberto Bobbio (1989, 25), political parties must be placed among subjects of economic, social, ideological, and religious conflicts constitutive for civil society. Simultaneously, modern political parties belong to authoritative institutions as well. This major change in the position of political parties is indicated by special legal and constitutional provisions defining the role and rights of political parties. They are totally integrated neither in the state nor in civil society but constitute "political society" that mediates between the state and civil society. The contemporary state largely became a "party-state"; the parliament became a site at which representatives of political parties rather than of citizens met to validate claims of their own political party in terms of generalized interests. The phenomenon of the party-state was particularly significant for the socialist state, which achieved institutional stability and uniformity by suppressing the plurality of political parties. However, a similar process of domination of political parties and their specific interests in the parliament must be regarded as an essential element in the ongoing transformations of the capitalist state, although it does not suppress differentiation to the same degree as the socialist state.

THE NEED FOR REGULATION

During the last century, the role of the most significant agents of power, that is, political parties and powerful economic actors, has changed significantly. An important consequence of these changes, to take just one example, was that the border between the state and civil society was becoming less and less transparent. In spite of these changes, the principal function of mass media remains basically unchanged. They still operate as they did from the very beginning, simultaneously in the realms of the state (politics) *and* economy (within or without civil society) and mediate between them. As Gouldner (1976) put it, they "stand *between* the public, on the one side, and, on the other, the official managers of institutions, organizations, movements, or the society's hegemonic elites." Thus the real core of the problem becomes the relationship of the media "to political parties here and elsewhere, [their] relations to the business world, to numerous groups and interests who influence and who are influenced by the public" (Weber [1924] 1976, 99).

The two spheres opposing the public are regulated by different principles: the political sphere (including the state) by the principle of maximization of power, and the economic sphere by the principle of maximization of profit. Both principles meet in the communication sphere—to the detriment of that structural part of society that is not governed by these principles, that is, *civil society in the strict sense,* which consists of civil movements, associations, and organizations. It assumes the materialization of communication rights and freedoms—freedom of thought, expression, press, association, assembly, and rights to privacy and to communicate.[9] Mass communication processes are subordinated to the principles dominant in the political and economic spheres through different forms of (indirect) control exercised by the state or private corporations, from censorship and propaganda to advertising and political marketing. The fundamental rights of individuals in civil society were shifted, by and large, to legal entities (corporations, political parties, and the state) that dominate the mass media either directly (as their owners) or indirectly (as the most influential sources of information and opinions, advertisers and information subsidizers). Although it is extremely difficult to pinpoint the often indirect influence of corporate politics on editorial decisions in the mass media, such influence has been confirmed in a number of cases (Bagdikian 1983).

The *political independence* of the media is a controversial issue because, as Garnham (1990, 110) argues, it is possible that "pursuit of political freedom may override the search for economic efficiency." This is one side of the contradiction between the two spheres. The other refers to political consequences (nonfreedom) brought about by the economic determination of mass communication so that "the extent of possible political freedom is constrained by the level of material productivity." The two spheres influencing the sphere of mass communication—economy and politics—are guided by different basic principles of action and value systems. If two conflicting systems of values and relations (economic and political) exist, and the media are dominated by them and/or mediate between them, why should the media be subjected to the laws of economy rather than polity, as in commercial systems, or polity rather than economy, as in paternal systems? The media are political institutions par excellence, not just commercial enterprises. By forcing *political communication* to channel itself via *commercial media,* public communication is transformed into consumerism, and citizens into consumers. If the mass media, by definition, link the two different (or even opposing) spheres of economy and politics and perform both political and economic functions, it is not rational for the media to be totally subordinated to the laws of either of them. Surely, I would not argue that they should be subject to *both* of them. If the political and economic spheres are regulated by their own intrinsic principles and values, the communication sphere should have the same right to be intrinsically regulated—by principles and values based on communication rights and freedoms. We should not forget that communication rather than commerce or politics is generically human ability and need.

Public communication is simply the fully developed democratic communication that Raymond Williams ([1962] 1976, 134) defined as the negation of authoritarian, paternal, and commercial restraints of communication and control over it. The idea of the democratization of the communication sphere and the media is based on the assumption that it is possible and necessary to abolish the centralized and bureaucratic management systems, the political and economic restrictions of human rights and freedoms, and to develop new communication technologies, knowledge, and critical consciousness. Central to the idea of public, or democratic, communication is the right to communicate as a basic human right that consists of two parts—the active part, or the right to transmit, and the passive part, or the right to receive.

> On the right to transmit, the basic principle of democracy is that since all are full members of the society, all have the right to speak as they wish or find. This is not only an individual right, but a social need, since democracy depends on the active participation and the free contribution of all its members. The right to receive is complementary to this: it is the means of participation and of common discussion. The institutions necessary to guarantee these freedoms must clearly be of a public-service kind. (Williams [1962] 1976, 134)

A number of the suppositions of democratic communication have not been fulfilled by any society yet. Thus we cannot even speak of public (in the strict sense of the word) communication in the history of humankind. However, it is even more important to answer the question of whether such a conception of public communication is at all feasible. Due to numerous conceptual changes and controversies that have arisen during the last decades, a clearly and accurately defined concept of publicness is needed primarily for *normative* aims because all democratic societies are facing the problem of how the media, old and new, can be made accessible to citizens and used as an instrument of the public, for the benefit of citizens and not just as a vehicle to reach and persuade potential consumers and voters as well as to generate profit and power.

Both in official discourses and among academic analysts, the question of how to foster democratization of communication and the media primarily applies to media *regulation.* Forms of regulations so far developed to democratize communication were basically directed to the materialization of the right to receive, that is, the *passive* right to communicate. This is particularly clear if we look at the definition of the common normative framework of public service broadcasting (PSB), which started to develop in Europe in the 1920s. Basically, the idea of PSB implies four postulates: (1) PSB has three basic *functions for the audiences:* education, information, and entertainment; (2) PSB should serve *different tastes* from highbrow and elites to lowbrow and popular; (3) PSB must assure *universal access to broadcasting programs* on the whole national territory and care for the appropriate technical quality of transmission; (4) PSB must supply programming for ethnic, linguistic, regional, religious, and other *minorities.*

Public service broadcasting faced a crisis in the 1980s due to the development of new communication technologies and, primarily, the ideology of privatization. But the realistic question at the moment is not, as Mulgan (1991, 259) suggests (and there is no reason not to agree), "whether there will be forms of public intervention in the future, but rather what form they could and should take, and how collective freedoms can be reconciled with those of individuals and minorities." According to Mulgan, at least three types of regulation and public control seem likely to survive in the future as a necessary condition for the realization of individual freedom and diversity: (1) traditional *content regulation* of the core mass media; regulators, governments, and other public institutions will retain some role as a medium for public opinion, standards, and values; (2) *infrastructure policies* to ensure universal access to basic communication networks of society; and (3) policies and laws regulating common standards to allow for interconnectivity and providing *free public services,* organization of common menus, and directory information services to guarantee easy access and competition among information providers.

For Mulgan it is not likely that, in the future, forms of regulation would touch the right to communicate as an active citizens' right. Yet would such an expectation really be utopian? In a *normatively ideal situation,* communication networks are to be like *the public spaces* of the modern city, the parks and streets, theaters, pubs, and cafes where all classes and groups of society mix, associate, and communicate. Access to communication networks is universal, not determined by the market or controlled by the state, and networks or channels of communication are common property (like the electromagnetic space) subject to public regulation and accountability. Such a possible transformation is based on the assumption that a form of democratic equilibrium between political, economic, and cultural spheres as resources of societal integration is obtained through the separation of powers. But how this radical democratic change is to be attained remains an open question.

Such an ideal situation is normatively defined by C. W. Mills's concept of the public in his *Power Elite:* In a public, according to Mills, (1) virtually as many people express opinions as receive them. (2) Public communications are so organized that there is a chance immediately and effectively to answer back any opinion expressed in public. Opinion formed by such discussion (3) readily finds an outlet in effective action, even against, if necessary, the prevailing system of authority. And (4) authoritative institutions do not penetrate the public, which is thus more or less autonomous in its operation. According to Hoynes (1994, 168–76), the ideal of democratic communication may be achieved when five general principles are materialized: (1) the principle of *social ownership* as the most crucial of the five principles, since it alone can facilitate, as Hoynes wrongly believes,[10] the implementation of all the others; (2) the principle of *diversity,* which requires the provision of a variety of perspectives created by the plurality of groups and political differences; (3) the principle of *participation,* which is based on the need to develop structures for active citizen involvement; (4) the principle of *interaction,* in order to allow more than one-way communication; (5) the principle of *criticism,* which is based on the necessity to critically compare different (political) orientations and opinions. Neither Mills's nor Hoynes's principles are practically materialized; on the contrary, communication networks are usually more like private clubs with exclusive access, privately owned and governed by the principle of profit maximization and/or power maximization. This does not imply that the media are not regulated at all; regulation is left to the marketplace or state control that, by definition, generate and multiply power. The fundamental question to be asked is what is the rationale for the transformation of *interactive* communication, which is human *generic ability* and *need,* into *one-way mass* communication, which is most *profitable.*

Regulation means maintaining *control* over human behavior; thus it always exists, but it may tend toward the establishment of either competition or monopoly. Control may be defined as an intentional (purposive) influence toward a predetermined goal. The purpose of control can be twofold. First, it can be aimed at achieving given ends, such as gaining hold of scarce resources (control over environment or *extrinsic control*). The subject of action is in control of the external environment, and it exercises control to bring the environment into line with what is desired. Second, self-control (*intrinsic control*) deals with (un)expected changes and threats—control is not aimed toward other ends but is an end in itself. Regulation and control are always purposive in the sense that they are directed toward some prior goal of the controlling agent.[11] Regulation may include the entire range from a monopoly (absolute control by a single agent) to the weakest and most probabilistic forms, that is, any kind of purposive influence on behavior, however insignificant.

With the development of direct and rapid communication links, the central issue of control becomes *access* to various types of complex control structures. Questions of purpose, of who and/or what is the subject of control, and who is the controller are inherently political. Within any society, there are actors or people who have ready and privileged access to communication channels, as well as those who are deprived of it. It is needless to say that such a division between the accessed and "unaccessed" is political by its very nature.

The problem of media regulation obviously involves a number of competing interests. At least the following distinct *classes of interest* can be identified with respect to their involvement in the mass media: (1) the owners' interest in using their media as a means of self-expression and in protecting a limited property interest; (2) demand from audiences for access to the media; recipients' interest in receiving or not receiving information, opinions, and so on; (3) various civil society groups' interest in having access to the media to publish their opinions; (4) society's interest in having the media perform their public service functions; (5) the government's interest in getting its viewpoints to the citizens and in maintaining the rights of all citizens. Yet governments and regulatory bodies in liberal democracies have relatively little room for media regulation. They are faced with strong and often incompatible pressures like increasing commercial pressures militating in favor of a greater number of channels provided with digital satellite technology; competitive pressures from neighboring countries that have been faster in developing new services; pressures from business interests wanting to develop these services; and advertisers wanting to use new, perhaps more efficient ways of delivering commercial messages. The fundamental problem of regulation is that of striking a proper balance between different actors in the game. In addition, with the development of satellite television and global computer-mediated communication networks, a juridical vacuum (or at least vagueness) came into existence regarding legal regulation. It seems that all these problems stimulate the tendency to *globalizing market regulation,* which would certainly provoke the *least number of legal perplexities* but at the same time, and with no less certainty, would (definitely) bury the idea of public communication. Despite all these problems (and perhaps because of them), media democratization *requires* a specific form of regulation according to its *specific purpose,* which is to limit the control and power held by commercial groups and political agents in order to protect and increase, and not to injure, the independence of the media and/or prevent coalitions between the media and the state or capital that go to the detriment of consumers.

The problem is well illustrated by the case of the professional enforcement of the *objectivity principle* (factual and balanced reporting) in journalism after World War I in the United States and later in Europe, a principle that "celebrates the canon of professional objectivity, with its stress on disinterested detachment, the separation of fact from opinion, the balancing of claim and counterclaim" (Curran 1991, 32). Objectivity is far from being a self-evident and "natural" characteristic of quality journalism. Newspapers have begun to develop as critical organs of (public) opinion rather than mere vehicle of news distribution. The freedom of the press that materialized with the bourgeois revolution has been fundamentally the extension (and adaptation to new technological possibilities and social needs) of the freedom of thought and opinion expression rather than of the freedom of information (Splichal 1994a, 73–75). In the early 1920s, when the idea of journalistic objectivity was adopted as a professional norm, it represented "a rigorous reporting procedure growing out of the broader cultural movement of *scientific naturalism*" (Streckfuss 1990, 973, emphasis added). It was also related to the need for professional education in journalism, advocated, for example, by Walter Lippmann. At that time, many newspapers were closely linked to political parties, and "objectivity" represented an alternative to politically partisan journalism. After that period, however, the cultural, political, and economic environment changed considerably. Mergers of newspapers became an everyday practice after the decline of the traditionally politicized party press. The new type of "objective journalism" was based on the growth of mass media monopoly and the spread of mass advertising that neutralize information, since news that was specific, views that were personal, and interpretations that were consonant with the attitudes and beliefs of only one part of the large audience might have affronted those with different opinions and thus reduced the readership or audience on which advertising revenues depended. The separation of news from editorial policy originated from the finding that "an 'imprudent' pursuit of the paper's policy might offend and limit its market" (Gouldner 1976, 96) both in terms of readers and (even more important) advertisers. Simultaneously, the separation of news from commentaries was blurred by the subordination of both to entertainment, which fundamentally limited diversity and fostered superficiality.

Paradoxically, journalists saw in the same principle of objectivity the assurance of their autonomy in relation to media owners and thus actually entered into coalition with them; as a result, the media systematically avoided complex and great ideological issues and placed everyday facts and events on the agenda. Jerry Mander produced a list of thirty-three "miscellaneous inherent biases" to show what kind of world television must inevitably transmit. One bias is clearly related to objectivity doctrine: "When there is a choice between objective events (incidents, data) and subjective information (perspectives, thoughts, feelings), the objective event will be chosen" (Mander 1978, 324). The principle of objectivity further implies that the one (e.g., personalities, charismatic leaders, symbols) is preferred to the many (e.g., a philosophy, political movements); hierarchy to democracy or collectivity; superficiality to depth; the conclusion to the process; doing to being; the specific to the general; quantity to quality; the finite to the infinite; death to life; and "facts concerning the moon are better television than poetry concerning the moon. Any facts work better than any poetry."

Such stereotyping of news obscures the existence of different perspectives and values, and perpetuates the illusion of objectivity. As David Paletz and Robert Entman (1981, 23) argue, "the mode of presentation is designed to persuade the audience of the credibility of the news stories and the legitimacy of the media which present them." But in fact, "as news reports, it therefore also censors and occludes aspects of life; its silences generate a kind of 'underprivileged' social reality, a social reality implicitly said (by the silence) to be unworthy of attention" (Gouldner 1976, 107). Objective reporting privileges stereotyped news and prefers "official voices and [tends] to leave unreported large areas of genuine relevance that authorities chose not to talk about. . . . It widened the chasm that is a constant threat to democracy—the difference between the realities of private power and the illusions of public imagery" (Bagdikian 1983, 182). This liberal perspective considers the media mainly a channel of information between the government and the governed, although it rejects a direct advocacy journalism.

Thus objective journalism is not simply a question of professional quality standards developed in the past century. It is mainly a question of the social role of the media in society and, of course, the nature of society itself, that is, social characteristics that influence the specific nature of journalism and its quality and objectivity. With a consistent separation from its contexts, news remains a pure "sensation," as Dewey wrote. Endeavors for objective reporting did not abolish stereotypes and the ideological nature of the media but rather helped replace one ideology with another. In addition, by reducing opinions to reporting facts (e.g., publicly expressed opinions of prominent individuals), they limited citizen access to the media. Indeed, as a consequence of the application of the objectivity principle, artificially arranged events intended exclusively for *opinion* expression and construction of public image (e.g., press conferences, election campaigns, party conventions) became "facts" and reporting them "news" whereas a direct journalist's or citizen's statement remained "opinion."

Similarly to the materialization of the objectivity principle, which does not result in an actual objectivity of the media, information subsidies do not primarily result in an easier citizen access to information but rather the publication of opinions as facts. Information subsidy is always interlinked with negotiations in which subsidizers try their best to tell journalists as little as possible and get in return as much media attention as possible. In this process, coalitions are formed between public and private bureaucracy and the media. The most customary subject of negotiations and agreements behind the back of audiences is confidential information ("off the record") given to journalists who do not publish it at all or only when its use value substantially decreases and it no longer has predictive value ("embargo"), perhaps with no reference to the source ("from sources close to . . ."). Perhaps the most important consequence of such coalitions is a rapid decline of citizen confidence in the media, which indicates an inflation of influence. Declining trust in journalism has revived discussions and controversies about public journalism[12] whose roots go back to Dewey's reflections on the interconnection between (social) sciences, newspapers, and interpersonal communication in the process of transforming Great Society into Great Community. The problem basically has not changed: how to interlink or aggregate local citizens' deliberations at the national or even the global level. Solutions to this problem are often paradoxical, so that even civil movements are forced to use corporate strategies (e.g., public relations) to make their opinions and alternative proposals public, whereas public journalism reporting local debates and publishing citizens' opinions remains confined to the local level.

The true sense of democratization is the prevention (or at least hindrance and control) of all actions and transactions behind the public's back. Democratic regulation is aiming to make influence on the mass communication process equally available to all citizens. From a *normative-theoretical* perspective, this calls not only for radical democratization of the media but also for political and economic systems that represent the societal context of the media. According to the model developed by Hans-Peter Krüger (1991), first, *public use of the media* should allow for symmetrical change between the diverging perspectives of participants and observers. If not, the potentially public media degenerate into economic enterprises or propaganda departments of the state or political parties. Second, institutional autonomization of *political competition* should be counteracted by (1) recognition of the public media as the fourth, "soft," or symbolic-argumentative, power in order to preclude its subordination under one of the three classic powers (legislative, executive, judicial); (2) an ever renewed "federalization" of all four powers to limit their drive toward centralization; (3) lowering the threshold of citizen participation in democratic political competition. Third, *economic competition* should be socioculturally regulated (1) through the political separation of powers; (2) through the limitation of the costs of bureaucratization caused by separation of powers; (3) through the extension of the customary models of codetermination, for example, by the inclusion of representatives of the public sphere.

One of the basic ideas behind the normative model of democratization of mass communication is that no citizen should have more institutionally guaranteed influence over public (or collective) affairs (e.g., in a process of public deliberation and debate about the best uses of state power) than any other, and that the society as a whole should be in control of the media, rather than any specific part of it. Equality does not mean a sort of mathematical equivalence that would make each individual actually substitutive for any other. It denotes, in John Dewey's words, "the unhampered share which each individual member of the community has in the consequences of associated action. It is equitable because it is measured by need and capacity to utilize, not by extraneous factors which deprive one in order that another may take and have. . . . It denotes effective regard for whatever is distinctive and unique in each, irrespective of physical and psychological inequalities" ([1927] 1991, 150–51).

THE RIGHT TO COMMUNICATE
AND ITS OPERATIONALIZATION

Mass media and, generally, any activity exhibiting influence can be controlled either internally or externally. Attempts at democratic regulation are often confronted with what we could call external sources of inequality of influence (e.g., inequality of income and wealth). Any universal provision of equal rights ensures equal availability of influence only under the provision that such external sources of inequality of influence do not exist. But this is not a very realistic assumption. Clearly, the view on which the number of votes citizens have should depend on their taxable income, or any other external inequality, would obviously be considered antidemocratic because citizens would be unequal in terms of votes. Yet this is usually not thought to be the case with regard to the unequal availability of influence in a stage prior to the voting process, which is (according to the "rationalist" model of public opinion) central to public opinion formation and expression. Citizens are extremely unequal in terms of their access to the media—to publish their opinions, to participate in public discussion, that is, in the "right to transmit," as Williams would put it. This is a typical example of external sources of inequality in which the abolition of legal limitations (e.g., censorship) does not represent a "positive condition," as Dewey would say, for intellectual freedom; what is needed is methods and instruments for control of *social* rather than individual conditions. This is the central problem of any attempt to regulate the media in contemporary complex societies in a way to overcome citizens' unequal influence in the formation and expression of public opinion.

From the perspective of a genuine democratization of communications, the concept of freedom of the press has definitely proved insufficient as an ethical and legal imperative. As Key argued, the fundamental significance of freedom of speech and the press was to enable deviants from dominant opinion "to play a critical role in the preservation of the vitality of a democratic order as they urge alterations and modifications better to achieve the aspirations of men" (Key [1961] 1967, 555). Every democratic system should, as Held maintains (1989, 270), help all citizens develop their nature and express their qualities, protect them from the arbitrary use of coercive power, involve them in the determination of the conditions of their association, and expand economic opportunities to maximize the availability of resources. This can only develop on the basis of an open information and communication system that provides informed decisions on public issues. The belief that "free competition" brings all significant opinions to the marketplace is either naiveté or ignorance in the period of globalized monopolization. The idea of the free marketplace of ideas rests on a number of false assumptions, for example, (1) that everyone has free access to the market, (2) that truth is not subjectively developed but rather objectively given, (3) that truth is always among the ideas in the marketplace, and (4) that people are able to discriminate between the truth and falseness (Hopkins 1996, 44). In the early development of mass media during the period of liberal capitalism, a free market system was perhaps quite an accurate approximation of the ideal of freedom of the press. During the period of media monopolization, however, the abstract principle of freedom of the press proved unsatisfactory to limit the manipulative practice of the press and to stimulate substantial reforms. Today it basically means that everyone can speak freely, provided that it is interesting for a large enough audience, which assures the media of a profitable circulation or audience share, and primarily a large enough interest on the part of advertisers. In fact, freedom of the press privileges *corporate* subjects against the rights of citizens. Minorities of all sorts are rarely visible in public, despite technological possibilities, because their interests and opinions dissenting from the majority may decrease the circulation or audience share, which would, in turn, reduce advertising income. Indeed, the measure of the importance of an opinion in the free marketplace of ideas is its commercial efficiency.

Jean D'Arcy has summarized the ideas about the necessity to surpass the classic bourgeois freedom of the press in the concept of *the right to communicate:*

> The rights to hear and be heard, to inform and to be informed, together may be regarded as the essential components of a "right to communicate." . . . The real-

ization of a "right to communicate" is a desirable objective for a democratic society, so that each individual may know he is entitled to be informed and to be heard, regardless of where he may live or work or travel in his own country. (D'Arcy, cited in Fisher 1981, 15)

Since then, the right to communicate, which substantially exceeds classical freedom of the press, has been at the center of international discussions on democratization of communication. Indeed, the new right to communicate is about returning the media to the public or civil society, to the citizens as active participants in communication rather than mere consumers. A number of treatises on the *right to communicate* have attempted to define more accurately the generic human ability and need to communicate. Four basic rights and freedoms can be defined as the cornerstones of the generic right to communicate: (1) the right to publish opinions in the mass media, as an extension of the traditional freedoms of thought and expression, and as a right complementary to the right to receive information;[13] (2) the right to participate in the management of the mass media and communication organizations; (3) the right of free association and mutual interlinkage for realizing individual and common needs; and (4) equality of citizens in rights and duties, of which the first requirement is that this equality is not limited by or dependent on social status or the uneven distribution of material resources.

The right to publish opinions is central to the right to communicate and is the fundamental condition for the democratic formation of public opinion. Basically, it extends the principle of publicity beyond the obligation of *corporate* power agents (primarily the state) to the *individual*'s right. It implies equal value for all individual opinions in society and thus eliminates the difference between privileged (ruling) and "incompetent" opinions. This naturally concerns only those opinions that determine the social hierarchy of *values*. All opinions must have equal significance in democratic discussion and decision making when they are based on evaluation and specific interests, not on professional knowledge or professional capability in making technical or instrumental decisions. Individual opinions certainly have, due to objective circumstances, a different final probability of being affirmed as common or even public opinion and thus of being turned into effective action. However, the initial probability must be based on a genuinely equal opportunity to publish opinions. In a democratic debate, the dominant opinion is formed from individual (publicly expressed) opinions that are not subordinated to authoritative intervention. But if these possibilities are equal only politically (while actually being unequal) the dominant opinion originates in power elites, which *post festum* try to secure publicity for their opinion: a publicly expressed opinion (of the elite) thus reduces the autonomy of the debate and the possibility of response and critique.

To achieve an equal initial probability for all individual opinions, communications have to be organized as a public good and managed and controlled by neither private nor state (i.e., particularistic) interests, but rather by society as a whole. Essentially, citizens have to have the right to participate in the management of communication organizations, for only on such a basis can the right to publish opinions be politically and legally materialized as an essential part of the right to communicate. One can hardly imagine a system, either on the local or the national level, in which everyone would contribute to discussions and/or decision making every time a controversial issue appears. It does not follow, however, that the (political) system cannot be transformed in order to make more citizens' participation possible. Many different strategies to democratize the communication sphere have been developed, for example, the model of a centrally controlled market economy, a mandated market economy model, and a regulated market economy model—with only limited effects on the democratization of the total communication sphere (see J. Curran 1991). They clearly have one important common denominator: they are trying to preserve the traditional values of public service broadcasting and connect them with growing pressures by private capital rather than radically enforce the ideas of democratization.

Different conceptualizations of public service media have in common the idea of the media whose operation ought to be based on public funding and not controlled by the state or dominated by commercial interests. Such a new public system certainly cannot be the *only* system; rather, it should compete with those developed by the state (paternal systems) and the market (commercial systems). But the fact that civil society would have its own communication system would make it less vulnerable than it is now, due to the share of *communicative power* it would gain and generate. Strictly speaking, in terms of my earlier differentiation between power and influence, communicative power can only be (and by definition is) *influence*. As Gunnar Andrén argues, central to the "power to communicate" is the idea of freedom of expression; but it also incorporates "positive freedoms." According to his normative definition,

> *a person has communicative power* to the extent that he (i) has consciously developed opinions and attitudes of his own; (ii) he knows how to express his opinions and attitudes in adequate ways; (iii) he has access to media where he can express his opinions and attitudes; (iv) by (iii) he can reach a large and/or influential audience or a particular audience which he wants to influence; (v) by (iv) he will, in

fact, influence the opinions, attitudes, or behaviors of other citizens in accordance
with his intentions. (Andrén 1993, 61)

As we have seen, attempts to develop public journalism and establish public newspapers, which go back to the nineteenth century, have not been very
effective until today. The future success of new ideas does not depend primarily on the feasibility of their assumptions and technological possibilities but on
the relations of social power. Whether or not citizens can acquire communicative power largely depends on the reduction of *externally* (primarily economically) produced inequalities in individuals' education, knowledge, wants,
and customs.

A sample solution of societal regulation to materialize the idea of the right to
publish opinions as the basis of the right to communicate is the idea of a *voucher
system*. A voucher system may guarantee equality of access to the media for all
citizens if they are provided with a voucher of a fixed "value" that they may contribute to any "opinion agent" (e.g., political party, interest group, association)
they want but is otherwise valueless (Brighouse 1995). The regulation should
of course prohibit market trading with vouchers, which is relatively easy to enforce. However, there are other persuasive arguments against the voucher regulation. A voucher system makes access to the public communication space more
useful to those in majorities than those in minorities: the larger the number of
supporters an option has, the greater its chance of gaining new adherents regardless of its relative rational preferability. Paradoxically, equal access to the
public space (media) for individuals itself yields unequal influence for individuals. This is congruent with the spiral of silence theory, which predicts that
when the media make one political option highly visible, individuals who initially did not support that option adopt the visible position as well. Obviously,
the voucher system would not solve the problem of unequal access of citizens
to the media; it might even make access more unequal and thus practically incite the spiral of silence process.

According to Harry Brighouse, the problem of unequal access might be better solved by the *fair marketplace of ideas*. The regulation should allocate *equal
time and space to each view* presented, or to each "public policy option," rather
than to each individual or opinion agent. This is an idealization; in practice,
space could normally be allocated only to political organizations (parties) or
tendencies (interest groups) that will de facto organize the allocation of space
to each issue. In other words, a number of individuals or parties who hold the
same opinion would receive altogether only one "unit" of time or space in the
media. This is not an entirely new idea. In 1926, Hayes argued that the U.S.
government should legally regulate the publication of newspapers in order to

support the development of an informed public opinion: according to Hayes, each newspaper should be obliged to give an equal amount of space to each of the four leading political parties in the last elections for the presentation of their ideas (Wilson 1962, 81). Many European countries regulate (public) television broadcasting in this way during parliamentary election campaigns. The ethical principle of fair and balanced reporting also reflects the same basic idea.

Yet there is a substantial difference between an ethical principle and its legal operationalization. In order to make a legal regulation effective, it should be based on *realistic assumptions*. The fair marketplace of ideas is based on three cardinal assumptions (Brighouse 1995), first, that the average level of individuals' will and willingness to be persuaded or influenced does not depend on his or her opinion and is about equal across adherents of different options. This seems a rather plausible assumption in a pluralistic society.

Second, each policy option or specific opinion on a given public issue requires equally complex arguments, and there is a symmetry of complexity between the arguments for and against the options. This, however, is very unlikely. Thus, allowing for different degrees of complexity, extra time should be given to more complex views, which is quite complicated and unrealistic in (political) practice. It may often be quite difficult to determine whether two options or opinions are (fundamentally) different or essentially represent the same option. It would be even more difficult to measure complexity of opinions or arguments. And it would be a hard task indeed to appoint a judge over this fair marketplace of ideas.

Third, the media should provide enough space and time for all existent options to be presented fully and accurately. This, again, is not likely at all, if measured by the time citizens are willing to spend attending public debates. It is quite likely, however, in terms of the availability and, primarily, information capacity of *new communication technologies*—cable TV, satellite TV, and computer-mediated communications (e.g., the Internet). Yet the available space and time must relate to public deliberation and debates rather than to individual expression of opinion (e.g., on the home page), which limits even the range of technological possibilities.

As Brighouse suggests, the problems of different complexity of arguments and limited time and space in the media could be partly resolved in an analogy with the parliamentary elections by the establishment of a threshold of support: only opinions having support above the threshold would be represented in the "fair marketplace of ideas" and not those below it (or they would be only partially). Thresholds are commonly used under proportional representation schemes for elections to legislative bodies of a limited size, or in the allocation of airtime to political parties during the election campaigns, so this is not an unusual restriction. But there is another fundamental problem with this idea: the massive wealth-based inequalities in terms of political influence and access to the media that exist in contemporary societies constitute a very substantial barrier for the implementation of the fair marketplace model. The power elites are not willing to give up their privileged access to the media. To make this model workable, extensive reforms of contemporary political, economic, and social regulations and practices would be needed in the first place.

Both the voucher model and the fair marketplace model represent attempts to separate opinion formation and expression in public debate from the basic inequalities among citizens that prevent them from having an equal opportunity to influence public affairs, in the same way that they have an equal opportunity to influence elections on the basis of their right to vote. Both propositions suggest that the only acceptable inequalities of influence in public discussion ought to be those arising from the power of a better argument and that socially produced inequalities should be minimized. The idea of equal availability of influence in the process of public debate clearly resembles Dewey's idea of an "organized public," but it expands it from face-to-face communication to the mass media. This may represent a bridge between Lippmann's emphasis on formal rules to which "outsiders" are sensitive and Dewey's emphasis on the need of full publicity in respect to all issues concerning the public and the assurance of freedom of expression. Yet both proposals lack of practical feasibility.

Unlike the two models discussed by Brighouse, James Fishkin's (1991) idea of *deliberative opinion polls* represents a kind of cross section between conventional public opinion polling, focus group discussions organized mainly by political parties (or research agencies in their behalf) to identify citizens' urgent problems, and direct democracy. Fishkin proposes the establishment of a public forum on the basis of public opinion polling—a random sample of citizens. Randomly sampled citizens ought to discuss in a series of meetings important problems defined or selected by themselves and question politicians they would choose; the debates should be broadcast by television. Unlike public opinion polls, individual opinions would not have equal value in these panels. Randomly selected participants could be interviewed before and after the discussion, which would help transcend the aggregate definition of public opinion in polling: the results of interviews would reveal how individual opinions are changed in the course of a free discussion.[14] In the long run, televised deliberative polls may threaten the monopoly of political elites and the media in agenda setting and thus significantly contribute to the democratization of public deliberations. Of course, Fishkin's proposal cannot ensure every citizen the right to participate in such discussions: what it can do, however, is *stimulate reasoning* about public issues among citizens at large.

Is the idea of the right to communicate as the fundamental principle of media regulation feasible at all? The affirmative answer to the question is in a *gradual progressiveness:* endeavors to democratize communication should be directed toward general societal and political reforms and reregulations of communication networks and mass media, necessary for the materialization of the passive and active right to communicate. The common denominator of these processes should be socialization of the central mass media and communication infrastructure, a process with three basic components: (1) social management and/or control of the media, (2) provision of financial resources (social information subsidies) for mass media operation on the principles of solidarity and reciprocity of all citizens, and (3) social influence (direct and/or indirect influence of citizens) on the formulation and implementation of communication and media policies and programs.

Socialization of mass communication denotes a process of reappropriating generic communication abilities and means by human beings in democratic societies. The modern history of socialism clearly disproved utopians who believed that it could be accomplished by a single action, once forever and even regardless of historical circumstances. Human and social relationships are far too complex to allow radical structural changes as a consequence of a single, one-dimensional action in any sphere of human activity, and there is no reason to believe that the communication sphere could be an exception. Thus there is little chance that abolishing private and/or state ownership of the media (or any similar action) would democratically reorder and genuinely socialize mass communication. Also, the idea of reappropriation cannot be understood in terms of property relations. In contrast to a commonplace equalization of socialization with a sort of nationalization of private property and its transformation into state or "public" ownership, the idea of the organization of communications as public goods does not imply the expropriation of the privately owned media. In his plea for the Great Community, John Dewey convincingly argued against socialists who demanded that "industry should be taken out of private hands," stressing that "the public has no hands except those of individual human beings. . . . The same causes which have led men to utilize concentrated political power to serve private purposes will continue to act to induce men to employ concentrated economic power in behalf of nonpublic aims" (Dewey [1927] 1991, 82). In other words, the demand that the media cease to be regulated by the principle of profit maximization and function for the benefit of citizens does not refer to the question of *ownership* but to that of *regulation*. Public service media are surrounded by private economy, which substantially limits their production autonomy (Negt and Kluge 1973, 191). As a consequence, even public service media react to the environment as business companies; for example, the results of the measurement of audiences become a sort of "television money" that determines the value of programming; they are managed according to managing principles used by any other company; and they are directly involved in transactions with private suppliers of programs and equipment that are often in a monopoly position. Hence the idea of socialization denotes *the need to acknowledge the specific nature of communication* and to liberate the (public service) media from their subordination to the principles of the free market. In this sense, socialization of mass communication is the precondition of the right to communicate as the individual's right and societal need.

In his pioneering book *Information Society as Post-Industrial Society,* Yoneji Masuda denoted the coming society as a society composed of interdependent "diverse voluntary communities," a "classless society, free of overruling power," a system with a "multicentered structure characterized by mutual cohesion" ([1980] 1983, 151). In the society to come, the private ownership of capital, free competition, and profit maximization as the key economic principles of industrial society ought to be replaced by "voluntary civil society characterized by the superiority of its infrastructure, as a type of both public capital and knowledge oriented human capital." The parliamentary system and majority rule as the main components of the political system in industrial societies ought to be substituted by participatory democracy; the political system should be founded on the principles of consensus, participation, and synergy, which pay regard to the opinions of minorities. All these and even more substantial changes that Masuda expected to see by the end of the twentieth century ought to result in a natural way from, or even be imposed by, the development of information technologies. Yet nothing has happened. Masuda's *computopia* is still (and primarily) a *utopia.* Technological revolution has never been *eo ipso* a soci(et)al revolution; without societal interests and society's will (or even against the ruling interests in industrial societies), technology by itself cannot produce revolutionary changes in social relationships.

I am not referring here to Masuda's ideas to criticize them or to prove how utopian they actually are. What seems to me significant is that the main problems he is discussing in *computopia* concern participation and social communication, opinion formation and expression. They are related to the fundamental assumptions of democratic communication, which have been discussed since the beginning of this century and were, for example, at the center of the controversy between Lippmann and Dewey in the 1920s. The ways and possibilities of democratic communication are fundamental to public opinion formation and expression; it is not by chance that, from the very beginning, the idea of the *regime of public opinion* (or opinion of the public) is closely connected with *freedom of the press*. For three centuries, newspapers and later the electronic media were a test case of possibilities of democratic communication and public opinion expression. But the fundamental and complex societal *assumptions* of the right to communicate were never materialized. Thus I must agree with Dewey that there is (still) no way to predict possible ways and degrees of participation of the masses in public opinion processes until "secrecy, prejudice, bias, misrepresentation, and propaganda as well as sheer ignorance are replaced by inquiry and publicity" ([1927] 1991, 209).

The global advance of information and communication technologies makes (at least from the technological point of view) access to communication means much easier than any technological solution in the past. However, instead of providing only passive access to the consumption sphere, democratization implies primarily the development of conditions for active participation, that is, a direct and indirect incorporation of citizens into the production and exchange of messages in different forms of communication from interpersonal communication to the mass media in which the individual can realize his or her interests and meet his or her needs in collaboration with others. Actual democratization is defined not only by the number of active participants in the communication processes but also by the expansion of the social basis of communication, that is, the new forms of communication and democracy contribute to the incorporation of heretofore excluded social categories and groups, for example, young people, women, socially, economically, or politically deprived groups, national, ethnic, linguistic, and religious minorities, and so on. In other words, democratization should eliminate the major sources of distorted communications and external sources of inequalities, for example, class and ownership privileges, gender preference, racial discrimination, age-grade exclusion, and political or professional elitism.

Ideas of a *radical diversity* in the new electronic media and, consequently, forms of communication in the postmodern age in general (e.g., in comparison with the newspaper as the typical medium of modernity) are in certain ways delusive. Despite all the changes indubitably brought about by new communication technologies, media, and networks, traditional or modern questions and processes of influence, consensuality, opinion expression, (political) competence, identity, freedom, equality, and media regulation continue to have fundamental importance in the communication development in postmodern society and still directly connect the communication sphere with that of politics. Beyond doubt, public opinion changes forms of political institutionalization, but it essentially preserves its democratic political significance. The changes are evolutionary rather than revolutionary; new communication technologies may indeed have a revolutionary character in the *technological* sense, but all its social consequences cannot transform the *cultural, political,* and *economic continuity.* All social revolutions in the past were likewise (alas!) not primarily a matter of technology and reason. Political public opinion has been inscribed in the foundations of democracy; the idea of its end is no more sensible and no less (though negatively) utopian than Masuda's image of an information society that we ought to enter at the beginning of the next millennium and leave behind all the burdens of controversies of the previous development. That is why the key issues of public/ness and public opinion generated in theoretical developments and controversies since the beginning of the twentieth century, starting with Tönnies, Lippmann, and Dewey, are not just the past that we can leave behind but are *the heritage we carry with us.*

Notes

CHAPTER 1:
PUBLICITY, THE PUBLIC, AND PUBLIC OPINION

1. Ginsberg's and Zaller's preference for "mass opinion" is not founded on the public opinion-mass opinion dichotomy, in which mass opinion is a *negation* of public opinion, as suggested, for example, by Tönnies (1922, 77–87) and later by Schmidtchen (1959).

2. Dewey conceives of the existence of officials as the "external mark" of the organization of the public, and the state is considered "the organization of the public effected through officials for the protection of the interests shared by its members" (Dewey [1927] 1954, 33).

3. At the dawn of public opinion polls Allport (1937) argued in the editorial of the first issue of *Public Opinion Quarterly* that with all other publics, it is never clear which individuals are "inside" the public and which are "outside," whereas national registers (e.g., the electoral register) make it perfectly clear.

4. However, Dewey ([1927] 1991) argued for the necessity of the transformation of "Great Society" into "Great Community," which would enable every individual to achieve a higher degree of participation.

5. It would be an exaggeration to attribute the authorship of this conception exclusively to Dewey, since his determination of the difference between the private and the public is not completely original. At least implicitly and not in relation to the public or public opinion, this differentiation can be found in Marx and explicitly in Engels's *Principles of Communism*. Engels's answer to the hypothetical question, What will be the influence of the communist social organization on the family? was that the abolition of private property would fundamentally alter the nature of the family, the relationship between the wife and the husband, and that between children and parents: "The gender

313

relationship will be changed into a purely *private relationship concerning only the persons affected* which the society is not allowed to interfere with" (Engels [1847] 1974, 377; emphasis added).

6. This was the most important reason for "publicity experts" to look for a new name for their work, public relations, with a positive (or at least neutral) connotation (Mayhew 1997, 202).

7. However, there is no commonly accepted distinction between opinion and attitude. The terms "attitude" and "opinion" are often used as synonyms, although social psychologists avoid using the term "opinion" in favor of "attitude." Thus Theodore Newcomb (1950, 176) suggested replacing the term "public opinion" with a more accurate one, which should be "group attitudes." Even Park ([1904] 1972) wrote interchangeably of "the public's attitudes" and "public opinion." Attitude is usually defined as "an individual's disposition to react with a certain degree of favorableness or unfavorableness to an object, behavior, institution, or event—or to any other discriminable aspect of the individual's world" (Ajzen, 1993, 41). As English and English ([1958] 1972, 293) argue, opinion is "intellectual," whereas attitude is "evaluative" (pro-con, positive-negative). In contrast to opinion, attitude is considered a hypothetical and operational construct: since it is not directly observable, it can only be *inferred* from measurable cognitive, affective, and conative *reactions* to the attitude object. Cognitive reactions are defined as expressions of beliefs. Although in social psychology, at least to my knowledge, believing is not contrasted with opining and knowing as distinct forms of holding for true, as conceptualized in the Kantian tradition (e.g., Tönnies), it is at least interesting to note that "attitude" is related to "belief" but not to "opinion." In my view, opinion is more complex than attitude, and it is objectively a more certain form of holding for true than belief (it is a more rational concept), although the latter might be more certain in subjective terms. According to the Oxford Dictionary, "attitude" came into English about 1710, thus later than "opinion" (but in the same way: from Latin via Italian and French), and at a time when the term "public opinion" had been already coined. For the history of the concept of attitude, see Fleming 1967. For a radical critique of the concept of attitude, see Blumer [1955] 1969.

8. Uncertainty should be considered both the cause of interaction and its result. However, the reduction of uncertainty can only be the consequence of, and the motive for, interaction.

9. Key distinguishes four types of consensus in relation to governmental action: (1) *supportive* consensus underpins existing governmental policies and actions; (2) *permissive* consensus permits government to act without fear of effective dissent but is not a direct antecedent of an action; (3) *decisive* or *directive* consensus is, in contrast, more than just an extensive agreement upon a question—it is a "consensual product of the confrontation of opposing ideas," a *compromise* that calls for immediate action; (4) *multiple* consensus is formed in all political groupings and structural parts of society and thus destroys popular support for factions of leadership that may oppose a policy ([1961] 1967, 29–39).

10. Many public opinion theorists were interested in the question of religious differences. Dewey, e.g., based the necessity of the elimination of religious issues from the domain of public opinion on the argument that in democratic societies religion passes from the public into the private domain because the consequences of unbelief become irrelevant for the broader community and not because of the impossibility of reaching consensus.

11. A typical example of such a restraint may be the exclusion of dissenting individuals or even whole groups from public discussion in nondemocratic societies.

12. Chaffee's conceptualization of coorientation is largely based on Carter (1965), who suggests reserving the term "coorientation" for the condition in which *two persons* interact with respect to *two objects* on the basis of an *attribute* relevant for the objects; the two objects and the attribute should be the same for both persons. Social interaction would mean "the more frequent condition in which two people are in some manner communicating with each other." Carter's idea of coorientation is based on the concept of attitude derived operationally from exclusive discrimination between two objects, or comparative judgment suggested by Thurstone. However, as Carter realizes, there is not much coorientation and interaction, so strictly defined, present in day-to-day communication.

13. For Park, however, this point can never be reached by the public because public opinion is not accepted as a *norm* by members of the public. Tönnies had a different view: opinion of the public is a form of social will and thus has a normative power in its own (ethical) field.

14. Huckfeldt and Sprague argue that "the overall change in interest and attentiveness is likely to be highest among those who do not regularly spend time on information search—the citizens whose opinions are likely to be least firmly tied to prevailing sentiment." Yet this would also imply that the least informed citizens are also the least conformable citizens (their opinions are not tied to prevailing sentiment); in fact, the opposite is the case.

15. In fact, Mayhew's "simulation" of a Parsonian reply to Habermas's critique brings us back to the ideas already present in early social-psychological balance models. Osgood's model, for example, deals with the attitudes persons hold toward a source of influence, or "influencer," and the objects of the source's assertions ("arguments"): a high confidence in a source may make its assertions acceptable despite the doubtfulness of its arguments, due to Festinger's mechanism of cognitive consonance.

16. Translator's note to §317 in Hegel [1821] 1971, 373.

17. Binkley (1928, 389) reports: "On the question when is opinion public, the round table was unable to come to a definite conclusion. The main points of disagreement were as follows: 1. whether there is and must of necessity be a single public opinion, or whether there may be a number of public opinions upon a given question; 2. whether opinion is public because of the subject matter to which it relates or the kind of persons who hold it; 3. what part of the public must concur in an opinion to make it public; 4. and must there be acquiescence by those who do not concur."

CHAPTER 2:
PUBLIC OPINION: THE SUBSTANCE OR PHANTOM OF
DEMOCRACY?

1. It is almost unnecessary to mention that the reader can find a comprehensive overview of eighteenth- and nineteenth-century theories of public opinion in Jürgen Habermas's anthological *Structural Transformation of the Public Sphere* (1962).

2. Great Britain is most often cited as an example of a civilized country, whereas Turkey is usually referred to as a typically noncivilized, barbaric country.

3. In Rousseau's words: "Je parle des moeurs, des coutumes, et surtout de l'opinion" (Rousseau [1762] 189, 276). This sentence is translated into English in different ways: "l'opinion" is translated as "opinion," "opinions," "public opinion," or is simply omitted. Elisabeth Noelle-Neumann ([1980] 1993, 82), in her interpretation of Rousseau's concept of (public) opinion as the custodian of morals and tradition, refers to the English translation (London: Nielsen 1953) in which F. Watkins mistakenly translates "l'opinion" into "public opinion." Elisabeth Noelle-Neumann used "opinion" and "public opinion" interchangeably in the interpretation of John Locke (see Peters 1995, 11).

4. Nevertheless, Rousseau clearly states that (1) the role of the censor is not to judge "the opinion of the people" but only to express it and (2) though censorship can contribute to the preservation of, for example, customs, it cannot change them.

5. And if these groups already exist, it is necessary (1) to ensure that there are as many of them as possible and (2) to prevent inequality among them.

6. Or in the positive formulation: "All maxims that *require* publicity (in order not to fail of their end) agree with both politics and morality" ([1795] 1983, 139).

7. Kant makes a sharp distinction between forms of rule *(forma regiminis)* and forms of government *(forma imperii);* democracy is a form of government that Kant considered despotic because it is not representative. Despotism is most tolerable when there is only one authority—in other words, the more autocratic, the more tolerable.

8. A century and a half later, Kant's concept would be adopted by one of the founding fathers of German science of journalism, Emil Dovifat ([1931] 1967, 117): "Opinion is still an insufficient 'holding for true' *(Fürwahrhalten)* which tends to establish through witnesses and confirmation."

9. The voice of the people is "the voice of God."

10. The debates of the sixth Rhineland provincial assembly.

11. In contrast to Tocqueville, whose *Democracy in America* he assessed—despite his general admiration of the work—rather critically ("it is not democracy in America he described, but democracy illustrated from America"), Bryce noted that "the tyranny of the majority does not strike one as a serious evil in the America of today" ([1887] 1995, 1567). Nevertheless, Bryce listed the tyranny of the majority, "which enslaves not only the legislatures, but individual thought and speech, checking literary progress, preventing the emergence of great men," among seven "clouds on the horizon" (p. 1569).

12. "It cannot absolutely be said that crowds do not reason and are not to be influenced by reasoning. However, the arguments they employ and those which are capable

of influencing them are, from a logical point of view, of such an inferior kind that it is only by way of analogy that they can be described as reasoning" (Le Bon [1895] 1930, 73). Yet Le Bon's contempt for crowds also extended to the crowds in parliamentary assemblies, which were characterized by "intellectual simplicity, irritability, suggestibility, the exaggeration of the sentiments and the preponderating influence of a few leaders" (p. 315).

13. In Freund's interpretation: "This opposition between community and society informs Tönnies's vision of the historical future. He considers socialism to be the achievement of mercantile and technocratic society, and at the same time appeals for a return to community. The class struggle, particularly the antagonism between capitalism and proletariat, constitutes the supreme form of antagonisms proper to society, but as such it also carries with it the hope of an imminent end to the anarchy which is characteristic of society and a rediscovery of the organic bonds which characterize communitarian life. The triumph of society, with its cosmopolitanism—the reign of public opinion—indicates its forthcoming dissolution, thanks to the expected reawakening of the vitality which is peculiar to organic will" (Freund 1978, 157).

14. Yet criticism also came from the opposite side. Carl Schmitt ([1928] 1954, 249), for example, criticized Tönnies's concept of public opinion, which was in many respects similar to the concept of the American pragmatists. Schmitt acknowledged that it was "the most important sociological research on the subject" but criticizes it for not fully advancing the political character of public opinion.

15. In 1934, George Gallup established in Princeton the American Institute of Public Opinion. By the end of 1936, opinion research had its first great triumph with Gallup's correct prediction of Roosevelt's victory in the U.S. presidential elections. In January 1937, the first issue of *Public Opinion Quarterly* was published at Princeton. The founder of the journal, Harword Childs, and its editor, Hadley Cantril, both professors at Princeton University, were also colleagues of Gallup. The introductory issue included Floyd H. Allport's article "Toward a Science of Public Opinion."

16. Childs (1965, 49–50) enumerated the following "major categories of the subject matter" discussed by *Public Opinion Quarterly*, which indicate trends in public opinion study and research: A. Public Opinion Polls, B. Public Opinion of Selected Groups on Specific Issues, C. Influence of Selected Factors in Formation of Public Opinion, D. Voting Behavior, E. Communication, F. Propaganda, G. Research, H. Theory. The latter category includes the following subcategories: 1. Definitions, 2. Models, 3. Hypotheses.

17. Allport's construction is as follows: "Those who have a common interest are said to constitute a 'public.' . . . This public becomes coterminous with the spread of an opinion upon certain issues. The public, in other words, would be defined as the number of people holding a certain opinion, and the people holding that opinion would be identified as those belonging to the public" (Allport 1937, 9). He even refers to Dewey, who supposedly "has recognized this confusion in the notion of the public" in his book *The Public and Its Problems*. But, in fact, Dewey intensely defended the concept of the public, which is "organized in and through those officers who act in behalf of its interests" (Dewey [1927] 1991, 28).

18. Obviously, Robert Park's (1904) book was forgotten by that time.

19. I enclosed Lyotard's term "consensus" in quotation marks because he should rather name it "agreement." As I have shown earlier, consensus substantially differs from agreement because, in contrast to agreement, it does not presuppose the abolishment of opinion differences. Neither it can be equated with majority opinion. Rather, consensus is defined in terms of minimizing the sum of differences among those participating in a discourse, or in society in general. In this sense, consensus is the purpose of a dialogue when a decision has to be made, for example, for the reason of regulating long-term social consequences of individual transactions, as discussed by Dewey (1927).

20. The "revisions" first appeared in the introduction to the German Suhrkamp edition published in 1990.

21. See, for example, Thompson 1990; Peters 1995; Mayhew 1997.

22. Anderson's conceptualization of imagined communities may also help explain why public opinion is so closely related to the idea of nation. See Anderson [1983] 1991, 11.

23. However, the very first market research was conducted much before Lazarsfeld; it is attributed to the advertising firm Ayer and Son, which in 1879 documented for a manufacturer of threshing equipment the quantity of threshable grain produced in the United States (Mayhew 1997, 196).

CHAPTER 3:
PUBLIC OPINION AS A FORM OF SOCIAL WILL:
TÖNNIES'S *CRITIQUE OF PUBLIC OPINION*

1. Except for shorter periods, Tönnies never lectured at universities despite his qualification *(Habilitation)* in 1881. Because of his liberal and materialist-rationalist views, the Prussian minister of education did not grant him a professorship until 1911, from which Tönnies retired only five years later (Rudolph 1995, 42–46). Thus Tönnies was without students who could have continued to develop his theoretical thought over time. His articles published before the appearance of *Critique* suggest that he had been systematically interested in public opinion; but they were scattered in various scientific journals, ranging from economics to psychology (Rudolph 1995, 239–43). Last but not least, his *Critique* was never published in English and thus remained out of reach for a significant part of the world, most of all the American academic community. Only parts of his article "Power and Value of Public Opinion" were published in an English translation from his extensive opus on public opinion. (Another good example of the consequences of such "isolation" is Habermas's *Strukturwandel der Öffentlichkeit,* which was published in Germany in 1962 and translated into English in 1989. Before 1989 his work was almost unknown among English-speaking scholars; after it was translated, it practically entered the basic literature overnight and has been reprinted seven times in six years; cf. Strum 1994.)

2. Only a few fragmentary references and only five more or less complete presentations of his ideas on public opinion were published between 1925 and 1997. For instance, following D. Koigen's (1925) review of *Kritik der öffentlichen Meinung* in the

German journal *Ethos,* Paul A. Palmer (1938) introduced the work to the English-speaking world after Tönnies's death in 1936. Later treatments appeared in Wilson's *Theories of Public Opinion* (1962), Gillian Lindt-Gollin and Albert E. Gollin's contribution to a Tönnies reader, edited by Werner J. Cahnman in 1973, and particularly in Hanno Hardt's *Social Theories of the Press: Early German and American Perspectives* (1979). Tönnies's ideas are present in major discussions of public opinion in the works of William Albig (1939; 1956), John Keane (1982; 1984), and Horst Pöttker (1993), who carried out a comparative analysis of Tönnies's and Noelle-Neumann's conceptualizations of public opinion. Examinations of Tönnies's sociological theory (e.g., Merz-Benz 1995; Rudolph 1995) completely overlook his theory of public opinion.

3. Understanding opinion of the public as social will also include an important dimension of social control, characteristic for all forms of social will; conceiving of public opinion as (merely) social control is characteristic of Elisabeth Noelle-Neumann's work and her spiral of silence.

4. It is probably redundant to stress that Tönnies compares public opinion with religion in a narrow sense—a system of concepts about God, world, and human beings related to specific forms of behavior, rituals, and norms of behavior in life generally, that is, as a system publicly presented (in the sense of "representative publicness") and symbolized by various "sacred things." Nevertheless, in practice it is nearly impossible to separate religion from the church or religious groups, organizations, and institutions (e.g., cults, sects) that behave as subjects of religion.

5. Distinguishing between Gemeinschaft and Gesellschaft apparently resembles Durkheim's differentiation between "mechanical solidarity," which characterizes primitive social structures, and "organic solidarity," which describes modern differentiated structures. Actually, Tönnies's concept of Gesellschaft signifies mechanical, instrumental, and rational relationships in societies, whereas Gemeinschaft indicates traditional organic bonds. About Tönnies's theoretical definition of the concept of Gemeinschaft, see, e.g., Rudolph 1995, 142–55.

6. A parallel between the public and the religious may be found in John Dewey ([1927] 1991) and Hannah Arendt ([1958] 1989). Dewey discusses the transfer of religious rites and beliefs from public to private domain as a consequence of the loss of the constitutive nature of religion for the entire community. "As long as the prevailing mentality thought that the consequences of piety and irreligion affected the entire community, religion was of necessity a public affair. Scrupulous adherence to the customary cult was of the highest political import." Accordingly, temples were public buildings as were formerly the agora in Greece and forum in Rome, and priests were "public officials" (p. 49). Arendt, on the other hand, compares feudalism with ancient Greece and Rome: in the Middle Ages, the Catholic Church "offered men a substitute for the citizenship which had formerly been the prerogative of municipal government." The rise from the private to the religious after the downfall of the Roman Empire corresponded in many ways, according to Arendt, to the rise from the private to the public in antiquity (p. 34).

7. Tönnies also clarifies the contrast between organic and reflexive wills with the difference between two forms of property, depending on whether the property is a matter of organic or reflexive will: "The property of an organic will is so deeply attached to

the essence of a person, with his/her soul, that parting with it necessarily creates a feeling of discomfort. The property of a reflexive will, to the contrary, causes happiness only in as much as it has the desirable result as an unconditionally desired consequence: this means that happiness effaces and often even compensates for the discomfort that is present also here" (Tönnies 1926, 19–20).

8. Wilhelm Bauer similarly, though less clearly, argued that public opinion "articulates and formulates not only the deliberative judgments of the rational elements within the collectivity but the evanescent *common will*, which somehow integrates and momentarily crystallizes the sporadic sentiments and loyalties of the masses of the population" (W. Bauer [1933] 1963, 670; emphasis added).

9. Tönnies encountered the distinction between public opinion and the opinion of the public in Löbl's book, *Kultur und Presse,* published in 1903, after he had already started to make the distinction between these concepts himself. See Tönnies 1922, 132.

10. Obviously this confusion is often due to printing errors, although this is not always the case. In his article about American sociology, for example, Tönnies refers to the title of his own book as "Kritik der Öffentlichen Meinung," which would signify a critique of his own theory of opinion of the public.

11. Tönnies translates Bryce's term "public opinion" as "die Öffentliche Meinung" (see Bryce [1888] 1995, and Tönnies 1922, 324–34).

12. A good example of translation problems is the English translation of Tönnies's article "Macht und Wert der Öffentlichen Meinung," in which the translator differentiates only between "public opinion" and "the public opinion."

13. Tönnies's distinction is similar to Robert Park's differentiation between the public and the crowd; see Park [1904] 1972. Conceptualizations of the difference between the mass and the public were characteristic of turn-of-the-century intellectual (primary social-psychological) discussions.

14. Schmidtchen's definition of public opinion as "an aggregate of relational phenomena" and "something which politically exists only in certain relations between the ruling power and the people" (Schmidtchen 1959, 255) is a typical example of difficulties pointed out by Tönnies: Schmidtchen merely indicates where public opinion can be found and does not define what it actually is.

15. An analogous idea is found in Wilson, who says that results of public opinion polls, even though they do not represent public opinion, nevertheless represent demands that political power must respect; they also limit the arbitrariness of power—which is the function of public opinion (or, rather, of an opinion of the public, according to Tönnies).

16. As an example of relying too much on "common sense," that is, on shallow carelessness, Tönnies quotes Bauer, who speaks of the "large city Massachussetts" (Tönnies 1916, 420 n.).

17. The concept of a large public was later adopted by Habermas ([1962] 1995, 37).

18. "The true public . . . has to purge itself of the self-interested groups who become confused with it." Tönnies knew Lippmann's work; he reviewed *Public Opinion,* issued the same year as his own *Critique,* for *Weltwirtschaftliches Archiv* in an article on American sociology (1927).

19. Moreover, Habermas mentions a possibility that some kind of new "critical publicity" could be initiated by mutual control of competing organizations, such as political parties and organized private interests ([1962] 1995, 209–210) which is, nevertheless, unrelated to any specific feature of the new media.

20. Wilhelm Bauer, *Die öffentliche Meinung und ihre geschichtlichen Grundlagen* (Tübingen: J. C. B. Mohr, 1914).

21. Marx similarly argues in his famous discussion about freedom of the press that the press can only be free if it is regulated by the laws of its own sphere rather than other spheres of human activities. And he adds: "A writer certainly has to earn in order to exist and write, but by no means he should exist and write in order to earn. . . . A writer does not consider his works as a *means*. They are a *means in themselves,* and they are so far from being a means for himself or the others that he sacrifices *his own* existence for *their* existence if necessary" (Marx [1842] 1969, 92).

22. The same sort of observation was already made by Tocqueville in his book *Democracy in America* ([1840] 1995) in which (chap. 21) he stated that "the leading opinions of men become similar in proportion as their conditions assimilate: such appears to me to be the general and permanent law."

23. Tönnies has always sharply argued against an unscientific and forceful separation of the natural and human sciences, which explains his frequent, and not always successful (metaphorical), use of scientific terms borrowed from physics to define social processes. The tendency to use metaphors instead of definitions sui generis expanded with polling: polls are presented as a *weathercock,* a *looking-* or *weather-glass,* a *thermometer,* or *sondage* in French (from medicine and navigation; means probing or sounding) intended to measure the *climate, pulse,* or *temperature* of public opinion, but, in fact, they are much more than a neutral "measuring instrument"—they construe public opinion.

24. Like Tönnies, Wilson connects fluidity with controversies but durability with tradition, in contrast to Tönnies. Similarly, the behaviorist operational definition of opinion as an attitude in the sense of "an explicit response approaching or avoiding the attitude object" implies relative stability—an attitude is more than a momentary reaction to a controversial issue or to a question asked in a survey.

25. In his discussion of propaganda, Tönnies frequently and exhaustively refers to James Bryce's voluminous works *Modern Democracies* and *The American Commonwealth.*

26. Tönnies alternates between "daily public opinion" (1922, 178) and "daily opinion of the public" (1922, 249).

CHAPTER 4:
PUBLIC OPINION AND PARTICIPATION:
THE DEWEY-LIPPMANN CONTROVERSY

1. In fact, Dewey wrote his book in reply to Lippmann's contemptuous attitudes toward the public and democratic ideals developed in his *Phantom Public.* Dewey

reviewed Lippmann's book in *New Republic* in December 1925; a month later, he gave a series of lectures on these issues at Kanyon College, which he edited and published in 1927 as *The Public and Its Problems,* in which he acknowledged his indebtedness to Lippmann's work "for ideas involved in my entire discussion even when it reaches conclusions diverging from his" (Dewey [1927] 1991, 117 n.).

2. Dewey postulated that "only if we start from a community as a fact, grasp the fact in thought so as to clarify and enhance its constituent elements, can we reach an idea of democracy which is not utopian" (Dewey [1927] 1991, 149).

3. Yet voting participation is a very specific, restrictive, and routine form of participation. Participation in polls (which does not depend primarily on the participants) has a similar character. Thus the major locus of the relation between public opinion and political participation is the "influence framework," i.e., public discussion on controversial issues.

4. Dewey does not use the term "state" in the sense of a concrete (modern) political *structure* or a system of institutions, but rather in the sense of general *functions* that are not only characteristic of the modern state but had to be performed in a certain way throughout history.

5. Dewey also sees significance in the fact that etymologically, "private" is defined in opposition to "official," a private person being one deprived of public position (p. 15).

6. Much later, this idea reappears in Habermas: "The political public sphere can fulfill its function of perceiving and thematizing encompassing social problems only insofar as it develops out of the communication taking place among *those who are potentially affected.* It is carried by a public recruited from the entire citizenry" ([1992] 1997, 365).

7. This also holds true for private ownership, which, like public ownership, can have socially favorable consequences; what is important is the regulation of the consequences, not the type of ownership itself.

8. Dewey does not specifically and explicitly define public opinion; nevertheless, it is obvious that Tönnies's conceptualization of opinion of the public is the closest to Dewey's ideas from among all his contemporaries.

9. The concept of community has a less specific meaning in Marx's than in Dewey's theory, but in either case it is close to Tönnies's concept of Gemeinschaft.

10. See also Dewey 1925, 54.

11. Dewey's almost blind confidence in social inquiry clearly contradicts his own assessment of the role of experts in the formation of the public, which is among the least utopian and the most critical parts of his discussion. Although Dewey, when speaking about intellectuals, clearly disagrees with Lippmann's trust in the impartiality of (political) scientists, his faith in autonomous and depoliticized social sciences actually resembles Lippmann's position.

12. Tönnies was markedly enthusiastic when he discovered that Lippmann made a difference between the plurality of public opinions and Public Opinion (with capital letters), but he wrongly perceived this difference as "the guidance of his work" (Tönnies 1927, 1**). In the first place, Lippmann's "public opinions" are not equal to Tönnies's "published opinions" and even less to "public opinion(s)." Lippmann's Public Opinion is not equal to Tönnies's "opinion of the public" (*die Öffentliche Meinung*). Tönnies partly blamed Lippmann for not clearly defining Public Opinion; thus, he had to rely

on "what a theorist can grasp," and that is "almost exclusively the opinion of a relatively weak minority (relative to the size of population) that can hardly be delineated and that acts as the intellectually dominant class, and it is certainly strongly influenced by politically and financially dominant classes which, in turn, [public opinion] affect." As was said earlier, however, Tönnies was a respectful critic and looked for commonalities rather than differences, which would help him to prove the validity of his own theory.

13. Wilson (1962, 82 n.) suggests that Lippmann's work was very influential in establishing the idea of publics in the terminology of public opinion studies.

14. Dewey would agree that public opinion only appears in a crisis situation "when it is not the product of methods of investigation and reporting constantly at work," which speaks in favor of the necessity to develop science and education ([1927] 1991, 178).

15. As noted earlier, Tönnies was so enthusiastic about Lippmann's use of capital letters that he believed there was no difference between Lippmann's concept and his own. Whereas the difference between Tönnies's Public Opinion (i.e., opinion of the public) and public opinion refers to the difference between two conceptual levels—normative and applied—Lippmann's difference is between private and publicly expressed or manifested opinions, as defined later by Harrisson (1940).

16. See, for example, Leyens, Yzerbyt, and Schadron 1994.

17. Lippmann defines public affairs as "those features of the world outside which have to do with the behavior of other human beings, in so far as that behavior crosses ours, is dependent upon us, or is interesting to us."

18. In his late (re)conceptualization of the public sphere, Habermas took a similar position by stressing a sharp separation between the roles of "the actors appearing in the arenas" and the roles of "the spectators in the galleries." The latter merely express favorable or unfavorable attitudes toward opinions formulated by the former ([1992] 1997, 374–75).

19. Making a distinction between insiders and outsiders is not always an easy task because the two roles are changeable in the course of time. That is why participation in the public is not permanent and why they are constantly being redefined in accordance to the controversial issue initiating the process of public opinion formation: "the actors in one affair are the spectators of another, and men are continually passing back and forth between the field where they are executives and the field where they are members of a public" (1925, 110).

20. Lippmann argues that elections based on majority rule historically and practically represent "sublimated and denatured civil war." Thus it was also argued that women should not be granted suffrage because they never carried arms.

21. Like the representative of the bourgeois class in Marx's *Debatten über Pressefreiheit und Publikation,* Lippmann considers a classical inconsistency that "community applies one ethical measure to the press and another to trade or manufacture," instead of treating the press as "a business pure and simple" ([1922] 1960, 321).

22. A technically more elaborate solution than that proposed by Dewey is Fishkin's idea of deliberative polls, which combines reciprocity characteristic of local communities with broad dispersion of participants typical of large (global) communities. This idea will be discussed in the final chapter.

23. Dewey assessed Lippmann's *The Phantom Public* as "a statement of faith in a pruned and temperate democratic theory" and "a powerful plea, from a new angle of approach, for democratization in governmental affairs" (Dewey 1925, 52, 53).

24. The notion of the new public has already been exposed to the inflation of meaning: in contrast to Aikens, Mayhew (1997) defines the new public as a postmodern version of mass.

25. The banal question already asked by Lippmann, that is, who has to pay for information—audiences, advertisers, or public funds—is becoming more and more important as new forms of information distribution develop. The significance of information subsidies, which is central to the problems of media diversity and access, will be discussed in chapter 7.

CHAPTER 5:
PUBLIC OPINION AS PANOPTICON:
A CRITIQUE OF THE SPIRAL OF SILENCE

1. Initially, Noelle-Neumann considered her spiral of silence a *theory of public opinion;* however, when faced with the criticism first expressed by Elihu Katz ([1981] 1983) and followed by many others, she presented the spiral of silence model as *not related to public opinion theory* (1985, 67).

2. Harrisson wrongly equated public opinion with a part of private opinion and subdivided it into (1) "the overt though often temporary opinion stated to a stranger by the private individual" and (2) "published opinion" in the newspapers (1940, 375), since he did not see the possibility that the opinion expressed (to strangers or in the media) by the private individual would differ from the opinion he had himself or expressed privately to his neighbors in primary groups.

3. A similar argumentation can be found in an early Habermas work on leisure, in which he points to the fundamental difference between the individual's free and individually disposable time. He criticizes the self-evident understanding of leisure as the time left after, and independent from working time. In contrast, he defines leisure in a developed capitalist society as a collectively disposable time, as "an artificially arranged system of rules one has obligatory to obey." Thus, according to Habermas, the majority of individuals cannot *have* leisure; rather, they can only *partake* of it (Habermas 1973, 63).

4. In probably the first systematic clustering of motives, McDougall identified eighteen main motives; one of them was "gregarious propensity," which equals to Noelle-Neumann's fear of isolation. Other attempts resulted in even longer lists of motives. See McClelland ([1985] 1995, 34–48).

5. In contrast to Noelle-Neumann, Susan Herbst (1993, 37), for example, persuasively argues that "quantitative data from polls and surveys are numerical symbols which have proven to be powerful, multilayered ones when used in political discourse."

6. Only in her response to the critics in the 1985 *Political Communication Yearbook,* Noelle-Neumann (1985, 70) admits that the two concepts should not be understood as being alternative and that elite (or effective) public opinion forms an "effective part of

public opinion in the comprehensive sense." However, she also stresses that public opinion does not necessarily "adopt the elite opinion," so it remains perfectly unclear what the role of elite public opinion is and how "public opinion in the comprehensive sense" is formed.

7. When briefly referring to Robert E. Park, a representative of the rationalistic approach, Noelle-Neumann ([1980] 1993, 223) cites an American monograph claiming that his dissertation on public opinion left Park exhausted and disappointed, and warns that "even today, a similar fate probably awaits authors who try to equate public opinion and rationality."

8. According to Weber, rationalization is a macrohistorical process that no society can evade. Thus the "derationalization" of public opinion suggested by Noelle-Neumann represents a historical regression. On the contrary, as Weber would argue, public opinion process is increasingly characterized by *instrumental rationalization*.

9. Moscovici stresses that this kind of selectivity is not related to any theoretical foundation; it merely reflects personal preferences of the researcher.

10. Lowell (1923, 167–68) exemplified this process with historical examples of Caesar, Bismarck, and Churchill.

11. In the *Oxford Advanced Learner's Dictionary of Current English* (1986) the verb *think* is defined as "use, exercise, the mind in order to form opinions, come to conclusions."

12. The difference between "animal society" and "culture" is similar to Tönnies's differentiation between organic and reflexive forms of social will, or between community and society: "Among humans reciprocity forces all individuals to accept uniformity in the formal aspects of social life, expressed in usage and fashion. This uniformity is purely formal and external; its importance dwindles the further the social forms are from the 'natural' forms of animal society. Thus in social life, in culture, it is seen that suggestive imitation—the primary form of reciprocity—only determines the style of life, but not life itself" (Park [1904] 1972, 43).

13. An interesting case is that Tönnies (1922, 200) used fashion as a metaphor of how easily public opinion, in contrast to the opinion of the public, may change; Noelle-Neumann takes fashion as a typical form of true public opinion: "Fashion should also be included among the forms of appearance of public opinion because it is more based on individuals' observation of the environment than on their own, and it only allows to choose between adaptation or isolation" (Noelle-Neumann 1979, 171).

14. See the recently published meta-analysis of survey studies on the spiral of silence by Caroll J. Glynn, Andrew F. Hayes, and James Shanahan (1997).

15. In his experiment, Solomon Asch (1951) put one person in the midst of seven confederates and asked each of them to identify among three lines the shortest one that was actually clearly distinguishable. The seven confederates were instructed in each trial to select an incorrect line, and then the experimental person had to make his choice. Asch found that thirteen, or one-fourth, of the fifty experimental persons selected the correct line in all twelve trials, despite the pressure to select the incorrect one; the next twenty-two experimental persons selected the incorrect line in one to five (i.e., less than half) trials; fifteen experimental persons selected the incorrect line in more than half of twelve trials, but no one selected it all twelve times.

16. Moscovici (1985, 383) reports that in a replication of Asch's study, two English authors exposed students (engineers, mathematicians, and chemists) to the influence of a unanimous majority of six confederates in a face-to-face situation, and they obtained dramatically different results: in only 1 out of 396 trials did a subject join the majority! The authors argue that the Asch effect is simply a product of specific time and culture.

17. See, for example, Tönnies 1922, 130; Lowell 1923, 121; Key [1961] 1967, 48; Harrisson 1940, 369–70; Kennamer 1990, 396.

18. Vincent Price and Hayg Oshagan (1995) give a very useful and systematic overview of various streams of social-psychological research that contributed (or may contribute) to public opinion research.

19. "Interest in something is, of course, a very vague term and usually does not refer to anything unambiguous. Sometimes one can plausibly assume that the measure of interest is also a measure of the importance of some implied future behavior or of some existing behavior or reaction" (Festinger, 1957, 147).

"By interest I mean . . . the 'run of attention.' Everywhere and always, certain interests, persons, or events are in the focus of attention; certain things are in fashion. Whatever has importance and prestige at the moment has power to direct for a time the currents of public opinion" (Park [1939] 1966, 172).

20. The difference between informational and normative influence is not related to Moscovici's differentiation between normative and coercive power. Both normative and informational influences operate to strengthen the cohesion of the group, and thus they can explain individuals' conformity but not negotiation and innovation.

21. Taylor operationalized the key variable in the model, conformity, as the willingness to donate money to the group that an individual favored rather than the willingness to speak out.

22. The original experiment comprised a majority of several "naive" subjects and a minority of two experimental confederates who looked at a series of obviously blue slides. When the two confederates claimed the slides were green, one-third of the experimental majority responded incorrectly that the slides were green.

23. As Elihu Katz ([1981] 1983) noted, "The Emperor's New Clothes" could be used as a classic example of pluralistic ignorance. In this H. C. Anderson fairy tale, a tailor duped a narcissistic emperor into believing that only wise men could see his new golden-threaded clothing, which actually did not exist. For fear of revealing their incompetence, the emperor's retinue thus acted as if they could see it; and so did the common people for fear of "negative sanctions." Only a child who had nothing to lose exclaimed, "The emperor is naked!"

24. Noelle-Neumann is familiar with the experiments on pluralistic ignorance and looking-glass perception conducted primarily in the United States. But she tends to limit validity of these tests to two extreme situations: (1) the polarization of public opinion or the division of society into two extreme opinion camps and (2) the "dual climate of opinion" that appears when "the climate the population perceives directly" differs from "the climate as portrayed by the media" ([1980] 1993, 124, 168).

25. A typical survey question used by Noelle-Neumann always included only two alternatives for each issue, for or against a political party, recognition of GDR, abortion, nuclear energy plants, and so on.

26. This is not to say that laboratory experiments are generally more appropriate than surveys. They are certainly *less* appropriate for the estimation of the absolute values of variables, e.g., the percentage of people who inaccurately perceive majority opinion. Yet they are more appropriate when we want to determine possible causes of some behavior, that is, the nature of relationship between variables. Unfortunately, a third form of data gathering—observation and participatory observation—is largely absent from behavioral studies.

27. For Wilson, public opinion as "the deep-seated and deeply felt social code of the masses exercises one form of control, but opinion as controversial must be less of an agency of social discipline. . . . On the other hand, propaganda seeks to shape opinion on both controversial and traditional issues . . . and it must assume that public opinion so formed will be an important agency of social control" (Wilson 1962, 108).

28. Primarily because Key's conceptualization of public opinion does not assume the existence of the public as any "particular sort of loosely structured association or other ghostly sociological entity," it was appropriate to justify polling as a method of research into public opinion. However, Key emphasized in his definition of public opinion its relevance for *governmental action.*

29. At the same time, similar attitudes against polling could be found in England and France. When *Bystander* commented on polling introduced by Harrisson's Institute of Public Opinion, it wrote, "This is called a Gallup survey and is probably one of the stupidest notions in existence. It suits America admirably, but it doesn't suit the people of this country" (Harrisson 1940, 379). In 1939, *Le Travailler de Gien* opposed to the alleged formation of Gallup's institute in France as though it might be appropriate for the "tractor country" (United States), but not for France (Blondiaux 1998, 281).

CHAPTER 6:
POLITICAL INSTITUTIONALIZATION OF PUBLIC OPINION:
CONTROVERSIES ON POLLING

1. Modern public opinion is, as a matter of course, conceptualized as a phenomenon closely linked with the *nation-state.* This self-comprehensibility was particularly emphasized by public opinion polling in which respondents are randomly selected from the population of citizens. Thus citizens represent a sort of "natural" population despite the fact that modern states at best exist no more than a few centuries (but often only a few decades or even a few years). Regardless of whether such equalization is justified or not, there obviously exist other forms of expression and representation of (public) opinion that are less (or not at all) institutionalized and involve relatively small numbers of individuals and/or groups.

2. Bryce ([1888] 1995) defines the following as the three fundamental forms of popular government: (1) government by the plenary assembly of citizens, (2) representative system, and (3) government by public opinion. According to Bryce, government by public opinion could be considered an attempt to apply the first form on a numerous population, or as a modification of the second form. Cf. Tönnies 1922, 323.

3. "Straw poll" is the name for sidewalk interviews with haphazardly selected respondents or mail surveys of available lists such as magazine subscribers, which newspapers used to supplement conventional news coverage of elections. According to *Encyclopedia Britannica*, "The straw poll began as an intermittent practice in U.S. journalism in 1824. In that year, the *Pennsylvanian* sent out reporters to inquire among the citizens of Wilmington, Delaware, whether they were going to vote for Henry Clay, Andrew Jackson, John Quincy Adams or William H. Crawford for president" ("Public Opinion Surveys," p. 744). Straw votes based on the principle of sampling have been conducted in the United States since the early 1900s, mostly by newspapers and periodicals. These early polls were concerned primarily with candidates, although some of them, especially the polls conducted since 1916 by the magazine *Literary Digest,* dealt, at times, with social issues. They were conducted by ballots printed in the newspapers or magazines, which readers could clip and return to the newspaper, by ballots left in stores, and by interviews. It was soon found that polls by clipped ballots could be and often were invalidated by impassioned party members or sympathizers who sent in large numbers of ballots in order to make a good showing of their candidate. The house-to-house method led to the first attempts to achieve a genuinely representative cross section of voters.

4. Yet straw polls were at their time clearly more democratic (or at least less exclusive) than general elections, since reporters took votes not only from potential voters (i.e., men) but also from women. See Herbst 1993, 78. Female suffrage was progressively introduced only after World War II.

5. It should be noted, however, that the first sharp critiques of polling (e.g., the one by Robert Lynd in 1940) were directed at assumptions about the democratic nature of polling and the participatory endowment of citizens.

6. For example, Susan Herbst (1993, 39) argues that "numbers *allow us* to communicate directly about the abstract notion of public opinion, just as IQ test scores *have enabled* educators to discuss something called 'intelligence'" (emphasis added).

7. The accumulation of social data has started much earlier; for example, the use of statistics about the population (birth and death rates) goes back to seventeenth-century England. See Hacking 1995, 16–17.

8. In 1928, the *American Journal of Sociology* published the well-known Luis L. Thurstone article "Attitudes Can Be Measured"; in 1932, Rensis Likert published in *Archives of Psychology* his important article "A Technique for the Measurement of Attitudes."

9. Hadley Cantril (collaborating with Gallup's institute) at Princeton and Paul Lazarsfeld at Columbia (working with the Roper Institute) have been the most important university promoters of survey methods and polls. See Blondiaux 1998, 227–37.

10. To predict the results of the U.S. presidential elections in 1936, Gallup used a combination of mail ballots and personal interviews with subjects selected on the basis

of quota sampling methods; his prediction underestimated the Roosevelt vote by 6.4 percent. Crossley developed a quota sample survey and likewise underestimated the Roosevelt vote by 6.4 percentage points. The Fortune poll, directed by Elmo Roper, used a weighted sample of only 4,500 people based on age, sex, geographical divisions, rural-urban districts, and economic class—and overestimated the Roosevelt vote by only 1.5 percentage points. On the other hand, *Literary Digest* mailed ballots to over 10 million respondents; 24 percent were returned. It predicted Alf Landon's victory with 59.1 percent of the popular vote and 370 electoral votes (and for Franklin Roosevelt 40.9 and 161, respectively). However, the prediction failed disastrously: Roosevelt received 60.2 percent of the popular vote and 523 out of 531 electoral votes. The straw poll was unreliable because the sample was not representative of the U.S. population: the mailing lists of *Literary Digest* were compiled from telephone directories and automobile registration files. Its circulation list contained over 20 million names. In the years 1916, 1920, 1924, and 1928, *Literary Digest* predictions based on polling showed an average error of 20, 21, 12, and 12 percent. After the *Literary Digest* debacle in 1936, the principle of sampling a representative cross section was no longer disputed, but the battles over what constitutes a representative sample quite properly became central. See Albig 1956, 180–82, 215.

11. In 1937, Tom Harrisson was an English anthropologist engaging in research on Borneo and New Hebrides when the idea occurred to him to use the same kind of methods to study his fellow citizens in England. Charles Madge, newspaper reporter and poet, established Mass Observation in England to explore the "mind of the masses." On February 12, 1937, the first thirty trained observers reported on their experiences of that day. Mass Observation has been interested persistently in what we call studies in depth, and in recording the variety of forms that make up the expression of opinions. In the first year, its observers reported on Coronation Day (May 12, 1937) the motives and fulfillments involved in smoking, pub going, and football (Albig 1956, 193).

12. In a similar presentation of historical developments in opinion expression, Herbst (1993, 61–66) summarizes them as a tendency toward "more structured techniques," in contrast to earlier "unstructured activities" (e.g., rioting), but she admits that structuring that is characteristic of polling, "may distance us from classical democratic notions of participation."

13. See Herbst 1993, chapter 7, for a detailed description of the development of crowd estimation in the United States. However, Herbst does not see a *fundamental (theoretical) contradiction* between *crowd* estimation and opinion of the *public*, as defined, for example, by R. E. Park. She discusses early crowd estimation practices as a historical form of "public opinion rationalization" that "indicated public opinion," while over the course of time (in the 1930s) it became clear that "high attendance at rallies was not necessarily an indicator of national public opinion" any more. Thus the impossibility of using crowd estimation to indicate public opinion is attributed to the emerging possibility that crowds are not "mobilized" but "manufactured" rather than to the *inherent contradiction* between the crowd and the public. The fact that *throughout history* police have been the most experienced and zealous "crowd estimators" is a cogent indicator of the latter position.

14. This also pertains to the present and the future: computer mediated communication may again affect the formation of public opinion and its nature.

15. Berger and Luckmann (1969) published a very illuminating discussion of institutionalization, or formation of institutions, its relation to habitualization, typification, historicness, and social control. I refer here to their complex definition of the concept of institution.

16. Albig quotes the results of a 1945 poll in Mexico, in which 81.2 percent of social scientists and 72.5 percent of journalists interviewed stated that public opinion polls had some influence on opinion.

17. Lemert (1981) reports how a study by Grothe of attitude changes among American tourists in the Soviet Union revealed the difference in respondents' differentiation between "Russian people" and "Soviet government" in the open-response items, whereas in the fixed-response items the object was the USSR. Whereas in the former case significant changes were found (increased favorability toward Russian people), in the latter case only insignificant changes were recorded.

18. "Dr. Gallup has always insisted that prediction serves a useful purpose, but without specifying what it is. One must conclude that the useful purpose is to demonstrate to commercial users of the polls that the data the pollsters report can be relied upon" (Rogers 1949, 122).

19. Similarly, Noelle-Neumann pointed out in her doctoral dissertation, which she defended in 1940 in Berlin, that in contrast to the United States, where public opinion polls had to be used in order to obtain information about people's opinions, "our biggest popular leaders had and have such a vital relationship with the masses they lead that they can comprehend them without such instruments of knowledge" (Noelle 1940, 1).

20. Rogers (1949, 40) argued that "voters are firmer in their preferences for and antagonisms against candidates than they are on issues. While he is in the polling booth, a voter will not mind nearly so much being against what he thinks is the prevailing sentiment as he may mind in giving his reply to a strange interviewer."

21. This argument is bounded to polling that gathers individuals' responses that express an *opinion,* that is, they are based at least on a certain level of *knowledge.* Questions structured like "Who is responsible, in your opinion, for yesterday's accident?" or "Which football team will win, in your opinion, in tomorrow's finals?" force the respondent to make a guess, like gambling, and they are not related to opinion formation. This type of "polling" was invented by the media, and its sole object is to produce attractive news.

22. Lindsay Rogers (1949) was the first to systematically criticize the unreflective practice of asking questions in polling. One of the most often reported cases of almost mysterious effects of variations in question wording on responses is that reported by Rugg (in Hogan, 1997), who analyzed split-ballot data gathered by Elmo Roper. Roper had asked half his sample whether "the United States should *forbid* speeches against democracy" and the other half whether "the United States should *allow*" such speeches. Whereas 46 percent of respondents opposed forbidding such speeches, only 25 percent of them would allow them—an astonishing difference of 21 percent! However, in a sim-

ilar experiment on "forbidding" or "not allowing" *pornographic films,* the effect of question wording disappeared.

In studying polls on abortion, Schuman and Presser found a difference of 15 percent in two surveys asking exactly the same question: "Do you think it should be possible for a pregnant woman to obtain a legal abortion if she is married and does not want any more children?" However, in one survey the question was placed after another question asking whether it should be possible to get a legal abortion "if there is a strong chance of a serious defect in the baby." In this case, the support for abortion rights in the other question was 15 percent lower than in the case when no such "introductory" question was asked (Hogan 1997, 169, 171).

23. However, from an action-oriented public opinion theory, this kind of interview response may be considered closer to a genuine (public) opinion expression than a methodologically faultless polling.

CHAPTER 7:
PUBLIC OPINION AND MASS MEDIA: QUESTIONS OF DEMOCRATIZATION AND REGULATION

1. G. H. Mead ([1934] 1962, 147) stressed the opposite side of the same relationship when he wrote that "[a] person who is saying something is saying to himself what he says to others; otherwise he does not know what he is talking about."

2. "Agenda setting" is commonly believed to be a recently developed concept. However, it goes back at least to Robert E. Park ([1904] 1972), who observed that "modern journalism, which is supposed to instruct and direct public opinion by reporting and discussing events, usually turns out to be simply a *mechanism for controlling collective attention*" (p. 57; emphasis added).

3. The passage continues with the following lucid thought, which is as valid today as it was seventy years ago: "The catastrophic, namely, crime, accident, family rows, personal clashes and conflicts, are the most obvious forms of breaches of continuity; they supply the element of shock which is the strictest meaning of sensation; they are the *new* par excellence, even though only the date of the newspaper could inform us whether they happened last year or this, so completely are they isolated from their connections."

4. A size of type.

5. Generally, the concept of public/ness is discussed in reference to European culture, but due to the lack of comparative research such a "self-worship" is very doubtful.

6. Strictly speaking, we may even see "dismediatization" in these processes, that is, a more direct access of political elites to the citizens through the media and the exclusion of intermediary organizations or "steps" in multistep communication flow.

7. It was probably Melvin DeFleur who first pointed to the fact that the relationship between the media and advertisers is based on a process that is more subtle and less visible, but nevertheless fundamental—the process in which the audience exchanges its

attention for what it receives from the media. "The distributor provides entertainment content (and often advertising), but the audience provides little back in a direct sense. However, it does provide its *attention*. In fact, it is precisely the attention of the audience that the distributor is attempting to solicit. He sells this 'commodity' directly to his financial backer or sponsor" (DeFleur 1963, 153).

8. To mention just one example from my own country, Slovenia, with a population of only 2 million. None of about 150 professional or scientific journals published in Slovenia could survive without substantial subsidies from the Ministry of Science. Similarly, without state subsidies a large part of other publications and cultural production (including movies) would disappear. Of course, the media providing services that the majority of consumers most desire would continue to exist, but this is probably not to say that all other media need state protection because they publish "words and ideas that trouble or confound," as Fowler and Brenner believe.

9. In this sense, civil society represents the "natural environment" of the public.

10. Why the regulation of communication and the media rather than the nature of the ownership (i.e., public, state, collective, private) determines the character of communication will be discussed later.

11. In a similar way, Csikszentmihalyi defines the difference between two ways in which "public opinion may be formed: The extrinsic process of public opinion formation exists when conscious agents of communication try to impose a certain set of beliefs or attitudes on the population at large. . . . Intrinsic opinion emerges out of more spontaneous, organic reactions, either to open debates or to concrete experiences" (1991, 292–93).

12. The "new" journalism is differently named, for example, public journalism, civic journalism, communitarian journalism, community journalism. It is not clear that the thing needs a specific name at all; Jay Rosen and Buzz Merritt agree that people could call it banana and get on with it (Black 1997, vii).

13. Considering all that has been said about the reduction of freedom of the press to entrepreneurial freedom, it cannot surprise us that some prophets of democracy, on the ground of freedom of the press, still regard even the internationally enacted citizens' right to reply as a repressive instrument because it "could force papers to double in size, making printing and distribution costs soar," and that would of course "endanger freedom of the press" (Schmidt 1996). Not press freedom but rather the entrepreneurial freedom of its owners!

14. In January 1996, Fishkin assembled 450 randomly selected U.S. citizens at the "deliberative poll" organized at the University of Texas at Austin. Six hours of proceedings were broadcast on the Public Broadcasting System. Mayhew (1997, 265) reports that the event had little effect on public consciousness, but several defenders of conventional public opinion polls considered the experiment subversive because participants in the discussion influenced each other, which violates (1) the basic principle of random sampling, that is, the independence of units, and (2) the principle of equal value of all individual opinions, which critics call undemocratic.

References

Adorno, Theodor W., and Max Horkheimer. [1956] 1980. *Sociološke studije (Soziologische Exkurse)*. Zagreb: Skolska knjiga.

Aikens, G. Scott. 1996. The Democratization of Systems of Public Opinion Formation. Paper presented at the International Symposium on Technology and Society, Princeton University, Princeton, N.J., June 21–22.

Ajzen, Icek. 1993. Attitude Theory and the Attitude-Behavior Relation. In *New Directions in Attitude Measurement*, edited by D. Krebs and P. Schmidt, 41–57. Berlin: Walter de Gruyter.

Albig, William. 1939. *Public Opinion*. New York: McGraw-Hill.

Albig, William. 1956. *Modern Public Opinion*. New York: McGraw-Hill.

Allport, Floyd H. 1937. Toward a Science of Public Opinion. *Public Opinion Quarterly* 1, 1:7–23.

Anderson, Benedict. [1983] 1991. *Imagined Communities: Reflections on the Origins and Spread of Nationalism*. London: Verso.

Andrén, Gunnar. 1993. A Concept of Freedom of Expression for Superindustrialized Societies. In *Communication and Democracy*, edited by S. Splichal and J. Wasko, 55–68. Norwood, N.J.: Ablex.

Arato, Andrew, and Jean Cohen. 1996. The Rise, Decline, and Reconstruction of the Concept of Civil Society. *Politična dumka—Political Thought* (Kiev) 1: 134–138.

Arendt, Hannah. [1958] 1989. *The Human Condition*. Chicago: University of Chicago Press.

Aronowitz, Stanley. 1993. Is a Democracy Possible? The Decline of the Public in the American Debate. In *The Phantom Public Sphere*, edited by B. Robins, 75–92. Minneapolis: University of Minnesota Press.

Asch, Solomon E. 1951. Effects of Group Pressure upon the Modification and Distortion of Judgments. In *Groups, Leadership and Men*, edited by H. Guetzkow, 177–190. New York: Russell and Russell.

Axford, Barrie, and Richard Huggins. 1999, in press. Public Opinion and Postmodern Populism: A Crisis of Democracy or the Transformation of Democratic Governance? In *Vox Populi—Vox dei?* Edited by S. Splichal. Cresskill, N.J.: Hampton.

Bagdikian, Ben H. 1983. *The Media Monopoly.* Boston: Beacon.

Baker, K. M. 1990. Public Opinion as Political Invention. In *Inventing the French Revolution: Essays on French Political Culture in the Eighteenth Century,* 167–199. Cambridge: Cambridge University Press.

Baran, Paul, and Paul Sweezy. [1967] 1978. *Monopolni kapital (Monopoly Capital).* Zagreb: Stvarnost.

Bašič Hrvatin, Sandra. 1996. Javnost in množični mediji. Ph.D. diss., Ljubljana: Fakulteta za družbene vede.

Bauer, Helmut. 1965. *Die Presse und die öffentliche Meinung.* München: Günter Olzog.

Bauer, Wilhelm. 1914. *Die öffentliche Meinung und ihre geschichtlichen Grundlagen.* Tübingen: J. C. B. Mohr.

Bauer, Wilhelm. 1930. *Die öffentliche Meinung in der Weltgeschichte.* Wildpark-Potsdam: Athenaion.

Bauer, Wilhelm. [1933] 1963. Public Opinion. In *Encyclopedia of the Social Sciences,* edited by E. R. A. Seligman, 669–674. New York: Macmillan.

Beaud, Paul. 1993. Common Knowledge. *Reseaux, French Journal of Communication* 1, 1:119–128.

Beaud, Paul, and Laurence Kaufmann. 1999, in press. Opinion Policing. In *Vox Populi—Vox dei?* Edited by S. Splichal. Cresskill, N.J.: Hampton.

Beniger, James R. 1986. *The Control Revolution: Technological and Economic Origins of the Information Society.* Cambridge, Ma.: Harvard University Press.

Beniger, James R. 1987. Toward an Old New Paradigm: The Half-Century Flirtation with Mass Society. *Public Opinion Quarterly* 51, 4, pt. 2:S46-S66.

Beniger, James R. 1992. The Impact of Polling on Public Opinion: Reconciling Foucault, Habermas, and Bourdieu. *International Journal of Public Opinion Research* 4, 3:204–219.

Bentham, Jeremy. [1791] 1994. Of Publicity. *Public Culture* 6, 3:581–595.

Bentham, Jeremy. [1787] 1995. *The Panopticon Writings.* Edited with an introduction by M. Božovič, London: Verso.

Berelson, Bernard. 1952. Democratic Theory and Public Opinion. *Public Opinion Quarterly.* Fall, 313–330.

Berelson, Bernard, and Morris Janowitz, eds. 1950. *Reader in Public Opinion and Mass Communication.* New York: Free Press.

Berelson, Bernard, Paul Lazarsfeld, and William McPhee. 1954. *Voting: A Study of Opinion Formation in a Presidential Election.* Chicago: University of Chicago Press.

Berger, Peter L., and Hansfried Kellner. 1981. *Sociology Reinterpreted: An Essay on Method and Vocation.* Garden City, N.J.: Anchor/Doubleday.

Berger, Peter L., and Thomas Luckmann. 1969. *Die gesellschaftliche Konstruktion der Wirklichkeit.* Frankfurt am Main: Fischer.

Bernays, Edward L. [1923] 1961. *Crystallizing Public Opinion.* New York: Liveright.

Bertalanffy, Ludwig von. 1971. *General System Theory.* Harmondsworth, U.K.: Penguin.

Binkley, Robert C. 1928. The Concept of Public Opinion in the Social Sciences. *Social Forces* 6:389–396.

Black, Jay, ed. 1997. *Mixed News: The Public/Civic/Communitarian Journalism Debate.* Mahwah, N.J.: Lawrence Erlbaum.

Blalock, Hubert M. 1960. *Social Statistics.* London: McGraw-Hill.

Blondiaux, Loic. 1998. *La fabrique de l'opinion.* Paris: Seuil.

Blumer, Herbert. 1948. Public Opinion and Public Opinion Polling. *American Sociological Review* 13:542–554.

Blumer, Herbert. [1946] 1966. The Mass, the Public, and Public Opinion. In *Reader in Public Opinion and Mass Communication,* edited by B. Berelson and M. Janowitz, 43–50. New York: Free Press.

Blumer, Herbert. 1972. Symbolic Interaction: An Approach to Human Communication. In *Approaches to Human Communication,* edited by R. W. Budd and B. D. Ruben, 401–419. Rochelle Park, N.J.: Spartan.

Blumer, Herbert. [1955] 1969. Attitudes and the Social Act. In *Symbolic Interactionism,* 90–100. Berkeley: University of California Press.

Blumler, Jay G. 1991. Broadcasting Policy in a Changing Information Environment. *Bulletin of the Institute of Journalism and Communication Studies* (University of Tokyo) 43:1–13.

Bobbio, Norberto. 1989. *Democracy and Dictatorship: The Nature and Limits of State Power.* Cambridge: Polity.

Boudon, Raymond, ed. 1993. *On Social Research and Its Language (The Heritage of Sociology)* by Paul F. Lazarsfeld. Edited and with an introduction by Raymond Boudon. Chicago: University of Chicago Press.

Bourdieu, Pierre. [1972] 1979. Public Opinion Does Not Exist. In *Communication and Class Struggle.* Vol. 1, *Capitalism, Imperialism,* edited by A. Mattelart and S. Siegelaub, 124–130. New York: International General.

Bourdieu, Pierre. 1985. Remarques à propos de la valeur scientifique et des effets politiques des enquêtes d'opinion. *Pouvoirs* 33:131–140.

Bourdieu, Pierre. 1991. *Language and Symbolic Power.* Edited and introduced by J. B. Thompson. Cambridge: Harvard University Press.

Bourdieu, Pierre. 1998. *On Television.* New York: New Press.

Borneman, Ernest. 1947. The Public Opinion Myth. *Harper's Magazine,* July 1947, 30–40.

Brighouse, Harry. 1995. Political Equality and the Funding of Political Speech. *Social Theory and Practice* 21, 3:473–500.

Bryce, James. [1888] 1995. *The American Commonwealth.* 2 vols. Indianapolis: Liberty Fund.

Bryce, James. [1887] 1995. The Predictions of Hamilton and de Tocqueville. In *The American Commonwealth.* Vol. 2, *1530–1570.* Indianapolis: Liberty Fund.

Buckley, Walter. 1967. *Sociology and Modern Systems Theory.* Englewood Cliffs, N.J.: Prentice-Hall.

Burke, Edmund. [1769] 1967. The British Empire and American Revolution. In *Selected Writings and Speeches of Edmund Burke on Reform, Revolution, and War,* edited by Ross J. S. Hoffman and Paul Levack, 46–112. New York: Knopf.

Cahalan, Don. 1989. The *Digest* Poll Rides Again. *Public Opinion Quarterly* 53, 1:129–133.

Cahnman, Werner J., ed. 1973. *Ferdinand Tönnies: A New Evaluation.* Edited and with an introduction by W. J. Cahnman. Leiden: Brill.

Calhoun, Craig. 1992. Introduction: Habermas and the Public Sphere. In *Habermas and the Public Sphere,* edited by C. Calhoun, 1–48. Cambridge: MIT Press.

Calhoun, Craig, ed. 1992. *Habermas and the Public Sphere.* Cambridge: MIT Press.

Carey, James W. 1982. The Mass Media and Critical Theory: An American View. In *Communication Yearbook 6,* edited by M. Burgoon, 18–33. Beverly Hills: Sage.

Carter, Richard F. 1965. Communication and Affective Relations. *Journalism Quarterly,* Spring, 203–212.

Chaffee, Steven H. 1969. Cognitive and Coorientational Theory in Communication Research. In *Mass Media and International Understanding,* edited by F. Vreg, 138–148. Ljubljana: Partizanska knjiga.

Childs, Harwood L. 1939. "By Public Opinion I Mean." *Public Opinion Quarterly,* April, 327–336.

Childs, Harwood L. 1965. *Public Opinion: Nature, Formation, and Role.* Princeton, N.J.: D. van Nostrand.

Chomsky, Noam. 1991. Force and Opinion. *Z Magazine,* July-August.

Cohen, Bernard P. 1980. *Developing Sociological Knowledge: Theory and Method.* Englewood Cliffs, N.J.: Prentice-Hall.

Cohen, Jean L., and Andrew Arato. 1992. *Civil Society and Political Theory.* Cambridge: MIT Press.

Coleman, James. 1978. Sociological Analysis and Social Policy. In *A History of Sociological Analysis,* edited by T. Bottomore and R. Nisbet, 677–703. New York: Basic Books.

Comstock, D. E. 1980. *A Method for Critical Research: Investigating the World to Change It.* Transforming Sociology Series, no. 72. Livermore: Red Feather Institute.

Converse, Philip E. 1962. Information Flow and the Stability of Partisan Attitudes. *Public Opinion Quarterly* 26:578–599.

Converse, Philip E. 1987. Changing Conceptions of Public Opinion in the Political Process. *Public Opinion Quarterly* 51, 4, pt. 2:S12-S24.

Cooley, Charles Horton. 1909. *Social Organization: A Study of the Larger Mind.* New York: Scribner's.

Coser, Lewis A. 1994. Consensus. In *Twentieth-Century Social Thought,* edited by W. Outhwaite and T. Bottomore, 108–109. Oxford: Blackwell.

Crespi, Irving. 1989. *Public Opinion, Polls, and Democracy.* Boulder: Westview.

Csikszentmihalyi, Mihaly. 1991. Reflections on the "Spiral of Silence." In *Communication Yearbook 14,* edited by J. A. Anderson, 288–297. Newbury Park: Sage.

Curran, James. 1991. Rethinking the Media as a Public Sphere. In *Communication and Citizenship,* edited by P. Dahlgreen and C. Sparks, 27–57. London: Routledge.

Dalton, Russell J. 1996. Democracy and Its Citizens: Patterns of Political Change. http://hypatia.ss.uci.edu/democ/papers/dalton.htm

DeFleur, Melvin L. 1963. *Theories of Mass Communication.* New York: McKay.

Deutsch, Morton, and Harold B. Gerard. 1955. A Study of Normative and Informational Social Influence upon Individual Judgment. *Journal of Abnormal and Social Psychology* 51, 629–636.

Dewey, John. 1922. Public Opinion by Walter Lippmann. *New Republic* 30:286–288.

Dewey, John. 1925. Practical Democracy. *New Republic* 45:2–54.

Dewey, John. 1931. *Philosophy and Civilization.* New York: Minton and Balch.

Dewey, John. [1927] 1991. *The Public and Its Problems.* Athens: Swallow.

Dovifat, Emil. [1931] 1967. *Zeitungslehre.* Vols. 1–2. Berlin: Walter de Gruyter.

Downing, John. 1984. *Radical Media: The Political Experience of Alternative Communication.* Boston: South End.

Eckhardt, Kenneth W., and Garry Hendershot. 1967. Dissonance-Congruence and the Perception of Public Opinion. *American Journal of Sociology* 73:226–234.

Engels, Friedrich. [1845] 1974. Die Lage der arbeitenden Klasse in England. In *Marx-Engels Werke,* 2:225–506. Berlin: Dietz Verlag.

Engels, Friedrich. [1847] 1974. Grundsätze des Komunismus. In *Marx-Engels Werke,* 4:361–380. Berlin: Dietz Verlag.

English, Horace B., and Ava C. English. [1958] 1972. *Obuhvatni rečnik psiholoskih i psihoanalitičkih pojmova (A comprehensive dictionary of psychological and psychoanalytical terms).* Beograd: Savremena administracija.

Ewen, Stuart. 1977. *Captains of Consciousness: Advertising and the Social Roots of the Consumer Culture.* New York: McGraw Hill.

Festinger, Leon. [1957] 1962. *A Theory of Cognitive Dissonance.* Stanford, Calif.: Stanford University Press.

Fisher, Desmond. 1981. *The Right to Communicate: A Status Report.* Paris: UNESCO.

Fishkin, James S. 1991. *Democracy and Deliberation: New Directions for Democratic Reform.* New Haven: Yale University Press.

Fishkin, James S. 1997. *The Voice of the People: Public Opinion and Democracy.* New Haven: Yale University Press.

Fleming, Donald. 1967. Attitude: The History of a Concept. In *Perspectives in American History,* edited by D. Flemming and B. Bailyn, 1:287–368. Cambridge, Mass.: Charles Warren Center for Studies in American History.

Foucault, Michel. 1977. *Discipline and Punish: The Birth of the Prison.* New York: Pantheon.

Foucault, Michel. [1976] 1993. Power as Knowledge. In *Social Theory: The Multicultural and Classic Readings,* edited by C. Lemert, 518–524. Boulder: Westview.

Fowler, Mark S., and Daniel L. Brenner. 1983. A Marketplace Approach to Broadcast Regulation. In *Mass Communication Review Yearbook,* edited by E. Wartela and D. C. Whitney, 4:645–695. Beverly Hills: Sage.

Freund, Julien. 1978. German Sociology in the Time of Max Weber. In *A History of Sociological Analysis,* edited by T. Bottomore and R. Nisbet, 149–186. New York: Basic Books.

Gallup, George H., and Saul F. Rae. 1940. *The Pulse of Democracy.* New York: Simon and Schuster.

Gandy, Oscar H., Jr. 1982. *Beyond Agenda Setting: Information Subsidies and Public Policy.* Norwood, N.J.: Ablex.

Gaonkar, Dilip Parameshwar, with Robert J. McCarthy Jr. 1994. Panopticism and Publicity: Bentham's Quest for Transparency. *Public Culture* 6, 3:547–578.

338   *References*

Garnham, Nicholas. 1990. *Capitalism and Communication: Global Culture and the Economics of Information.* London: Sage.

Gawiser, Sheldon R., and G. Evans Witt. 1994. *A Journalist's Guide to Public Opinion Polls.* Westport, Conn.: Praeger.

Ginsberg, Benjamin. 1986. *The Captive Public: How Mass Opinion Promotes State Power.* New York: Basic Books.

Ginsberg, Benjamin. 1989. How Polling Transforms Public Opinion. In *Manipulating Public Opinion,* edited by M. Margolis and G. A. Mauser, 271–293. Pacific Grove, Calif.: Brooks/Cole.

Glynn, Carroll J., and Jack M. McLeod. 1984. Public Opinion du Jour: An Examination of the Spiral of Silence. *Public Opinion Quarterly* 48, 4:731–740.

Glynn, Carroll J., and Jack M. McLeod. 1985. Implications of the Spiral of Silence Theory for Communication and Public Opinion Research. In *Political Communication Yearbook,* edited by K. R. Sanders, L. L. Kaid, and D. Nimmo, 43–65. Carbondale: Southern Illinois University Press.

Glynn, Carroll J., Andrew F. Hayes, and James Shanahan. 1997. Perceived Support for One's Opinions and Willingness to Speak Out: A Meta-Analysis of Survey Studies on the 'Spiral of Silence.' *Public Opinion Quarterly* 61, 3:452–463.

Gollin, Gillian Lindt, and Albert E. Gollin. 1973. Tönnies on Public Opinion. In *Ferdinand Tönnies: A New Evaluation,* edited by J. Cahnmann, 181–203. Leiden: E.J. Brill.

Gouldner, Alvin W. 1976. *The Dialectic of Ideology and Technology: The Origins, Grammar, and Future of Ideology.* New York: Seabury.

Graber, Doris. 1982. The Impact of Media Research on Public Opinion Studies. In *Mass Communication Review Yearbook,* edited by D. C. Whitney and E. Wartella, 3:555–564. Beverly Hills: Sage.

Graber, Doris A. 1984. *Processing the News: How People Tame the Information Tide.* New York: Longman.

Habermas, Jürgen. 1973. *Arbeit, Freizeit, Konsum.* Gravenhage: van Eversdijck.

Habermas, Jürgen. [1964] 1979. The Public Sphere. In *Communication and Class Struggle.* Vol. 1, *Capitalism, Imperialism,* edited by A. Mattelart and S. Siegelaub, 198–201. New York: International General.

Habermas, Jürgen. [1965] 1980. *Teorija i praksa (Theorie und Praxis).* Beograd: Kultura.

Habermas, Jürgen. 1981. *Theorie des kommunikativen Handelns.* Frankfurt: Suhrkamp.

Habermas, Jürgen. [1962] 1989. Javnost (leksikonsko geslo). In J. Habermas, *Strukturne spremembe javnosti,* 293–299. Ljubljana: Studia Humanitatis.

Habermas, Jürgen. 1990. Vorwort zur Neuauflage. *Strukturwandel der Öffentlichkeit.* Frankfurt: Suhrkamp.

Habermas, Jürgen. 1992a. Further Reflections on the Public Sphere. In *Habermas and the Public Sphere,* edited by C. Calhoun, 421–461. Cambridge: MIT Press.

Habermas, Jürgen. 1992b. *Faktizität und Geltung: Beiträge zur Diskurstheorie des Rechts und des demokratischen Rechtsstaats.* Frankfurt: Suhrkamp.

Habermas, Jürgen. [1962] 1995. *The Structural Transformation of the Public Sphere: An Inquiry into a Category of Bourgeois Society.* Cambridge: MIT Press.

Habermas, Jürgen. [1992] 1997. *Between Facts and Norms: Contributions to a Discourse Theory of Law and Democracy.* Translated by W. Rehg. Cambridge: Polity.

Hacking, Ian. [1990] 1995. *The Taming of Chance.* Cambridge: Cambridge University Press.

Hardt, Hanno. 1979. *Social Theories of the Press: Early German and American Perspectives.* Beverly Hills: Sage.

Hardt, Hanno. 1983. Press Freedom in Western Societies. In *Comparative Mass Media Systems,* edited by L. J. Martin and A. G. Chaundhary, 291–308. New York: Longman.

Hardt, Hanno. 1992. *Critical Communication Studies: Communication, History, and Theory in America.* London: Routledge.

Hardt, Hanno. 1996. The Making of the Public Sphere: Class Relations and Communication in the United States. *Javnost—The Public* 3, 1:7–23.

Harrisson, Tom. 1940. What Is Public Opinion? *The Political Quarterly* 11:368–383.

Hauser, Gerard A. 1985. Common Sense in the Public Sphere: A Rhetorical Grounding for Publics. *Informatologia Yugoslavica* 17, 1–2:67–75.

Hauser, Gerard A. 1997. On Publics and Public Spheres: A Response to Philips. *Communication Monographs* 64, 3:275–279.

Hegel, Georg Wilhelm Friedrich. [1821] 1971. *Philosophy of Right.* Translated with notes by T. M. Knox. London: Oxford University Press.

Heider, Fritz. 1946. Attitudes and Cognitive Information. *Journal of Psychology* 21:107–112.

Held, David. 1987. *Models of Democracy.* Cambridge: Polity.

Hennis, Wilhelm. 1957. *Meinungsforschung und repräsentative Demokratie: Zur Kritik politischen Umfragen.* Tübingen: J. C. B. Mohr/Paul Siebeck.

Herbst, Susan. 1992. Surveys in the Public Sphere: Applying Bourdieu's Critique of Opinion Polls. *International Journal of Public Opinion Research* 4, 3:220–229.

Herbst, Susan. 1993. *Numbered Voices: How Opinion Polling Has Shaped American Politics.* Chicago: University of Chicago Press.

Hočevar, Meta. 1996. Arhitektura je prostor sprave, scenografija pa prostor konflikta. Interview by T. Brate. *Razgledi* 24:2–8.

Hoffman, Ross J.S., and Paul Levack. [1949] 1967. Introduction: Burke's Philosophy of Politics. In *Selected Writings and Speeches of Edmund Burke on Reform, Revolution, and War,* xi–xxxvii. New York: Knopf.

Hogan, Michael J. 1997. George Gallup and the Rhetoric of Scientific Democracy. *Communication Monographs* 64, 2:161–179.

Holm, Kurt, 1975. Die Frage. In *Die Befragung,* edited by K. Holm, 2:32–91. München: Francke.

Holston, James, and Arjun Appadurai. 1996. Cities and Citizenship. *Public Culture* 8, 2:187–204.

Hopkins, W. Watt. 1996. The Supreme Court Defines the Marketplace of Ideas. *Journalism and Mass Communication Quarterly* 73, 1:40–52.

Horkheimer, Max. [1936] 1976. *Tradicionalna i kritička teorija (Tradizionalle und kritische Theorie).* Beograd: BIGZ.

Hoynes, William. 1994. *Public Television for Sale: Media, the Market, and the Public Sphere*. Boulder: Westview.

Huckfeldt, Robert, and John Sprague. 1995. *Citizens, Politics, and Social Communication: Information and Influence in an Election Campaign*. Cambridge: Cambridge University Press.

Hunziker, Peter. 1981. Gesellschaftliche Strukturbedingungen der öffentlichen Meinung. *Media Perspektiven* 7:515–520.

Irion, Frederick C. 1950. *Public Opinion and Propaganda*. New York: Crowell.

Jakubowicz, Karol. 1994. Civil Society, Independent Public Sphere, and Information Society. In *Information Society and Civil Society*, edited by S. Splichal, A. Calabrese, and C. Sparks, 78–102. West Lafayette, Ind.: Purdue University Press.

Jaworski, Adam. 1993. *The Power of Silence: Social and Pragmatic Perspectives*. Newbury Park: Sage.

Jensen, Klaus Bruhn. 1995. *The Social Semiotics of Mass Communication*. London: Sage.

Johnson, Nicholas. 1994. An Autonomous Media. Background paper prepared for the Commission on Radio and Television Policy-Aspen Institute Session, May 4–7, 1994, Aspen Wye Woods Conference Center, Maryland.

Jowett, Garth S., and Victoria O'Donnell. 1992. *Propaganda and Persuasion*. Newbury Park: Sage.

Kant, Immanuel. [1781] 1952. *The Critique of Pure Reason*. Chicago: Encyclopaedia Britannica.

Kant, Immanuel. [1784] 1965a. Beantwortung der Frage: Was ist Aufklärung? In *Immanuel Kant: Politische Schriften*, 1–8. Köln: Westdeutscher Verlag.

Kant, Immanuel. [1798] 1965b. Streit der Fakultäten. In *Immanuel Kant: Politische Schriften*, 151–166. Köln: Westdeutscher Verlag.

Kant, Immanuel. [1795] 1983. To Perpetual Peace. In *Immanuel Kant: Perpetual Peace and Other Essays*, 107–144. Cambridge, Ind.: Hackett.

Katz, Daniel. [1966] 1972. Attitude Formation and Public Opinion. In *Political Attitudes and Public Opinion*, edited by D. D. Nimmo and C. M. Bonjean, 13–26. New York: McKay.

Katz, Elihu. 1957. The Two-Step Flow of Communication: An Up-to-Date Report on an Hypothesis. *Public Opinion Quarterly* 21, 1:61–78.

Katz, Elihu. [1981] 1983. Publicity and Pluralistic Ignorance: Notes on "The Spiral of Silence." In *Mass Communication Review Yearbook*, edited by E. Wartela and D. C. Whitney, 4:89–100. Beverly Hills: Sage.

Katz, Elihu. 1987. Communication Research since Lazarsfeld. *Public Opinion Quarterly* 51, 4, pt. 2:S25-S45.

Katz, Elihu, and Paul F. Lazarsfeld. 1955. *Personal Influence: The Part Played by People in the Flow of Mass Communication*. Glencoe, Ill.: Free Press.

Keane, John. 1982. Elements of a Radical Theory of Public Life: From Tönnies to Habermas and Beyond. *Canadian Journal of Political and Social Theory* 3:11–49.

Keane, John. 1984. *Public Life and Late Capitalism: Toward a Socialist Theory of Democracy*. Cambridge: Cambridge University Press.

Keane, John. 1988. Despotism and Democracy. In *Civil Society and the State: New European Perspectives*. Edited by J. Keane. London: Verso.

Keane, John. 1992. *Mediji in demokracija*. Ljubljana: Znanstveno in publicistično sredisče.

Kennamer, J. David. 1990. Self-serving Biases in Perceiving the Opinions of Others. *Communication Research* 17, 3:393–404.

Key, V. O., Jr. [1961] 1967. *Public Opinion and American Democracy*. New York: Knopf.

Key, V. O., Jr., with Alexander Heard. 1949. *Southern Politics: In State and Nation*. New York: Knopf.

Klapp, Orin E. 1957. The Concept of Consensus and Its Importance. *Sociology and Social Research* 41:336–342.

Klapper, Joseph T. 1960. *The Effects of Mass Communication*. Glencoe, Ill.: Free Press.

Kracauer, Siegfried. 1952. The Challenge of Qualitative Content Analysis. *Public Opinion Quarterly*, Winter, 631–642.

Krassa, Michael A. 1988. Social Groups, Selective Perception, and Behavioral Contagion in Public Opinion. *Social Networks* 10, 2:109–136.

Kreiling, Albert, and Norman Sims. 1981. Symbolic Interactionism, Progressive Thought, and Chicago Journalism. In *Foundations for Communication Studies,* edited by J. Soloski, 5–38. Iowa City: Center for Communication Study.

Krüger, Hans-Peter. 1991. Radical Democratization. *Praxis International* 11, 1:18–36.

Kutzi, Jupp. 1962. *Propaganda und öffentliche Meinung*. Kempten/Allgäu: Albert Pröpster.

Lang, Kurt. 1979. The Critical Functions of Empirical Communication Research: Observations on German-American Influences. *Media, Culture, and Society* 1, 2:83–96.

Lasch, Christopher. 1995. Journalism, Publicity, and the Lost Art of Argument. *Media Studies Journal* 9, 1:81–92.

Lasswell, Harold D. 1957. The Impact of Public Opinion on Our Society. *Public Opinion Quarterly* 21, 1:33–38.

Lasswell, Harold D. [1948] 1966. The Structure and Function of Communication in Society. In *Reader in Public Opinion and Communication,* edited by B. Berelson and M. Janowitz, 178–190. New York: Free Press.

Lasswell, Harold D. 1981. Nations and Classes: The Symbols of Identification. In *Reader in Public Opinion and Mass Communication,* edited by M. Janowitz and P. Hirsch, 17–28. 3d ed. New York: Free Press.

Laufer, Romain, and Catherine Paradeise. 1990. *Marketing Democracy: Public Opinion and Media Formation in Democratic Societies*. New Brunswick: Transaction.

Lazareff, Alexandre. 1984. *Le droit des sondages politiques*. Paris: LDJ.

Lazarsfeld, Paul. 1957. Public Opinion and Classical Tradition. *Public Opinion Quarterly* 21, 1:39–53.

Lazarsfeld, Paul, Bernard Berelson, and Hazel Gaudet. 1940. *The People's Choice*. New York: Columbia University Press.

Le Bon, Gustave. [1895] 1930. *The Crowd: A Study of the Popular Mind*. London: Ernest Benn.

Lemert, James B. 1981. *Does Mass Communication Change Public Opinion after All? A New Approach to Effects Analysis*. Chicago: Nelson-Hall.

Leyens, Jacques-Philippe, Vincent Yzerbyt, and Georges Schadron. 1994. *Stereotypes and Social Cognition.* London: Sage.

Lindt-Gollin, Gillian, and Albert E. Gollin. 1973. Tönnies on Public Opinion. In *Ferdinand Tönnies: A New Evaluation,* edited by W. J. Cahnman, 181–203. Leiden: Brill.

Lippmann, Walter. 1925. *The Phantom Public.* New York: Harcourt, Brace.

Lippmann, Walter. [1922] 1960. *Public Opinion.* New York: Macmillan.

Lowell, Abbott Lawrence. 1923. *Public Opinion in War and Peace.* Cambridge: Harvard University Press.

Lowery, Shearon, and Melvin L. DeFleur. 1983. *Milestones in Mass Communication Research: Media Effects.* New York: Longman.

Luhmann, Niklas. 1969. *Legitimation durch Verfahren.* Neuwied: Luchterhand.

Luhmann, Niklas. 1971. Systemtheoretische Argumentation. In *Theorie der Gesellschaft oder Sozialtechnologie.* Edited by J. Habermas and N. Luhmann. Frankfurt: Suhrkamp.

Luhmann, Niklas. 1974. Öffentliche Meinung. In *Zur Theorie der politischen Kommunikation.* Edited by W. R. Langenbucher. München: R. Piper Verlag.

Luhmann, Niklas. 1994. An Interview with David Sciulli. *Theory, Culture, and Society* 11, 2:37–69.

Luhmann, Niklas. 1996. *Die Realität der Massenmedien.* Opladen: Westdeutscher Verlag.

Lukes, Steven. 1994. Power. In *Twentieth-Century Social Thought,* edited by W. Outhwaite and T. Bottomore, 504–505. Oxford: Blackwell.

Luthar, Breda. 1996. Analiza medijskih vplivov v semiotični družbi. *Teorija in praksa* 33, 2:181–193.

Lynd, Robert S. 1940. Democracy in Reverse. *Public Opinion Quarterly* 4, 2:218–220.

Lyotard, Jean-Franҫois. 1979. *La condition postmoderne.* Paris: Minuit.

MacKinnon, William A. [1828] 1971. *On the Rise, Progress, and Present State of Public Opinion, in Great Britain, and Other Parts of the World.* Shannon: Irish University Press.

Mander, Jerry. 1978. *Four Arguments for the Elimination of Television.* New York: Quill.

Marx, Karl. [1842] 1969. Die Verhandlungen des 6. rheinischen Landtags. In *Pressefreiheit und Zensur,* by K. Marx and F. Engels, 44–99. Frankfurt: Europäische Verlagsanstalt.

Marx, Karl. [1842] 1974. Debatten über Pressefreiheit und Publikation der Landständischen Verhandlungen. In *Marx-Engels Werke,* 1:28–77. Berlin: Dietz Verlag.

Marx, Karl. [1843] 1974. Zur Kritik der Hegelschen Rechtsphilosophie. In *Marx-Engels Werke,* 1:202–336. Berlin: Dietz Verlag.

Marx, Karl. [1905] 1974. Theorien über den Mehrwert. In *Marx-Engels Werke,* 26:1. Berlin: Dietz Verlag.

Masuda, Yoneji. [1980] 1983. *The Information Society as Post-Industrial Society.* Washington, D.C.: World Future Society.

Mattelart, Armand, and Jean-Marie Piemme. 1984. Twenty-Three Guidelines for a Political Debate on Communication in Europe. In *The Critical Communications Review.* Vol. 2, *Changing Patterns of Communications Control,* edited by V. Mosco and J. Wasko, 211–223. Norwood, N.J.: Ablex.

Maus, Heinz. 1973. Zur Vorgeschichte der empirischen Sozialforschung. In *Handbuch der empirischen Sozialforschung,* edited by R. König, 1:21–56. Stuttgart: Ferdinand Enke Verlag.

Mayhew, Leon H. 1997. *The New Public: Professional Communication and the Means of Social Influence.* Cambridge: Cambridge University Press.

McClelland, David C. [1985] 1995. *Human Motivation.* Cambridge: Cambridge University Press.

McDougall, William. 1920. *The Group Mind.* New York: Putnam's.

McLeod, Jack, Zhogdang Pan, and Dianne Rucinski. 1995. Levels of Analysis in Public Opinion Research. In *Public Opinion and the Communication of Consent,* edited by T. L. Glasser and C. T. Salmon, 55–87. New York: Guilford.

McQuail, Denis, and Sven Windahl. 1981. *Communication Models.* London: Longman.

Mead, George Herbert. [1934] 1962. *Mind, Self, and Society.* Chicago: University of Chicago Press.

Mead, Margaret. [1937] 1965. Public Opinion Mechanisms among Primitive Peoples. In *Public Opinion and Propaganda,* edited by D. Katz, D. Cartwright, S. Eldersveld, and A. McClung Lee, 87–94. New York: Holt, Rinehart, and Winston.

Merkle, Daniel M. 1996. Review: The National Issues Convention Deliberative Poll. *Public Opinion Quarterly* 60, 4:588–619.

Merritt, Davis. 1995. *Public Journalism and Public Life: Why Telling the News Is Not Enough.* Hillsdale, N.J.: Lawrence Erlbaum.

Merten, Klaus. 1985. Some Silence in the Spiral of Silence. In *Political Communication Yearbook,* edited by K. R. Sanders, L. L. Kaid, and D. Nimmo, 31–42. Carbondale: Southern Illinois University Press.

Merton, Robert K. [1949] 1993. Manifest and Latent Functions. In *Social Theory,* edited by C. Lemert, 328–334. Boulder: Westview.

Merz-Benz, Peter-Ulrich. 1995. *Tiefsinn und Scharfsinn: Ferdinand Tönnies' begriffliche Konstitution der Sozialwelt.* Frankfurt: Suhrkamp.

Meyrowitz, Joshua. 1985. *No Sense of Place: The Impact of Electronic Media on Social Behavior.* New York: Oxford University Press.

Michelat, Guy, and Michel Simon. 1985. Les "sans réponse" aux questions politiques. *Pouvoirs* 33:41–56.

Mill, John Stuart. [1859] 1985. *On Liberty.* London: Penguin.

Miller, Peter V. 1995. The Industry of Public Opinion. In *Public Opinion and the Communication of Consent,* edited by T. L. Glasser and C. T. Salmon, 105–131. New York: Guilford.

Miller, Warren E., and Donald E. Stokes. [1963] 1972. Constituency Influence in Congress. In *Political Attitudes and Public Opinion,* edited by D. D. Nimmo and C. M. Bonjean, 543–561. New York: McKay.

Mills, C. Wright. [1956] 1968. *The Power Elite.* London: Oxford University Press.

Mitchell, Duncan G., ed. 1968. *A Dictionary of Sociology.* London: Routledge and Kegan Paul.

Moore, David W. 1995. *The Superpollsters: How They Measure and Manipulate Public Opinion in America.* New York: Four Walls Eight Windows.

Moscovici, Serge, and Willem Doise. 1994. *Conflict and Consensus: A General Theory of Collective Decisions.* London: Sage.

Moscovici, Serge. 1976. *Social Influence and Social Change.* London: Academic.

Moscovici, Serge. 1985. Social Influence and Conformity. In *Handbook of Social Psychology,* edited by G. Lindzey and E. Arondson, 2:347–412. New York: Random House.

Moscovici, Serge. 1991. Silent Majorities and Loud Minorities. In *Communication Yearbook 14,* edited by J. A. Anderson, 298–308. Newbury Park: Sage.

Mueller, Claus. 1973. *The Politics of Communication.* New York: Oxford University Press.

Mulgan, Geoffrey. 1991. *Communication and Control.* Cambridge: Polity.

Negt, Oskar. 1980. Mass Media: Tools of Domination or Instruments of Emancipation? Aspects of the Frankfurt School's Communications Analysis. In *The Myths of Information: Technology and Postindustrial Culture,* edited by K. Woodward, 65–87. London: Routledge and Kegan Paul.

Negt, Oskar, and Alexander Kluge. 1973. *Öffentlichkeit und Erfahrung: Zur Organisationsanalyse von bürgerlicher und proletarischer Öffentlichkeit.* Frankfurt: Suhrkamp.

Neidhardt, Friedhelm, ed. 1994. Öffentlichkeit, öffentliche Meinung, soziale Bewegungen. *Kölner Zeitschrift für Soziologie.* Sonderheft 34. Opladen: Westdeutscher Verlag.

Neuman, W. Russell. 1991. *The Future of the Mass Audience.* Cambridge: Cambridge University Press.

Newcomb, Theodore M. 1950. *Social Psychology.* New York: Dryden.

Newcomb, Theodore M. 1953. An Approach to the Study of Communicative Acts. *Psychological Review* 60:393–404.

Nielsen, Kai. 1995. Reconceptualizing Civil Society for Now: Some Somewhat Gramscian Turnings. In *Toward a Global Civil Society,* edited by M. Walzer, 41–68. Providence, R.I.: Berghahn Books.

Noelle, Elisabeth. 1940. *Amerikanische Massenbefragungen über Politik und Presse.* Inaugural Dissertation. Berlin: Friedrich-Wilhelms-Universität.

Noelle-Neumann, Elisabeth. 1974. The Spiral of Silence: A Theory of Public Opinion. *Journal of Communication* 24, 2:43–51.

Noelle-Neumann, Elisabeth. 1977. Turbulences in the Climate of Opinion: Methodological Applications of the Spiral of Silence Theory. *Public Opinion Quarterly* 41, 2:143–158.

Noelle-Neumann, Elisabeth. 1979. *Öffentlichkeit als Bedrohung.* Edited by J. Wilke. Freiburg: Karl Alber.

Noelle-Neumann, Elisabeth. 1985. The Spiral of Silence: A Response. In *Political Communication Yearbook,* edited by K. R. Sanders, L. L. Kaid, and D. Nimmo, 66–94. Carbondale: Southern Illinois University Press.

Noelle-Neumann, Elisabeth. [1980] 1993. *The Spiral of Silence: Public Opinion—Our Social Skin.* Chicago: University of Chicago Press.

Noelle-Neumann, Elisabeth. 1991. The Theory of Public Opinion: The Concept of the Spiral of Silence. In *Communication Yearbook* 14, edited by J. A. Anderson, 256–287. Newbury Park: Sage.

Noelle-Neumann, Elisabeth. 1995. Public Opinion and Rationality. In *Public Opinion and the Communication of Consent,* edited by T. L. Glasser and C. T. Salmon, 33–54. New York: Guilford.

Ogle, Marbury Bladen. 1950. *Public Opinion and Political Dynamics.* Boston: Houghton Mifflin.

O'Gorman, Hubert J., Stephen L. Garry. 1976. Pluralistic Ignorance: A Replication and Extension. *Public Opinion Quarterly* 40, 4:449–458.

Olien, Clarice N., George A. Donohue, and Philip J. Tichenor. 1995. Conflict, Consensus, and Public Opinion. In *Public Opinion and the Communication of Consent,* edited by T. L. Glasser and C. T. Salmon, 301–322. New York: Guilford.

Osgood, Charles E., and Percy H. Tannenbaum. 1955. The Principle of Congruity in the Prediction of Attitude Change. *Psychological Review* 62:42–55.

Otto, Ulla. 1966. Die Problematik des Begriffs der öffentlichen Meinung. *Publizistik* 2:99–130.

Ozouf, Mona. 1987. Quelques remarques sur la notion d'opinion publique au XVIIIe siècle. *Reseaux* 22:79–103.

Page, Benjamin I., and Robert Y. Shapiro. 1989. Educating and Manipulating the Public. In *Manipulating Public Opinion,* edited by M. Margolis and G. A. Mauser, 294–320. Pacific Grove, Calif.: Brooks/Cole.

Paget, Edwin H. 1929. Sudden Changes in Group Opinion. *Social Forces* 7, 3:438–444.

Paletz, David, and Robert Entman. 1981. *Media, Power, Politics.* New York: Free Press.

Palmer, Paul A. 1938. Ferdinand Tönnies's Theory of Public Opinion. *Public Opinion Quarterly* 2, 4:584–595.

Park, Robert E. [1939] 1966. Reflections on Communication and Culture. In *Reader in Public Opinion and Communication,* edited by B. Berelson and M. Janowitz, 167–177. New York: Free Press.

Park, Robert E. [1904] 1972. *The Crowd and the Public.* Edited by H. Elsner Jr. Chicago: University of Chicago Press.

Peer, Limor. 1992. The Practice of Opinion Polling as a Disciplinary Mechanism: A Foucauldian Perspective. *International Journal of Public Opinion Research* 4, 3:230–242.

Peters, John Durham. 1989. Democracy and American Mass Communication Theory: Dewey, Lippmann, Lazarsfeld. *Communication* 11, 3:199–220.

Peters, John Durham. 1989a. Satan and Savior: Mass Communication in Progressive Thought. *Critical Studies in Mass Communication* 6, 3:247–263.

Peters, John Durham. 1993. Distrust or Representation: Habermas on the Public Sphere. *Media, Culture and Society* 15:541–571.

Peters, John Durham. 1995. Historical Tensions in the Concept of Public Opinion. In *Public Opinion and the Communication of Consent,* edited by T. L. Glasser and C. T. Salmon, 3–32. New York: Guilford.

Peters, John Durham. 1997a. Why Dewey Wasn't So Right and Lippmann Wasn't So Wrong: Recasting the Lippmann-Dewey Debate. Paper presented at the International Communication Association, May 1997, Montréal.

Peters, John Durham. 1997b. Realism in Social Representation and the Fate of the Public. *Javnost—The Public* 4, 2:5–16.

Pool, Ithiel de Sola. 1983. *Technologies of Freedom.* Cambridge, Mass.: Belknap.

Porter, Theodore M. [1990] 1995. *Trust in Numbers: The Pursuit of Objectivity in Science and Public Life.* Princeton, N.J.: Princeton University Press.

Poster, Mark. 1984. *Foucault, Marxism and History: Mode of Production versus Mode of Information.* Cambridge: Polity.

Pöttker, Horst. 1993. Ferdinand Tönnies und die Schweigespirale. Zur Mutation einer Theorie über die öffentliche Meinung. In *Theorien öffentlicher Kommunikation. Problemfelder, Positionen, Perspektiven,* edited by G. Bentele and M. Rühl, 203–213. München: Ölschläger.

Price, Vincent. 1992. *Public Opinion.* Newbury Park, Calif.: Sage.

Price, Vincent, and Scott Allen. 1990. Opinion Spirals, Silent and Otherwise. *Communication Research* 17, 3:369–392.

Price, Vincent, and Hayg Oshagan. 1995. Social-Psychological Perspectives on Public Opinion. In *Public Opinion and the Communication of Consent,* edited by T. L. Glasser and C. T. Salmon, 177–216. New York: Guilford.

Ridgeway, Cecilia R. 1981. Nonconformity, Competence, and Influence in Groups: A Test of Two Theories. *American Sociological Review* 46, 3:333–347.

Roach, Colleen. 1993. Reflections on Communication and Cultural Rights and the Rights of People. In *Communication and Democracy,* edited by S. Splichal and J. Wasko, 169–186. Norwood, N.J.: Ablex.

Robbins, Bruce. 1993. Introduction to *The Phantom Public Sphere,* edited by B. Robbins, i–xxvi. Minneapolis: University of Minnesota Press.

Robinson, Gertrude J. 1984. The Study of "Schools of Thought." In Communication Studies: A Paradigmatic Approach. Paper presented at the IAMCR conference, Prague.

Rogers, Everett. 1981. The Empirical and the Critical Schools of Communication Research. *Communication Yearbook, 5.* New Brunswick: Transaction Books.

Rogers, Lindsay. 1949. *The Pollsters: Public Opinion, Politics, and Democratic Leadership.* New York: Knopf.

Roper, Elmo. 1942. *Why Public Opinion Research?* New York: Institute of Life Insurance.

Rousseau, Jean Jacques. [1762] 189?. *Contrat social ou principes du droit politique.* Paris: Garnier.

Rousseau, Jean Jacques. [1762] 1947. *The Social Contract.* Translated by C. Frankel. New York: Hafner.

Rudolph, Günther. 1995. *Die philosophisch-soziologischen Grundpositionen von Ferdinand Tönnies: Ein Beitrag zur Geschichte und Kritik der bürgerlichen Soziologie.* Hamburg: Rolf Fechner Verlag.

Rusciano, Frank Louis. 1989. *Isolation and Paradox: Defining "the Public" in Modern Political Analysis.* New York: Greenwood.

Salmon, Charles T., and Gerald D. Kline. 1985. The Spiral of Silence Ten Years Later: An Examination and Evaluation. In *Political Communication Yearbook,* edited by K. R. Sanders, L. L. Kaid, and D. Nimmo, 3–29. Carbondale: Southern Illinois University Press.

Schacht, Richard L. 1972. Hegel on Freedom. In *Hegel: A Collection of Critical Essays,* edited by A. MacIntyre, 289–328. Garden City, N.Y.: Anchor.

Scheff, Thomas J. 1967. Toward a Sociological Model of Consensus. *American Sociological Review* 32, 1:32–46.

Scherer, Helmut. 1990. *Massenmedien, Meinungsklima, und Einstellung: Eine Untersuchung zur Theorie der Schweigespirale*. Opladen: Westdeutscher Verlag.

Scheuch, Erwin K. 1973. Das Interview in der Sozialforschung. In *Handbuch der empirischen Sozialforschung*, edited by R. König, 2:66–190. Stuttgart: Ferdinand Enke.

Schmidt, Josephine. 1996. A Media Blizzard Overwhelms Eastern Europe. *Nieman Reports*, Summer, 39–47.

Schmidtchen, Gerhard. 1959. *Die befragte Nation: Über den Einfluss der Meinungsforschung auf die Politik*. Freiburg: Romabach.

Schmitt, Carl. [1928] 1954. *Verfassungslehre*. Berlin: Duncker and Humbolt.

Schramm, Wilbur. 1997. *The Beginnings of Communication Study in America*. Edited by S. H. Chaffee and E. M. Rogers. Thousand Oaks: Sage.

Schudson, Michael. 1997. Why Conversation Is Not the Soul of Democracy. *Critical Studies in Mass Communication* 14, 4:297–309.

Seeman, Melvin. 1993. A Historical Perspective on Attitude Research. In *New Directions in Attitude Measurement*, edited by D. Krebs and P. Schmidt, 3–20. Berlin: Walter de Gruyter.

Sennett, Richard. 1978. *The Fall of Public Man: On Social Psychology of Capitalism*. New York: Vintage Books.

Shamir, Jacob, and Michal Shamir. 1997. Pluralistic Ignorance across Issues and over Time: Information Cues and Biases. *Public Opinion Quarterly* 61, 2:227–260.

Singer, Eleanor. 1987. Editor's introduction. *Public Opinion Quarterly* 51, 4, pt. 2:S1-S3.

Škerlep, Andrej. 1996. Analiza družbenega konteksta komunikacijskih procesov. Ph.D. diss., Ljubljana: Fakulteta za družbene vede.

Smith, Tom W. 1987. The Art of Asking Questions, 1936–1985. *Public Opinion Quarterly* 51, 4, pt. 2:S95-S108.

Smythe, Dallas W., and Trinh Van Dinh. 1983. On Critical and Administrative Research: A New Critical Analysis. *Journal of Communication*, Summer, 117–127.

Sparks, Colin. 1995. The Media as a Power for Democracy. *Javnost—The Public* 2, 1:46–62.

Speier, Hans. 1995. The Rise of Public Opinion. In *Propaganda*, edited by R. Jackall, 26–46. New York: New York University Press.

Splichal, Slavko. 1981. *Množično komuniciranje med svobodo in odtujitvijo*. Maribor: Obzorja.

Splichal, Slavko. 1981a. Od javnog do slobodnog mnjenja. O kategorijama građanskog društva u "revolucionarnoj" komunikologiji. *Naše teme* 25, 10:1609–1616.

Splichal, Slavko. 1987. "Public Opinion" and the Controversies in Communication Science. *Media, Culture and Society* 9, 2:237–261.

Splichal, Slavko. 1990. *Statistična analiza besedil*. Ljubljana: FDV.

Splichal, Slavko. 1994. Pomlad javnosti. *Javnost—The Public* 1, 1:7–22.

Splichal, Slavko. 1994a. *Media beyond Socialism: Theory and Practice in East-Central Europe*. Boulder: Westview.

Squire, Peverill. 1988. Why the 1936 *Literary Digest* Poll Failed. *Public Opinion Quarterly* 52, 1:125–133.

Streckfuss, Richard. 1990. Objectivity in Journalism: A Search and a Reassessment. *Journalism Quarterly* 67, 4:973–983.

Strum, Arthur. 1994. A Bibliography of the Concept *Öffentlichkeit*. *New German Critique* 61:161–202.

Sutton, Jane. 1993. The Marginalization of Sophistical Rhetoric and the Loss of History. In *Rethinking the History of Rhetoric*, edited by T. Poulakos, 75–90. Boulder: Westview.

Tarde, Gabriel. 1898. L'opinion et la foule. *La Revue de Paris* 4.

Taylor, D. Garth. 1982. Pluralistic Ignorance and the Spiral of Silence: A Formal Analysis. *Public Opinion Quarterly* 46, 3:311–335.

Thompson, John B. 1990. *Ideology and Modern Culture.* Stanford: Stanford University Press.

Thompson, John B. 1993. The Theory of the Public Sphere. *Theory, Culture, and Society* 10, 3:173–190.

Thompson, John B. 1995. *The Media and Modernity: A Social Theory of the Media.* Stanford, Calif.: Stanford University Press.

Thurstone, Luis L. 1928. Attitudes Can Be Measured. *American Journal of Sociology* 33:539–554.

Tocqueville, Alexis de. [1840] [1912] 1995. *Democracy in America.* http://darwin.clas.virginia.edu/~tsawyer/DETOC/ Originially scanned and corrected by Thomas G. Roche at the University of Virginia (June 15, 1995) from *Democracy in America*, by Alexis de Tocqueville; translated by Henry Reeve. New York: D. Appleton, 1912.

Tokinoya, Hiroshi. 1996. A Study on the Spiral of Silence in Japan. *Keio Communication Review* 18:33–46.

Tönnies, Ferdinand. 1916. Zur Theorie der öffentlichen Meinung. *Schmollers Jahrbuch für Gesetzgebung, Verwaltung, und Volkswirtschaft im Deutschen Reiche* 40, 4:2001–2030.

Tönnies, Ferdinand. 1922. *Kritik der öffentlichen Meinung.* Berlin: Julius Springer.

Tönnies, Ferdinand. 1923. Macht und Wert der Öffentlichen Meinung. *Die Dioskuren: Jahrbuch für Geisteswissenschaften* 2, 2:72–99.

Tönnies, Ferdinand. 1926. *Das Eigentum.* Wien: W. Braumüller.

Tönnies, Ferdinand. 1927. Amerikanische Soziologie. *Weltwirtschaftliches Archiv* 26, 2:1**–10**.

Tönnies, Ferdinand. 1928. Die öffentliche Meinung in unserer Klassik. *Archiv für Buchgewerbe und Gebrauchsgraphik* 4:31–49.

Tönnies, Ferdinand. 1928a. Die Öffentliche Meinung Deutschlands in ihren jüngsten Phasen. *Die Bötcherstrasse* 1, 1:36–42.

Tönnies, Ferdinand. [1923] 1971. The Power and Value of Public Opinion. In *Ferdinand Tönnies on Sociology: Pure, Applied and Empirical*, edited by W. J. Cahnman and R. Heberle, 251–265. Chicago: University of Chicago Press.

Tönnies, Ferdinand. [1887] 1991. *Gemeinschaft und Gesellschaft.* Darmstadt: Wissenschaftliche Buchgesellschaft.

Touraine, Alain. 1996. *Les médias: nouveau forum politique ou destruction de l'opinion publique?* Barcelona: Centre d'Investigació de la Comunicació.

Vreg, France. 1980. *Javno mnenje in samoupravna demokracija.* Maribor: Obzorja.

Warner, Michael. 1992. The Mass Public and the Mass Subject. In *Habermas and the Public Sphere,* edited by C. Calhoun, 377–401. Cambridge: MIT Press.

Weaver, David. 1984. Media Agenda-Setting and Public Opinion: Is There a Link? In *Communication Yearbook 8,* edited by R. N. Bostrom and B. H. Westley, 680–691. Beverly Hills: Sage.

Weber, Max. [1924] 1976. Toward a Sociology of the Press. *Journal of Communication* 26, 3:96–101.

West, Cornel. 1989. *The American Evasion of Philosophy: A Genealogy of Pragmatism.* Madison: University of Wisconsin Press.

Westley, Bruce H., and Malcolm S. MacLean. 1957. A Conceptual Model for Communication Research. *Journalism Quarterly* 34:31–38.

Williams, Raymond. [1962] 1976. *Communications.* Harmondsworth, U.K.: Penguin.

Wilson, Francis Graham. 1962. *A Theory of Public Opinion.* Chicago: Regnery.

Wirth, Louis. 1948. Consensus and Mass Communication. *American Sociological Review* 13, 1:1–15.

Zaller, John R. 1992. *The Nature and Origins of Mass Opinion.* Cambridge: Cambridge University Press.

Zaller, John. 1994. Positive Constructs of Public Opinion. *Critical Studies in Mass Communication* 11, 276–287.

Zolo, Danilo. 1992. *Democracy and Complexity: A Realist Approach.* University Park: Pennsylvania State University Press.

Index

access: control of, 298; inequality in, 302, 305–7
accessibility: mediated, 18; Noelle-Neumann on, 192; public as, 17–18; regulation and, 296–97
acclamation, 12–13, 45; in ancient Greece, 256
accuracy, in cognitive coorientation model, 41–42
active public, 16
activist subculture, 251
adjective theories, 2, 171
Adorno, Theodor, on method, 92
advertising, 285; changes in, 280–81; versus publicity, 26; and public opinion polling, 231
agate square system, 280
agenda setting by media, 272, 274–75, 331n2
aggregate states of opinion of the public, 110, 112, 124–26; Noelle-Neumann on, 196
agitation, and opinion formation, 125
agreement, criteria for, 42
Aikens, Scott, 166–67
Albig, William, 93, 213; on consensus, 190; on ignorance, 257; on polling, 231, 239, 247, 252, 264

Allport, Floyd H., 80–81, 217; on consensus, 42; Noelle-Neumann and, 173, 175–76; and polling, 224; on polling, 267
American pragmatism, 73; criticism of, 76; Habermas and, 87; on omnicompetent individual, 162
Anderson, Benedict, 89
Andrén, Gunnar, 305–6
animal society, versus culture, 325n12
anthropology, on public sphere, 5
Arendt, Hannah: on definition of public, 18; on publicity, 282; on public sphere, 19
Ariosto, Lodovico, 66
Aristotle, 88, 151, 256
art, Dewey on, 149–50, 162
Asch, Solomon, 182, 201–2, 215, 325n15, 326n16
attention, selective, 208
attentive public, 16
attitudes, 314n7; dimensions of, 266
attitudinal variables, interval scales for, 212
audience: interest in media regulation, 298; role in mass media, 14

351

atized, 282; versus morals, 21; and polling, 252–53; public opinion and, 29; visibility and, 283
popular opinion, Noelle-Neumann on, 179
populism, mass media and, 253
Poster, Mark, on Foucault, 175
Postmodern theories on public opinion, 83–89
power: versus authority, 185; versus control, 183–84; control and, 9; versus influence, 182–83; Noelle-Neumann on, 184; range of, 183
power of public opinion: critique of, 185–86; Noelle-Neumann on, 182–86
Powers, Joshua, 232
power sphere, versus public sphere, 23–24
preference norm, 38–39, 48
press. *See* journalism; mass media; newspapers
principle of publicity, 20–21, 26; Bentham on, 58–60; Dewey on, 142; and individual, 304; Kant on, 63–65, 282; Lippmann on, 157; and public opinion, 274; and public sphere, 23
private: as attribute of social institutions, 17–20. *See also* public-private distinction
private opinion, public opinion polling and, 214
private sphere, communication technologies and, 84
probability, 228–29
propaganda, 290–91; Lippmann on, 155; and opinion formation, 125
psychological research, and public opinion theories, 72–78
public, 2, 6; as attribute of social institutions, 17–20; versus civil society, 36; concept of, 2–3, 5–6, 16; contradiction with opinion, 48–52; versus

crowd, 8–10, 72; decline of, 25, 30, 234–38; definitions of, 8, 10–11, 17–18; Dewey-Lippmann controversy and, 152–53; Dewey on, 16, 20, 139–50; eclipse of, 147–48, 150; globalization of, 283; versus individual, 17, 20; large, 23, 89; Lippmann on, 156–59; versus mass, 2, 6, 10–11, 252; Noelle-Neumann on, 174, 191–92; requirements for, 10; roots of concept of, 49; as social collectivity, 7–17; Tönnies on, 117–18, 194–96; types of, 16
public authority, 12
public communication, 295–96
publicity, 2, 6; versus advertising, 26; changing function of, 277–86; critical, 281; Dewey on, 148–49; Hegel on, 65; Kant on, 273; Marx on, 67; pragmatists on, 75; principle of (*see* principle of publicity); representative, 18; of statistics, 229–30; Tönnies on, 119; types of, 14–15, 119
public journalism, 301
public/ness, 2, 6, 90; feudal representative, 3; and human rights, 6; limitations of concept, 56; semantic dimensions of, 6–7
public opinion, 2, 6–7, 90; abandonment of concept of, 4–5; approaches to, 33–34; contradictions in, 48–52; definitional categories for, 55; definitional difficulties with, 2–4, 80–81, 176; definitions of, 10, 34, 73, 110–13, 173–74, 216, 320n14; and democracy, 28–29, 50–51, 53–98; dimensions of, 31, 32*f;* disappearance of, 199–214; evolution of, 224; expression of, 214–19, 273–77 (*see also* freedom of public expression); formation of (*see* opinion formation); general model of, 27–35; global, 33; and government (*see* government by public

+

About the Author

Slavko Splichal is professor of communication at the Faculty of Social Sciences, University of Ljubljana, Slovenia. He is founder (1987) and convenor of the International Colloquia on Communication and Culture, director of the European Institute for Communication and Culture, and editor of its journal *Javnost—The Public*. For four years he served as deputy secretary-general of the International Association for Media and Communication Research (1992–1996). His recent English-language publications include *Communication and Democracy* (co-edited with J. Wasko, Ablex, 1993), *Journalists for the 21st Century* (co-authored with Colin Sparks, Ablex, 1994), *Media in Transition* (co-edited with Ildiko Kovats, Hungarian Academy of Sciences, 1993), *Media Beyond Socialism: Theory and Practice in Postsocialist Countries* (Westview, 1994), *Information Society & Civil Society* (co-edited with A. Calabrese and C. Sparks, Purdue University Press, 1995), and a number of articles in major communications research journals, particularly on media theory, research methods, public opinion, and political communication. He has served on the editorial board of *Gazette, Journalism Studies, Journal of Communication, New Media & Society, Reseaux, Teorija in praksa,* and *Zeszyty Prasoznawcze.*